The Complete BOCUSE

Translated from the French by
Carmella Abramowitz-Moreau
Design: Alice Leroy
Editorial Assistance: Anya Glazer
and Louisa-Claire Dunnigan
Copyediting: Penelope Isaac
Typesetting: Gravemaker+Scott
Proofreading: Helen Woodhall
Color Separation: IGS-CP, Paris
Printed in Portugal by Printer Portuguesa

Originally published in French as
Toute la cuisine de Paul Bocuse

English-language edition

87, quai Panhard et Levassor
75647 Paris Cedex 13

editions.flammarion.com

13 14 15 4 3 2

ISBN: 978-2-08-020095-2

Dépôt légal: 10/2012

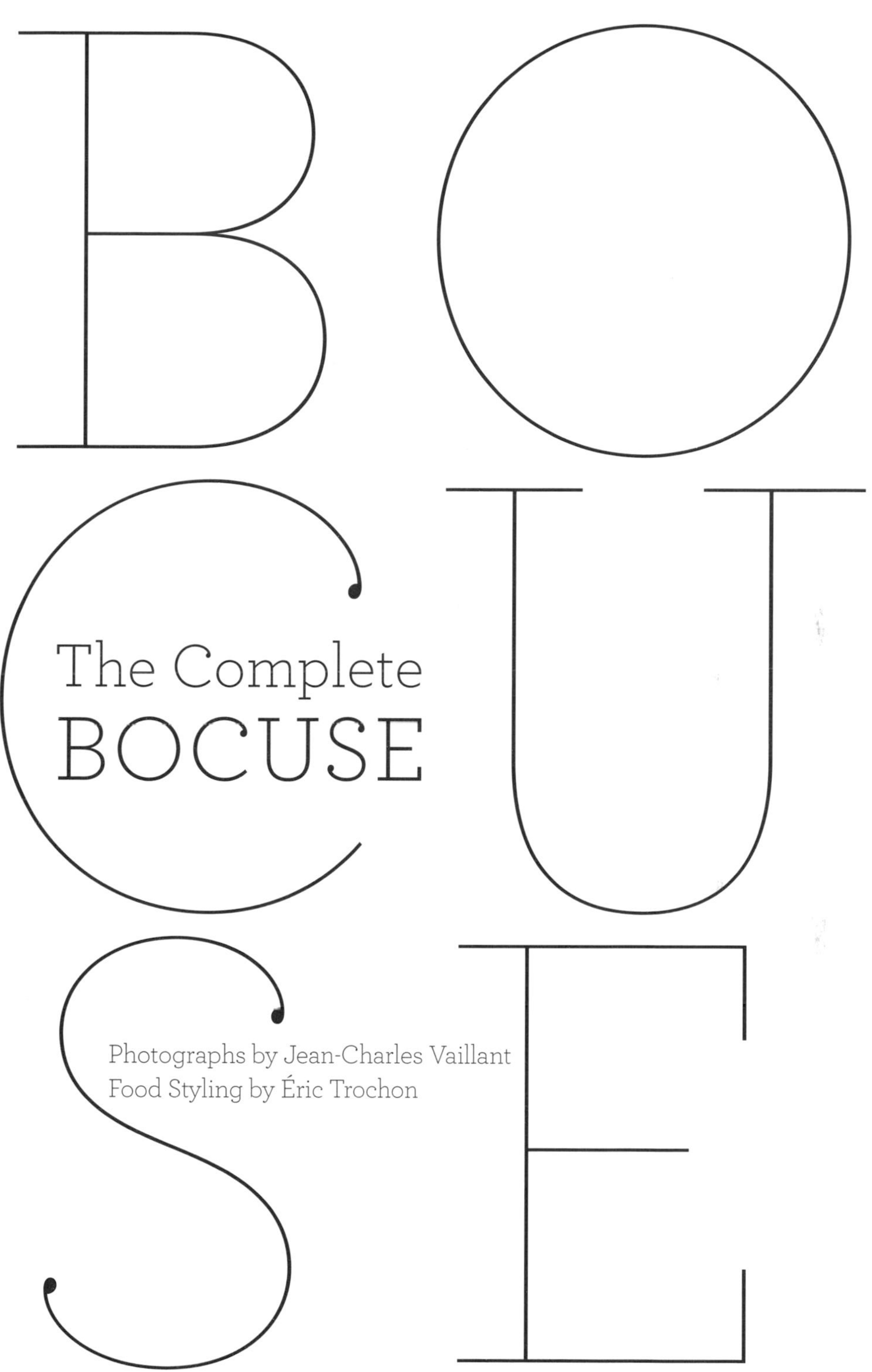

The Complete BOCUSE

Photographs by Jean-Charles Vaillant
Food Styling by Éric Trochon

Flammarion

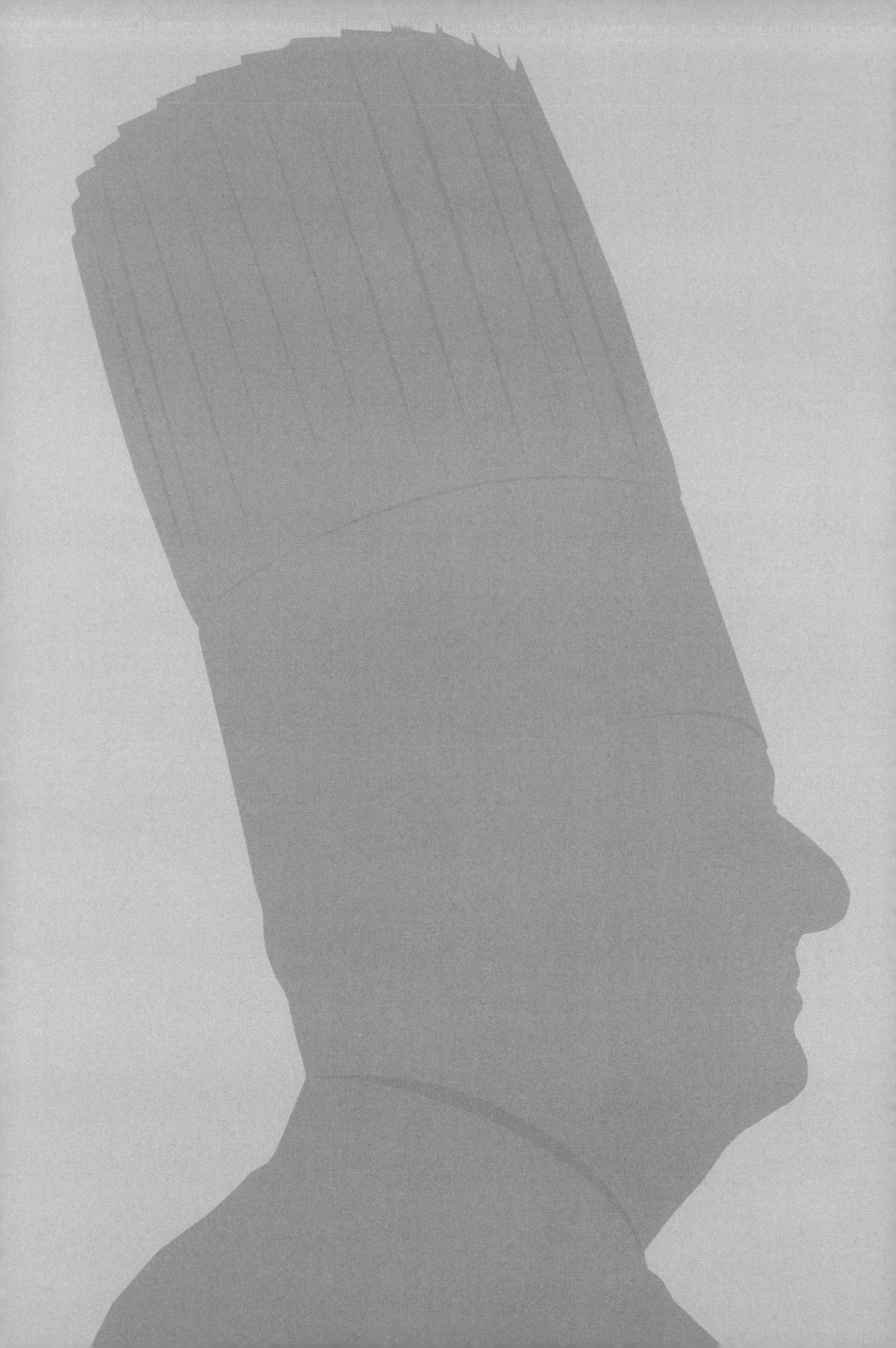

Contents

Savory

Sweet

SOUP

Oxtail Consommé
Oxtail clair

SERVES 4
PREPARATION TIME: 20 MINUTES
COOKING TIME:
4 HOURS 30 MINUTES

- 3 lb. (1.5 kg) oxtail
- 3 onions
- 3 medium-sized carrots
- 7 tablespoons (3 ½ oz./100 g) butter
- 1 bouquet garni (1 sprig parsley, ½ bay leaf, 1 sprig thyme)
- 1 celery stick
- Scant ½ cup (100 ml) Madeira wine
- Scant ½ cup (100 ml) cognac
- 14 cups (3.5 liters) stock, divided
- 2 cups (500 ml) water
- 3 turnips
- 1 celery heart (tender part of innermost ribs)
- Salt and pepper

Preheat the oven to 350°F (180°C). Cut the oxtail into pieces and quarter the onions and carrots. Brown the oxtail pieces and vegetables in the butter in an ovenproof dish.

When this is done, transfer all the pieces to a large cooking pot over the burner. Add the bouquet garni and the stick of celery. Then pour in half the Madeira wine and cognac, wait a little, and pour in the rest. Gently simmer to reduce the cooking liquid, and then pour in 12 cups (3 liters) of the stock and the 2 cups (500 ml) water.

Cook over low heat for 4 hours. The liquid should simmer gently and not come to a fast boil.

Cut the turnips into olive shapes and the celery heart into pieces. Cook them in the remaining stock. Filter the liquid in which the meat has cooked through a sieve.

Select the choicest pieces of oxtail–one per person–and add to each plate a tablespoon of carrots, turnips, and celery. Pour the strained consommé over the meat and vegetables.

Serve very hot.

SERVES 1
PREPARATION TIME: 20 MINUTES
COOKING TIME: 40 MINUTES

Elysée Truffle Soup
Soupe aux truffes Elysée

2 tablespoons of finely diced mixed carrots, onions, celery, and mushrooms in equal proportions

Butter for sautéing

2 oz. (50 g) fresh raw truffles

⅔ oz. (20 g) foie gras

1 cup (250 ml) chicken stock

2 ½ oz. (60 g) puff pastry

1 egg yolk

Special equipment: a small ovenproof soup dish, such as one you would use for a portion of onion soup

Sauté the diced vegetables gently in butter. Slice the truffle irregularly and cut the foie gras into differently sized pieces.

Preheat the oven to 425°F (220°C).

Place the sautéed vegetables in a soup bowl together with the truffle slices, pieces of foie gras, and the chicken stock.

Roll out the puff pastry very thinly and brush it with egg yolk. Fit it snugly over the soup bowl so that the contents are airtight.

Place the soup bowl in the oven. It will cook fairly quickly. The puff pastry will rise and turn a lovely golden color when it is done.

To enjoy this soup, break the puff pastry with a spoon so that the crumbs fall into the bowl.

This truffle soup was created specially for M. Valéry Giscard d'Estaing, former French president, and his wife, and served at a sumptuous dinner for the finest French cooks. It was at this reception that the President awarded me the Croix de la Légion d'Honneur, for my work as an ambassador of French cuisine, on Tuesday February 25, 1975.

SERVES 8
PREPARATION TIME: 15 MINUTES
SOAKING TIME: 2 HOURS
COOKING TIME: 3 HOURS

---

2 ¼ lb. (1 kg) salted pig's head
3 carrots
2 medium-sized turnips
1 small round cabbage
4 leeks
3 ½ oz. (100 g) green lentils, preferably Puy lentils, and water for soaking
16 cups (4 liters) water
1 loaf farmhouse or brown bread
Salt and pepper

Auvergne-Style Soup
Soupe auvergnate

Peel and wash the vegetables. Remove the cores from the carrots if they are hard. Soak the lentils for 2 hours in cold water and then drain them.

Combine the water, pig's head, and vegetables in a small pot. Season with salt and pepper and simmer gently for 3 hours.

To serve, place slices of bread in the soup bowls and pour the broth over. Serve the pork and vegetables separately on a dish.

Ardennes-Style Soup
Soupe ardennaise

SERVES 6
PREPARATION TIME: 20 MINUTES
COOKING TIME: 1 HOUR

- 6 Belgian endives
- 2 leeks, white parts only
- 2 medium-sized potatoes
- 1 ⅓ sticks (5 oz./150 g) unsalted butter, divided
- 4 cups (1 liter) water
- 2 teaspoons salt (10 g) salt, divided
- 2 cups (500 ml) milk
- ½ very thin baguette or 3 ½ oz. (100 g) bread

Peel and clean the vegetables. Cut the Belgian endives and leek whites into julienne strips and finely slice the potatoes. Heat 3 tablespoons (50 g) butter in a pot and add the vegetables. Cover the pot with the lid and stew gently for 15 minutes. The vegetables should be softened, not browned. Pour in the water and add 1 ¾ teaspoons salt. Simmer over low heat for 45 minutes. When done, add the milk.

Cut the thin baguette or other bread into very thin slices. Toast them lightly in the oven and place them in the tureen with the remaining butter.

Adjust the seasoning. Pour the boiling soup over the bread just before serving.

Nîmes-Style Soup
Soupe nîmoise

SERVES 6
PREPARATION TIME: 15 MINUTES
COOKING TIME:
1 HOUR 15 MINUTES

- 3 leeks, white part only
- 10 oz. (300 g) green cabbage
- 1 celery heart (tender part of innermost ribs)
- 3 tablespoons (50 g) butter
- 3 ½ oz. (100 g) barley or rice
- 1 pinch crushed fresh basil
- 1 tablespoon (15 g) salt
- 8 ½ cups (2 liters) water
- Grated Gruyère cheese to serve

Cut the vegetables into julienne strips. Heat the butter and gently stew the vegetables, stirring from time to time. When they are softened, add the barley, basil, and salt. Pour in the water and cook for 45 minutes.

If you are using rice, proceed as follows: add the water to the vegetables and cook for 15 minutes. Add the rice and cook for a further 30 minutes.

Serve the soup with a bowl of grated Gruyère cheese.

SERVES 4
PREPARATION TIME: 15 MINUTES
COOKING TIME: 50 MINUTES

Savoy-Style Soup
Soupe savoyarde

- 2 oz. (50 g) fatback (cut of pork fat from pig's back)
- 4 leeks
- 1 onion
- 1 celery stalk
- 2 medium-sized potatoes
- 4 cups (1 liter) water
- 2 cups (500 ml) milk
- 3 ½ oz. (100 g) bread
- Grated Gruyère or Parmesan cheese
- Salt

Trim the rind and cut the fatback into small dice. Melt the dice in a pot. Cut the leeks, onion, and celery into julienne strips. Finely slice the potatoes. Stew the vegetables gently with the pot covered for 15 minutes, stirring from time to time. Pour in the water, season lightly with salt, and cook for 35 minutes. Pour in the milk and bring to a boil for just a moment.

Cut the bread into small pieces and arrange them on a baking tray. Sprinkle them with grated cheese and grill them under the broiler.

Place the bread with the cheese in a tureen and pour the boiling soup over just before serving.

SERVES 4 TO 6
PREPARATION TIME: 20 MINUTES
COOKING TIME: 40 MINUTES

Lyon-Style Soup au Gratin
Gratinée lyonnaise

- 1 ¼ lb. (600 g) yellow onions
- 1 ⅓ sticks (5 oz./150 g) unsalted butter
- 2 tablespoons flour
- 11 cups (2.5 liters) water
- 1 small bouquet garni
- 7 oz. (200 g) bread, preferably a thin baguette (known in France as a *flûte*)
- 9 oz. (250 g) Gruyère cheese, grated
- 4 egg yolks
- 1 small glass of aged Madeira wine
- Salt and freshly ground pepper

Finely slice the onions. Melt the butter in a large skillet and sauté the sliced onions until they are nicely colored but not too browned.

Sprinkle the flour over the onions, tilting the skillet or stirring a few times so that the flour cooks as it would for a roux. Then transfer the onions into a pot containing the 10 ½ cups (2.5 liters) water. Season with salt and pepper and add the bouquet garni. Bring to a boil and leave to simmer gently for about 30 minutes.

Remove the bouquet garni from the pot and push the onions through a sieve or process them through a food mill.

Finely slice the bread and then cut it into sticks. Dry them out in a heated oven, and then place them at the bottom of an oven-proof soup tureen. Place half the grated cheese between the pieces of bread.

Heat the oven to 450°F 475°F (240°C).

Adjust the seasoning of the soup and pour it over the bread. Generously sprinkle the remaining cheese on top of the soup so that it is covered.

Place the tureen in a very hot oven. The Gruyère will melt and the surface should turn a lovely golden color.

Put the four egg yolks into a bowl and stir in the Madeira wine. Present the tureen of soup to the guests, then pour the egg and Madeira mixture into the soup tureen, stirring immediately with the ladle so that the soup becomes thickened and perfectly smooth (this is known as *touiller* in French).

This is a popular soup in Lyon, where it is usually enjoyed in the evening with family and friends, or after the theater.

SERVES 6
PREPARATION TIME: 30 MINUTES
COOKING TIME: 50 MINUTES
CHILLING TIME: 2 HOURS

2 ¼ lb. (1 kg) leeks

1 lb. (500 g) floury potatoes such as Yukon Gold

5 ½ tablespoons (3 oz./80 g) butter

8 ½ cups (2 liters) water

1 sprig thyme

1 sprig parsley

1 ¼ cups (300 ml) whipping cream

10 chives, chopped

Salt and pepper

Vichyssoise

Remove the outer skins of the leeks, cut them lengthways in four, and wash carefully. Discard the green tops and slice the white parts finely.

Peel the potatoes, wash them, and cut them into large cubes.

Melt the butter in a large cooking pot. Add the sliced leeks and allow them to soften gently, without browning.

Add the cubed potatoes and mix well. Pour the 8 ½ cups (2 liters) water into the pot and add the thyme and parsley. Bring to a boil and allow to simmer for about 35 minutes.

Drain the leeks and potatoes, setting aside some of the cooking liquid, and remove the thyme and parsley.

Purée the vegetables in a food processor. Return the puréed vegetables to the cooking pot with a ladleful of cooking liquid and the whipping cream.

Over medium heat, bring the soup back to a boil, whipping constantly. Chill for 2 hours before serving.

Just before serving, adjust the seasoning. Pour the vichyssoise into consommé bowls and sprinkle with chopped chives.

SERVES 6
PREPARATION TIME: 30 MINUTES
COOKING TIME:
2 HOURS 20 MINUTES

½ lb. (250 g) fresh borlotti beans (also known as cranberry beans)

½ lb. (250 g) fresh cannellini beans

7 oz. (200 g) French green beans

6 carrots

2 medium-sized potatoes

2 zucchini (courgettes)

1 leek

1 white onion

13 cups (3 liters) water

7 oz. (200 g) pork rind

3 ½ oz. (100 g) small macaroni

5 oz. (150 g) Parmesan cheese, grated

3 ½ oz. (100 g) Gruyère cheese, grated

Salt and pepper

PISTOU

1 lb. (500 g) ripe tomatoes

6 garlic cloves

10 sprigs basil

1 small glass olive oil

Salt and pepper

Pistou Soup
Soupe au pistou

Shell the borlotti and cannellini beans. Top and tail the green beans and remove the strings. Wash all the other vegetables, then peel them, except for the zucchini. Cut them all into small dice.

Take a large pot and pour in the water. Add the pork rind. Bring to a boil, skimming the surface. Season with salt and pepper.

Add the cubed vegetables and green beans. Simmer gently for 2 hours. Add the small macaroni and cook for a further 15 minutes.

To prepare the *pistou*, peel and seed the tomatoes. Place them in a colander to drain them of their liquid.

Peel the garlic cloves and crush them using a mortar and pestle. Remove the leaves from the basil stalks, chop them, and add them to the mortar.

Take a few cooked diced potatoes from the soup and add them to the garlic mixture. Work these ingredients well until you have a smooth paste, either by hand or in a food processor. Season it with salt and pepper.

Gradually incorporate in the olive oil, as you would to make a mayonnaise. When the mixture is quite homogenous, add the chopped drained tomatoes.

Pour the boiling soup into a tureen. Add the *pistou* and mix it in thoroughly. Cover with a lid and wait for 10 minutes before serving it, accompanied with grated Parmesan and Gruyère.

SERVES 10
PREPARATION TIME: 20 MINUTES
COOKING TIME: 1 HOUR

Mussel Soup
Soupe de moules

4 quarts (4 liters) Bouchot or other fine mussels
2 cloves garlic
3 shallots
10 oz. (300 g) onions
10 oz. (300 g) leeks, white part only
1 bottle Pouilly-Fuissé, divided
2 oz. (50 g) parsley
7 tablespoons (3 ½ oz./100 g) butter
1 cup (250 ml) olive oil
2 oz. (50 g) fresh fennel, diced
13 cups (3 liters) water
9 lb. (4 kg) Mediterranean fish, or other rock fish
3 ½ lb. (1.5 kg) tomatoes, peeled and cut into pieces
½ bay leaf
1 sprig thyme
About 4 threads saffron
1 cup (250 ml) crème fraîche
Salt and pepper
Toasted bread
Grated cheese

Crush the garlic and chop the shallots. Chop the onions and cut the leeks into julienne slices. Put the mussels in a pot with 1 cup (250 ml) of the white wine and the garlic, shallots, parsley, and butter. Cook until they open. Strain off, reserving the liquid, and keep the mussels warm. Heat the olive oil in a large pot (capacity approx. 35 cups/10 quarts/9 liters). Add the onions, leeks, and fennel and cook gently for 5 minutes. Then pour in the water, remaining wine, the cooking liquid from the mussels, and add the fish, tomatoes, herbs, and seasoning. Cook for 40 minutes.

Strain the broth through a very fine sieve or chinois, pressing down on the ingredients to extract the liquid and the flesh of the fish. Pour the strained soup into a pot and bring it to a boil. At the last moment, add the mussels and incorporate the cream.

Cook for 2 minutes.

Serve the soup in a tureen, with the croutons and grated cheese as accompaniments.

SERVES 4
PREPARATION TIME: 15 MINUTES
COOKING TIME: 45 MINUTES

Dubarry Soup or Creamed Cauliflower Soup
Potage Dubarry ou crème de chou-fleur

- 1 ¼ lb. (600 g) cauliflower
- 1 stick plus 1 tablespoon (4 ½ oz./130 g) butter, divided
- 12 oz. (350 g) potatoes, peeled and quartered
- 4 cups (1 liter) milk
- 1 cup (250 ml) clear stock, chicken or veal, or water
- 1 tablespoon (15 g) salt
- Scant ½ cup (100 ml) crème fraîche, heavy cream, or boiling milk
- 1 pinch chopped chervil leaves
- Croutons, diced and browned in butter

Trim and blanch the cauliflower. Refresh it under cold water and drain well. Melt 7 tablespoons (3 ½ oz./100 g) butter in a pot and place the cauliflower pieces in it. Cook very gently for 20 minutes. Add the quartered potatoes, the milk, the white stock (or water), and the tablespoon (15 g) of salt. Simmer gently for 20 minutes.

Strain through cheesecloth or a fine sieve, pressing down hard on the vegetables. Return the liquid to a pot and bring to a boil. Remove from the heat and adjust the consistency by adding some boiling milk or cream.

Just before serving, stir the remaining butter into the soup. Sprinkle with the chervil leaves and add the croutons.

SERVES 4
PREPARATION TIME: 15 MINUTES
COOKING TIME: 40 MINUTES

Watercress and Potato Soup
Soupe cresson-pommes de terre

- 1 ½ cups tightly packed (75 g) watercress leaves
- 1 lb. (500 g) potatoes
- 6 cups (1.5 liter) water
- 1 ½ teaspoons (10 g) kosher salt
- 6 tablespoons (100 ml) crème fraîche or heavy cream
- ½ stick (50g) butter
- Salt and pepper

Bring the water and salt to a boil in a large saucepan.

Remove the stems of the watercress and wash the leaves carefully. Peel the potatoes, wash them quickly and cut them into quarters. Add the potatoes to the water and boil uncovered for 25 minutes.

Lift the potatoes out of the water with a slotted spoon and mash or puree them by hand or in a food processor or food mill. Put them back into the water, stir, then add the watercress and boil gently for 10 minutes more. Add the cream and butter, lower the heat, and simmer (do not boil), stirring frequently, for 5 minutes longer.

Season as needed, then pour the soup into a soup tureen and serve.

Gazpacho

SERVES 4
PREPARATION TIME: 20 MINUTES
CHILLING TIME: 4 HOURS

1 ¾ lb. (800 g) tomatoes
1 large onion
2 cloves garlic
1 red bell pepper
1 medium cucumber
2 cups (500 ml) cold water
4 tablespoons olive oil
1 tablespoon red wine vinegar
Salt and pepper
10 ice cubes
10 to 12 slices of French bread, or squares of ordinary bread (optional)

Run the tomatoes under hot water and peel them. Peel the onion and garlic. Cut the pepper in half, remove its seeds and rinse it. Peel the cucumber, cut it in half lengthwise and remove its seeds. Finely chop all the vegetables and place in a large mixing bowl. Season generously with salt and pepper, and add the water. Puree in a blender or food processor–this will have to be done in several batches. Pour each batch of pureed ingredients into a soup tureen.

When done, whisk 2 tablespoons of the olive oil and vinegar into the soup, taste for salt and pepper, and place the tureen in the refrigerator for 3 to 4 hours to chill before serving.

To serve, coarsely crush the ice cubes by wrapping them in a towel and hitting them with a rolling pin. Add to the soup and serve.

If you like, make croutons by browning the bread in the remaining olive oil. Serve them on the side.

SERVES 4
PREPARATION TIME: 15 MINUTES
COOKING TIME: 35 MINUTES

Home-Style Vegetable Soup
Soupe bonne femme

1 large onion, peeled
2 medium potatoes
1 large or 2 small leeks
About 9 oz. (250 g) young green cabbage
6 cups (1.5 liter) water
1 ½ teaspoons (10 g) kosher salt
7 tablespoons (100 g) butter, divided
2 cups tightly packed (100 g) sorrel leaves
Nutmeg
Salt and pepper

Bring the water and kosher salt to a boil in a large saucepan. Peel the onions and potatoes. Wash all the vegetables. Thinly slice the onion, leeks, and cabbage, and dice the potatoes. In another large saucepan, melt 5 tablespoons (70 g) of the butter; when it is sizzling hot, add the onions and leeks. Lightly brown the vegetables over moderate heat, then add the cabbage and stir until it has melted down. Pour the boiling water into the pot with the vegetables, add the potatoes, and simmer uncovered for 30 minutes. Chop then add the sorrel and cook for 5 minutes more.

Warm the soup tureen by pouring a little boiling water into it, swirling it around and pouring it out.

Add a little nutmeg, salt, and pepper to taste, then pour the soup into the tureen. Stir the remaining 2 tablespoons (30 g) of butter into it and serve.

SERVES 8
PREPARATION TIME: 20 MINUTES
COOKING TIME: 35 MINUTES

Crayfish Bisque
Bisque d'écrevisses

- 20 crayfish, 1 ½ oz. (40 g) apiece
- 5 oz. (150 g) rice
- 4 cups (1 liter) white stock, veal or chicken, divided
- 1 ½ oz. (40 g) carrots
- 1 ½ oz. (40 g) onion
- 1 sprig thyme
- 1 small piece bay leaf
- Scant ½ cup (100 ml) cognac
- 1 cup (200 ml) dry white wine
- 1 ⅓ sticks (5 oz./150 g) unsalted butter
- Crème fraîche (optional)
- Salt and pink peppercorns or piment d'Espelette

Carefully wash the rice and cook it in 3 cups (750 ml) of the stock.

While it is cooking, cut the carrot and onion into very fine dice (this makes a mirepoix). Gently melt a knob of butter in a sauté pan and sweat the diced vegetables, ensuring they do not color.

Add the thyme and bay leaf piece. Increase the heat to maximum and add the crayfish to the aromatic base. Season with salt and pepper.

Sauté the crayfish quickly–they will immediately turn red. Pour over the cognac and flambé. As quickly as possible, pour over the white wine to extinguish the flames. Cook for 8 minutes.

Pour the sautéd mirepoix into a mortar or food processor. Using a few tablespoons of the stock, rinse out the pan and add this too.

Remove the flesh from the tails of half the crayfish. Place the crayfish flesh in a little stock and put the shells into a large mortar (or processor). Crush the shells into a fine paste. Drain the rice and incorporate the rice and the crayfish flesh to the crushed shells immediately. Crush the mixture again with the pestle, or process it, until the texture is creamy. Then strain it through a fine sieve, pressing all the liquid through until all that remains are the dried-out, powdered shells.

Return the mixture to a pot and bring to a brisk boil. Dilute the creamed crayfish with white stock or crème fraîche until the consistency is right. Remove from the heat and incorporate the remaining butter. Season lightly with the red peppercorns or piment d'Espelette.

To serve, slice the whole crayfish tails and garnish the soup with them.

When it is ready, this soup should be the same red as the cooked crayfish.

SERVES 4
PREPARATION TIME: 10 MINUTES
COOKING TIME: 35 MINUTES

Leek and Potato Soup
Soupe poireaux-pommes de terre

1 lb. (500 g) potatoes
4 medium leeks
6 cups (1.5 liter) water
1 ½ teaspoons (10 g) kosher salt
2 tablespoons (30 g) butter
6 tablespoons (100 ml) crème fraîche or heavy cream
Pepper
Pork rind (optional)

In a large saucepan, bring the water and salt to a boil.

Peel, wash, and dice the potatoes. Peel and carefully wash the leeks, and dice them using scissors.

In another large saucepan, melt the butter, add the leeks and cook over low heat until they have softened completely. Pour in the boiling water, add the potatoes, and cook uncovered over moderate heat for 20 minutes, then stir in the cream, add a little pepper, cook 5 minutes more, and serve.

Variation: In Lyon, a version of this soup is made using a local preparation called *couennes cuites en paquets*–"pork rind cooked in packets." You can make something similar by buying large pieces of fresh pork rind and cutting them into strips about 16 in. (40 cm) long and 2 in. (5 cm) wide. Fold each piece in four, like an accordion, and tie kitchen string tightly around the middle; the result will be the size and shape of a bow tie (in fact, in Lyon, bow ties are called *paquets de couennes*). Add two of these "packets" to the soup 10 minutes before it has finished cooking. Serve them in a separate bowl with a little of the soup to keep them warm, and eat them with Black Olives (see p. 556) and mustard (if making the soup this way, don't add the cream).

Note: The pork rind that can be bought in Lyon is fresh but pre-cooked. Since this will not be readily available elsewhere, use the pork rind that has cooked in the Boiled Pork Dinner (see p. 333) or simply place pork rind in cold water, bring to a boil, and poach for 1½ hours. Allow it to cool before cutting, tying, and cooking it in the soup as described above (when tying, be careful not to allow the string to cut the rind).

SERVES 4
PREPARATION TIME: 15 MINUTES
COOKING TIME: 35 MINUTES

Herb Soup
Soupe aux herbes

- 2 small onions, peeled
- About 8 oz. (250 g) young green cabbage
- 10 lettuce leaves
- 20 radish greens
- 20 celery leaves
- 15 sorrel leaves
- 1 small bunch chervil
- 10 young nettle tips (optional, see Note)
- 5 tablespoons (70 g) butter
- 6 cups (1.5 liters) water
- 1 ½ teaspoons (10 g) kosher salt
- Pepper
- Nutmeg
- 2 egg yolks
- 6 tablespoons crème fraîche or heavy cream

Bring the water and salt to a boil in a large saucepan.

Carefully wash all the vegetables. Keep the sorrel, chervil, and nettle tips, if using, aside. Finely slice the remaining vegetables.

In another large saucepan, melt 3 tablespoons (40 g) of the butter, add the sliced onions and cook until they begin to color. Add all the other vegetables except the sorrel, chervil, and nettle tips, if using. Stir and cook until the vegetables have softened, then add the boiling water, the sorrel, chervil, and nettle tips, and cook at a gentle boil for 20 minutes, uncovered.

Add a little pepper and nutmeg, and salt if needed.

Place the egg yolks and cream in a mixing bowl and beat with a whisk to combine. Remove the soup from the heat and whisk 2 ladlefuls into the egg-cream mixture; then pour back into the saucepan, stirring constantly with a wooden spoon. Stir in the remaining 2 tablespoons (30 g) of butter, pour the mixture into a warm soup tureen, and serve.

Note: The shoots of young nettles in the spring (or the tender tips of older nettles) are excellent in soup. Gather them yourself, but wear gloves to pick them.

SERVES 4 TO 5
PREPARATION TIME: 15 MINUTES
COOKING TIME: 35 MINUTES

Country-Style Vegetable Soup
Soupe paysanne

6 cups (1.5 liter) water
2 teaspoons (15 g) kosher salt
1 onion
4 carrots
2 small turnips
2 stalks celery
2 leeks
About 8 oz. (250 g) young green cabbage
1 bunch chervil
5 tablespoons (70 g) butter, divided
½ loaf (125 g) of French bread
Salt and pepper
1 cup (100 g) freshly grated Gruyère cheese

Bring the water and salt to a boil in a large saucepan.

Peel the onion, carrots, turnips, and celery, and carefully wash all the vegetables. Set aside in a colander. Keep the chervil apart. On a cutting board, cut all the vegetables into fine julienne strips.

In another large saucepan, melt 3 tablespoons (40 g) of the butter; when sizzling hot, add the onions and leeks, lower the heat, and cook to soften but not color. Add the carrots, turnips, celery, and cabbage and cook, stirring frequently, until all the vegetables have softened; then pour the boiling salted water into the pot and cook, covered, over low heat for 30 minutes.

Cut the bread in half lengthwise and chop the chervil. Toast the bread under the broiler and cut it into thick slices; then place it in a warm soup tureen, sprinkle with the chervil, and pour in the soup.

Stir the remaining 2 tablespoons (30 g) of butter into the soup, salt and pepper to taste, and serve with a bowl of freshly grated Gruyère cheese on the side.

Minestrone

SERVES 4 TO 6
SOAKING TIME: ABOUT 2 HOURS
PREPARATION TIME: 30 MINUTES
COOKING TIME:
1 HOUR 20 MINUTES

- 1 cup (185 g) shelled fresh white beans, or ½ cup (90 g) dried white beans
- 4 oz. (125 g) salt pork or slab bacon
- 4 oz. (125 g) green beans, cut into small pieces
- 2 carrots
- 3 medium potatoes
- 2 turnips
- 4 stalks celery
- 3 leeks, white part only
- 1 cup (185 g) shelled fresh green peas
- 2 very large tomatoes
- 2 cloves garlic
- 12 fresh basil leaves
- 9 cups (2 liters) cold water
- 1 ½ teaspoons (10 g) salt
- 4 tablespoons (60 ml) olive oil
- 3 ½ oz. (100 g) spaghetti
- Salt and pepper
- Freshly grated Parmesan or Gruyère cheese (for serving)

If using dried white beans, soak them overnight, then put them in the 8½ cups (2 liters) cold salted water, bring to a boil, and simmer for 45 minutes before adding the other ingredients. Fresh white beans can just be added with the other vegetables.

If using salt pork, soak it in cold water for an hour and a half before making the soup (bacon need not be soaked). Cut the salt pork or bacon into small cubes.

String the fresh green beans, run them under cold water, cut into small pieces and set aside. Peel the carrots, potatoes, turnips, and celery; rinse them quickly and dice them. Set aside.

Slice the white parts of the leeks into quarters, wash them carefully, finely slice them, and set aside. Shell the green peas, and set aside. Frozen peas may be used instead.

Run the tomatoes under hot water, peel and dice them. Peel the garlic. Wash the basil leaves, and pat them dry. Set aside.

Bring the water and salt to a boil in a large pot, add the white beans, carrots, leeks, and salt pork or bacon. Cover and cook for 40 minutes, then add the potatoes, turnips, and celery. Fifteen minutes later, add the green beans and peas, and cook 15 minutes more.

While the soup is cooking, place the tomatoes in a bowl, mix them with the garlic, basil, and olive oil, and crush with a fork. Set aside.

Spoon a ladleful of soup into the tomato mixture, stir well, then pour back into the soup. Break the spaghetti into small pieces, add to the soup and finish cooking, uncovered, for 10 minutes. Add salt and pepper to taste, then pour the soup into a warm soup tureen and serve with a bowl of freshly grated Parmesan or Gruyère cheese on the side.

Tapioca Soup
Soupe au tapioca

SERVES 4
PREPARATION TIME: 10 MINUTES
COOKING TIME: 20 MINUTES

- 4 cups (1 liter) water or beef bouillon (see Pot-au-Feu, p. 264)
- 1 teaspoon (7 g) kosher salt (if using water)
- ⅓ cup (70 g) tapioca
- 4 egg yolks
- 2 tablespoons (30 g) softened butter, broken into pieces
- 1 cups (100 g) grated Gruyère cheese
- Nutmeg
- 6 tablespoons (100 ml) crème fraîche or heavy cream
- Pepper

Bring the water and salt or the beef bouillon to a boil in a large saucepan, sprinkle in the tapioca, stirring constantly, and boil for 5 minutes, stirring frequently.

In a bowl, whisk the egg yolks together, then add the softened butter, grated cheese, a little nutmeg, and finally the cream, little by little.

Remove the soup from the heat and add 2 ladlefuls to the egg mixture, whisking constantly, then pour the contents of the bowl into the soup and whisk to combine. Place back over low heat and simmer slowly (do not boil) for 5 minutes, stirring constantly. Add a little pepper and serve.

SERVES 4
PREPARATION TIME: 15 MINUTES
RESTING TIME: 45 MINUTES
CHILLING TIME: ABOUT 4 HOURS

3 cucumbers, about 1 ½ lb. (700 g) in total

3 tablespoons finely chopped chives

2 small cloves garlic

15 walnut meats

2 tablespoons olive oil

2 cups (500 ml) plain yogurt

Salt and pepper

Cold Cucumber Soup
Potage au concombre

Cut the cucumbers in half lengthwise and scoop out the seeds with a spoon. Cut the pulp into little cubes, place in a mixing bowl, sprinkle generously with salt, and leave for 45 minutes before making the soup.

Wash the chives and peel the garlic, and finely chop them both on a cutting board. Separately chop the walnut meats. Set aside.

Place the salted cucumber in a colander and rinse thoroughly under cold running water, then spread out on a clean towel to dry.

In a large bowl, mix together the cucumber, walnuts, garlic, olive oil, yogurt, and two tablespoons of the chives, and season with salt and pepper. The mixture should be thick and creamy, so stir just long enough to mix everything together, and then blend in a food processor. Pour into a soup tureen and place in the refrigerator for 3 to 4 hours. Just before serving, sprinkle with the remaining tablespoon of chives.

SERVES 4 TO 6
PREPARATION TIME: 45 MINUTES
COOKING TIME:
3 HOURS 10 MINUTES

1 ¾ lb. (800 g) beef shank
1 marrow bone
2 quarts (2 liters) cold water
2 teaspoons (15 g) kosher salt
3 medium carrots
½ small celeriac, or 3 stalks of celery
2 medium leeks
About 9 oz. (250 g) young green cabbage
2 cloves garlic
2 shallots
1 large onion
2 tablespoons (30 g) butter
4 medium tomatoes
1 clove
4 medium potatoes
1 large cooked beet
Pepper
4 to 6 tablespoons crème fraîche or heavy cream
4 to 6 teaspoons red wine vinegar

Polish-Style Soup
Potage polonais

This soup, which could make a whole meal, is best if the beef and most of the vegetables are cooked a day in advance.

A day before serving: Place the meat and marrow bone in a large pot, pour in the water, and add the salt. Bring to a boil, skimming off any foam that rises.

Peel and wash the carrots and celeriac or celery, and cut them into fine julienne strips. Cut the leeks lengthwise into quarters, thinly slice the cabbage, and wash them. On a cutting board, peel and chop the garlic, shallots, and onion.

In another pot, melt the butter, add the onion, garlic, and shallots, and simmer for 5 minutes. Meanwhile pass the tomatoes under boiling water, peel them, and cut them into quarters. Add the tomatoes to the pot with the vegetables and cook 1 minute longer. Then add the carrots, celeriac (or celery), leeks, and cabbage. Cover, and simmer for 15 minutes. Add the vegetables to the pot with the meat, as well as a little pepper and the clove. Cook over low heat for 2 hours, then remove from the heat and allow to cool completely. When cold, the soup may be refrigerated.

The next day: Remove the pot from the refrigerator 1½ hours before dinner. Peel, rinse, and dice the potatoes. Forty-five minutes before serving, reheat the soup, add the potatoes, and simmer for 35 minutes. Peel and dice the beet, add to the soup and cook 10 minutes more.

To serve, lift the meat and marrow bone out of the soup and serve on a separate platter. Put a tablespoon of cream into each soup bowl as well as a teaspoon of vinegar. Ladle the hot soup into the bowls and serve, with any remaining soup in a tureen, and the platter of meat on the side.

Cream of Asparagus Soup
Velouté d'asperges

SERVES 4
PREPARATION TIME: 15 MINUTES
COOKING TIME: 25 TO 30 MINUTES

- 1 ¼ lb. (600 g) asparagus
- 1 medium onion
- 4 sprigs of parsley
- 4 cups (1 liter) water
- 1 teaspoon (7 g) kosher salt
- 1 tablespoon cornstarch
- 2 tablespoons water
- 3 ½ tablespoons (50 g) softened butter
- 6 tablespoons (100 ml) crème fraîche or heavy cream
- Salt and pepper

Take the scales off green asparagus or peel white asparagus using a vegetable peeler (be careful not to damage the tips). Wash the asparagus in cold water, cut off the tips, and cut the rest of each asparagus into slices. Peel the onion. Wash the parsley and tie it in a bunch.

Bring the water and salt to a boil in a large saucepan, add the asparagus, onion, and parsley, and boil gently for 20 minutes.

Lift out all the vegetables from the saucepan using a slotted spoon, leaving only the liquid. Discard the onion and parsley and set aside the asparagus.

Lower the heat so that the liquid in the pot just simmers. Mix the cornstarch with 2 tablespoons of cold water and stir into the liquid. Then raise the heat and bring the liquid back to a boil, stirring constantly. Lower the heat once more, stir in the butter and cream, put the asparagus back into the pot, and cook for 3 to 4 minutes longer. Taste for salt and pepper and serve.

SERVES 4
PREPARATION TIME: 15 MINUTES
COOKING TIME: 20 MINUTES

Cream of Oyster Soup
Velouté aux huîtres

1 lb. (500 g) potatoes
1 lb. (500 g) leeks
3 tablespoons (40 g) butter
6 cups (1.5 liter) hot water
1 scant tablespoon kosher salt
16 oysters in their shells
1 bunch chervil
6 tablespoons (100 ml) crème fraîche or heavy cream
Salt and pepper

Peel the potatoes, wash them under cold water, and dice them. Then cut the leeks lengthwise into quarters, carefully wash them under hot water and cut them into fine julienne strips. Heat the butter in a large saucepan; when it begins to foam, add the leeks and potatoes, and stir over moderate heat until the leeks have softened. Add the hot water and salt, cover, and simmer for 20 minutes.

Place a sieve over a bowl, line with a doubled-over piece of cheesecloth, and open the oysters over the sieve to strain and catch their liquid. Place the oysters in a small saucepan with their strained liquid and bring just barely to a boil. Then remove from the heat, lift the oysters out of the liquid, and set aside reserving the liquid. Check the oysters to be sure there are no bits of shell caught in them.

Quickly wash the chervil, pat it dry with paper towel and roughly chop it. Set aside.

Strain the oyster liquid into the soup, then purée the soup in a blender or food processor. Do this in several batches. Blend the cream into the last batch.

Place the blended soup back in the pot, taste for salt and pepper, and heat until very hot but not boiling. Place four oysters in each warm soup plate and pour the hot soup over them. Sprinkle with a little pepper and the chervil and serve.

SERVES 4
PREPARATION TIME: 20 MINUTES
COOKING TIME: 35 MINUTES

Winter Squash Soup
Soupe de courge

1 ½ lb. (700 g) winter squash

2 medium potatoes (about 10 oz./300g), peeled and diced

2 medium leeks

6 cups (1.5 liter) cold water

1 ½ teaspoons (10 g) kosher salt

4 tablespoons (60 g) butter, plus butter for browning the croutons

Salt and pepper

12 slices French bread, or 4 slices ordinary bread cut into quarters

6 tablespoons (100 ml) crème fraîche or heavy cream

Nutmeg

Peel and seed the winter squash, rinse it under cold water and cut into cubes of roughly 1 in. (2 cm). Peel, rinse, and dice the potatoes. Clean and slice the leeks.

Place the winter squash and potatoes in a large saucepan with the water and salt, and bring to a boil. Meanwhile, melt the butter in a frying pan, add the leeks and cook slowly until they have melted down, then add them to the saucepan. Boil the soup over moderate heat, uncovered, for 20 minutes, then purée it in a blender, food processor, or by using a food mill. The result should be creamy; add salt and pepper and cook for 5 to 7 minutes more over low heat.

Brown the slices of bread in butter to make croutons, place them on a plate, and cover with a clean cloth to keep them warm.

Pour the cream into a warm soup tureen and stir in the soup little by little. Add a little nutmeg and serve with the croutons on the side.

SERVES 6
PREPARATION TIME: 30 MINUTES
COOKING TIME: ABOUT 1 HOUR

Cabbage Soup
Soupe au chou

- 14 oz. (400 g) pork breast, partially salt-cured
- 12 cups (3 liters) water
- 1 large green cabbage
- 5 potatoes
- 3 carrots
- 2 turnips
- 2 leeks
- 1 large onion
- 1 clove
- 1 tablespoon lard
- Kosher salt
- White peppercorns
- 6 slices country bread

Pour the 12 cups (3 liters) water into a large cooking pot and add the pork breast. Bring to a boil and simmer for 10 minutes, skimming off any foam that rises to the surface. Peel, wash, and quarter the cabbage.

Blanch the quartered cabbage for 5 minutes in boiling water and remove.

Peel the potatoes, carrots, turnips, leeks, and onion. Stud the onion with the clove. Wash the other vegetables and, with the exception of the potatoes, chop them roughly.

Add the cabbage, the chopped carrots, turnips, and leeks, the onion, and the lard to the pot.

Bring to a boil again and add a handful of kosher salt and a few white peppercorns. Cover and simmer for 25 minutes. Quarter the potatoes, add them to the soup, and cook for a further 20 minutes.

To serve, place a slice of country bread in each soup plate and pour the soup over it.

SERVES 6
PREPARATION TIME: 30 MINUTES
COOKING TIME: 30 MINUTES

- 1 small pumpkin, about 4 ½ lb. (2 kg)
- 2 cups (500 ml) chicken stock
- ¾ cup (200 g) heavy cream
- Salt and pepper
- Nutmeg
- 10 croutons
- A few sprigs of chervil, chopped

Pumpkin Soup
Soupe au potiron

Cut off the top of the pumpkin. Hollow out the seeds and most of the flesh carefully, making sure you don't pierce the skin.

Remove the long fibers and seeds from the pumpkin flesh and cut it into pieces. Steam the pumpkin pieces for 20 minutes.

Heat the chicken stock.

Blend the pumpkin pieces using a food processor, gradually pouring in the boiling chicken stock, until it is quite smooth. Return the liquid to the pot, stir in the cream, and mix well. Season with salt, pepper, and a little freshly grated nutmeg. Gently increase the heat and allow to boil very briefly.

Cut the croutons into small cubes.

Pour the soup into the hollowed out pumpkin and scatter with the diced croutons. Sprinkle with chopped chervil.

SERVES 4
PREPARATION TIME: 20 MINUTES
COOKING TIME: 45 MINUTES

Onion Soup
Soupe à l'oignon

- 4 medium onions
- 4 tablespoons (60 g) butter, divided
- 2 tablespoons (12 g) flour
- 6 cups (1.5 liter) beef bouillon (see Pot-au-Feu, p. 264) or water
- 1 loaf (250 g) of French bread
- 1 cup (100 g) freshly grated Gruyère cheese
- Pepper
- 3 tablespoons (30 g) bread crumbs

Peel and slice the onions. Melt 2 tablespoons (30 g) of the butter in a large saucepan, add the onions, and brown lightly. Stir in the flour and, when it begins to color, add the bouillon or water, stirring constantly. Cook uncovered over moderate heat for 15 minutes.

Cut the bread in half lengthwise. Toast the bread under the broiler, then cut it into thick slices.

Preheat the oven to 350°F (180°C).

In an ovenproof soup tureen, place a third of the bread. Sprinkle it with a quarter of the grated cheese, 2 teaspoons of the remaining butter, softened, and a little pepper. Make three layers in this way, then pour the soup into the tureen, sprinkle with the bread crumbs and the remaining cheese, and place in the oven for 20 minutes or until the cheese and bread crumbs have browned. Serve immediately.

Variation: A richer soup can be made by beating three egg yolks in a bowl with a few spoonfuls of heavy cream, a little port, and a pinch of nutmeg. Whisk in a ladleful of the soup and simmer (do not boil), stirring constantly until the mixture begins to thicken. Pour this mixture into the tureen over the bread and cheese, add the remaining soup, and finish as described above.

This soup is traditionally served to French party guests in the early morning hours but can be enjoyed at any meal.

COLD APPETIZERS

SERVES 4
PREPARATION TIME: 20 MINUTES
COOKING TIME: 30 MINUTES

Salad Niçoise
Salade niçoise

- 10 oz. (300 g) potatoes
- 10 oz. (300 g) ripe tomatoes
- 10 oz. (300 g) green beans
- 1 butterhead (Boston) lettuce, heart only
- 1 onion
- 3 tablespoons olive oil
- 1 tablespoon red wine vinegar
- Salt and freshly ground pepper
- A few sprigs of chervil

Use equal proportions of potatoes, tomatoes, and green beans.

Boil the potatoes, peel them, and slice them thinly. Peel the tomatoes (plunge them very briefly in boiling water), remove the base, seed, and quarter them. Trim the beans and boil them in salted water–they should retain their crunch.

Wash and dry the lettuce leaves and combine them with the potatoes, tomatoes, and beans. Finely chop the onion. Season with the oil, vinegar, salt, and pepper, and garnish with the chopped onion.

Just before serving, sprinkle with a generous handful of chervil leaves.

SERVES 4
PREPARATION TIME: 15 MINUTES
COOKING TIME: 6 MINUTES
MARINATING TIME: 2 DAYS

1 small red cabbage or Savoy cabbage

1 clove garlic

½ bay leaf, broken into small pieces

1 ¾ cups (400 ml) white wine vinegar

3 tablespoons walnut oil

Table salt and freshly ground pepper

Red Cabbage or Savoy Cabbage Salad
Salade de chou rouge ou chou de Milan

Remove the outer leaves of the small cabbage and pick the inner leaves off. Trim the ribs, wash the leaves, and drain them. Arrange them in small piles to cut them into fine julienne strips. Prepare using either of the two methods given below.

First method

Boil the julienned cabbage for 6 minutes and drain thoroughly. Arrange the slices in a mixing bowl in layers; on top of each layer sprinkle a little table salt and freshly ground black pepper, and insert the garlic clove and ½ bay leaf. Bring the vinegar briefly to a boil and allow to cool. Pour the cooled vinegar over the cabbage so it is completely covered. Leave to marinate in an airtight container in the refrigerator for 2 days, checking periodically that the cabbage is well covered with the vinegar. When it is ready, you can use it:

a) as it is;

b) drained and seasoned with walnut oil, using 3 tablespoons per 5 oz. (150 g) cabbage;

c) seasoned and combined with an equal weight of finely sliced tart apples.

Second method

Bring the vinegar to a boil in a saucepan. Add the julienned cabbage and bring to a brisk boil. Then leave to cool. Drain, but not thoroughly (leave some of the cooking liquid), and just before serving, season with salt, pepper, and oil.

Each of these methods softens the cabbage and makes it more easily digestible.

Lyonnaise Cream Cheese with *Fines Herbes*
Cervelles des canuts

SERVES 4
PREPARATION TIME: 15 MINUTES
COOKING TIME: ABOUT 5 MINUTES
CHILLING TIME: 2 HOURS

- 1 clove garlic
- 1 shallot
- A few sprigs chervil
- Several chives
- A few sprigs tarragon
- A few sprigs parsley
- 7 oz. (200 g) *fromage blanc* cream cheese
- Scant ½ cup (100 ml) crème fraîche or thick cream
- 2 tablespoons olive oil
- ½ tablespoon wine vinegar
- 1 French loaf (baguette)
- Salt and pepper
- 1 bunch pink radishes (optional), washed and sliced

Peel the garlic clove and shallot. Chop them finely and set aside in a bowl.

Carefully wash the chervil, chives, tarragon, and parsley. Remove the stalks from the parsley. Using a pair of scissors, cut the herbs finely in a bowl. You should have about a tablespoon of each herb.

Place the *fromage blanc* in a mixing bowl and whisk in the crème fraîche. Stir in the oil and vinegar, and season with salt and pepper. Combine well. Then add the chopped garlic and shallot and, lastly, the herbs. Mix thoroughly and chill for about 2 hours.

Serve well chilled.

About 15 minutes before serving, cut the baguette lengthways and grill it under the broiler. Serve the cream cheese mixture accompanied by the toast; it is also delicious with sliced pink radishes.

Note: Fromage blanc *("white cheese") is a light cheese whose consistency is between that of a fairly thick yogurt and cream cheese. The moisture content is anything up to 80 percent. If you cannot find fromage blanc, make your own mix with ricotta, Quark, or farmer's cheese, and sour cream, or blend cottage cheese and yogurt until smooth.*

Lyon was a major silk-weaving center for many centuries; the silk-weavers were known as the canuts, and this inspired the French title of the dish. It is still served in the restaurants of Lyon.

Oriental-Style Small Red Mullets
Petits rougets à l'orientale

SERVES 6
PREPARATION TIME: 10 MINUTES
COOKING TIME: 8 TO 10 MINUTES
CHILLING TIME: 1 HOUR

---

12 small red mullets
4 tomatoes
1 clove garlic
4 tablespoons olive oil
Scant ½ cup (100 ml) dry white wine
1 sprig thyme
½ bay leaf
1 pinch saffron threads
Salt and freshly ground pepper
1 lemon, peeled and sliced, for garnish

Plunge the tomatoes briefly in boiling water and remove their skins. Remove the seeds and chop the flesh. Crush the garlic clove. Lightly oil an ovenproof dish large enough to hold the fish.

Preheat the oven to 350°C/180°F.

Remove the gills from the mullet but do not gut them. Pat them dry and place them, side by side, in the dish. Season them with salt and freshly ground pepper. Combine the oil, white wine, tomato pulp, herbs, and spices and pour this mixture over the mullet. Place in the oven and cook for 10 minutes. Leave to cool in the dish then place in the refrigerator for about 1 hour.

Serve chilled, each mullet garnished with a slice of peeled lemon.

SERVES 6
PREPARATION TIME: 20 MINUTES
COOKING TIME: 10 MINUTES
CHILLING TIME: 1 HOUR

Marinated Mackerel
Maquereaux marinés

- 12 small mackerel, gutted and cleaned
- Salt and freshly ground pepper
- 1 lemon, peeled and thinly sliced, for garnish

COOKED MARINADE

- 1 medium-sized carrot
- 1 large onion
- Dry white wine
- Vinegar
- 1 sprig thyme
- ½ bay leaf

Thinly slice the carrot and onion. Cook the marinade for 20 minutes: use two-thirds dry white wine, one-third vinegar, the thinly sliced carrot and onion, the thyme, and half bay leaf.

Preheat the oven to 350°F (180°C). Arrange the mackerel in an ovenproof ceramic dish. Season them with salt and freshly ground pepper. Cover the mackerel with the marinade and cook for 8 to 10 minutes. Leave to cool in the dish and chill for about 1 hour.

To serve, garnish each mackerel with a thin slice of lemon.

SERVES 4
PREPARATION TIME: 10 MINUTES

Belgian Endive Salad
Endives

¼ cup (50 g) raisins
1 lb. (500 g) Belgian endives
15 to 20 walnut meats
1 teaspoon Dijon mustard
2 teaspoons sherry vinegar
2 tablespoons walnut oil
Salt and pepper

Soak the raisins in a bowl of lukewarm water.

Wash the Belgian endives and remove the base of each one. Cut each into four pieces lengthwise, slicing each section directly into a large salad bowl. Drain the raisins. Sprinkle the raisins and nuts over the endives. Make a dressing by whisking together the mustard, vinegar, oil, salt, and pepper. Pour this onto the salad just before serving. Toss and serve.

SERVES 4
PREPARATION TIME: 15 MINUTES
COOKING TIME: ABOUT 10 MINUTES

Mushroom and Green Bean Salad
Champignons en salade

- 12 oz. (350 g) green beans, strings and ends removed
- 12 oz. (350 g) fresh mushrooms
- 2 shallots
- 2 tablespoons red wine vinegar
- 2 teaspoons Dijon mustard
- 6 tablespoons salad oil
- Salt and pepper

Peel the green beans, rinse them and cook them in 8 cups (2 liters) lightly salted boiling water for 10 minutes. Drain in a colander and cool under cold running water. Place on a clean towel to dry.

Cut off any dirt on the stem of each mushroom, then wash the mushrooms in cold water, pat them dry and cut into thin slices. Place in a salad bowl with the green beans. Peel the shallots, finely chop them, and scatter over the salad.

Make a dressing by whisking together the vinegar, mustard, oil, salt, and pepper. Pour the dressing onto the salad just before serving, toss gently, and serve.

SERVES 6
PREPARATION TIME: 10 MINUTES

1 oz. (30 g) sweet onion
3 tablespoons (50 g) butter
6 large green or red bell peppers
12 oz. (350 g) soft cream cheese
⅔ oz. (20 g) chives, chopped
⅔ oz. (20 g) finest quality Hungarian paprika
⅓ oz. (10 g) cumin seeds
Table salt and white pepper

Hungarian Cheese
Fromage hongroise

Finely chop the onion, gently sauté it in the butter, and allow it to cool. Wash and dry the peppers and remove the seeds and ribs. Pat them dry.

Combine the cream cheese with the cooled chopped onion and add the chives, paprika, cumin seeds, and salt and pepper. Mix thoroughly.

Stuff the peppers with this preparation, and serve them on a cheese platter.

SERVES 4
PREPARATION TIME: 7 MINUTES
COOKING TIME: ABOUT 40 MINUTES

Boiled Artichokes
Artichauts

- 4 artichokes
- 2 tablespoons kosher salt
- 1 teaspoon Dijon mustard
- 1 tablespoon red wine vinegar
- 3 tablespoons walnut oil
- Salt and pepper

Choose only artichokes that are firm and green, not bruised or discolored from shipping. Cook them in an enameled or stainless steel pot to avoid discoloration.

Bring 17 cups (4 liters) water and the salt to a boil.

Cut off the stem of each artichoke and remove the leaves around the base. Rinse in hot water before placing them in the pot to cook. The artichokes should simmer, not boil, for 40 minutes. When done, lift them out of the pot and place them, leaves down, in a colander next to the sink to drain.

Make an oil and vinegar dressing by combining the mustard, vinegar, walnut oil, and a little salt and pepper.

Serve the artichokes warm with the dressing in small individual bowls.

Note: To eat, pull off each leaf and dip the fleshy end in the dressing before scraping off the flesh between your teeth. Discard the rest of the leaf.

Greek-Style Artichokes
Artichauts à la grecque

SERVES 6
PREPARATION TIME: 15 MINUTES
COOKING TIME: 25 MINUTES

- 12 small artichokes
- 12 small white onions
- 1 tablespoon (15 g) salt
- Juice of 3 lemons
- 10 peppercorns
- 1 sprig thyme
- ½ bay leaf
- 1 stick celery
- 1 pinch dried fennel seeds, or 1 stalk fennel
- 15 coriander seeds
- ¾ cup (200 ml) olive oil

Remove the stalks of the artichokes and cut off just under 1 in. (2 cm) of the tips of the leaves. Cut the artichokes into quarters.

Prepare the marinade: Wrap the aromatic ingredients–peppercorns, thyme, bay leaf, celery, fennel, and coriander–in a small muslin bag. Bring 2 cups (500 ml) water to a boil with the salt, lemon juice, and aromatics. Leave to boil for 5 minutes before adding the oil, artichoke quarters and onions to the boiling marinade. Cook for about 20 minutes, or until you can easily detach a leaf from an artichoke bottom. Remove the artichoke pieces and transfer them to a dish. Chill and serve cold.

Mushroom Salad
Salade de champignons

SERVES 4
PREPARATION TIME: 15 MINUTES

10 oz. (300 g) medium-sized firm white button mushrooms

1 pinch sugar

Juice of 1 lemon

1 tablespoon crème fraîche or oil

Aromatic herbs, such as tarragon, chervil, chopped fennel, thyme flowers, crushed garlic, or spices of your choice

Salt and freshly ground pepper

Clean, wash, and carefully dry the mushrooms. Finely slice them and place them in a salad dish. Season with salt and freshly ground pepper, sugar, lemon juice, and crème fraîche (or oil). Season with herbs or spices of your choice and serve chilled.

SERVES 4
PREPARATION TIME: 10 MINUTES
COOKING TIME: 8 TO 9 MINUTES

Green Salad
Laitue

1 medium butterhead (Boston) lettuce
2 eggs
1 small can of anchovies in oil
1 teaspoon Dijon mustard
1 tablespoon red wine vinegar
2 tablespoons salad oil
Salt and pepper

Carefully wash and drain the lettuce. Remove the thick rib from each leaf.

Prepare the hard-boiled eggs. This should take 8 or 9 minutes, depending on whether or not the eggs have been refrigerated. Once cooked, run the eggs under cold water and peel them when they have cooled down. Cut the eggs in half lengthwise, sprinkle with salt, and place in a small serving dish.

Roll each anchovy up on itself, then place the little rolls in another small serving dish.

In a bowl, whisk together the mustard, vinegar, oil, salt, and pepper. Place the lettuce in a salad bowl, add the dressing, and toss to mix. Serve immediately, with the eggs and anchovies on the side.

SERVES 4
PREPARATION TIME: 10 MINUTES
COOKING TIME: 8 TO 9 MINUTES

Red and Green Chicory Salad
Chicorée verte et rouge

- 4 ½ oz. (125 g) green chicory (see Note)
- 4 ½ oz. (125 g) red treviso chicory (see Note)
- 2 eggs
- 1 celery heart (tender part of innermost ribs)
- 1 tablespoon red wine vinegar
- 1 teaspoon Dijon mustard
- 3 tablespoons salad oil
- Salt and pepper
- 2 oz. (50 g) black olives (about 10)

Cut the base off each little chicory. Wash the leaves carefully and set aside. Prepare the hard-boiled eggs. This should take 8 or 9 minutes, depending on whether or not the eggs have been refrigerated. Wash the celery and remove the stringy filaments by breaking the base toward the rounded, ridged side and pulling it up toward the leaves. Dice the celery.

In a salad bowl, whisk together the vinegar, mustard, and oil, then season with a little salt and pepper.

Once cooked, run the hard-boiled eggs under cold water and peel them when they have cooled down. Slice the eggs into the salad bowl. Add the chicory, olives, and celery. Toss gently and serve immediately.

Note: This kind of chicory forms tiny loose-leafed heads and is either red or green. Its characteristic bitter taste makes substitutions difficult, although other types of chicory and red varieties of lettuce mixed together–2 cups tightly packed (125 g) of each–are worth trying.

SERVES 4
PREPARATION TIME: 10 MINUTES

Lamb's Lettuce and Beet Salad
Mâche ou doucette à la betterave rouge

8 oz. (250 g) lamb's lettuce (see Note)
1 celery heart (tender part of innermost ribs)
1 small cooked beet
1 teaspoon Dijon mustard
1 tablespoon red wine vinegar
2 tablespoons walnut oil
Salt and pepper

Cut off the base of each bunch of lamb's lettuce, then wash carefully, and drain thoroughly.

Remove the stringy parts of the celery. Wash and dice the celery. Peel and dice the beet.

In a salad bowl, whisk together the mustard, vinegar, oil, salt, and pepper. When ready to serve, place the lettuce, celery, and beets in the bowl and toss. Serve immediately.

Note: Lamb's lettuce is particularly small-leafed and tender; if it is not available, try using very young spinach leaves with the same seasoning.

SERVES 4
PREPARATION TIME: 10 MINUTES

Curly-Leaf Endive Salad
Frisée

- 1 medium head of curly-leaf endive or escarole
- 2 cloves garlic
- 8 × 1 in. (2.5 cm) squares of toasted bread (croutons)
- 1 teaspoon Dijon mustard
- 1 tablespoon red wine vinegar
- 2 tablespoons salad oil
- Salt and pepper

Carefully wash, drain, and coarsely chop the endives.

Peel the cloves of garlic and slice them in half lengthwise. Rub each crouton with garlic. Set aside.

In a large salad bowl, whisk together the mustard, vinegar, oil, salt, and pepper. Then place the croutons in the bowl and stir to coat them with the dressing. Add the endives, toss, and serve immediately.

SERVES 4
PREPARATION TIME: 15 MINUTES
COOKING TIME: 18 TO 25 MINUTES

2 ¼ lb. (1 kg) asparagus
2 tablespoons kosher salt
1 teaspoon Dijon mustard
1 tablespoon red wine vinegar
3 tablespoons olive oil
Salt and pepper
1 egg white

Asparagus Salad
Asperges

Break off the tough, stringy base of each asparagus; then, if using large white ones, peel them with a vegetable peeler. Small green asparagus simply need to have the scales along the stem removed.

Wash the asparagus under cold running water and divide them into two or three bunches. Tie each bunch with kitchen string both at the bottom and toward the tip end.

Bring 10 cups (2.5 liters) water and the salt to a boil in a large pot. Drop the asparagus into the water, bring back to a boil, then lower the heat and simmer for 18 to 25 minutes, depending on size: the tip of a knife should easily penetrate the stem of the asparagus when done. Lift the asparagus out of the pot and leave them on a clean cloth to drain. Remove the strings.

Serve the asparagus warm with a vinaigrette mousseline. To make this, whisk together the mustard, vinegar, and oil, with a little salt and pepper. Beat the egg white until thick and foamy, but not stiff, then gently whisk it into the sauce just before serving.

Variation: The asparagus may also be served cold with a simple Vinaigrette (see p. 542) or as a hot side dish with Hollandaise Sauce (see p. 548).

SERVES 4
PREPARATION TIME: 20 MINUTES
COOKING TIME: 7 MINUTES

Dandelion Green and Bacon Salad
Pissenlit au lard

- 12 oz. (350 g) dandelion greens
- 7 oz. (200 g) salt pork or slab bacon
- 1 teaspoon Dijon mustard
- 1 tablespoon red wine vinegar
- 3 tablespoons olive oil
- Salt and pepper

Carefully wash the dandelion greens: cut each little bunch in half lengthwise, and shake them in a bowl of cold water to remove any dirt. Drain thoroughly. Place in a large salad bowl and set aside.

In a mixing bowl, whisk together the mustard, vinegar, oil, salt, and pepper; set aside.

Remove the bacon rinds. Cut the bacon into ½-in. (1-cm) cubes and brown in an ungreased frying pan. This should take about 7 minutes. Pour off all the fat and add the bacon to the dandelion greens. Add the dressing, toss, and serve immediately.

Variation: Small squares of toasted bread (croutons) may be rubbed with half a clove of garlic and added to the salad just before serving.

If preferred, the bacon can be cut into four slices and each slice cut in half.

SERVES 4
PREPARATION TIME: 10 MINUTES
CHILLING TIME: 30 MINUTES

3 cucumbers weighing 1 ¼-1 ½ lb. (600 to 700 g) in total

1 bunch chives

2 tablespoons crème fraîche or heavy cream, or half an individual plain yogurt

1 tablespoon lemon juice

Salt and pepper

Cucumber and Cream Salad
Concombres à la crème

Cucumbers are easier to digest if they have been peeled and salted before being used in salads.

Peel the cucumbers and cut them into slices. Place them on a large plate, salt, then turn the pieces over and salt again. Leave the cucumbers in the refrigerator for 30 minutes before making the salad.

Remove the cucumbers from the refrigerator, place in a colander, and rinse off under cold running water. Leave them to dry on a paper towel. Finely chop the chives. Make a sauce by stirring together the cream, lemon juice, chives, salt, and pepper. Place the cucumbers on individual plates, spoon the sauce over them, and serve.

SERVES 4
PREPARATION TIME: 25 MINUTES

Chicken Salad
Poulet en salade

- Both breasts from a roasted or boiled chicken
- 1 small butterhead (Boston) lettuce
- Tender pale leaves from a curly-leaf endive
- 1 celery heart (tender part of innermost ribs)
- 3 ½ oz. (100 g) Gruyère cheese
- 4 new baby onions
- 1 clove garlic (optional)
- 3 large tomatoes
- 1 scant cup (100 g) black olives
- 1 cup (100 g) walnut meats
- 1 tablespoon sherry vinegar
- 3 tablespoons olive oil
- Salt and pepper

This salad could be a meal in itself–it's especially nice on a summer evening.

Carefully wash, and coarsely chop the lettuce and endive leaves. Wash and dice the celery into cubes of roughly ½ in. (1 cm). Dice the Gruyère cheese. Peel and finely slice the onions. Peel and finely chop the garlic (if using).

Cut the chicken breasts into strips.

Run the tomatoes under hot water, peel them, and chop them.

Place the chicken, lettuce, endives, celery, onion, cheese, olives, tomatoes, and nuts all in a salad bowl and chill until ready to serve.

In a small bowl, whisk together the vinegar, oil, salt, pepper, and garlic (if using). Pour over the salad, toss, and serve immediately.

SERVES 4
PREPARATION TIME:
1 HOUR 15 MINUTES

Cantaloupe and Prosciutto
Melons et jambon de Parme

4 small or 2 large cantaloupes
Crushed ice
8 very thin slices prosciutto

Make sure your melons are perfectly ripe. If you keep them in the refrigerator, it is best to first place them in a plastic bag because a truly ripe melon will impregnate everything with its aroma. Otherwise, place the uncut melons in a large bowl of ice water and leave for 1 hour before serving.

This dish can be served in various ways; I find the following one particularly attractive. Place some crushed ice on a large serving platter. If using small canteloupes, cut off the very top of each one just below the stem and reserve. Scoop out all the seeds with a spoon, then place two slices of ham around the opening of each melon, pleating it so it will look like a fancy collar coming out of the melon. Place the "top" with the stem back in place and serve.

If the melons are large, simply cut them in half, scoop out the seeds, place the ham in each half as described above, and serve.

This is delicious served with a glass of red port.

Tabbouleh
Taboulé

SERVES 4
PREPARATION TIME: 20 MINUTES
COOKING TIME: 20 MINUTES

4 oz. (125 g) couscous
5 tablespoons (75 ml) olive oil
Juice of 2 lemons
2 sprigs fresh mint
A few chives
7 oz. (200 g) tomatoes
3 ½ oz. (100 g) peas, fresh or frozen
Salt and pepper

Feel free to add other herbs depending on your tastes, though my personal preference is for this, the simplest, version.

Prepare the couscous according to the manufacturer's directions. When it is cooked, place it in a salad bowl. Combine the olive oil, lemon juice, salt, and pepper and pour over the couscous. Mix well and leave to cool.

Finely chop the mint leaves and snip the chives. Dip the tomatoes in boiling water and peel them. Chop them into small dice. Transfer them to a plate, season with salt and pepper, and sprinkle with the herbs.

Cook the peas: if you are using fresh peas, boil them in 2 cups (500 ml) salted water; if you are using frozen peas, follow the directions on the packet. Drain and refresh them. When the couscous and peas have both cooled, combine them and add the herbed tomatoes. Adjust the seasoning, transfer to a salad bowl, and place in the refrigerator. Tabbouleh must be served well chilled.

SERVES 4
PREPARATION TIME: 15 TO 20 MINUTES
COOKING TIME: 25 MINUTES

Rice and Crabmeat Salad
Salade de riz

- About 7 oz. (200 g) finest quality crabmeat
- ¾ cup (150 g) long-grain rice
- 1 pinch saffron
- ⅔ cup (100 g) shelled peas
- ½ cup (120 ml) Mayonnaise (see p. 552)
- 20 black olives
- Salt

Bring 3 cups (750 ml) water to a boil in a medium saucepan, salt lightly, add the saffron, and stir. Add the rice and cook at a moderate boil, uncovered, for 15 minutes. Drain thoroughly, then place in a salad bowl.

In another saucepan, boil the peas for 10 to 12 minutes, or until tender, in lightly salted water. If using frozen peas, follow the instructions indicated on the pack. Drain, then add to the bowl with the rice.

Separate four nice pieces of claw meat from the crab and set aside. Break up the rest of the meat, removing any cartilage, and set aside on another plate.

When the rice and peas have cooled completely, add the bits of crabmeat.

Stir in the Mayonnaise just before serving. Decorate by placing the reserved claw meat on top of the salad. Arrange the olives around it.

SERVES 4
PREPARATION TIME: 40 MINUTES
COOKING TIME: 30 MINUTES

Potato Salad with Lyonnaise Pistachio Sausage
Salade de pommes de terre et saucisson pistaché

- 1 dried Lyonnaise sausage with pistachio nuts
- 2 ¼ lb. (1 kg) yellow, firm potatoes, such as Yukon Gold or Estima
- 1 handful kosher salt
- Scant ½ cup (100 ml) white wine
- 2 tablespoons Dijon mustard
- 1 tablespoon white wine vinegar
- 3 tablespoons peanut oil (or other neutral oil)
- Salt and freshly ground pepper
- 2 shallots
- 5 sprigs chervil
- 2 sprigs flat-leaf parsley

Prepare the ingredients for this salad so that you can serve it while the sliced sausage is still warm.

Place the sausage in a pot and cover it completely with cold water. Bring to a simmer and leave to simmer gently for 30 minutes. Remove the pot from the heat and leave the sausage in it for a further 5 minutes.

Wash the potatoes and place them in a pot of cold water with a handful of kosher salt. Bring to a boil and cook for about 20 minutes, or until done (check with the tip of a knife; they should remain relatively firm for this salad).

While they are still warm, peel and slice them. Immediately pour over the white wine.

Prepare the vinaigrette: combine the mustard, vinegar, salt, pepper, and oil. Pour the vinaigrette over the sliced potatoes.

Peel the shallots and chop them finely. Pick the leaves off the chervil and chop both herbs.

Cut the sausage into thick slices.

Arrange the sliced potatoes and still-warm sausage slices on a serving dish. Scatter with the chopped shallots, parsley, and chervil.

Baby Artichokes *à la Barigoule*
Artichauts "barigoule"

SERVES 4
PREPARATION TIME: 20 MINUTES
COOKING TIME: 45 MINUTES

- 8 baby artichokes weighing about 1 ¼ lb. (600 g) in total
- 8 baby onions
- 4 medium mushrooms
- 4 large tomatoes
- 4 oz. (125 g) salt pork or bacon
- 3 tablespoons olive oil
- 2 cloves garlic
- 1 sprig thyme
- ¼ bay leaf
- Salt and pepper

Bring 10 cups (2.5 liters) water to a boil in a large pot.

Cut off the leaves of each artichoke about a third of the way down from the top. Cut off the stems, then remove the tough outer leaves around the base and cut each artichoke into four pieces. Use a little spoon to scoop out the choke in the center of each piece. Quickly rinse the artichokes in warm water, then drop them into the boiling water, cook for 15 minutes, and drain.

Meanwhile, peel the onions. If small, leave them whole. Cut off any dirt on the stem of each mushroom, then wash the mushrooms and cut them into quarters. Blanch the tomatoes, peel them and chop them. Remove the rind from the bacon or salt pork. Dice the bacon or salt pork into ½-in. (1-cm) cubes and brown in an ungreased frying pan for 5 to 7 minutes.

Heat the oil in a high-sided frying pan or cast-iron pot. Add the tomatoes, mushrooms, onions, garlic, thyme, bay leaf, and salt pork or bacon. Cook for 10 to 20 minutes, or until half of the moisture from the vegetables has evaporated, then add the artichokes, salt, and pepper. Cover the pan and simmer for 25 minutes.

Serve immediately, either in the pan used to cook the artichokes or in a serving dish.

Note: Artichokes cooked this way are excellent cold as well as hot.

SERVES 6 TO 8
PREPARATION TIME: 1 HOUR
COOKING TIME: 40 MINUTES

Mixed Raw Vegetable Platter
Hors-d'œuvre variés

- 1 lb. (500 g) new potatoes
- 2 tablespoons olive oil
- 8 oz. (225 g) green beans
- 4 eggs
- 1 small butterhead (Boston) lettuce
- 1 bunch radishes
- 4 small celery hearts (tender part of innermost ribs)
- 1 cucumber
- 4 medium tomatoes
- 4 baby artichokes
- A little lemon juice
- 1 lb. (500 g) broad beans
- 7-oz. (200-g) can of tuna packed in oil
- 1-oz. (30-g) can of anchovies packed in oil
- 1 scant cup (150 g) black olives
- Anchovy Paste (see p. 555)
- 3 teaspoons Dijon mustard
- 3 tablespoons red wine vinegar
- 9 tablespoons olive oil
- Salt and pepper
- 1 loaf whole-wheat or country-style bread
- Butter

Wash the potatoes, boil them in their skins for 30 minutes, then peel and slice them. Place in a serving dish, sprinkle with salt and pepper, and spoon 2 tablespoons of olive oil over them. Stir gently and leave to cool.

String the green beans, wash them, and drain them. Drop the green beans into a large pot of lightly salted boiling water, and simmer for 10 to 15 minutes. Taste to see if they're done (they shouldn't be too cooked). Drain the beans in a colander, cool quickly under cold running water, and set aside.

Boil the eggs for 9 minutes if taken straight from the refrigerator, otherwise 8 minutes, until hard-boiled. Drain and cool under running water. Remove the shells, cut each egg in half lengthwise, and set aside.

Wash the lettuce, remove the rib from the center of each leaf, place the leaves on a platter or in a bowl, and set aside.

Cut the leaves off the radishes, carefully wash the radishes, and set aside.

Wash the celery, place in a serving dish, and set aside.

Peel the cucumber, cut it into thick slices, place in a large bowl, and sprinkle generously with salt. Leave for 20 minutes. Then place sliced cucumber in a colander and rinse under cold running water. After drying slices on a paper towel, put them in a serving dish, and set aside.

Wash the tomatoes and wipe them dry, cut out the stems and cut the tomatoes into wedges with a stainless steel knife, place them in a serving dish, sprinkle with salt, and set aside.

Cut off the stems of the artichokes and dip the artichokes in a large bowl of cold water mixed with a little lemon juice; shake them to wash and remove any dirt, drain, place on a plate, and set aside.

Shell the broad beans and remove the little skin that surrounds each bean.

Place in a bowl and reserve.

Place the tuna in a small serving dish and the anchovies in another; place the olives in a third bowl.

Try to present each ingredient in an attractive bowl of appropriate dimensions. Place everything in the refrigerator for about 1 hour before serving.

To serve, place the anchovy paste in a small bowl and prepare an oil and vinegar dressing by mixing together the mustard, vinegar, olive oil, and a little salt and pepper.

Toast one or two large slices of bread per person. Then serve the vegetables, eggs, fish, sauces, and a dish of butter all at once. Place everything on the table and let your guests serve themselves, dipping the vegetables into one of the sauces or simply eating them plain with a little salt and butter.

Serving suggestions: This vegetable platter takes a little while to make, but it's worth the trouble. It's the perfect thing to serve before (or with) shish kebabs or barbecued pork or lamb. It can also be served alone at lunchtime or as a light late-summer dinner.

WARM APPETIZERS

SERVES 4
PREPARATION TIME: 30 MINUTES
COOKING TIME: 15 MINUTES

Parmesan Soufflés
Soufflés au Parmesan

1 ⅔ cups (400 ml) milk
4 eggs, separated
2 teaspoons milk
¾ cup (2 ½ oz./75 g) flour
2 oz. (60 g) Parmesan or Gruyère cheese, grated
2 tablespoons (30 g) butter, plus extra for greasing the molds
Salt and pepper
Nutmeg to taste

Preheat the oven to 350°F (180°C).

Butter four small soufflé molds or porcelain ramekins. Bring the milk to a boil and leave it to cool a little. Dilute the egg yolks with the 2 teaspoons of milk. Then pour the slightly cooled milk little by little over the flour, stirring all the time, until you have a perfectly smooth mixture with no lumps. Season with salt and add a pinch of pepper and a little nutmeg. Bring this back to a boil, stirring constantly. As soon as it begins boiling, remove the pan from the heat and immediately stir in the cheese, butter, and yolks diluted with milk.

Whisk the 4 egg whites to firm peaks and carefully fold them into the milk mixture. Make sure you don't deflate the whisked whites.

Fill the soufflé molds or ramekins with the batter three-quarters to the top and bake for 10 minutes. The soufflés should be well risen with a lovely crust.

Serve immediately.

SERVES 6
PREPARATION TIME: 20 MINUTES
COOKING TIME: 30 MINUTES

Ham Soufflés
Soufflés au jambon

2 cups (500 ml) Béchamel or White Sauce (see p. 536)
8 oz. (250 g) cooked lean ham
2 tablespoons (30 g) butter
1 pinch paprika
3 eggs, separated

Preheat the oven to 350°F (180°C).

Butter a soufflé dish or individual ramekins. Heat the béchamel sauce. Grind or process the ham finely with the butter. Push the mixture through a fine-meshed sieve and stir it into the hot béchamel sauce with the paprika. Incorporate the three egg yolks. Whisk the egg whites to firm peaks and fold them in carefully. Make sure you don't deflate the whisked whites.

Pour the mixture into the soufflé dish to three-quarters to the top and bake for about 30 minutes, until the batter has doubled in volume and risen well above the rim.

Serve immediately.

Poached Sausage with Warm Potato Salad
Saucisson chaud, pommes à l'huile

SERVES 4
PREPARATION TIME: 20 MINUTES
COOKING TIME: 30 MINUTES

- 1 large or 2 medium pure pork poaching sausages (*saucisson de Lyon* or other), weighing 1 ¾ lb. (800 g) in total
- 1 ¼ lb. (600 g) new potatoes
- ½ bunch chives
- 3 tablespoons olive oil
- 1 ½ tablespoons white wine vinegar
- 1 ½ tablespoons white wine
- Salt and pepper

Wash the potatoes, place them in a large pot with some water and a little salt, and bring to a boil. Cook for 30 minutes.

Prick the sausage in several places with a pin or the tip of a knife, then place it in another pot with 8 cups (2 liters) of cold water, lightly salted. Bring just to a boil, then immediately lower the heat and simmer for 25 minutes (do not boil).

Wash the chives and pat them dry using paper towel. Use scissors to finely chop the chives and set aside.

The potatoes and sausage should finish cooking at about the same time. Keep the sausage warm by covering the pot and removing it from the heat while making the potato salad.

Check whether the potatoes are done with the tip of a knife: they should be slightly firm. Once cooked, peel the potatoes while they are still hot. Cut the potatoes into thick slices, and place them in a salad bowl with the olive oil, vinegar, white wine, salt, pepper, and chives. Toss gently.

Lift the sausage out of the water, cut it into thick slices, and place it on a warm platter.

Serve with the bowl of warm potato salad on the side.

Variation: You may make a mustard dressing to serve with the sausage at the table if you like. Make a Vinaigrette (see p. 542), but use lemon juice instead of vinegar, and double the mustard measurement.

SERVES 4
PREPARATION TIME: 20 MINUTES
COOKING TIME: 50 MINUTES

Endives with Ham
Endives au jambon

2 ¼ lb. (1 kg) Belgian endives
1 ½ teaspoons (10 g) salt
Juice of ½ lemon
1½ tablespoons (20 g) butter
4 slices ham
Generous ¾ cup (200 ml) crème fraîche or heavy cream
1 cup (100 g) grated Gruyère cheese
Pepper

Preheat the oven to 350°F (180°C).

Remove the outer leaves from the endives. Use a small knife to hollow out the base of each endive, then rinse them off under hot water.

Bring 6 cups (1.5 liters) water, salt, and lemon juice to a boil, add the endives, cook for 20 minutes, and drain.

Place the endives head to tail in a buttered baking dish. Cut the ham into small pieces, and sprinkle over the endives. Pour in the cream and spread it out evenly. Sprinkle with the grated cheese and a little pepper, then bake for 25 to 30 minutes, or until golden brown.

Serve the endives in the baking dish.

SERVES 6
PREPARATION TIME: 25 MINUTES
COOKING TIME: 15 MINUTES

Chicken Croquettes
Croquettes de volaille

- 8 oz. (250 g) cooked chicken
- 3 ½ oz. (100 g) lean cooked ham or pickled tongue
- 2 oz. (50 g) raw truffles, preferably in season
- 3 ½ oz. (100 g) mushrooms
- 3 tablespoons (50g) butter
- 1 ⅔ cups (400 ml) white chicken broth thickened with flour (a velouté)
- 3 egg yolks
- 2 oz. (50 g) stale bread, crusts removed
- 1 egg
- ½ cup (1 ¾ oz./50 g) flour plus a pinch for the bread crumbs
- Oil for frying
- Tomato Sauce for serving (see p. 544)

Cut the chicken, ham or tongue, truffles, and mushrooms into fine dice. Use a suitably large sauté pan and heat the butter in it over high heat. When it is sizzling, throw in the mushrooms. A few seconds later, add the truffles, and then the thickened chicken broth. Still over high heat, cook until reduced by half. Add the diced chicken and ham or tongue and bring back to a boil. As soon as it boils, remove the pan from the heat and stir in the three egg yolks. Combine well and pour the mixture into a buttered dish. Spread it out and dab it with a piece of butter. Leave to cool.

While it is cooling, crush the stale bread together with a pinch of flour in a folded kitchen cloth. Push it through a medium-meshed sieve or colander. This will make fresh bread crumbs. Alternatively, you may use ready-made bread crumbs, though homemade are better.

Beat the remaining egg in a bowl.

When the mixture has cooled, divide it into 2 oz. (50 g) portions. Shape each one into a cork shape by rolling lightly on a floured board. Dip each in the beaten egg and then into the bread crumbs.

Just before serving, fry the croquettes in very hot oil. They should be crisp and golden on the outside and creamy inside.

Drain on a piece of paper towel and serve accompanied with Tomato Sauce.

Brioche Sausage Roll
Saucisson en brioche

SERVES 5 TO 6
PREPARATION TIME: 30 MINUTES
COOKING TIME:
1 HOUR 20 MINUTES

- 1 dried pork sausage for cooking, weighing about 2 ¼ lb. (1 kg) and about 12 in. (30 cm) long (at specialty charcuterie counters)
- 1 cup (250 ml) Beaujolais wine or other fruity red wine
- 1 lb. (500 g) Brioche Dough (see p. 561)
- 1 egg yolk
- Flour for dusting

Place the dried sausage in cold water in a pan over minimum heat. Cook it, ensuring that the water does not boil, for 30 minutes. Then remove the pan from the heat and leave the sausage to cool a little. Preheat the oven to 475°F (240°C), or as high as your oven will go. While the sausage is still warm, remove it from the pan and peel off the casing. Roast it for a few minutes. The sausage will render some of its fat, which you should discard. Deglaze the dish with Beaujolais wine, return to the stovetop, and reduce until dry.

Roll out the brioche dough until it is just a little longer than the sausage, and is 6 in. (15 cm) wide. At this stage, you may reserve a little dough for decoration if you wish.

Brush the sausage with a little egg yolk and sprinkle it with flour. Brush the edge of the dough lightly with water to ensure that the two sides stick together so that the brioche will stay firmly closed and then roll the sausage up in it.

Brush the dough all over with the remaining egg yolk, and decorate it with a few cutout shapes of dough or simply with the tip of a knife.

Place the enclosed sausage on a baking tray and leave the dough to rise a little. Bake in a hot oven at 425°F (220°C) for about 30 minutes, until the brioche is a lovely golden color.

To serve, cut into slices. A fine Périgueux sauce is an excellent accompaniment to this dish.

Note: Périgueux sauce is Madeira sauce to which finely chopped or diced truffles are added. It is named after the town of Périgueux in the Périgord region of France, renowned for its truffles.

Warm Lentil Salad
Salade de lentilles

SERVES 4
PREPARATION TIME: 15 MINUTES
COOKING TIME: 1 HOUR 30 MINUTES
SOAKING TIME: 12 HOURS

- 1 onion
- 1 ½ cups or 10 ½ oz. (300 g) lentils, preferably dark green or tan
- 5 oz. (150 g) salt pork or slab bacon
- 1 small bunch chives
- 1 shallot
- 1 teaspoon Dijon mustard
- 1 tablespoon red wine vinegar
- 3 tablespoons walnut oil
- Salt and pepper
- Country-style bread for serving

Peel the onion. Wash the lentils under cold water in a colander. Place the lentils in a large saucepan with 8 cups (2 liters) cold water. Salt lightly, add the onion, and bring to a boil. Lower the heat, cover the pan, and simmer for 1 ½ hours, or until the lentils are tender but not falling apart.

Remove the rinds and cut the salt pork or bacon into ½-in. (1-cm) cubes. Wash and finely chop the chives. Peel and chop the shallot, and set aside. Fifteen minutes before serving, fry the salt pork or bacon until the pieces have browned on all sides, then pour off the fat, remove from the heat, and cover the pan to keep warm.

Make a dressing by whisking together the mustard, vinegar, oil, salt, and pepper.

Once the lentils are done, remove the onion and drain the lentils in a sieve or colander. Place them in a large salad bowl with the chives, shallots, and dressing. Toss gently to season, and place the pieces of bacon on top. Serve warm with country-style bread.

Warm Potato Salad
Salade de pommes de terre

SERVES 4
PREPARATION TIME: 15 MINUTES
COOKING TIME: 30 MINUTES

1 ¾ lb. (800 g) potatoes
1 shallot
1 small bunch chives
1 teaspoon Dijon mustard
1 tablespoon red wine vinegar
3 tablespoons olive oil
Salt and pepper

Wash the potatoes, but don't peel them. Place them in a pot with 6 cups (1.5 liters) water, salt lightly, and bring to a boil. Cook covered for 30 minutes or until a knife penetrates them easily.

Meanwhile, peel and finely chop the shallot on a cutting board. Wash and dry the chives, and finely chop them using scissors. Set aside.

Once cooked, drain the potatoes in a colander, rinse them rapidly under cold running water to cool them slightly, and peel them while they are still warm (the skins will come off easily).

Cut the potatoes into thick slices and place them in a salad bowl. Make a dressing by whisking together the mustard, vinegar, oil, salt, and pepper. Pour over the potatoes, add the shallot and chives, then toss gently so as not to crush the potatoes. Serve.

SERVES 4
PREPARATION TIME: 15 MINUTES
COOKING TIME: 25 MINUTES

Risotto with Chicken Livers
Risotto aux foies de volailles

Heaped ½ cup (4 ½ oz./125 g) rice
6 large mushrooms
1 shallot
1 medium-sized onion
4 tablespoons (60 g) butter, divided
2 cups (500 ml) clear stock
6 chicken livers
1 tablespoon thickened veal *jus* (either store-bought or leftovers from a roast, thickened with a little flour)
Salt and pepper

Cut the mushrooms into quarters and chop the shallot. Set aside.

Chop the onion finely and sauté it gently in a sauté pan in one-third of the butter until it is transparent. Add the rice and heat in the butter. Pour in the clear stock, cover with the lid, and cook gently for 18 minutes. Then carefully stir in another third of the butter, and pour it into a warmed dish.

Cut the chicken livers into halves and season them with salt and pepper. Heat the last third of the butter in a very hot pan and sauté the livers lightly. Do not overcook. Transfer them to the dish of rice, and quickly cook the quartered mushrooms and chopped shallot. Remove from the heat and incorporate the thickened veal jus. Drizzle the *jus* over the livers and rice.

Note: The rice should be well cooked but not sticky–the grains should separate.

Gougère

SERVES 4
PREPARATION TIME: 20 MINUTES
COOKING TIME: 25 MINUTES

- 3 ½ oz. (100 g) Gruyère cheese
- 4 tablespoons (60 g) butter, plus butter for the soufflé dish
- Generous ½ cup (150 ml) water
- 1 scant cup (125 g) flour
- 3 eggs, separated
- Salt
- Nutmeg

Preheat the oven to 425°F (210°C).

Grate the Gruyère cheese and set aside.

Melt the butter with a little salt in a saucepan, then pour in the water and bring to a boil. Add the flour all at once, stirring constantly until the batter is smooth, detaches from the sides of the saucepan, and forms a ball around the spoon. Remove the pan from the heat and beat in the egg yolks one by one; then stir in the grated cheese and a little nutmeg.

Lightly butter a 6-in. (15-cm) soufflé mold or four individual ramekins, and place in the oven while finishing the batter.

Beat the egg whites until stiff, add a quarter of them to the batter, stirring them in with the whisk; then incorporate the rest of the egg whites in the same way. Remember to keep an eye on the buttered mold(s)–the butter should just start to brown lightly. Remove the mold(s) from the oven, pour in the batter, return to the oven, and bake for 25 minutes or until the blade of the knife comes out clean when stuck into the center of the gougère. Serve as soon as it comes out of the oven.

Serving suggestions: A gougère can be served alone as an entrée or as an accompaniment to meat, especially roast beef or lamb.

SERVES 4
PREPARATION TIME: 15 MINUTES
COOKING TIME: 30 TO 35 MINUTES

4 large quenelles, either store-bought or homemade
3 tablespoons (40 g) butter
½ cup (40 g) grated Gruyère cheese
Salt and freshly ground pepper
A little grated nutmeg
Shelled shrimps (optional)

Quenelles au Gratin

Buy or make your favorite quenelles: poultry, pike, etc.

Preheat the oven to 425°F (210°C).

Generously butter an ovenproof dish and arrange the quenelles in it. Bake for about 15 to 20 minutes, keeping a careful eye on it. About 15 minutes before the end of the cooking time, sprinkle the quenelles with the grated cheese. Season with salt, pepper, and grated nutmeg. Return the dish to the oven and finish baking until the top is crisp. If you like, add shelled shrimp to this dish.

QUICHES & TARTS

SERVES 4
PREPARATION TIME: 20 MINUTES
RESTING TIME:
1 HOUR 30 MINUTES
COOKING TIME: 35 MINUTES

DOUGH

5 tablespoons (75 g) butter

1 ½ cups (150 g) flour

½ teaspoon (4 g) salt

2 tablespoons water

(A frozen crust can be used instead.)

FILLING

4 oz. (125 g) slab bacon or prosciutto

2 eggs

6 tablespoons (100 ml) crème fraîche or heavy cream

1 oz. (30g) butter

Salt and pepper

Nutmeg

Quiche Lorraine

If you are preparing a crust from scratch, place the flour and salt in a large mixing bowl. Take the butter out of the refrigerator an hour before beginning the crust. Break the butter into the bowl in little nut-sized pieces, then use your fingers to "pinch" the flour and butter together. Work quickly to make a crumbly mixture, then add the water and quickly form the dough into a ball, working it as little as possible. Cover the ball of dough with a clean cloth and leave for 1 ½ hours before baking.

If you are using a frozen crust, simply defrost it.

Meanwhile, remove the rind from the bacon and cut into ½-in. (1-cm) cubes; or, if using prosciutto, cut into strips. Fry the bacon or prosciutto in an ungreased frying pan until the pieces have browned.

Preheat the oven to 450°F–475°F (240°C).

Roll out the dough on a well-floured surface to make a circle about ¼ in. (5 mm) thick. Lightly butter an 8-in. (20-cm) pie pan, line with the dough, and prick the bottom with a fork. Place the pieces of bacon evenly over the bottom, gently pushing them into the dough, then place in the oven for 15 minutes.

Whisk the eggs and cream together in a mixing bowl. Add a little salt, pepper, and nutmeg. When the 15 minutes of baking time is up, pour this mixture into the pie pan, dot with butter, lower the oven temperature to 300°F (150°C), and bake 20 minutes more. If the quiche colors too much while baking, cover with a piece of aluminum foil.

Serve hot from the oven.

SERVES 4 TO 5
PREPARATION TIME: 30 MINUTES
RESTING TIME:
1 HOUR 30 MINUTES
COOKING TIME: 35 MINUTES

DOUGH

2 ¼ cups (200 g) flour

¾ teaspoon (5 g) salt

7 tablespoons (100 g) softened butter

3 tablespoons water

FILLING

2 ¼ lb. (1 kg) spinach

4 teaspoons (30 g) salt

2 eggs

Generous ¾ cup (200 ml) crème fraîche or heavy cream

¾ cup (100 g) Gruyère cheese, grated

Salt and pepper

Nutmeg

Spinach Quiche
Tarte aux épinards

Make the dough as described in the recipe for Shortcrust Pastry (see p. 568), but use the measurements given here.

Preheat the oven to 425°F (210°C).

Remove the stem from each leaf of spinach, then wash the spinach carefully in a sink full of cold water. Bring 3 ½ quarts (3.5 liters) of water and the salt to a boil. Drain the spinach and drop it into the boiling water, boil for 5 minutes from the time the water comes back to a boil, then drain in a colander and cool under cold running water. Squeeze all the water out of the spinach using the palm of your hand, then chop it coarsely with a knife. Season with salt and pepper and set aside.

Roll out the dough on a well-floured table into a circle about ¼ in. (5 mm) thick, and line a 9 ½-in. (24-cm) pie pan with it. Prick the bottom with a fork.

Place the eggs in a large bowl with the cream and grated cheese, and beat to combine. Season generously with salt and pepper, add a little nutmeg, then stir in the cooked spinach. Pour this mixture into the pie pan and bake for 20 minutes, then lower the heat to 350°F (180°C) and continue baking 10 minutes more. Turn off the oven, but leave the quiche inside for 3 more minutes.

Serve hot.

SERVES 8
PREPARATION TIME: 30 MINUTES
COOKING TIME: 40 MINUTES

Alsatian Cheese Cake
Tarte alsacienne au fromage blanc

- 2 cups (500 ml) milk
- 1 lb. (500 g) *fromage blanc* (substitute Quark, yogurt cheese, or buttermilk cheese; see Note p. 56)
- 1 ¼ cups (9 oz./250 g) sugar
- 1 ¼ cups (120 g) flour
- 3 eggs
- ⅓ cup (150 ml) crème fraîche or heavy cream
- 14 oz. (400 g) Puff Pastry (see p. 565)
- Butter to grease the tart pan
- Special equipment: a tart pan with a detachable base

Set the *fromage blanc* in a colander lined with cheesecloth to drain.

Bring the milk to a boil.

Beat together the *fromage blanc* and sugar in a mixing bowl. Stir in the flour, followed by the eggs, one by one, and lastly, the cream. When they are thoroughly combined, gradually stir in the hot milk.

Preheat the oven to 425°F (210°C).

Butter the tart pan. Roll out the puff pastry so that it fits the pan, drape it over a rolling pin, and transfer to the pan. Prick the dough with a fork. Pour the cream cheese mixture into the pan and bake for about 35 minutes, until golden.

When the visible part of the pastry crust is done (it should be lightly browned), switch off the oven, but leave the tart inside for at least 5 minutes with the door slightly ajar.

When you remove the tart from the oven, take it out of the tart pan and leave to cool on a rack.

Serve still warm or cool.

Flammenküche

SERVES 6
PREPARATION TIME: 20 MINUTES
COOKING TIME: 15 MINUTES

- 10 oz. (300 g) onions
- 2 teaspoons (10 g) butter, plus a little extra for the baking tray
- 8 oz. (250 g) bacon
- 5 oz. (150 g) *fromage blanc*
- ¾ cup (200 ml) crème fraîche or heavy cream
- ⅓ cup (90 ml) canola (rapeseed) oil
- 1 ¼ lb. (600 g) Bread Dough (see p. 567)
- Salt

Peel and slice the onions. Soften them a little in the butter, ensuring that they do not color.

Remove the rind from the bacon and dice. Blanch the dice for 1 minute in boiling water. Refresh under cold water and dry.

Combine the *fromage blanc* and cream. Season with salt and incorporate 4 tablespoons of the canola oil.

Preheat the oven to 450°F-475°F (240°C).

Roll out the bread dough as thinly as possible. Lightly butter the baking tray and transfer the dough to it. Lift up the edges and roll them over to make a rim for your tart.

Spread out the softened onions, arrange the bacon bits over it, and pour over the cream and cream cheese mixture. Drizzle with the remaining canola oil.

Bake for about 10 minutes.

Brocciu Tart
Tarte au brocciu

SERVES 6
PREPARATION TIME: 15 MINUTES
COOKING TIME: 45 MINUTES

- 1 organic or unsprayed lemon, or scant ¼ cup (50 ml) eau-de-vie (brandy or fruit-based spirit)
- 1 lb. (500 g) brocciu (a Corsican specialty of unsalted fresh goat or ewe's milk cheese; substitute any fresh goat or ewe's milk cheese)
- 5 eggs
- 1 ¼ cups (9 oz./250 g) sugar
- 1 knob of butter

Preheat the oven to 450°F-475°F (240°C).

Finely grate the lemon zest, if using.

In a mixing bowl, crush the cheese using a fork.

Whisk the eggs and sugar together until the mixture is thick and pale. Pour it over the cheese and mix well. Stir in the grated lemon zest or spirits.

Butter a baking pan and pour the batter into it. Place in the oven and immediately lower the temperature to 300°F (150°C). Bake for 45 minutes.

Serve warm or cool.

PÂTÉS & TERRINES

Duck Foie Gras Terrine
Terrine de fois gras de canard au naturel

SERVES 12 TO 15
PREPARATION TIME: 45 MINUTES
SOAKING TIME: 2 HOURS
CHILLING TIME: 24 HOURS
COOKING TIME: 30 MINUTES

3 fine duck livers, each 1 ¼ lb. to 1 lb. 5 oz. (500-600 g) (the livers should come from specially fattened ducks)

SEASONING

2 teaspoons plus a scant ½ teaspoon (12 g) fine table salt

6 turns (2 g) of the pepper mill

A little freshly grated nutmeg

2 sheets (4 g) gelatin

⅔ cup (150 ml) port wine

The seasoning of foie gras prior to cooking is all-important. Use your scales for maximum accuracy. Foie gras is best prepared a day ahead.

Soak the duck livers for 2 hours in warm water, no hotter than 98°F (37°C).

Dab them dry and use your hands to open them up.

Carefully remove any bile you may find (it is a dark greenish color). Then remove all the veins and nerves you can see.

Combine the spices to make the seasoning. Soften the gelatin sheets in cold water. When they are rubbery, wring out the water and place them in the port. Stir until just dissolved.

Place the livers in a terrine and season them with the spices. Pour over the port. Cover the terrine and chill for 24 hours.

The next day, preheat the oven to 350°F (180°C). Place the terrine in the oven and immediately switch off the heat. Cook for 30 minutes, until the core temperature reaches 104°F (40°C).

Leave to cool in a cool place, and then chill before serving.

SERVES 6
PREPARATION TIME: 30 MINUTES
MARINATING TIME: 2 HOURS
COOKING TIME:
1 HOUR 30 MINUTES

TERRINE FORCEMEAT

14 oz. (400 g) veal fillet (cushion)
14 oz. (400 g) pork fillet
1 lb. (500 g) fresh fatback (cut of pork fat from pig's back)
1 oz. (2 tablespoons or 30 g) salt
1 sprig thyme
1 or 2 bay leaves
Freshly ground pepper
3 eggs
Scant ¼ cup (5 ml) cognac or other brandy
10 oz. (300 g) lean cooked ham
Bard: sufficient to line the terrine and cover the pâté
Special equipment: a 10 × 4 × 3 in. (25 × 10 × 7 cm high) terrine and a wooden board cut to the size of the top of the terrine

Veal Terrine
Terrine de veau

Prepare the forcemeat. Carefully remove the nerves, cartilage, external fat, and silver skin from the veal and the pork fillets, and remove the rind of the fatback, reserving half of the fatback for later. Finely chop the veal, pork, and fatback and season with salt and freshly ground pepper. When the mixture is quite smooth, incorporate the eggs one by one, and then the cognac. Leave to marinate for 2 hours in the refrigerator.

Prepare the meat layers. Cut the ham into strips. Line the terrine with the strips of bard. Spoon in a layer of forcemeat, then a layer of fatback and ham; and then another layer of forcemeat. Continue until you have used up all the ingredients.

Cover with a strip of bard and make a small hole in the center. Insert the thyme and bay leaf bits at each side of the hole. Cover the terrine with its lid and place it in a large dish filled with water. Cook at 425°F (210°C) for at least 1 hour 30 minutes.

The cooking time will vary according to the shape of the terrine and your ingredients. You will know that the terrine is done when the liquid that comes out simmering at the edge of the meat has completely clarified. This means that the juices have been transformed into meat glaze and stuck to the dish.

Remove the terrine from the oven, take off the lid, and put the wooden board on the top. Place a weight of about 8 oz. (250 g) over it. The terrine is weighted down to ensure that the forcemeat stays smooth as it cools. If you don't do this, it will be difficult to slice, as the pieces will disintegrate when you cut them.

Don't exceed the recommended weight: too much will cause the fat to exude, detracting from the flavors of the pâté.

To serve, wash and dry the terrine. Fold a clean white napkin, center it on a platter, and serve the terrine on this.

SERVES 8
PREPARATION TIME: 30 MINUTES
COOKING TIME:
1 HOUR 15 MINUTES

1 large duckling

4 oz. (125 g) firm white button mushrooms

1 lb. (500 g) unsweetened Shortcrust Pastry (see p. 568), rolled out

2 ¼ lb. (1 kg) forcemeat, made with chicken or veal (see p. 131)

A few thyme flowers, crushed

A few bay leaves, ground

1 egg, beaten

¾ cup (200 ml) Madeira Sauce (see p. 526)

Truffles for garnish, as many as you wish

Gaston Richard's Hot or Cold Duckling Pâté
Pâté chaud ou froid de caneton Gaston Richard

Pan-roast the duck for 15 minutes: it should be very rare. Remove the two wings with the breasts. Remove the skin and cut the flesh into long strips. Thinly slice the mushrooms and cook them rapidly in the dish you have used for the duckling so that they can absorb the flavors of the meat and the cooking juices.

Butter a charlotte mold and line it with the pastry. Spoon in a layer of forcemeat just under ½ in. (1 cm) thick.

Arrange a layer of duckling strips over the forcemeat, and then a layer of mushroom slices. If you wish, you can add some raw truffle slices. Then spread over another layer of forcemeat, continuing until you have used all the ingredients, and finishing with a layer of forcemeat. Sprinkle the top with a pinch of thyme flowers and ground bay leaves. Cover with some of the thinly rolled out dough, ensuring that it encloses the pâté completely. Wet the edges of the dough to seal it. Brush the dough with the beaten egg, make a few decorative incisions and, in the center, cut out a small vent so that the steam can escape. Cook at 350°F (180°C) for 1 hour.

To serve, turn the pâté out onto a round dish. Carefully cut the slices, stopping at ½ in. (1 cm) from the base and carefully work each slice free. Drizzle a tablespoonful of Madeira sauce over the forcemeat and serve the remaining sauce in a sauce dish.

You may decorate the top just before serving: take a large mushroom head and either slice it thinly or canelle it (make regular incisions around it so that it resembles a flower) and sauté it in butter. Place this in the center, surrounded by truffle shavings. Pour the Madeira sauce over it. If you serve this dish cold, do not use any sauce.

Gaston Richard was a renowned French chef and one of my mentors.

SERVES 6 TO 8
PREPARATION TIME: 30 MINUTES
COOKING TIME:
1 HOUR 30 MINUTES

Antonin Carême's Morel Timbale
Timbale de morilles Antonin Carême

- 2 cups plus scant ½ cup (600 ml) Béchamel or White Sauce (see p. 536)
- 14 oz. (400 g) *godiveau* (delicate forcemeat of veal or poultry and fat) or sausage meat
- 2 oz. (50 g) truffles, finely chopped
- 2 ¼ lb. (1 kg) freshly gathered morel mushrooms
- 7 tablespoons (3 ½ oz./100 g) butter, divided
- Juice of ¼ lemon
- ⅔ cup (150 ml) crème fraîche or heavy cream
- 5 egg yolks
- Salt and pepper

Prepare the béchamel or white sauce. Prepare the *godiveau*, if using, and combine it with the finely chopped truffles, or combine the sausage meat with the truffles.

Trim the earthy base of the morel mushrooms and wash them carefully several times, paying particular attention to the cavities where grit (and insects) tend to lodge. Set aside 12 of the finest morels with about 3 ½ oz. (100 g) of the stems.

Using 4 tablespoons (60 g) butter, a pinch of salt, the lemon juice, and 2 tablespoons water, cook the remaining morels in a pan with the lid on. If the morels are large, cut them into halves or quarters. Boil for 7 minutes. Drain them, keeping the cooking liquid in a bowl, and set them aside. Reserve 2 tablespoons of the liquid to use later.

To finish the béchamel sauce, add the cream and remaining morel cooking liquid to it and reduce until you have 1 ⅔ cups (400 ml). Remove from the heat. Dilute the 5 egg yolks with 1 tablespoon cream and 2 tablespoons cooking liquid. To combine the egg yolks with the béchamel, pour a little béchamel into the egg yolks, whisking as you do so, to heat them. Gradually pour this mixture back in to the béchamel, whisking briskly all the time. Return to the heat, still whisking, and remove just before it begins to boil. The sauce should be very thick and should on no account come to a boil. Add the cooked morels and stir them in. Leave to cool in a bowl.

Preheat the oven to 300°F (150°C). Generously grease a cake pan, and spoon in three-quarters of the *godiveau* or sausage meat–the layer should be just under 1 in. (2 cm) thick. Then pour in the béchamel-morel mixture, stopping when you reach a height just below 1 in. (2 cm) from the rim. Cover with the remaining *godiveau* or sausage meat and smooth it over. Make a parchment paper lid and butter it on one side. Fit it snugly over the top. Place the mold in an ovenproof dish and pour hot water into the dish, stopping when it is 1 in. (3 cm) from the rim of the mold. Poach the timbale in the oven for 55 minutes.

Eel Pâté
Pâté d'anguilles

SERVES 6
PREPARATION TIME: 30 MINUTES
MARINATING TIME: 2 HOURS
COOKING TIME: 2 HOURS

- 3 lb. (1.4 kg) freshwater eels
- 2 teaspoons plus a scant ½ teaspoon (12 g) fine table salt
- Generous serving of pepper (5 g)
- Freshly ground nutmeg
- Drizzle of olive oil
- ⅔ cup (200 ml) dry white wine, divided
- 2 tablespoons cognac
- 3 shallots
- 7 tablespoons (3 ½ oz./100 g) butter, divided
- 1 bunch parsley, chopped
- 4 hardboiled eggs, sliced
- 1 rolled-out piece of Half Puff Pastry (see pp. 565–66), about ⅛ in. (4 mm) thick and the size of a normal serving plate
- 1 egg, beaten
- ¾ cup (200 ml) fish-flavored *demi-glace* (see Glossary)

Skin, wash, and gut the eels. Cut them in two lengthways, making an incision on each side of the central bone, which you should remove completely.

Cut the fillets into angled slices of about 3 in. (8 cm). Bring a pot of well-salted water to a boil and put in the eel slices. Remove them as soon as the water comes to a boil again. Refresh them under cold water and drain them. Pat them dry and season with the salt, pepper, nutmeg, a drizzle of oil, half of the white wine, and the cognac. Leave to marinate for 2 hours.

Chop the shallots. Heat a large sauté pan and soften the chopped shallots in about 3 tablespoons (50 g) butter. Drain the eels, setting aside the marinade. When the shallots are softened, add the well-dried slices of eel and cook for 10 minutes. Lastly, sprinkle them with some of the chopped parsley.

Preheat the oven to 350°F (180°C).

Place the slices in a layer in a deep, round ovenproof porcelain or ceramic dish. When you have filled in one layer, arrange a layer of sliced hardboiled eggs sprinkled with chopped parsley.

Pour in the remaining white wine and the marinade until the eel slices and hardboiled eggs are practically covered. Cube 2 tablespoons (30 g) butter and dot the cubes around the top. Cover with the rolled-out pastry cut to exactly the dimensions of the dish.

Baste the top of the dough with the beaten egg. Make shallow incisions to draw a rose or leaf pattern. In the center, make a vent with the tip of a knife so that the steam can escape. Cook in the oven for 1 hour 30 minutes.

Just before serving, heat the demi-glace. Remove it from the heat and add the remaining butter to it. If necessary, add a spoonful of fish fumet. Pour this sauce into the center of the pâté through the small incision.

SERVES 6
PREPARATION TIME: 30 MINUTES
CHILLING TIME: 4 HOURS

1 lb. (500 g) cooked lean ham

¾ cup (200 ml) velouté sauce, well chilled

1 ⅔ cups (400 ml) thick crème fraîche

⅔ cup (150 ml) light-colored Madeira-flavored aspic or flavored gelatin, divided

Salt and pepper

Crushed ice for chilling and setting the aspic

Cold Ham Mousse
Mousse froide de jambon

Cut the ham into very small pieces and crush finely with a mortar and pestle or using a food processor. When it is uniformly crumbed, gradually add the well-chilled velouté sauce.

Pour this mixture into a fine-mesh sieve and push it through. Lightly whip the cream and heat the Madeira aspic until barely melted. Place the strained mixture in a bowl over crushed ice and stir briskly with a flexible spatula or spoon, gradually incorporating two-thirds of the Madeira aspic. Check the seasoning and then fold in the lightly whipped cream.

Take an appropriately sized mold and pour in half of the remaining melted Madeira aspic. Rotate on a bed of crushed ice to trigger the jelling process, not forgetting the sides.

When the aspic has set, fill the mold with the ham mousse, top with the remaining aspic, and leave to chill in the refrigerator for 4 hours.

To turn it out onto an immaculate silver dish, dip the mold for 1 second in hot water, dry it so that no drops will fall onto the dish, and place the dish over the mold. Quickly turn it over so that the mold is above the dish and remove it.

A pink mousse will be visible beneath the shiny, transparent layer of aspic. Serve immediately.

Note: The base of a velouté sauce is a roux, equal amounts of butter and flour cooked together until they begin to color. Then a stock is whisked in until the sauce is smooth.

SERVES 6
PREPARATION TIME: 40 MINUTES
COOKING TIME:
1 HOUR 15 MINUTES

9 oz. (250 g) pork fat or fresh fatback

9 oz. (250 g) lean pork or veal, all sinews removed

1 lb. (500 g) pork liver

3 tablespoons plus 1 teaspoon (50 g) fine table salt

1 pinch four-spice mixture (a typical French blend of black pepper, nutmeg, ginger, and cloves)

2 shallots

1 medium-sized onion

Scant ¼ cup (50 ml) cognac

½ lb. soft bread, soaked in milk

1 tablespoon chopped parsley

3 eggs, germinal discs (small, circular, white spot on the surface of the yolk) removed

4 strips of fresh bard for lining

1 bay leaf

1 sprig thyme

Soft dough of flour and water to seal the terrine

Special equipment: a 10 × 4 × 3 in. (25 × 10 × 7 cm high) terrine with a lid, and a wooden board cut to the size of the top of the terrine

Pork Liver Pâté
Pâté de foie de porc

Cut the pork fat (or fresh fatback), the pork or veal, and the liver into 1 in. (2 cm) cubes. Place all the cubes separately on a dish and season with all the salt and spices.

Finely chop the shallots and onion. Melt the fat or fatback partially in a sauté pan until it sizzles a little. Turn the heat to high and sauté the liver. As soon as it is seared, sprinkle with the chopped onion and shallots and sauté for a few seconds. Add the meat to sear it. Remove immediately from the heat and pour in the cognac. Stir until the bits of all the ingredients stuck to the pan have dissolved. Transfer all the contents to a bowl and leave to cool.

When cooled, mince either in a mincing machine or a blender, but not too finely. Press the milk out of the bread and add it to the meat mixture with the chopped parsley and the three eggs. (You should remove the germinal discs that would otherwise form coagulated white spots in the pâté.) Mix thoroughly until smooth.

To check the seasoning, poach a small ball of the mixture in boiling water. Adjust the seasoning by carefully adding salt and spices.

Line the bottom and sides of a pâté terrine with 3 strips of fresh bard. Fill with the mixture and cover with the last strip of fat. The terrine should be filled to the top, so choose it accordingly. Top with the bay leaf and sprig of thyme. Cover with the lid and seal it with a cord of soft dough made of water and flour.

To cook, place the terrine in a roasting dish with hot water. You will have to top up the level as it cooks. Place in a 300°F (150°C) oven for about 1 hour.

(*Continued overleaf*)

To test for doneness:
- Check the fat that rises to the top: it will be cloudy at first but clarified when the pâte is just ready.

- As the fat clarifies, it leaves the jus it carries at the edge of the terrine. When this jus is transformed into meat glace, the pâté is done.

- Insert a fine trussing needle into the pâté and leave it for 2 minutes. When you remove it, it should be really hot, a sign that the pâté is well cooked.

Remove it from the oven and take off the lid. Leave to cool for 15 minutes, cover with film, and then place a snugly fitting wooden board over it, weighted down with a weight of about 1 lb. (500 g). Leave to cool completely under pressure. The pressure allows all the elements that make up the pâté to combine thoroughly without ridding it of the still-liquid fatty matter.

If there is insufficient pressure, the pâté will break up when cut; if there is too much pressure, the fat will be exuded, making the pâté dry and causing it to lose its flavors and smoothness.

To serve, wash the terrine out, return the pâté to it, and present it on a rectangular dish covered with a napkin. At the table, cut it into very thin slices of ⅕ in. (5 mm).

Country Pâté
Pâté de campagne

SERVES 8 TO 10
PREPARATION TIME: 45 MINUTES
COOKING TIME:
1 HOUR 30 MINUTES

1 ¾ lb. (800 g) boned loin of pork (UK: spare rib or blade)
9 oz. (250 g) pork liver
7 oz. (200 g) fatback
1 ½ tablespoons plus 1 scant teaspoon (25 g) salt
A generous sprinkling (5 g) ground pepper
1 pinch four-spice mixture (a typical French blend of black pepper, nutmeg, ginger, and cloves)
1 shallot
1 clove garlic
3 eggs
1 tablespoon cognac
1 large strip of bard for lining
Special equipment:
a 10 × 4 × 3 in. (25 × 10 × 7 cm high) terrine with a lid

Mince the loin, liver, and fatback separately. Place all three in a large mixing bowl and season with salt, pepper, and the four-spice mix.

Preheat the oven to 350°F (180°C).

Peel and chop the shallot and garlic clove very finely. Add them to the meat mixture and mix well. Incorporate the whole eggs and the cognac and mix well again.

Line a terrine with three-quarters of the bard. Spoon the mixture into the terrine and cover with the remaining strip of bard. Place the lid on and cook in the oven for 1 hour 30 minutes.

To check for doneness, insert the blade of a knife. It should come out smooth without any traces of blood. Leave to cool.

Forcemeat for Pâtés and Terrines

PREPARATION TIME: 20 MINUTES

14 oz. (400 g) veal fillet (cushion)
14 oz. (400 g) pork fillet
1 lb. (500 g) fresh fatback
1 oz. (30 g) herbed salt
3 eggs
Scant ½ cup (100 ml) cognac

If you are using this forcemeat for a game pâté or terrine, use poultry meat or the meat of the same animal instead of veal.

Carefully remove any sinews from all the meat as well as the silver skin. Dice it and chop or crush or process it finely. When the mixture is quite smooth, stir in the salt, then the eggs, one by one, and lastly, the cognac. Check the seasoning by poaching a little of the mixture in boiling water and then tasting it. Proceed according to the instructions in the recipe.

EGGS

SERVES 6
PREPARATION TIME: 15 MINUTES
COOKING TIME: 15 MINUTES

14 oz. (400 g) spinach
2 oz. (50 g) lean ham
4 tablespoons (60 g) butter, divided, plus a little extra for the dishes
6 eggs
Salt and pepper
Freshly grated nutmeg

Baked Eggs Florentine
Oeufs sur la plat à la florentine

Pick the spinach leaves off the stalks and boil them briefly in well salted water. While they are cooking, finely dice the ham. Drain and refresh the spinach, and press it down hard over a colander to remove the water. Push through a sieve to make a purée.

Melt 2 tablespoons (30 g) butter in a sauté pan and when it is sizzling transfer the spinach purée to the pan. Season with salt, pepper, and a touch of freshly grated nutmeg. Heat through quickly and remove from the stovetop. Stir in almost all the remaining butter (set aside 1 teaspoon or 5 g) and the finely diced ham.

Preheat the oven to 425°F (210°C).

Butter six shirred egg dishes and smooth out a thin layer of diced ham and then a layer of spinach purée over each. Heat over the stove and then break an egg into each dish. Melt the remaining butter and drizzle a few drops over each one. Sprinkle a pinch of salt over the whites and cook in the oven until the white is milky and completely coagulated, and the eggs are shiny, about 15 minutes.

SERVES 4
PREPARATION TIME: 5 MINUTES
COOKING TIME: ABOUT 12 MINUTES

4 tablespoons (60 g) butter
8 fresh eggs
4 tablespoons vinegar
Salt and pepper
4 slices toasted country-style or whole-wheat bread

Fried Eggs
Œufs sur le plat

At least one hour ahead of time, remove the eggs from the refrigerator.

Preheat the oven to 300°F (150°C).

Use one small ovenproof dish per person. Place 1 tablespoon of butter in each one and melt over moderate heat. When the butter starts to foam, break two eggs into each dish and continue cooking over very low heat for 3 to 4 minutes, or until the white is half cooked; then place in the oven to finish cooking for 3 minutes more. Remove from the oven, season with salt and pepper, and add 1 tablespoon of vinegar to each dish.

Serve with toast.

SERVES 4
PREPARATION TIME: 15 MINUTES
COOKING TIME: ABOUT 40 MINUTES

Eggs Poached in Beaujolais
Œufs à la beaujolaise

8 eggs
4 tablespoons (60 g) softened butter
2 tablespoons (12 g) flour
2 medium onions or 6 baby onions
1 clove garlic
Small bunch parsley
Bouquet garni, made with 1 sprig thyme, ¼ bay leaf, 1 stalk celery, and white of 1 leek
1 bottle Beaujolais wine
1 teaspoon kosher salt
Pepper

Make a beurre manié by placing 2 tablespoons of softened butter in a small bowl with the flour and mixing the two together with your fingers until smooth. Break the mixture into pea-sized pieces and set aside.

Peel the onions and the garlic. Crush the garlic using a fork, and chop the onions. Mince the parsley.

Peel and wash the celery and the leek. Cut the leek lengthwise into quarters. Tie together the leek, celery, thyme, and bay leaf with kitchen string.

Melt the remaining 2 tablespoons of butter in a high-sided frying pan (preferably not aluminum). Add the onions and cook to color lightly; then add the wine, garlic, bouquet garni, salt, and pepper. Bring to a boil, lower the heat immediately, and simmer uncovered for 20 minutes. Lift the onions out with a slotted spoon and set aside.

Strain the wine through a sieve into a bowl, then pour it back into the pan and heat to simmering. Break an egg into a teacup, then slide it gently into the hot wine (you can poach up to four eggs at a time). Poach the eggs for 4 minutes, then lift them out with a slotted spoon. Place them on a plate and cover with aluminum foil to keep warm while poaching the second batch of eggs. Place these eggs on a plate and cover with foil as well. Add the beurre manié piece by piece to the wine and bring to a boil, stirring constantly. Lower the heat once more, place the onions back in the pan to warm up, taste, and add salt and pepper if needed.

Place two eggs on each dinner plate, spoon the sauce and onions around them, sprinkle with the parsley, and serve.

If you like, you can serve the eggs with croutons browned in a little butter and rubbed with half a clove of garlic.

SERVES 4
PREPARATION TIME: 10 MINUTES
COOKING TIME: 20 MINUTES

Eggs *en Cocotte* with Tomatoes
Oeufs en cocotte aux tomates

- 1 onion (optional), plus butter for cooking
- 2 ripe tomatoes
- 1 tablespoon plus 1 teaspoon (20 g) butter, divided
- 4 eggs
- A few leaves of flat-leaf parsley, chopped
- Salt and pepper

If using, chop the onion finely and soften it in butter without browning it. Set aside. Remove the base from the tomatoes and dip them very briefly in boiling water. Peel them immediately, cut them in two, and remove the seeds.

Dice the tomatoes and sauté them in the same pan with half the butter (2 teaspoons or 10 g). Season with salt and pepper. Cook until the tomatoes are reduced to the texture of preserves.

Preheat the oven to 375°F (190°C).

Butter the ramekins and smooth the puréed tomatoes into the bottom, setting aside a little for garnish. Break an egg into each dish and place in a dish of hot water. Bake for about 20 minutes, until the whites are coagulated. As soon as they are done, drop in a half-teaspoon of puréed tomatoes and sprinkle with a little chopped parsley.

If you are using onion, add it to the ramekin before spooning in the tomato purée.

SERVES 4
PREPARATION TIME: 20 MINUTES
COOKING TIME: 20 MINUTES

Soft-Boiled Eggs Béarnaise
Oeufs mollets béarnaise

- 2 tablespoons (30 g) butter
- 8 artichoke bottoms, cooked in a *blanc* (see Glossary)
- 8 soft-boiled eggs
- 1 ⅔ cups (400 ml) Béarnaise Sauce (see p. 530)
- Salt and freshly ground pepper

If you are using fresh artichokes, simmer the bottoms in water with lemon juice and a little flour until slightly softened but not cooked through.

Melt the butter in a sauté pan and add the artichoke bottoms. Season with a pinch of salt and freshly ground pepper and leave to simmer for 15 minutes over low heat, turning them once. Transfer them to a pre-heated dish and pour in the butter from the pan.

Place a shelled soft-boiled egg in each artichoke bottom and cover with the béarnaise sauce, serving the remaining sauce in a dish on the side.

SERVES 6
PREPARATION TIME: 20 MINUTES
COOKING TIME: 30 MINUTES

Fried Eggs Milanese
Oeufs frits à la milanaise

- 5 oz. (150 g) spaghetti or macaroni
- 2 tablespoons Tomato Sauce (see p. 544), plus extra for serving, or
- 2 tomatoes
- 3 tablespoons plus 1 teaspoon (50 g) butter
- ⅓ cup grated Parmesan or Gruyère cheese
- 6 eggs
- 3 tomatoes
- A few leaves fried parsley
- Salt and pepper

If you do not have the tomato sauce, peel and seed the two tomatoes. Season them with salt and pepper and soften them with a little butter in a small sauté pan. Bring 4 cups (1 liter) of water to a boil with 2 teaspoons (10 g) salt. Throw the pasta in and cook according to manufacturer's instructions. Drain well and return to the pot. Season with salt and pepper and add the tomato sauce or softened tomatoes.

Combine the pasta with the butter and cheese, taking care not to break it.

Butter a timbale mold generously and spoon the pasta mixture in. Rap the timbale a few times on a cloth to ensure that the mixture is well packed. Place in a dish of hot water and cook in the oven at 375°F (190°C) for 18 to 20 minutes. Remove and leave to rest for 5 minutes. Turn the oven up to "broil." Fry the eggs in an oil bath, halve the tomatoes, and broil them. Fry a few parsley leaves for garnish. Turn the pasta out of the mold onto a preheated round dish.

Arrange the 6 fried eggs, alternating them with the broiled tomato halves, around the timbale. Top each tomato half with a fried parsley leaf.

Serve accompanied by a bowl of Tomato Sauce.

SERVES 6
PREPARATION TIME: 40 MINUTES
COOKING TIME: 35 MINUTES

Hard-Boiled Eggs *à la Tripe*
Oeufs "à la tripe"

1 lb. (500 g) onions
7 tablespoons (3 ½ oz./100 g) butter
6 ½ tablespoons (40 g) flour
3 ½ cups (800 ml) chicken stock or milk
9 eggs
1 pinch freshly grated nutmeg
Salt and pepper

Peel the onions, cut them in two, and then into fine slices.

Blanch them for 5 minutes in boiling water and drain.

Place them in large pot and sweat them to dry out their liquid. Add the butter and stir with a wooden spoon until they are golden.

When the color is right, sprinkle with the flour and mix it in.

Gradually pour in the stock (or milk), stirring constantly. Season with salt, pepper, and freshly grated nutmeg.

Leave to simmer gently, still stirring constantly, for 20 minutes.

Hard-boil the eggs. Shell them and slice them using an egg slicer or small mandoline.

Pour half of the onion mixture into a deep dish. Arrange the still-hot egg slices over it and then cover with the remaining sauce.

The name of this dish means "eggs cooked like tripe." Written up in cookbooks since the seventeenth century, it is one of the oldest dishes in the Cordon Bleu repertoire.

SERVES 2
PREPARATION TIME: 10 MINUTES
COOKING TIME: 8 TO 10 MINUTES

3 eggs
A few leaves parsley, chopped
1 scallion or a few chives
2 teaspoons (10 g) butter, plus 2 extra knobs to provide gloss for the cooked omelet
Salt

Herb Omelet
Omelette aux fines herbes

Break the eggs into a mixing bowl. Just before you are ready to cook, season them with salt and beat them, but not too much (they should not be foamy). Add a teaspoon of freshly chopped parsley and a finely snipped scallion or some chives.

Heat the butter over very high heat until it sizzles and begins to brown. Pour the beaten eggs into the pan. When they come into contact with the hot butter, the eggs will begin to coagulate first around the rim of the pan. Using a fork, quickly move the cooked edges to the center; this will ensure that the omelet cooks evenly.

When the omelet reaches the desired consistency (well done, medium, or runny), leave for a further two seconds on the heat. Using your left hand, tilt the pan toward the heat, and with the fork in your right hand, roll the omelet to the far edge. Rap your left hand with your right hand to knock the pan. The omelet will rise into the correctly rolled position. Quickly add a knob of butter to make the omelet nice and shiny, then turn it onto a pre-heated long dish. Adjust the shape if necessary. Fit another knob of butter onto the tip of a knife and use it to "varnish" the omelet.

SERVES 4
PREPARATION TIME: 15 MINUTES
COOKING TIME: 30 MINUTES
(5 MINUTES PER EGG)

8 soft-boiled eggs, kept warm in a little salted water

4 large onions

2 tablespoons (30 g) butter

8 tablespoons Béchamel or White Sauce (see p. 536)

2 tablespoons cream or 2 knobs butter

8 large mushroom heads

A few drops of lemon juice

Salt

Soft-Boiled Eggs Soubise
Oeufs mollets soubise

Dice the onions, boil them for 5 minutes, and drain. Place the diced onion in a small pot with the butter and a pinch of salt and simmer very gently with the lid on. Be careful that it remains white. When cooked, push through a fine-meshed sieve. You should have 1 ¼ cup (300 ml) of purée. Transfer it to a sauté pan. Add the béchamel sauce, bring to a boil, and remove immediately from the heat. Stir in the cream or butter and taste to adjust the seasoning.

Broil the mushrooms or stew them in butter with just a few drops of lemon juice. If using the stewing method, pour all the butter into the Soubise purée after cooking the mushrooms.

Arrange the mushrooms on a preheated round dish. Shell the eggs and top each mushroom with a soft-boiled egg. Cover with the creamed onion purée, which should be smooth.

Paprika-Stuffed Eggs
Oeufs farcis au paprika

SERVES 4
PREPARATION TIME: 20 MINUTES
COOKING TIME: 8 TO 9 MINUTES FOR THE EGGS

- 4 hard-boiled eggs
- Scant ¼ cup (50 ml) heavy cream
- 1 pinch salt
- 1 pinch paprika

Gently cook the eggs until they are hard-boiled. Shell them and cut them in two lengthways.

Place the yolks in a bowl and crush them finely with a fork. Work in the heavy cream. Season this creamy paste with a pinch of fine table salt and paprika, according to taste. Fill the half egg whites with this cream, rounding and smoothing off the tops of the mixture.

Serve in small dishes.

Scrambled Eggs with Tomato and Basil
Oeufs à la tomate

SERVES 2
PREPARATION TIME: 10 MINUTES
COOKING TIME: 25 MINUTES

- 5 eggs
- 5 ripe tomatoes
- 2 tablespoons olive oil
- 5 basil leaves
- Salt and pepper

Blanch and peel the tomatoes, then cut into halves or quarters. Season with salt and pepper.

Heat the oil in a frying pan and add the tomatoes. Cook uncovered over moderate heat for 15 to 20 minutes, or until their water has evaporated, stirring frequently.

Wash and chop the basil, and set aside.

Break the eggs into a mixing bowl, season with salt and pepper, and beat lightly with a fork or whisk (the eggs should not be perfectly mixed). Pour them into the pan with the tomatoes and cook over moderate heat for about 2 minutes, stirring to cook the eggs.

Serve, sprinkled with the fresh basil.

SERVES 4
PREPARATION TIME: 10 MINUTES
COOKING TIME: 15 TO 20 MINUTES

- 10 eggs
- 5 oz. (150 g) truffles
- 2 tablespoons (30 g) butter, plus a little extra to make the toast
- 8 round pieces bread
- Salt and pepper

Scrambled Eggs with Truffles
Oeufs brouillés aux truffes

Butter 4 small dariole molds and place one generous slice of truffle in each. Dice the remaining truffles and stew them in butter.

Prepare creamy scrambled eggs with 6 of the eggs. Incorporate the diced truffles. Add the 4 remaining raw eggs. As you mix them in, season with salt and pepper.

Fill the molds with the mixture and poach them in a bain-marie for 15 to 20 minutes. While they are cooking, brown the slices of bread in clarified butter.

Serve accompanied by a very light *demi-glace* sauce (see Glossary) flavored with truffle essence.

This dish is known as oeufs moulés Verdi, *Verdi molded eggs.*

SERVES 4
PREPARATION TIME: 20 MINUTES
COOKING TIME: 8 TO 9 MINUTES

Eggs Mimosa
Oeufs mimosa

4 eggs
1 small bunch chives
1 butterhead (Boston) lettuce
1 cup (250 ml) Mayonnaise (see p. 552)
8 black olives
2 very large ripe tomatoes
Salt
1 lemon
7-oz. (200-g) can of tuna packed in oil (optional)

Prepare the hard-boiled eggs. If they have just been removed from the refrigerator, cook them for about 9 minutes rather than 8.

Wash and dry the chives, and use scissors to finely chop them. Carefully wash and dry the lettuce without removing the ribs. Set aside.

Once cooked, run the hard-boiled eggs under cold water and peel them when they have cooled down.

Cut the hard-boiled eggs in half lengthwise and separate the yolks from the whites. Put three half-yolks on a plate and reserve; crush the other yolks with a fork. Place the crushed yolks in a bowl with the chives, reserving a spoonful for garnish, then add mayonnaise a spoonful at a time to make a thick, smooth paste (there will be mayonnaise left over). Spoon this mixture into the hard-boiled egg whites, and top each half-"egg" with a black olive.

Decorate the edge of a round serving platter with some lettuce leaves, then place 4 cupped lettuce leaves in the center. Wash the tomatoes, remove the stem from each tomato, and wipe the tomatoes dry. Cut the tomatoes in half, then place half a tomato in each cupped lettuce leaf, cut side up. Lightly salt the tomatoes, then place one half-"egg" on each half-tomato.

Crush the remaining egg yolks with a fork or grind them through a food mill, and sprinkle them over the garnished platter.

Sprinkle with chives and serve with the remaining mayonnaise and the lemon wedges, with or without some tuna served in a separate dish.

SERVES 4
PREPARATION TIME: 15 MINUTES
COOKING TIME:
3 MINUTES PER EGG

8 eggs
1 tablespoon white (crystal) vinegar

Poached Eggs
Oeufs pochés

At least an hour and a half ahead of time, remove the eggs from the refrigerator. Absolutely the freshest eggs are essential here. You will also need two high-sided frying pans: one to poach the eggs in and the other in which to keep the cooked eggs warm while poaching the others.

Bring 2 cups (500 ml) of water to a boil in a small frying pan with 1 tablespoon of vinegar. In a large frying pan, heat 4 cups (1 liter) of water to warm but not boiling.

Break an egg into a teacup, then slide it gently into the boiling water with the vinegar. Lower the heat so the water simmers but does not boil, and poach the egg for 3 ½ minutes. Lift it out of the water with a slotted spoon and place it in the warm water while poaching the remaining eggs one by one. Be careful not to break the yolks, both when you crack the eggs and when you lift them out of the water. With a little practice, you will be able to poach two, three, even four eggs at a time, but if you do, increase the amount of water and vinegar in the first pan (only two eggs can be poached in the amounts given), and use a larger frying pan.

Once all the eggs are poached, lift them out of the warm water and leave for a few seconds on a clean towel (or on a paper towel folded over twice) to drain before serving.

Serving suggestions: Serve with the Dandelion Green and Bacon Salad (see p. 75) or with Spinach (see p. 474).

SERVES 3
PREPARATION TIME: 10 MINUTES
COOKING TIME: 15 MINUTES

Ham and Eggs
Oeufs au jambon

- 3 tablespoons (40 g) butter
- 3 slices (about 4-5 oz./125-150 g) precooked country-style ham
- 6 eggs
- Salt and pepper
- 3 slices toasted country-style or whole-wheat bread

At least an hour ahead of time, take all the ingredients out of the refrigerator.

Preheat the oven to 300°F (150°C).

Melt the butter in a large porcelain or enameled cast-iron baking dish, add the ham, and brown lightly on both sides.

Break the eggs into a small bowl, two at a time, and carefully slide them onto the ham. Continue cooking over very low heat for at least 5 minutes, or until the white is about half cooked; then place in the oven to finish cooking for about 3 minutes. Season with salt and pepper just before serving.

Serve with toast.

SERVES 8
PREPARATION TIME: 10 MINUTES
COOKING TIME:
ABOUT 15 MINUTES

- 8 eggs
- 6 tablespoons (90 g) softened butter
- 5 ½ tablespoons crème fraîche or heavy cream
- Salt and pepper
- 4 slices bread
- 8 small cilantro leaves

Baked Eggs with Cream
Oeufs cocotte à la crème

At least one hour ahead of time, take the eggs out of the refrigerator.

Preheat the oven to 350°F (180°C).

Butter eight little ramekins; place 1 teaspoon of cream and a little salt and pepper in each one. One at a time, break the eggs into a teacup, then gently slide each one into a ramekin and top with 1 teaspoon of cream.

Line a large roasting pan with waxed paper, place the ramekins in the pan, and pour in enough hot water to come halfway up the sides of the ramekins (the paper will keep the water from bubbling up too much and spilling into the ramekins later). Heat on top of the stove until the water is simmering but not boiling. Place the pan in the oven and bake for 4 minutes, or until the egg whites are opaque.

Remove the crust from the bread. Toast the bread, butter it, then cut each slice into "fingers" about ½ in. (1 cm) wide.

Rinse the cilantro leaves.

Remove the roasting pan from the oven, lift the ramekins out, and wipe each one dry. Place each ramekin on a plate, place a cilantro leaf in the center of each one, and surround the ramekin with a few pieces of toast.

Serve immediately.

SERVES 4
PREPARATION TIME:
5 TO 10 MINUTES
COOKING TIME: 15 MINUTES

- 8 thin slices Canadian bacon or 4 slices ham cut in half
- 4 tablespoons (60 g) butter
- 8 eggs
- Salt and pepper
- 8 slices toast

Bacon and Eggs
Oeufs au bacon

At least one hour ahead of time, take all the ingredients out of the refrigerator.

I like to serve eggs and bacon cooked in individual porcelain or enameled cast-iron dishes.

Brown the Canadian bacon or ham in a nonstick frying pan.

Melt 1 tablespoon (15 g) of butter in each of the individual dishes, then place two pieces of bacon or ham in each one.

Break the eggs into a small bowl, two at a time, then carefully slide them into each dish. Salt and pepper lightly. Cook over very low heat for about 4 minutes, or until the white is half cooked; then raise the heat and finish cooking for about 3 minutes.

Serve with toast.

SERVES 1
PREPARATION TIME: 5 MINUTES
COOKING TIME: 3 TO 4 MINUTES

Soft-Boiled Eggs
Oeufs à la coque

2 eggs
1 slice country-style or ordinary bread
Butter
Salt

If the eggs have been refrigerated, take them out of the refrigerator at least one hour ahead of time.

Bring a small saucepan of water just to a boil.

In the meantime, toast and butter the bread, then cut it into "fingers" about ½-in. (1-cm) wide. Sprinkle with a little salt and set aside.

When the water is on the verge of boiling, carefully lower the eggs, one at a time, into the saucepan using a spoon. Simmer for 3 ½ to 4 minutes, then lift the eggs out of the saucepan, place in eggcups, and serve, surrounded by the pieces of toast.

Excellent for breakfast with tea or coffee.

SERVES 4
PREPARATION TIME: 5 MINUTES
COOKING TIME: 10 TO 12 MINUTES

Souffléed Cheese Omelet
Omelette soufflée au fromage

7 eggs

6 tablespoons (100ml) crème fraîche or heavy cream

3 ⅓ oz. (100 g) old Mimolette cheese (see Note)

Salt and pepper

A little freshly grated nutmeg

1 ½ tablespoons (20 g) softened butter, for greasing the dish

About one hour ahead of time, take the eggs out of the refrigerator.

Preheat the oven to 425°F (210°C).

Separate the yolks from the whites of the eggs. Place the yolks in a mixing bowl with the cream. Grate the cheese and add to the bowl with the yolks, along with a little salt, pepper, and nutmeg. Beat with a spoon to combine.

In a large mixing bowl, beat the whites until stiff; then fold a quarter into the yolks and cheese mixture using a wooden spoon or spatula. When smooth, fold in the remaining whites. Lightly butter a medium-sized baking dish, pour in the batter, and bake for 10 to 12 minutes, or until golden brown on top. Remove from the oven and serve immediately.

Note: Mimolette is a hard cheese from Holland. Edam, Gouda, or even a mild Cheddar could be used instead.

SERVES 4
PREPARATION TIME: 10 MINUTES
COOKING TIME: 15 MINUTES

Potato and Bacon Omelet
Omelette aux pommes de terre et au lard

7 eggs
3 ½ oz. (100 g) slab bacon
2 medium (10 oz./300 g) potatoes, boiled
3 tablespoons (40 g) butter
Salt and pepper
1 tablespoon cold water

About one hour ahead of time, take the eggs out of the refrigerator.

Remove the bacon rind and dice the bacon. Fry the bacon in a very large ungreased frying pan. Cook slowly so that the fat will melt and the bacon will brown; turn the pieces over several times for even browning.

Dice or thinly slice the potatoes.

Remove the bacon from the pan and place on a paper towel to drain. Discard the fat. Wipe the frying pan with a clean paper towel, then melt the butter in it. When the butter starts to foam, add the potatoes and brown over moderate heat, turning them over carefully so they do not break. Break the eggs into a mixing bowl, season with salt and pepper, add 1 tablespoon of cold water, and beat with a fork just enough to break the yolks and mix them slightly with the whites; they should not be well mixed. Put the pieces of bacon back into the pan, then add the eggs. Cook for 5 to 6 minutes, or until done. Then slide the omelet onto a warm serving platter, giving it a gentle flip so that it will fold over onto itself. Serve immediately.

Serving suggestions: This omelet is excellent with a Green Salad (see p. 68).

Variation: The omelet may be cooked separately and the browned bacon and potatoes added afterward, once the omelet has been slid onto the serving platter.

Note: The omelet is done when the surface is set and creamy but not dry.

SERVES 4
PREPARATION TIME: 10 MINUTES
COOKING TIME: 35 MINUTES

8 eggs
8 oz. (250 g) fresh wild mushrooms, preferably morels (see Note)
3 tablespoons (40 g) butter
Salt and pepper

Wild Mushroom Omelet
Omelette aux champignons

At least one hour ahead of time, take all the ingredients out of the refrigerator.

Cut off any dirt from the stems of the mushrooms, then wash the mushrooms and cut them in half lengthwise or into slices. Melt half the butter in a very large frying pan. Add the mushrooms, salt, and pepper, and cook over moderate heat, stirring frequently, until all the liquid from the mushrooms has evaporated (about 10 to 15 minutes).

Break the eggs into a mixing bowl, season with salt and pepper, and beat lightly with a fork. Pour the mushrooms into the bowl with the eggs.

Melt the remaining butter in the pan. When hot, pour in the egg and mushroom mixture and cook for 5 to 10 minutes, or until done. Slide the omelet out of the pan and onto a warm serving platter, giving the pan a gentle flip when the omelet is halfway onto the platter so that it will fold over onto itself. Serve immediately.

Note: Although morels are called for in this recipe, many other wild mushrooms could be used instead (e.g., boletus, Japanese shitake mushrooms). About ¾ cup (25 g) top-quality dried wild mushrooms may also be used. Soak them for about 20 minutes in warm water (or follow the directions on the package), then add them with ½ cup (120 ml) of their water to the melted butter and cook as described for the fresh mushrooms.

Unless you have a very large frying pan, make two omelets, using half the egg and mushroom mixture each time.

SERVES 4
PREPARATION TIME: 15 MINUTES
COOKING TIME: 15 MINUTES

8 eggs

About 5 oz. (150 g) chanterelle mushrooms (see Note)

5 tablespoons (75 g) butter, divided

6 tablespoons (100 ml) crème fraîche or heavy cream

Salt and pepper

8 slices toast

Creamy Scrambled Eggs with Chanterelles
Oeufs brouillés aux chanterelles

At least one hour ahead of time, take the eggs out of the refrigerator.

Cut off any dirt from the base of each mushroom, then wash them quickly, drain, and dry on a towel.

Melt 2 tablespoons (30 g) of butter in a frying pan over moderate heat, and add the mushrooms. At first, they will release some liquid; as soon as this liquid has evaporated, lower the heat and simmer (the butter absorbed by the mushrooms will now reappear in the pan).

Melt 3 tablespoons (45 g) of butter in the top of a double boiler. Break the eggs into a bowl, add salt and pepper, whisk lightly, then pour into the melted butter. Continue whisking until the eggs are creamy; then stir in the cream with a wooden spoon. Stir constantly as the eggs are cooking, so they won't stick to the pan; when they are thick and creamy and coat the spoon, they arc done.

Remove the double boiler from the heat and stir the mushrooms into the eggs.

Serve immediately with buttered toast.

Note: Although chanterelles are called for here, many other wild mushrooms could be used instead (e.g., boletus, Japanese shitake mushrooms). About ½ cup (15 g) top-quality dried wild mushrooms may also be used. Soak them for about 20 minutes in warm water (or follow the directions on the package), then add them with 6 tablespoons (100 ml) of their water to the melted butter and cook as described for the fresh mushrooms.

Eggs scrambled in this way are not stiff but thick and creamy (almost like a sauce), so you may prefer to serve them in bowls and eat them with a spoon.

SERVES 4
PREPARATION TIME: 5 MINUTES
COOKING TIME: 8 TO 10 MINUTES

Creamy Scrambled Eggs with Salmon
Oeufs brouillés au saumon fumé

- 2 thin slices (4 oz./115 g) smoked salmon
- 2 tablespoons (30 g) butter
- 8 eggs
- 6 tablespoons (100 ml) crème fraîche or heavy cream
- Salt and pepper
- 8 slices toasted country-style or whole-wheat bread

At least one hour ahead of time, take all the ingredients out of the refrigerator.

Cut the salmon into thin strips.

Melt the butter in a double boiler. Whisk the eggs just enough to mix, and add the salmon, salt, and pepper. Pour the eggs into the butter and stir with a wooden spoon until very thick and creamy. Add the cream, stir to combine, and remove from the heat. Season with a little more pepper. Serve with buttered toast.

Note: Eggs scrambled in this way are not stiff but thick and creamy (almost like a sauce), so you may prefer to serve them in bowls and eat them with a spoon.

SERVES 4
PREPARATION TIME: 45 MINUTES
COOKING TIME: 1 HOUR

Eggs Toupinel
Oeufs Toupinel

- 4 large potatoes of uniform size
- Kosher salt
- 2 tablespoons vinegar
- 4 eggs
- 3 tablespoons (50 g) butter
- Scant ¼ cup (50 ml) crème fraîche or heavy cream
- A little grated nutmeg
- 5 oz. (150 g) cooked ham
- Salt and pepper

MORNAY SAUCE

- 1 cup (250 ml) milk, just boiled
- 1 tablespoon plus 1 teaspoon (20 g) butter
- 1 tablespoon plus 2 teaspoons (10 g) flour
- Salt and pepper
- A little grated nutmeg
- 2 tablespoons (20 g) grated Parmesan
- ½ cup (50 g) grated Gruyère
- 1 egg yolk

Wash and dry the potatoes. Put them on a bed of kosher salt in a broiler (dripping pan) and cook them at 450°F-475°F (240°C) for 35 minutes.

To prepare the Mornay sauce, bring the milk to a boil and remove from the heat. Melt the butter in a small pot and quickly stir in the flour. Leave for a few seconds and then pour in the boiling milk, stirring as you do so. Season with salt, pepper, and nutmeg, and leave to simmer gently for 10 minutes, stirring all the time. Remove from the heat and whip in the grated cheeses and the egg yolk. Set aside in a warm place.

Heat 4 cups (1 liter) water in a large pot and add the vinegar. Break an egg into a cup and drop it gently into the simmering liquid. Leave to poach for 3 minutes while the water simmers gently. Carefully remove it with a slotted spoon and place on a piece of paper towel. Repeat for the three other eggs.

When the potatoes are done, remove them from the oven. (Leave the oven on–you will need it later.)

Cut off a lid from the cooked potatoes using a knife with a sharp tip. Scoop out two-thirds of each potato, taking care not to pierce the skin. Mash the flesh with the butter and cream.

Season with salt and pepper and add a little grated nutmeg.

Fill the potatoes with this mixture, making a small cavity at the top.

Chop the ham and arrange it in the cavities with a spoonful of Mornay sauce.

Top with a poached egg and pour over the sauce. Cook in the oven for 4 to 5 minutes.

Oeufs Toupinel *is a dish created in the late nineteenth century and apparently named for a vaudeville play that was being performed at the time.*

Eggs Piperade
Oeufs à la piperade

SERVES 6
PREPARATION TIME: 20 MINUTES
COOKING TIME: 35 MINUTES

- 3 medium-sized onions
- 1 lb. (500 g) small Espelette peppers, or other sweet bell peppers
- 2 ¼ lb. (1 kg) tomatoes
- 2 cloves garlic
- Scant ¼ cup (50 ml) olive oil
- 9 eggs
- 6 thick slices Bayonne ham, or other mildly smoked, salt-cured ham
- Salt and freshly ground pepper

Peel and chop the onions.

Seed the peppers and cut them into short 1-in. (2-cm) strips.

Peel and seed the tomatoes and quarter them.

Peel the garlic cloves and slice them thinly.

Heat the oil in a large pan over high heat. Sauté the onions and sliced garlic cloves, leaving them to cook gently for 10 minutes. Add the sliced bell peppers and cook for 5 minutes to allow them to color. Add the tomatoes and cook at medium heat for 15 minutes. Break the eggs one by one into a mixing bowl and beat them with a fork. Pour into the pan over the vegetables.

Stir with a wooden spoon until the eggs are the creamy consistency of scrambled eggs.

Season with salt and pepper and pour into a warmed serving dish.

Quickly heat the ham slices in a pan over high heat, just 3 seconds on each side.

Arrange them over the eggs and serve immediately.

Piperade is a specialty from the Basque region, near the French-Spanish border, comprising stewed tomatoes and sweet bell peppers.

FISH

SERVES 4
PREPARATION TIME: 20 MINUTES
COOKING TIME: 40 MINUTES

Pike with Frogs' Legs
Brochetons "Tatan Nano"

- 4 pike, 5-6 oz. (150-180 g) apiece
- 24 large frogs' legs
- Bouquet garni
- 1 egg white and 2 egg yolks
- Scant cup (200 ml) cream
- ⅔ oz. (20 g) shallots
- 3 ½ oz. (100 g) mushrooms
- Scant ½ cup (100 ml) white wine
- 7 oz. (200 g) spinach leaves
- 1 stick plus 6 tablespoons (200 g) butter
- Salt and pepper

Scale, trim, and remove the gills of the pike. Make an incision in the back to remove the spine and, using the back of a spoon to push back the flesh, remove the small bones. Bone the frogs' legs. Make sure you have frogs' legs that have not been frozen, as freezing causes the flesh to swell with water.

Use the pike bones and frogs' leg bones to make a fumet. Stew the bouquet garni and then pour the strained liquid in.

Pound or process the flesh of the frogs' legs together with the egg white. Push through a fine sieve to eliminate any sinews. Whip half of the cream over a bowl placed over a larger bowl containing ice, as you would for a quenelle stuffing, seasoning it well. Fold it carefully into the strained frogs' legs mixture, still over the ice.

Fill each pike with the stuffing. To close, pull the edges together: they are gelatinous and will stick together easily.

Chop the shallots and sauté them gently in butter. Slice the mushrooms and sauté them in the same pan. Butter a dish and arrange a bed of shallots and mushrooms in it. Place the stuffed pike on top and pour in the white wine and some fumet. Season and cover with buttered parchment paper. Braise at low heat for about 15 minutes. During this time, blanch the spinach leaves briefly, refresh, and drain them well. Season. Drain the pike on a cloth and remove the skins. Trim. Wrap the pike in the spinach, leaving the head apparent.

Using the cooking liquid, make a velouté whipped with butter and thickened with the egg yolks. This will make a creamy white wine sauce that will glaze your dish. Use the method for a sabayon: emulsify the egg yolks with the rest of the cream in a double boiler. Arrange the pike on a serving platter. Arrange a line of sliced mushrooms on each one and drizzle over the sauce, strained through cheesecloth. Glaze in a hot oven (425°F/210°C) or under the salamander just before serving.

SERVES 6 TO 8
SOAKING TIME: 24 HOURS
PREPARATION TIME: 15 MINUTES
COOKING TIME: 25 MINUTES

Homemade Cod Brandade
Brandade de morue à la ménagère

- 1 lb. (500 g) salted cod, with very white flesh
- ¾ cup to 1 ¼ cups (200–300 ml) virgin olive oil, divided
- 1 clove garlic, crushed
- Scant ½ cup (100 ml) cream or milk
- 3 ½ oz. (100 g) mashed potatoes (precook the potatoes in their skins or steam them)
- 1 pinch finely ground white pepper
- Salt, if needed
- Juice of 1 lemon
- Croutons

Leave the cod to soak in cold water for 24 hours to remove some of its salt. If necessary, change the water several times. Salt cod should be purchased in large, flattened, and dried pieces on the bone with the skin still attached. If unavailable, fillets may be used. In either case, before cooking, the fish should be cut into large pieces and soaked for 24 hours in the following manner:

Turn a plate upside down in a large bowl or pot so that the fish will not rest directly on the bottom (all the salt falls to the bottom), and place the fish, skin side up, on top of it. Fill the bowl or pot with cold water and add a few ice cubes; change the water at least four times (six to eight is preferable) and add a few ice cubes each time. Before cooking, drain the cod and pat it dry with a clean cloth.

Poach the cod in water. Cut it into several pieces and place it in a pot with 6 ½ pints (3 liters) water. Bring to a boil and, as soon as it boils, remove the pot from direct heat, placing it just on the edge of the burner or over minimal heat with a heat diffuser. Leave to poach for 10 to 12 minutes.

Drain the pieces of fish and remove both the black and white skin as well as the bones. Flake off the flesh.

In a heavy-bottomed pot, heat a scant ½ cup (100 ml) of the oil. Add the flaked cod and the crushed garlic clove.

Briskly stir the ingredients together with a wooden spoon until the fish is reduced to a fine paste. Then lower the heat, continuing to stir briskly as you incorporate the remaining oil and the cream or milk.

To finish, mix in the hot mashed potatoes thoroughly. Season with the finely ground white pepper, and if necessary add a little salt. Lastly, stir in the lemon juice well. Your brandade is now finished: it will be a light, smooth paste and the color will be white.

Serve it hot on a platter, shaped into a dome and surrounded by small croutons fried golden brown in oil or butter.

SERVES 4
PREPARATION TIME: 45 MINUTES
COOKING TIME: 1 HOUR

FUMET

4 cups (1 liter) well-seasoned fish fumet prepared with the trout bones

Bouquet garni

MOUSSE

1 ¼ lb. (600 g) flesh of freshwater trout (retaining the bones for the fumet)

4 teaspoons (20 g) salt

15 turns of the pepper mill

4 egg whites

4 cups (1 liter) double cream (minimum 40 percent butterfat)

CRAYFISH COULIS

2 ¼ lb. (1 kg) red clawed crayfish

7 tablespoons (100 g) butter

Scant ½ cup (100 ml) cognac

Scant ½ cup (100 ml) cream

BEURRE MANIÉ

1 tablespoon flour

1 ¾ teaspoons butter

Salt and pepper

Special equipment: a savarin mold

Hot Freshwater Trout Mousse with Crayfish Coulis
Mousse chaude de truite de rivière au coulis d'écrevisse

Prepare a fumet using the trout bones, 4 cups (1 liter) water and a bouquet garni. Cook for 20 minutes, strain, and set aside.

Preheat the oven to 350°F (180°C).

To make the mousse, grind or process the flesh of the trout with the salt and pepper until smooth. Incorporate the egg whites and push through a sieve. When the mixture is quite smooth, stand the bowl over ice and mix in the double cream.

Butter a large savarin mold and fill it with the mousse. Place the mold in a baking pan and pour in boiling water halfway to the rim. It should take 45 minutes to cook in the oven.

Next make the crayfish coulis. Plunge the crayfish into boiling water. Section the tails and remove the shells. Set the tails aside. Pound the shells using a pestle and mortar or grind them in a food processor. Sauté them in a pan with butter to enhance their red color.

Add the cognac. Reduce it by half, then pour in the well-seasoned trout fumet. Cook for a few minutes over very low heat. Thicken slightly with the beurre manié and then adjust the seasoning. Stir in the cream and push the mixture through a chinois.

While the mousse is cooking, prepare the crayfish tails for garnish: stew them in butter, season them, and add a little very hot coulis.

To serve, turn the hot trout mousse out onto a large round silver or china platter. Place the prepared crayfish tails in the center.

Serve a dish of coulis on the side, as well as a dish of rice pilaf.

Variation: You may use individual savarin molds. To make this dish even more stylish, scatter with a few truffle shavings and surround the dish with decorative pieces of puff pastry (see p. 565).

SERVES 6
PREPARATION TIME: 1 HOUR
COOKING TIME:
1 HOUR 15 MINUTES

- 3 ½ lb. (1.5 kg) fresh fish, including:
  - Scorpion fish
  - Red scorpion fish
  - Whiting
  - Mullet
  - Great weever (or sting fish)
  - John Dory
  - Conger eel or other lean rockfish
  - Rock lobster
- 2 oz. (60 g) onions
- 1 medium-sized leek, white part only
- Scant ½ cup (100 ml) olive oil
- 2 tomatoes, peeled, seeded, and crushed, keeping the liquid
- ½ oz. (15 g) crushed garlic
- 1 generous pinch roughly chopped parsley
- 1 sprig thyme
- 1 bay leaf
- 1 sprig savory
- 1 branch fennel
- 1 small pinch aniseed
- 1 pinch saffron threads (this should be the dominant note)
- 3 tablespoons (40 g) unsalted butter
- Salt and pepper
- Croutons rubbed with garlic

Bouillabaisse

Clean, scale, gut, and trim the fish, and section their heads. Prepare about 8 cups (2 liters) fumet (stock) using the heads of the fish you will be using for the soup, or else with the bones of sole and brill and turbot heads. Do not salt.

Finely chop the onions and leek and place them in a soup pot with 2 tablespoons oil. Add the tomatoes and their liquid. Heat gently until they are all cooked through, but do not color. Arrange all the prepared fish, except the lobster, in the pot. Add the condiments and sprinkle with a generous pinch of salt (about 2 teaspoons or 8 g) and freshly ground pepper. Cover completely with the unsalted fish fumet. Cube the butter, add it to the pot, and pour in the remaining oil.

Turn the heat up to maximum. As soon as the liquid begins to boil, cut the live lobster into slices and add to the pot. Cook at a high boil for 15 minutes. As the contents boil, the fish fumet, oil, and butter become emulsified and combine, attaining the consistency of a creamed soup. This exceptionally tasty dish must be served as soon as it is ready, otherwise its natural thick and smooth texture–its most notable characteristic–rapidly disappears.

Rub croutons with garlic, drizzle them with oil, and grill them in the oven. Then put them in a soup tureen.

Carefully drain the pieces of fish and serve them on a platter. Check the seasoning in the soup, then pour the boiling soup over the croutons. The seasoning will give your bouillabaisse its distinctive note and mark it as one of high quality. The dominant note is set by the saffron, which also gives the bouillabaisse its flavor and golden color. You will need a fine palate to use the fennel and aniseed in the right proportions. It is a good idea to try to re-create the flavors of previously tasted fine bouillabaisses.

Note: Some cooks add shellfish such as mussels and cockles, but we don't advise this: the flavor of the mussels may be overpowering and shellfish often deposit sand.

Sea Bass Wrapped in Seaweed, *à la* Michel Guérard
Loup au varech à la façon de Michel Guérard

SERVES 4
PREPARATION TIME: 15 MINUTES
COOKING TIME: 30 MINUTES

1 sea bass weighing 3 ½-4 lb. (1.5-1.8 kg)

2 generous handfuls fresh rockweed (a type of seaweed found on the coasts of the North Sea and Atlantic and Pacific Oceans)

1 cup (250 ml) dry white wine

SAUCE

1 tomato

2 oz. (30 g) assorted fresh herbs, including parsley, chervil, tarragon, basil, and chives

1 mild chili pepper

Juice of 2 lemons

Scant ½ cup (100 ml) extra virgin olive oil

Salt and pepper

Preheat the oven to 400°F (200°C).

Place one-third of the rockweed at the bottom of a rectangular ovenproof dish. Gut, trim, and season the sea bass, place it in the dish, and cover it with the remaining rockweed. Pour over the white wine and cover with a sheet of aluminum foil. Place in the oven for about 30 minutes.

While the fish is cooking, prepare the sauce. Peel and finely chop the tomato. Chop the herbs and finely dice the chili pepper. Combine the three ingredients in a mixing bowl and season with salt and pepper. Stir in the lemon juice and olive oil.

To serve, carefully place the fish on a platter accompanied by the sauce in a sauceboat.

Variation: If you do not have chives, substitute a little chopped shallot or onion.

You may also cook the sea bass in a fish kettle over low heat, covered with the lid.

SERVES 4
PREPARATION TIME: 20 MINUTES
COOKING TIME: 40 MINUTES

Baked Cod
Cabillaud à la ménagère

- 1 large piece cod, about 1 ½ lb. (600 g), preferably cut from the central, thick part of the body
- 14 oz. (400 g) new potatoes
- 3 ½ oz. (100 g) small new onions
- 3 tablespoons (50 g) butter, melted
- 1 tablespoon olive oil (optional)
- 1 pinch chopped parsley
- 1 lemon, quartered
- Salt and pepper

Preheat the oven to 350°F (180°C).

Scale and wash the fish.

Generously butter an earthenware dish large enough to hold the fish and the vegetables. Season the fish all over generously with salt and pepper. Arrange small new potatoes and onions around it. If the vegetables are not new, first boil them briefly, drain, and season with table salt. Drizzle the melted butter over the fish and vegetables and cook in the oven, spooning frequently with the cooking liquid–if you like you can add 1 tablespoon of olive oil to it. The onions should comprise one quarter of the total garnish. Make sure that they stand firmly on the base of the dish so that they are in constant contact with the buttery cooking juices. This way, they will turn a nice golden color.

Just before serving the fish in the cooking dish, sprinkle the fish and vegetables with the freshly chopped parsley. On the side, serve the lemon quarters to squeeze over the fish when it is served into warmed plates.

Poaching and grilling are two other cooking methods that are very suitable for cod. Cut it into 1-in. (2-cm) slices and serve it with one of the sauces recommended for poached or grilled fish.

Court Bouillon

MAKES ABOUT 2 QUARTS (2 LITERS)
PREPARATION TIME: 10 MINUTES
COOKING TIME: 15 TO 20 MINUTES

- 1 leek, split lengthwise
- 2 stalks celery
- 2 sprigs thyme
- 1 small bunch parsley
- ¼ bay leaf
- Sprig of fennel leaves or a little fresh ginger (optional)
- 2 carrots, peeled and quartered
- 1 medium onion, stuck with a clove
- 1 ¼ cups (300 ml) dry white wine
- 7 ½ cups (1 ¾ liters) water
- 1 tablespoon (7 g) kosher salt
- 5 peppercorns

Peel and carefully rinse the vegetables. Cut the leek lengthwise into quarters.

Make a bouquet garni by tying together the leek, celery, thyme, parsley, bay leaf, and fennel or ginger (if desired).

Place the bouquet garni in a large pot with the quartered carrots, the onion stuck with a clove, wine, water, salt, and peppercorns. Bring to a boil and boil gently for 15 minutes uncovered; then remove from the heat and allow to cool completely before using.

Note: A court bouillon is an aromatic liquid used for poaching fish. Any fish can be poached in a court bouillon: pike, salmon, even lobsters or scallops. It can be made well in advance and kept in the refrigerator until you are ready to poach your fish. When the time comes, place the fish in the cold court bouillon, bring to a boil, then immediately lower the heat and poach the fish until it is cooked (cooking times are indicated in specific recipes). Generally, if you intend to eat a fish or large shellfish (lobster, etc.) cold, simply place it in the cold court bouillon, bring to a boil, then remove from the heat and cover the pot (the time it takes for the court bouillon to cool will be long enough to cook the fish).

SERVES 4
SOAKING TIME: 24 TO 48 HOURS
PREPARATION TIME: 25 MINUTES
COOKING TIME: 40 MINUTES

1 ½ lb. (700 g) dried salt cod with bones and skin or 1 ¼ lb. (600 g) salt cod fillets

1 ¾ lb. (800 g) potatoes, in their skins

6 tablespoons (100 ml) cooking oil

1 large clove garlic

1 small bunch parsley

1 whole egg

6 tablespoons (100 ml) whipping cream

Salt and pepper

Sautéed Salt Cod and Potatoes
Morue poêlée

Salt cod should be purchased in large, flattened, and dried pieces on the bone with the skin still attached. If unavailable, fillets may be used. In either case, before cooking the fish should be cut into large pieces and soaked for 24 hours using the following method:

Turn a plate upside down in a large bowl or pot so that the fish will not rest directly on the bottom (all the salt falls to the bottom), and place the fish, skin side up, on top of it. Fill the bowl or pot with cold water and add a few ice cubes; change the water at least four times (six to eight is preferable) and add a few ice cubes each time. Before cooking, drain the cod and pat it dry with a clean cloth.

Cook the potatoes in a large pot of lightly salted water for 30 minutes. Drain, rinse rapidly under running water to cool slightly, and remove their skins while still hot (they will peel very easily). Cut the potatoes into thick slices or large cubes, place in a bowl, cover, and set aside.

While the potatoes are cooking, cook the cod. Place it in a large pot, immerse in cold water, and bring to a boil. As soon as the water boils, cover the pot and remove from the heat. Leave the fish in the water for 20 minutes, then drain, carefully remove the skin and bones, and break the cod into small flaky pieces with your fingers.

Heat the oil in a large frying pan; when hot, add the potatoes and cod, lower the heat, and cook for 10 to 12 minutes, or until very hot, stirring frequently. Generously pepper and taste for salt (it probably won't need any).

While the cod and potatoes are cooking, peel the garlic, wash the parsley, and remove the stems from the parsley. On a cutting board, finely chop the garlic and the parsley separately and set aside.

When the cod and potatoes are hot, whisk the egg and cream together in a mixing bowl. Remove the frying pan from the heat and quickly stir in the egg and cream mixture. Pour into a hot serving dish, sprinkle with parsley and garlic, and serve immediately.

SERVES 6 TO 8
PREPARATION TIME: 1 HOUR
COOKING TIME:
1 HOUR 30 MINUTES

1 Mediterranean sea bass, weighing about 6 ½ lb. (3 kg)

5 sprigs chervil, leaves picked

5 sprigs tarragon, leaves picked

2 pieces Puff Pastry (see p. 565) large enough to encase the fish

1 egg yolk, lightly beaten

Salt and pepper

Mediterranean Sea Bass in a Pastry Case
Loup de la Méditerranée en croûte

Gut the fish and remove the skin, being careful not to damage the flesh and leaving the head and tail intact. Make an incision along the back until you reach the central bone. Insert leaves of freshly picked chervil and tarragon into the opening. Season with salt and pepper and close up the fish. Repeat the procedure at the stomach.

Preheat the oven to 425°F (220°C).

Roll out the two pieces of puff pastry until they are a little longer and wider than the fish. Place the fish on one of them and cover it with the other. To seal the fish within the pastry case, simply press the two sides of pastry together all around the fish so that its shape can be clearly seen.

Using a very thin knife, cut away the surplus pastry and use a little of it to shape the fin. Draw a few lines lengthways on the fin and use the remaining pastry to shape the gills and an eye. Baste the pastry with the egg yolk, then draw out the scales, using a very small, half-moon-shaped cooking cutter. This is fine work that requires a great deal of patience and skill.

Place the sea bass on a baking dish in the hot oven. As soon as the pastry begins to color, lower the temperature to 350°F (180°C) so that the encased fish can cook evenly and to avoid burning the pastry. Cook for about 1 hour 30 minutes.

To serve, place on a serving platter and cut it at the table. Accompany with melted butter or a beurre blanc sauce.

Variation: Before wrapping in pastry, you may also stuff the sea bass with a delicate lobster mousse.

Note: Mediterranean sea bass, with its delicate white flesh and well-flavored refined taste, can be cooked in many ways: poached or braised, and even served cold, but the most popular methods involve either grilling it with fennel or preparing it in a pastry case.

SERVES 6 TO 8
PREPARATION TIME: 20 MINUTES
COOKING TIME: 1 HOUR

Salmon Koulibiac
Coulibiac de saumon

12 oz. (350 g) salmon
2 tablespoons (30 g) butter
1 medium-sized onion
2 oz. (50 g) mushrooms
1 lb. (500 g) unsweetened Brioche Dough (see p. 561)
3 ½ oz. (100 g) large-grained couscous (semolina) cooked in a white stock
1 hard-boiled egg, roughly chopped
9 oz. (250 g) butter, melted

Cut the salmon into ¼-in. (5-mm) slices. Make sure there are no bones left in the salmon. Season them and sear them in the 2 tablespoons of butter. Remove from the pan. Chop the onion and mushrooms and soften them in the same butter. Leave to cool and then scatter over the salmon.

Preheat the oven to 200°F/90°C.

Roll out the brioche pastry and arrange the ingredients–the salmon mixture, the couscous, and the egg–in layers over it. Fold the dough over to wrap it all up, seal the ends, and turn the koulibiac over onto a baking tray. Cover it with a clean cloth and cook in the oven for 20 minutes. Then baste it with melted butter and make a few incisions. Make a little vent in the center to allow the steam to escape.

Turn the heat up to 425°F (210°C) and cook for about 35 minutes more. Just before serving, pour a few spoonfuls of melted butter into the vent in the center.

The cooked, seasoned couscous should separate like grains of rice and yet remain soft.

The Troisgros Brothers' Salmon Fillet with Sorrel
Escalope de saumon à l'oseille des frères Troisgros

SERVES 8 TO 10
PREPARATION TIME: 30 MINUTES
COOKING TIME: 10 MINUTES

- 3 ½ lb. (1.5 kg) fresh salmon, cut into thin slices
- 3 ½ oz. (100 g) sorrel
- 3 oz. (80 g) shallots
- 1 cup (250 ml) dry white wine
- 1 cup (250 ml) Noilly Prat
- 1 cup (250 ml) fish fumet
- 2 cups (500 ml) cream
- Scant ½ cup (100 ml) oil
- Salt and pepper
- Puff Pastry garnish (optional, see p. 565)

Prepare the sorrel: cook it in boiling water, then refresh and drain well. Chop the shallots.

In a pot, reduce the white wine, Noilly, and fish fumet, together with the chopped shallots. When the liquid is syrupy, strain it through a fine-meshed sieve and add the cream. Reduce again until it thickens. Season with salt and pepper and incorporate the well-drained sorrel.

Season the salmon slices well with salt and pepper and pan-fry them in hot oil. Do not allow them to dry out: just a few seconds is sufficient to cook them on both sides. To serve, arrange the salmon on warmed plates. Cover them with the sorrel sauce, or serve it separately. To garnish, add an attractive flower shape of puff pastry.

Braised Tuna
Thon braisé à la ménagère

SERVES 6 TO 8
SOAKING TIME: 1 HOUR
PREPARATION TIME: 10 MINUTES
COOKING TIME: 40 MINUTES

- 1 piece fresh tuna weighing approximately 2 ¾ lb. (1.2 kg)
- 2 oz. (50 g) chopped onions
- Scant ¼ cup (50 ml) virgin olive oil
- 10 oz. (300 g) tomato pulp
- 1 cup (250 ml) white wine
- 1 small bouquet garni comprising a bay leaf, thyme, rosemary, and parsley
- Salt and pepper

Soak the piece of tuna in cold water for about 1 hour to remove any traces of blood.

In a cast-iron pot, sauté the chopped onions in olive oil without allowing them to brown. Season the tuna with salt and pepper and place it on top of the chopped onions. Leave for 5 minutes and then turn it over. Add the tomato pulp, the white wine, and the bouquet garni. Season again.

Put the lid on the pot and leave to simmer gently over low heat for about 30 minutes. When the tuna is cooked, transfer it to a serving dish. Just before serving, pour over the sauce, which should have thickened.

Serve with a timbale of Creole rice.

SERVES 4
PREPARATION TIME: 5 MINUTES

Raw Salmon Renga-Ya
Saumon cru Renga-Ya

4 oz. (120 g) slice of raw, sushi-quality salmon
1 tablespoon olive oil
Juice of ¼ lemon
1 pinch chives
Salt and pepper

Slice the salmon just before serving. Place the slices on very cold plates. Season with salt and a little freshly ground pepper. Drizzle the olive oil and lemon juice over and scatter the chives on the top.

Serve with hot toast. If you wish, add a spoonful of caviar to the center of each slice.

I took the inspiration for this recipe from Japanese cuisine.

SERVES 2
PREPARATION TIME: 10 MINUTES
COOKING TIME: 10 MINUTES

- 1 lb. (500 g) sole (1 large sole)
- 2 tablespoons olive oil, divided
- 4 tablespoons flour
- 5 ½ tablespoons (80 g) butter, divided
- Juice of ½ lemon
- 1 teaspoon chopped parsley
- 1 lemon for garnish
- Salt and pepper

Sole Meunière

The white skin must be left on the sole; simply scrape it well to remove the scales.

Combine a few drops of oil with a little salt and pepper and season the fish with this. Then dust it with flour (a sole meunière is always dusted with flour).

Using an oval pan, preferably (having a pan the size of the fish saves using unnecessary butter, which often burns), heat 2 tablespoons (30 g) butter and 1 tablespoon olive oil. When the fat begins to smoke, place the fish in it and cook over high heat. When the sole comes into contact with very hot butter, it is sufficiently well seared for it not to stick. Ensure, however, that the butter does not boil.

After 5 to 6 minutes, turn the sole over with a spatula and leave until it is cooked through.

Heat a serving platter well. Cut a half-lemon lengthways and make decorative incisions in the zest. Cut thin slices and garnish the dish with a row of these slices.

Squeeze out a few drops of lemon juice over the fish. Scatter with the chopped parsley. Add 3 ½ tablespoons (50 g) butter to the pan and heat it until it browns. Pour it over the sole.

When the very hot butter and damp parsley come into contact, they form a foam that will cover the sole, which should be served immediately.

SERVES 4
PREPARATION TIME: 15 MINUTES
COOKING TIME: 30 MINUTES

Mediterranean Red Mullet and *Pistou* Sauce
Rougets de la Méditerranée, sauce au pistou

8 red mullet weighing about 3 ½ oz. (100 g) apiece

COURT BOUILLON

2 cups (500 ml) white wine
1 cup (250 ml) spring water
2 oz. (50 g) carrots, sliced
2 oz. (50 g) onions, chopped
2 oz. (50 g) kosher salt
½ oz. (15 g) parsley sprigs
½ oz. (15 g) celery stalks
½ oz. (15 g) leek, sliced
½ bay leaf
1 small sprig thyme
1 tablespoon plus 1 heaped teaspoon (⅓ oz./10 g) black peppercorns
2 cloves
2 coriander seeds
4 orange slices
4 lemon slices

PISTOU SAUCE

¾ cup (200 g) olive oil
⅔ oz. (20 g) basil, chopped
⅓ oz. (10 g) parsley, chopped
¼ oz. (5 g) tarragon, chopped
¼ oz. (5 g) chervil, chopped
¼ oz. (5 g) chives, chopped
Juice of 1 lemon
2 teaspoons (10 g) salt
3 grinds black pepper

Prepare a court bouillon with all the ingredients in the list and boil it for 15 minutes. Place the mullet in the pot, bring to a boil, and immediately remove from the heat. Leave to poach for 15 minutes.

Combine all the ingredients for the *pistou* sauce and leave the mixture in a moderately warm place.

Serve the sauce with the warm mullet, or in summer the mullet may be eaten cold.

Note: For this delicious dish, choose really fresh mullet. Select only fish with bright eyes and an attractive red color.

SERVES 4
PREPARATION TIME: 15 MINUTES
COOKING TIME: 15 MINUTES

Monkfish
Lotte

4 slices monkfish (anglerfish) weighing 1 ¾ lb. (800 g) in total

Flour

2 tablespoons (30 g) butter

1 clove garlic, whole and unpeeled

1 tablespoon lemon juice

Generous ½ cup (150 ml) dry white wine

Salt and pepper

Roll the slices of fish in flour, then shake to remove any excess. Salt and pepper each slice on both sides.

Melt the butter in a large frying pan; when it begins to foam, place the slices of fish in the pan, add the garlic, and cook over moderate heat for 7 minutes on each side. Remove the fish with a slotted spatula and place on a warm serving platter.

Add the lemon juice and wine to the pan, and boil rapidly, scraping the bottom of the pan with a wooden spoon, for a few seconds. The sauce should thicken slightly. Add a little salt and pepper; then pour the sauce over the fish and serve.

Serving suggestions: Serve with Rice (see p. 510) or steamed potatoes and with a dish of butter on the side.

SERVES 4
PREPARATION TIME: 10 MINUTES
COOKING TIME: 20 MINUTES

Roasted Monkfish
Rôti de lotte

A 1 ¾ lb. (800 g) piece (preferably toward the tail) of monkfish (anglerfish), skinned

1 large clove garlic

¼ cup (60 ml) olive oil

1 tablespoon lemon juice

Salt and pepper

Preheat the oven to 450°F-475°F (240°C), or as high as your oven will go.

Pat the fish dry with a clean towel. Peel the garlic and cut it into quarters. Lard the fish with garlic by making four incisions with a knife and sliding a piece of garlic into each one. Place the fish in a roasting pan, pour the oil over it, then roll the fish in the oil. Add the lemon juice, and sprinkle with salt and pepper. Bake in the oven for 20 minutes, basting from time to time.

Serve the fish in the dish in which it was cooked.

Cod Lyonnaise
Morue à la lyonnaise

SERVES 4
SOAKING TIME: 24 TO 48 HOURS
PREPARATION TIME: 20 MINUTES
COOKING TIME: 40 MINUTES

1 lb. (500 g) salted cod
3 medium-sized potatoes
3 medium-sized onions
1 tablespoon plus 1 teaspoon (20 g) butter
2 tablespoons oil
1 pinch fresh chopped parsley
½ tablespoon vinegar
Salt and pepper

To prepare the salted cod for cooking, see instructions p. 179.

Poach the salted cod and remove the skin and bones. Flake it and dry it at low heat until all the cooking water has evaporated.

Peel the potatoes and cook them in salted water. Cut them into slices.

Finely cut the onions into julienne slices and sauté with the butter and oil. When they are cooked and only barely colored, add the cooked potatoes and sauté them until lightly browned.

Then add the prepared cod and sauté for a few moments over high heat. Check the seasoning and add some freshly ground pepper.

Just before serving, scatter the cod with the chopped parsley. Transfer to the serving platter and bring the vinegar to a boil rapidly in the sauté pan. Pour it over the cod.

SERVES 4
PREPARATION TIME: 15 MINUTES
COOKING TIME: 10 MINUTES

Cod with Melted Butter Sauce
Tranches de cabillaud au beurre fondu

4 slices fresh cod weighing 2 lb. (900 g) in total

COURT BOUILLON
1 leek
2 stalks celery
2 sprigs thyme
1 small bunch parsley
¼ bay leaf
2 carrots
1 medium onion
1 clove
1 ¼ cups (300 ml) dry white wine
3 cups (750 ml) water
Salt

MELTED BUTTER SAUCE
1 tablespoon lemon juice
7 tablespoons (100 g) softened butter
Salt and pepper

Finely chopped parsley (optional)
Finely chopped chives (optional)

Several hours or a day in advance, make the court bouillon: Peel and carefully rinse the vegetables. Cut the leek lengthwise into quarters. Make a bouquet garni by tying together the leek, celery, thyme, parsley, and bay leaf. Cut the carrots into quarters. Place the bouquet garni in a large pot with the carrots, the onion stuck with a clove, wine, and very lightly salted water. Bring to a boil and boil gently for 15 minutes uncovered; then remove from the heat and allow to cool completely before using.

Place the slices of fish in the cold liquid, bring to a boil, then immediately lower the heat and simmer for 10 minutes.

For the melted butter sauce, break the butter into ten pieces. When the fish is almost done, place the lemon juice and butter in the top of a double boiler, add a little salt and pepper, and set into place over a little simmering water in the bottom of the double boiler. Melt the butter, stirring constantly. As soon as the butter has melted, the sauce is ready to serve.

Lift the fish out of the court bouillon with a slotted spoon and place it on a warm serving platter. If desired, stir the freshly chopped herbs into the sauce. Serve on the side in a sauceboat.

This dish is often served with potatoes that have been peeled and boiled in salted water to which a little olive oil has been added.

Turbot with Mixed Vegetables
Turbotin aux légumes

SERVES 4
PREPARATION TIME: 15 MINUTES
COOKING TIME: 10 MINUTES

- 1 turbot (or other flatfish) weighing 3 ½ lb. (1.5 kg)
- 2 carrots
- ¼ celeriac
- 1 leek
- 4 tablespoons (60 g) softened butter
- Bouquet garni, made with 2 sprigs thyme, ¼ bay leaf, and 2 sprigs parsley tied together
- 1 cup (250 ml) dry white wine
- Salt and pepper

Ask the fish seller to cut off the head and fins, and to cut the fish into four pieces.

Preheat the oven to 425°F (210°C).

Bring water and salt to boil in a pot. Peel and wash the vegetables, and on a cutting board slice them into fine julienne strips.

Cook all the vegetables in the pot of lightly salted boiling water for 7 to 8 minutes, drain, cool under running water, and pat dry with a clean cloth. Butter a baking dish, spread the vegetables over the bottom, and place the pieces of fish on top. Season with salt and pepper, and place the bouquet garni in the dish. Add the white wine and bake in the oven for about 10 minutes. To serve, remove the bouquet garni and serve the fish and vegetables in the baking dish.

Serving suggestions: Serve with Rice (see p. 510) or fresh pasta.

SERVES 5 OR 6
PREPARATION TIME: 20 MINUTES
COOKING TIME: 15 MINUTES

Skate with Browned Butter
Raie bouclée au beurre "noisette"

- 4 lb. (1.8 kg) skate
- 1 stalk celery
- 1 small leek
- 1 sprig thyme
- ¼ bay leaf
- Generous ½ cup (150 ml) white wine vinegar
- 3 tablespoons (30 g) kosher salt
- 4 peppercorns, coarsely crushed
- 1 bunch parsley
- 4 tablespoons (60 ml) Dijon mustard
- 6 tablespoons (60 g) capers
- 1 tablespoon red wine vinegar
- 1 ¼ sticks (150 g) butter
- Salt and pepper

In a large, wide pot, bring 8 cups (2 liters) water to a boil, then add the skate and boil for 2 minutes, a piece at a time. Drain, place on a cutting board, and use a small knife to remove the skin.

Cut the fish into equal portions, then place the pieces back in the pot. Pour in enough cold water to cover. Wash the celery and leek and split the leek lengthwise. Make a bouquet garni by tying together the celery, leek, thyme, and bay leaf with twine, and add it to the pot with the fish along with the vinegar, kosher salt, and peppercorns. Bring to a boil, then immediately remove the pot from the heat. Cover, and leave the skate in the hot water for 10 minutes to cook.

While the skate is cooking, carefully wash the parsley and chop it coarsely. Spread the mustard over the bottom of a large porcelain or earthenware dish. Lift the skate out of its cooking liquid with a slotted spoon or spatula, and place it in the dish with the mustard. Sprinkle with salt, pepper, and parsley, then add the capers and red wine vinegar.

Meanwhile, melt the butter in a frying pan until it begins to color. Pour the butter immediately into the platter with the fish and serve.

Serve with steamed potatoes.

SERVES 4
SOAKING TIME: 24 TO 48 HOURS
PREPARATION TIME: 1 HOUR
COOKING TIME: 45 MINUTES

1 ½–1 ¾ lb. (700–800 g) dried salt cod with bones and skin, or 1 ¼–1 ½ lb. (600–700 g) salt cod fillets

2 large red or yellow bell peppers

1 large onion

4 tomatoes

1 clove garlic

1 fresh chili pepper

1 cup (240ml) olive oil, divided

Generous ½ cup (100 g) black olives

Generous ½ cup (150 ml) dry white wine

1 lb. (500 g) potatoes

Salt

Portuguese-Style Salt Cod
Morue à la portugaise

Prepare the salt cod for cooking according to the instructions on page 179.

Preheat the oven to 450°F–475°F (240°C), or as high as your oven will go.

Wash the bell peppers, wipe them dry, cut out the stem, and remove the seeds. Brush each pepper with oil, then place them on a rack in the oven for 15 minutes, turning over once. Remove the peppers from the oven and peel off the skin using your fingers and a paring knife, then cut the peppers into strips and set aside.

Peel and slice the onion. Run the tomatoes under hot water, peel them and remove the seeds. Coarsely chop the tomatoes. Peel the garlic and crush it with a fork. Finely slice the chili pepper and remove its seeds.

Drain the salt cod, pat it dry with a clean cloth, remove the skin and bones, then cut it into pieces about 2 in. (5 cm) on a side. Heat 8 tablespoons (120 ml) of oil in a large, high-sided frying pan, add the cod, and cook over moderate heat for 5 minutes a side. Remove with a slotted spatula and place on a warm serving platter. Cover the platter, and place the cod inside the still warm oven while cooking the vegetables.

Place the remaining ½ cup (120 ml) of oil in a cast-iron or earthenware pot.

When hot, add the bell peppers, chili pepper, onion, garlic, tomatoes, and olives. Simmer for 8 minutes. Add the wine, bring to a boil, lower the heat, and simmer slowly for 15 minutes more.

While the vegetables are cooking, peel the potatoes and boil them in lightly salted water for 30 minutes.

Add the cod to the pot with the vegetables and simmer together for 8 minutes. Serve in its cooking pot, with the potatoes in a serving dish on the side.

SERVES 4
PREPARATION TIME: 15 MINUTES
COOKING TIME: 30 MINUTES

Fresh Tuna and Tomatoes
Rôti de thon

- 1 ¾ lb. (800 g) fresh tuna, in one piece (see Note)
- 2 medium (200 g) onions
- 3 medium (400 g) ripe tomatoes
- ¼ cup (60 ml) olive oil
- 1 clove garlic, whole and unpeeled
- Bouquet garni, made of thyme, bay leaf, and parsley
- Generous ½ cup (150 ml) dry white wine
- Salt and pepper
- Chopped tarragon (optional)

Peel and slice the onions. Peel the tomatoes and cut them into quarters.

Heat the oil in a large frying pan, brown the tuna on both sides, add the onion, and allow to color lightly, then add the tomatoes, garlic, and bouquet garni.

Cook over moderate heat for 15 minutes, turning once; then add the wine, salt, and pepper. Cover the pan and finish cooking over low heat for 15 minutes more.

Just before serving, sprinkle with the fresh tarragon (if desired).

Serving suggestions: Serve with Rice (see p. 510) or steamed potatoes.

Note: Red tuna is best. Try to get a slice from the middle of the fish if possible.

Any large, meaty fish, such as swordfish, can be cooked in the same way.

SERVES 5 TO 6
PREPARATION TIME: 20 MINUTES
COOKING TIME: 35 MINUTES

- 3 lb. (1.4 kg) eel, skinned, cleaned, and cut into 1-in. (2.5-cm) thick pieces
- 3 lb. (1.4 kg) carp, scaled, cleaned, and cut into 1-in. (2.5-cm) thick pieces
- 2 medium (200 g) onions
- 4 cloves garlic
- 1 carrot
- Bouquet garni made with white of 1 leek, 1 stalk celery, 1 sprig thyme, ¼ bay leaf, and 4 sprigs parsley, tied together
- 2 bottles red wine (preferably from Burgundy)
- 4 peppercorns, coarsely crushed in a mortar
- 1 tablespoon (10 g) flour
- 3 tablespoons (50 ml) water
- 3½ tablespoons (50 g) butter
- Salt

Carp and Eel Stewed in Red Wine
Matelote d'anguille et de carpe

Ask the fish seller to prepare the fish and cut it into pieces.

Peel the onions, garlic cloves, and carrot. Carefully wash the celery and leek, and tie together the components of the bouquet garni with twine.

Place the onions, garlic, carrots, and bouquet garni in a large saucepan, add the wine and pepper, bring to a boil, and simmer for 30 minutes.

While the wine and vegetables are cooking, remove as many small, hairlike bones from the pieces of fish as possible, using a pair of tweezers. Season with salt.

Stir 3 tablespoons of water, little by little, into the tablespoon of flour to make a smooth, thin mixture.

Remove the wine and vegetables from the heat and take out the bouquet garni. Whisk in the flour mixture, then blend in a blender or food processor (this will have to be done in several batches): this forms the sauce.

Melt the butter in a large, high-sided frying pan or pot, add the fish, and cook over low heat for 5 minutes. Pour the sauce over the fish and cook for another 5 or 6 minutes.

Lift the pieces of fish out of the pan using a slotted spoon and place them in a warm serving dish. Boil the sauce rapidly for a minute or two if it seems too liquid, taste for salt and pepper, then pour over the fish and serve.

Serving suggestions: This fish stew is excellent served with Spinach (see p. 474), Poached Eggs (see p. 152), and small squares of bread (croutons) fried in a little butter and rubbed with garlic. Soft-boiled eggs, cooked for 6 minutes and carefully peeled, may be used instead of poached eggs if you find them easier to prepare.

SERVES 4
SOAKING TIME: 6 HOURS
PREPARATION TIME: 25 MINUTES
COOKING TIME: 25 MINUTES

1 ¾ lb. (800 g) smoked haddock
1 quart (1 liter) milk
½ medium onion, sliced
Bouquet garni made of thyme, bay leaf, and parsley
1 large tomato
1 clove garlic
2 onions
5½ tablespoons (80 g) butter
A pinch of saffron
1 tablespoon flour
Generous ½ cup (150 ml) dry white wine
6 tablespoons (100 ml) crème fraîche or heavy cream
Salt and pepper

Smoked Haddock with Cream Sauce
Haddock à la crème

Peel off the skin of the haddock (if there is any), and cut it into four or eight pieces. Place the fish on a platter or in a bowl. Add milk (enough to cover), the slices of onion, and the bouquet garni. Allow to soak for 6 hours (this will desalt the fish and make it tender).

Run the tomato under boiling water, peel it, finely chop it and set aside in a bowl. Peel and finely chop the garlic and onions on a cutting board.

Drain the haddock and pat it dry with a clean cloth. Melt the butter in a large frying pan. When it foams up, add the fish, and cook for 5 minutes on each side over moderate heat, shaking the pan constantly to keep it from sticking (see Note). Lift the cooked fish out of the pan with a slotted spatula, place it on a serving platter, cover, and keep warm while making the sauce.

Add the tomato, garlic, and onions to the pan, and simmer for 5 minutes. Sprinkle in the saffron and flour, stir to combine, then add the wine, stirring constantly. Simmer very gently for 8 minutes. Stir in the cream and continue cooking very slowly, over very low heat, for 5 to 6 minutes more. Add pepper, salt if needed, then strain the sauce, stirring and pressing on the vegetables to extract all the liquid. Pour the sauce over the fish and serve immediately.

Serving suggestions: Serve with Rice (see p. 510) or steamed potatoes.

Note: Unless you have a very large frying pan, it will be necessary to cook the haddock in two batches. In this case, use half of the butter each time. If you prefer, the sauce may be spooned onto the plates and the fish placed on top to serve (see photograph).

SERVES 4
PREPARATION TIME: 20 MINUTES
COOKING TIME: 30 MINUTES

Porgy Provençal
Daurade provençale au four

One 3 lb. (1.4 kg) porgy or sea bream
1 small (50 g) onion
1 ¾ oz. (50 g) shallots
8 oz. (250 g) tomatoes
8 oz. (250 g) fresh mushrooms
2 tablespoons olive oil
Bouquet garni, made with thyme, bay leaf, and parsley
⅓ cup (75 ml) dry white wine
Salt and pepper
1 lemon, quartered

Peel and finely slice the onion and shallot. Blanch the tomatoes to peel them easily; once peeled, cut them into quarters. Cut off any dirt from the stems of the mushrooms, then quickly dip the mushrooms in water with a little lemon juice squeezed in to wash them. Drain them and pat them dry; only slice the mushrooms right before use.

Preheat the oven to 350°F (180°C).

Scale and gut the fish, run it under cold water, and pat it dry using a clean towel. Brush the fish inside and out with a little oil, then place the bouquet garni inside it. Pour the remaining oil into a baking dish, add the fish, and surround it with the onion, shallot, tomatoes, and mushrooms. Salt and pepper, then pour in the white wine. Bake for 20 minutes. Turn off the oven, but leave the fish inside for 7 minutes more to finish cooking. Serve the fish in the dish it cooked in, garnished with lemon wedges.

Serving suggestions: Serve with Rice (see p. 510) or boiled potatoes.

Hake with Cream Sauce
Colin en tranches

SERVES 4
PREPARATION TIME: 10 MINUTES
COOKING TIME: 25 MINUTES

- 4 slices hake weighing 2 lb. (900 g) in total
- 1 shallot
- 3 tablespoons (40 g) softened butter (for the dish)
- About 2 tablespoons olive oil
- Generous ½ cup (150 ml) dry white wine
- 6 tablespoons (100 ml) crème fraîche or heavy cream
- Salt and pepper

Preheat the oven to 450°F-475°F (240°C), or as high as your oven will go.

Peel the shallot and finely chop it on a cutting board. Carefully pat the fish dry with a clean towel.

Butter a baking dish large enough to hold all the fish flat on the bottom. Sprinkle in the shallots, arrange the slices of fish on top after brushing each one on both sides with oil. Salt lightly, pepper, and add the white wine. Bake for 20 minutes.

Remove the fish from the oven. Lift out of the dish with a slotted spatula, and place on a warm serving platter. Pour the cream into the baking dish and heat on top of the stove until the sauce just comes to a boil, stirring constantly. Taste for salt and pepper, then spoon the sauce over the fish and serve immediately.

SERVES 6
PREPARATION TIME: 10 MINUTES
COOKING TIME: 15 MINUTES

Red Mullet en Papillote
Rougets en papillotes

- 6 red mullet (goatfish) weighing about 9 oz. (250 g) each
- 3 shallots
- 2 medium tomatoes
- 4 large button mushrooms
- 2 tablespoons olive oil
- Fennel seeds
- Salt and pepper
- 1 lemon

Preheat the oven to 350°F (180°C).

Scale the fish and remove the gills, but don't clean otherwise. Peel and finely chop the shallots. Blanch the tomatoes, peel them, and chop them. Wash the mushrooms in water with a little lemon juice squeezed in and slice them. Set all the vegetables aside. Brush the fish with oil, then place each one on a piece of aluminum foil or parchment paper about 14 in. (35 cm) square. Use a sharp knife to make several little incisions in the sides of each fish, and insert one or two fennel seeds into each cut. Place a little tomato, shallot, and mushroom over and under each fish and season with salt and pepper. Then fold and squeeze the edges of the foil or parchment together to enclose the fish. Don't wrap the fish too tightly: there should be a pocket of air above each one to allow the steam to circulate while the fish is cooking.

Once all the fish are wrapped up, place them on a baking sheet and bake in the oven for 15 minutes. Cut the lemon into quarters.

Serve the fish hot in the foil or parchment they baked in, with wedges of lemon on the side.

Serving suggestions: Serve with Melted Butter Sauce (see Cod with Melted Butter Sauce, p. 194) or Mustard Sauce (see p. 543)

Note: Other fish can be cooked in exactly the same way but they should be cleaned before cooking.

SERVES 4
PREPARATION TIME: 15 MINUTES
COOKING TIME: 10 TO 12 MINUTES

Trout or Whiting Meunière
Truites ou merlans meunière

- 4 trout or whiting weighing about 10 oz. (300 g) each
- 1 small bunch parsley
- 4 tablespoons flour
- 4 tablespoons (60 g) butter, divided
- 1 tablespoon olive oil
- 2 cloves garlic, unpeeled
- Salt and pepper
- 1 lemon

Ask the fish seller to clean the fish by removing the gills and cleaning without opening the stomach.

Carefully wash the parsley and remove the stems. Finely chop the parsley and set aside.

Salt and pepper the fish, then roll them in flour, and shake them to remove any excess before cooking.

Heat 2 tablespoons (30 g) of butter and the oil in a large frying pan. When it starts to foam, add the fish and garlic. Cook over high heat for about 6 minutes on each side, carefully turning them over once with a spatula (they should be browned on both sides).

Lift the fish out of the pan with a slotted spatula. Place them on a warm serving platter and sprinkle with parsley. Cut the lemon into quarters to garnish. Add the remaining butter to the frying pan, heat to melt, and pour over the fish. Serve immediately.

Mackerel Marinated in Vinegar
Maquereaux au vinaigre de vin blanc

SERVES 4
PREPARATION TIME: 45 MINUTES
RESTING TIME: 12 HOURS
COOKING TIME: 20 MINUTES

8 baby mackerel weighing about 2 lb. (900 g) in total, cleaned (see Note)

2 onions

2 carrots

2 cloves garlic

Bouquet garni, made with 1 stalk celery, 1 sprig thyme, 4 sprigs parsley, and ¼ bay leaf

2 cups (500 ml) water

1 whole clove

12 peppercorns

1 tablespoon (15 g) kosher salt

1 lemon

2 cups (500 ml) white wine vinegar

When buying the fish, make sure to pick shiny mackerel with bright eyes. Carefully clean them, run them under cold water and pat them dry using a clean towel. Set aside on a plate.

Peel the onions, carrots, garlic, and celery. Wash the parsley. Slice the onions and the carrots. Crush the garlic using a fork. Tie together the bouquet garni made with thyme, bay leaf, parsley, and celery.

In a medium saucepan, bring the water to a boil before adding the onions, carrots, crushed garlic, bouquet garni, and whole clove. Boil over moderate heat for 12 minutes.

Place the mackerel in a deep porcelain serving dish and sprinkle with the peppercorns and kosher salt. Peel the lemon and cut it into thin slices. Lay the slices of lemon on top of the fish. Add the vinegar to the saucepan with the water and vegetables, bring to a rolling boil, and pour immediately over the fish. The fish should be completely immersed; if there is too much liquid, discard any extra, but place all the vegetables and seasonings in with the fish. Leave to cool overnight (the fish will cook while cooling). Serve cold.

This dish can be refrigerated if it is stored in a glass dish.

Note: This recipe is for very small fish weighing about 4½ oz. (125 g) each. If only large fish are available, fillet them and proceed exactly as described above.

SERVES 6
PREPARATION TIME: 15 MINUTES
COOKING TIME: 50 MINUTES

Baked Carp
Carpe au four

- 3 ½ lb. (1.5 kg) carp
- 3 shallots
- 1 small bunch parsley
- 4 medium (100 g) button mushrooms
- 3 ½ tablespoons (50 g) softened butter
- 1 ¼ cups (300 ml) dry white wine
- Salt and pepper

Ask the fish seller to scale and clean the carp.

Preheat the oven to 350°F (180°C).

Peel the shallots. Wash the parsley and remove its stems. Chop the shallots and the parsley separately. Cut any dirt off the stems of the mushrooms, carefully wash them and then slice them.

Use the butter to grease a baking dish–earthenware or porcelain–just large enough to hold the carp comfortably. Salt and pepper the fish inside and out, then place it in the dish. Around the fish, arrange the shallots, mushrooms, any roe or milt that was inside the fish, and half the parsley. Then sprinkle everything with salt and pepper. Add the wine and bake for 50 minutes, basting occasionally. Five minutes before the fish is done, sprinkle the remaining parsley over it.

Serve the fish in the cooking dish.

SHELLFISH & CRUSTACEANS

SERVES 6
PREPARATION TIME: 30 MINUTES
COOKING TIME: 20 MINUTES

Bordeaux-Style Crayfish
Écrevisses à la bordelaise

- 24 freshwater crayfish
- 1 medium-sized carrot
- 1 onion
- 2 shallots
- 1 ⅓ sticks (150 g) unsalted butter, divided
- 1 sprig thyme
- 1 bay leaf
- Scant ½ cup (100 ml) cognac
- 1 ¼ cups (300 ml) white wine
- 3 tablespoons tomato paste
- 1 sprig chervil
- 1 sprig tarragon
- Salt

Wash the freshwater crayfish and remove any eggs. Cut the carrot into tiny dice. Cut the onion and shallots into tiny dice. Stew these vegetables gently with 3 tablespoons (50 g) butter, the prepared crayfish, a pinch of salt, the thyme, and bay leaf. Then turn up the heat until the crayfish turn a bright red. Pour in the cognac, white wine, and tomato paste. Cover with the lid and cook for 8 to 10 minutes, still over high heat. Transfer the crayfish to a serving dish and keep warm.

Reduce the sauce by half. Remove from the heat and add the remaining butter and a pinch each of chopped chervil and tarragon.

Pour the sauce over the crayfish.

SERVES 3 TO 4
PREPARATION TIME: 20 MINUTES
COOKING TIME: 25 MINUTES

Lobster *à l'Américaine*
Homard à l'américaine

1 live lobster weighing 1 ¾-2 lb. (800-900 g)
1 medium onion
2 shallots
2 medium tomatoes
¼ clove garlic
4 tablespoons oil
¾ cup (200 ml) dry white wine
¼ cup (50 ml) fish fumet (see Glossary)
4 tablespoons cognac, divided
3 sprigs tarragon
1 small pinch cayenne pepper

FOR THE REDUCTION
7 tablespoons (100 g) butter, divided
1 sprig chervil, leaves chopped
1 sprig tarragon, leaves chopped
1 sprig parsley, leaves chopped
Salt and freshly ground pepper

Cut the lobster as follows: Holding the lobster in your left hand, and with the tail and claws stretched out, cut the claws where they meet the body. Break the shell and cut the tail into 5 or 6 rings. Split the thorax into two parts lengthways. Remove the small membrane pouch near the head–it contains sand. Quickly set aside in a bowl the creamy tomalley and the pink coral and cover with plastic wrap so that they do not spoil.

Finely chop the onion and the shallots. Peel, seed, and roughly chop the tomatoes. If you do not have tomatoes, substitute a scant ½ cup (100 ml) tomato purée. Crush the garlic.

Heat the oil in a sauté dish over high heat. Place the lobster pieces in the smoking oil. Season with salt and freshly ground pepper and sauté until the shell is red. Remove the lobster pieces and set aside, keeping warm. Add the finely chopped onion to the oil and soften it without allowing it to color; stir frequently. When it is almost done, add the finely chopped shallots and crushed garlic. Drain and discard the oil. Pour in the wine, fish fumet (or water if you do not have fumet), and 2 tablespoons cognac. Add the tomatoes (or tomato purée), the sprigs of tarragon, and the cayenne pepper. Arrange the pieces of lobster over the aromatic ingredients and put the lid on. Cook for 20 minutes. Transfer the lobster pieces to a serving dish and keep warm. Remove the tarragon from the cooking liquid and reduce the liquid by half. Mix the creamy parts (tomalley and coral) with 3 ½ tablespoons (50 g) butter, a sprig of chervil and tarragon. Remove the sauce from the heat just before it boils; stir in the remaining 3 ½ tablespoons (50 g) butter and 2 tablespoons cognac. Pour the sauce over the lobster and sprinkle it with chopped parsley.

Serving suggestions: Serve with Rice Pilaf (see p. 504).

Note: For this dish, it is essential to have a live lobster.

It has become more and more common to extract the flesh from the lobster before serving, making it much easier for guests to eat.

GRAND VIN DE BORDEAUX

SERVES 4
PREPARATION TIME: 30 TO 40 MINUTES
COOKING TIME: 45 MINUTES

2 live lobsters, 1 ½ lb. (700 g) apiece
6 small potatoes
7 oz. (200 g) very fine French green beans
3 ½ oz. (100 g) carrots
3 ½ oz. (100 g) turnips, carved into garlic clove shapes
3 ½ oz. (100 g) freshly shelled garden peas
10 tablespoons (150 g) butter, divided
3 shallots
6 small white onions
1 cup (250 ml) dry white wine
1 cup ((250 ml) chicken stock
A few sprigs tarragon, leaves picked
A few sprigs chervil, leaves picked
Salt and freshly ground pepper

Spring Lobster
Homard printanier

In separate pots of salted boiling water, blanch the potatoes and green beans. They should remain firm. Chop the carrots, and cook the carrots and turnips separately in salted cold water. Drain all the vegetables and refresh with cold water; drain once more.

Throw the peas into salted boiling water. Leave them to simmer for 4 to 6 minutes. Drain, refresh under cold water, and drain once again.

To prepare the lobsters, insert a knife into the middle of the line where the tail and thorax meet. This will kill the lobsters instantly. Slice through to separate the tail and cut the tail into four slices. Slit the thorax lengthways and remove the membrane pouch that contains sand. Set aside the coral. Break the claws.

Finely chop the shallots and set aside.

In a sauté dish, heat 7 tablespoons (100 g) butter and sauté the lobster pieces for 3 to 4 minutes. Add the shallots and onions, stirring for a few moments; then add the blanched vegetables. Season with salt and freshly ground pepper. Cook for a further 5 minutes, stirring well to combine. Add the wine and stock, cover with the lid, and cook for about 10 minutes.

Pour the cooking liquid into another pan and set the sauté pan containing the lobster and vegetables to the side of the burner, or over minimal heat to keep warm. Place the pan containing the cooking liquid over a medium heat and reduce for about 15 minutes. Thoroughly mix the rest of the butter with the coral and then whip it into the reduced sauce. At the last minute, add the tarragon and chervil leaves.

Pour the sauce over the lobsters and bring it all back to a boil, stirring for a further 5 minutes.

Serve immediately.

Grilled Rock Lobster
Langouste grillée

SERVES 2
PREPARATION TIME: 15 MINUTES
COOKING TIME: 20 MINUTES

- 1 live rock lobster weighing 1 ¾ lb. (800 g), or 2 rock lobsters, 14 oz. (400 g) apiece
- Scant ¼ cup (50 ml) melted butter
- A few sprigs parsley
- Fine salt and freshly ground pepper

Prepare a large pot of salted boiling water. Plunge the rock lobster (or lobsters) in for 2 to 3 minutes to kill them and firm up the flesh.

Remove from the pot and slit it lengthways in two. Season the flesh with salt and pepper and brush it well with melted butter.

Cook the lobster, flesh side down, on a grill pan over medium heat. Allow about 15 minutes for it to cook; be careful that it does not dry out.

To serve, arrange the rock lobster halves on napkins or linen-faced paper. Garnish the edge of the dish with sprigs of parsley.

To accompany, serve a timbale of Creole rice.

Serving suggestions: Choron Sauce (see p. 242) and American sauce should be served on the side. American sauce is a thickened sauce made using small crabs, lobster, or crayfish.

Note: You can prepare other types of lobster in the same way.

SERVES 8 TO 10
PREPARATION TIME: 10 MINUTES
COOKING TIME: 15 MINUTES

Lyon-Style Frogs' Legs
Grenouilles à la lyonnaise

- 50 large frogs' legs
- 2 onions
- 2 tablespoons (30 g) butter
- 2 tablespoons flour
- 1 tablespoon vinegar
- Salt and freshly ground pepper
- A few leaves parsley, chopped

Cut the onions into julienne slices and soften them in butter.

Dust the frogs' legs with flour and shake them well to remove any excess. Heat the butter in a pan until it sizzles and put the frogs' legs in. Sauté them over high heat until they brown slightly. Season with fine table salt and freshly ground pepper, and add the softened onions. Transfer to a serving platter.

When you are ready to serve, pour the vinegar into the burning hot pan and pour the liquid over the frogs' legs.

Sprinkle with chopped parsley.

SERVES 4 (A DOZEN PER PERSON)
PREPARATION TIME: 10 MINUTES
COOKING TIME: 10 MINUTES

Burgundy-Style Snails
Escargots à la bourguignonne

50 prepared snails plus their shells
White bread crumbs

SPECIAL SNAIL BUTTER
⅓ oz. (10 g) garlic
1 oz. (30 g) shallot
⅔ oz. (20 g) parsley
2 ½ teaspoons (12 g) salt
6 turns of the pepper mill (2 g)
2 ¼ sticks (250 g) butter, softened

Crush the garlic. Finely chop the shallots and the parsley. Add the three ingredients to the butter with the salt and pepper.

Combine thoroughly.

Preheat the oven to 425°F (210°C).

Place a knob of the prepared butter in each shell. If using canned snails, drain them. Then place a snail in each one; this will push the butter to the bottom of the shell. Close the shell by adding a little more prepared butter.

Pour just a little water into an ovenproof dish and arrange the shells in it. Place the filled shells in this. Sprinkle a few white bread crumbs over each snail and cook in the oven for 8 minutes.

Serve straight from the oven.

SERVES 4 TO 6
PREPARATION TIME: 20 MINUTES
COOKING TIME: 30 MINUTES

4 ½ lb. (2 kg) live freshwater crayfish

Knob of butter for sautéing the shells

2 oz. (50 g) onions

2 oz. (50 g) carrots

Scant ½ cup (100 ml) cognac, divided

2 cups (500 ml) dry white wine

1 tablespoon tomato purée

1 small bouquet garni with a generous portion of tarragon

1 pinch cayenne pepper

⅓ cup (30 g) flour

5 ½ tablespoons (80 g) butter, divided

2 oz. (50 g) truffles

1 cup (250 ml) cream

Scant ½ cup (100 ml) Hollandaise Sauce (see p. 548)

Salt and pepper

Fernand Point's Crayfish Tail Gratin
Gratin de queues d'écrevisses Fernand Point

Prepare a large pot of salted boiling water and plunge the crayfish in for 5 minutes. Drain them immediately and remove the shells from the tails and large claws. Crush the shells.

Add a knob of butter to a pot and sauté the crushed shells. Cut the onions and carrots into very small dice and add them to the pot.

Flambé the aromatic base with half the cognac. Pour in the white wine and a little water so that there is enough liquid to cover the ingredients. Add the tomato purée and the bouquet garni. Season with salt and pepper and a small pinch of cayenne pepper.

Cook over low heat for about 20 minutes. While it is cooking, prepare a beurre manié: combine ⅓ cup (30 g) flour with 2 tablespoons (30 g) butter. Strain the cooking liquid through a chinois and thicken it with the beurre manié to make the sauce.

Sweat the shelled tails and claws in 3 tablespoons (50 g) butter and deglaze with the remaining cognac. Cut the truffles into julienne slices. Add the cream and cooking liquid sauce, then the julienned truffle. Bring to a boil for a few minutes and remove from the heat. Incorporate the hollandaise sauce.

Adjust the seasoning and arrange the preparation in individual ovenproof porcelain dishes.

Glaze with a salamander to brown the top lightly, or place briefly under the broiler.

Serve this fine dish immediately.

Fernand Point is known as one of the fathers of modern French cuisine. His restaurant La Pyramide in Vienne, near Lyon, received three Michelin stars in 1933, and he trained a host of great French chefs, including the Troisgros brothers, Michel Guérard, and myself.

Stuffed Clams
Palourdes farcies

SERVES 4
PREPARATION TIME: 20 MINUTES
COOKING TIME: 10 MINUTES

- 4 dozen clams
- 1 ⅓ sticks (150 g) unsalted butter, room temperature
- 6 cloves garlic
- 1 bunch parsley
- ¼ cup (30 g) bread crumbs
- Kosher salt
- Salt and pepper

Take the butter out of the refrigerator ahead of time to bring it to room temperature.

Wash the clams under plenty of running water to remove their sand, then place them in a large pot with a little salted water. Cover with the lid and place over high heat. Shake the pot from time to time, holding the lid in place.

Remove the clams as they open. Take off the top shell of each clam.

Preheat the oven to 475°F (240°C), or as high as your oven will go.

Soften the butter until it is a creamy texture (you will have a *beurre pommade*).

Peel the garlic cloves. Wash the parsley and pick the leaves off. Finely chop the garlic and parsley together, then combine them with the butter, adding the bread crumbs.

Work the mixture well and season with salt and pepper.

Fill each clam with the butter preparation.

Fill a broiling pan with a layer of kosher salt to keep the clams horizontal and place them snugly in the salt, or in specially indented dishes.

Brown them in the oven for 2 to 3 minutes.

Serve immediately with slices of country bread.

SERVES 6
PREPARATION TIME: 10 MINUTES
COOKING TIME: 15 MINUTES

1 lb. (500 g) sea scallops or bay scallops
Flour
4 tablespoons (60 g) butter
1 tablespoon lemon juice
⅓ cup (75 ml) white vermouth
Generous ¾ cup (200 ml) crème fraîche or heavy cream
Salt and pepper

Scallop Fricassee with Cream Sauce
Fricassée de coquilles Saint-Jacques à la crème

To ensure the freshness of the scallops, ask the fish seller not to remove their shells until the moment you buy them, or, better still, do it yourself. Carefully wash the scallops.

Season the scallops with salt and pepper, roll them in flour, and shake them lightly to remove any excess before cooking.

Heat the butter in a large enameled cast-iron frying pan. When very hot, add the scallops and cook over moderate heat for 4 to 6 minutes if using sea scallops, 2 to 3 minutes if using bay scallops. Shake the pan frequently and turn the scallops over halfway through cooking.

Pour the lemon juice over the scallops, stir in the vermouth, then pour over the cream, stirring to scrape any juices from the bottom of the pan into the sauce. Bring the cream just to a boil, add a little salt and pepper, and serve.

Serving suggestions: This is delicious with Broccoli (see p. 465).

Moules Marinière

SERVES 4
PREPARATION TIME: 30 MINUTES
COOKING TIME: 15 MINUTES

- 4 quarts (4 liters) mussels (see Note)
- 4 new onions
- 2 stalks celery
- 1 small bunch parsley
- 5 tablespoons (75 g) butter
- 2 cups (500 ml) dry white wine
- Pepper
- Juice of ½ lemon

Mussels should be tightly closed or–if they are open–should close tightly when scraped or tapped with the blade of a knife; if they stay open, it means they are dead and could be dangerous if eaten (don't worry, however, if the mussels open and close after being cleaned: they are simply breathing).

Clean the mussels one by one, scraping off any barnacles or mud, and pulling out the little "beard" that protrudes from the shell. Wash the mussels under cold running water (don't let them sit in water), and place in a large bowl as they are cleaned. Once clean, they should be shiny.

Peel and slice the onions. Remove the tough outer fibers from the celery, wash, and dice the stalks. Wash the parsley, remove its stems, then coarsely chop the parsley on a cutting board.

Melt the butter in a large pot, add the onions, the celery, and half the parsley. Cook until the vegetables just begin to brown. Pour in the wine, add a little pepper, and bring to a boil. Cover the pot and remove from the heat. Leave for 5 to 7 minutes before cooking the mussels.

Add the mussels and lemon juice to the pot, cover, and return to the stove over high heat. Keep an eye on the mussels: once each mussel has opened, remove it with a slotted spoon. Remove one shell from each mussel, then place them in a large serving bowl (discard any mussels that haven't opened).

Line a sieve with a piece of doubled-over cheesecloth and strain the mussels' cooking liquid into the bowl with the mussels. Sprinkle with the remaining parsley and serve immediately.

Note: 4 quarts of mussels weigh about 6 lb. (2.8 kg); other small shellfish, such as clams, can be prepared in exactly the same way.

SERVES 4
PREPARATION TIME: 40 MINUTES
COOKING TIME: 30 MINUTES

Mussels in Creamy White Wine Sauce
Moules au vin blanc

4 quarts (4 liters) mussels (see Note)
4 medium new onions
2 shallots
6 baby carrots
5 tablespoons (75 g) butter, divided
3 cups (750 ml) dry white wine
Salt and pepper
1 bunch parsley
4 tablespoons (25 g) flour
Generous ¾ cup (200 ml) heavy cream

Peel the onions, shallots, and carrots, and coarsely chop them on a cutting board. Melt 3 ½ tablespoons (50 g) butter in a large pot. Add the onions, shallots, and carrots, and simmer for 15 minutes. Add 2 cups (500ml) of the wine, salt, a little pepper, and cook slowly for 7 more minutes.

Meanwhile, clean the mussels. Mussels should be tightly closed or–if they are open–should close tightly when scraped or tapped with the blade of a knife; if they stay open, it means they are dead and could be dangerous if eaten (don't worry, however, if the mussels open and close after being cleaned: they are simply breathing).

Clean the mussels one by one, scraping off any barnacles or mud, and pulling out the little "beard" that protrudes from the shell. Wash the mussels under cold running water (don't let them sit in water), and place in a large bowl as they are cleaned. Once clean, they should be shiny.

Place the mussels in a second pot, add the rest of the wine and a little pepper, bring to a boil, and cover the pot. As the mussels open, lift them out of the pot with a slotted spoon and discard one shell from each one. Place the mussels in a bowl and keep warm while finishing preparing the sauce.

Line a sieve with a piece of doubled-over cheesecloth and strain the mussels' cooking liquid into the pot with the vegetables; taste for seasoning. Wash the parsley, remove its stems and coarsely chop the parsley on a cutting board. Set aside. Make a beurre manié by mixing the remaining 1 ½ tablespoons (25 g) softened butter with the flour with your fingers until smooth, then break it into pea-sized pieces.

Whisk the cream into the boiling sauce; then whisk in the pieces of beurre manié. When the sauce is creamy, sprinkle the parsley over the mussels, add the sauce, and serve immediately.

Note: 4 quarts of mussels weigh about 6 lb. (2.8 kg); other small shellfish, such as clams, can be prepared in exactly the same way.

MEAT

BEEF

SERVES 6
PREPARATION TIME: 15 MINUTES
COOKING TIME: 20 MINUTES

Boiled Beef
Boeuf à la ficelle

- 4 ½ lb. (2 kg) beef tenderloin or fillet of beef, trimmed
- Just under 1 oz. (25 g) kosher salt
- 1 ¾ teaspoons (5 g) black peppercorns
- 1 onion, studded with 3 cloves
- 1 sprig parsley
- 1 sprig chervil
- 1 sprig tarragon
- 6 leeks, white part only
- 2 celery hearts (tender part of innermost ribs)
- 3 tomatoes
- 7 oz. (200 g) carrots and turnips, cut into sticks
- Croutons
- Grated Gruyère

Pour 13 cups (6 ⅓ pints/3 liters) of water into a large pot. Add the seasoning, the aromatic ingredients, and the vegetables. Bring to a boil and leave to boil for 5 minutes.

Tie a length of string around the beef, drop the beef into the broth and tie the string to the pot handle so that you can remove it easily.

Skim the surface thoroughly and leave at a very gentle simmer. Allow, on average, 10 to 15 minutes per pound (500 g) of meat, as you would for a roast beef; it should be pinky-red when you cut it.

Serve the fillet of beef surrounded by the vegetables.

Add a little butter to the broth and serve it with small croutons and grated Gruyère.

Serving suggestions: This dish is excellent accompanied by Tomato Sauce (see p. 544) flavored with tarragon and chives. Alternatively, you can simply serve the fillet with kosher salt, gherkins, and small pickled onions. A remoulade sauce is another possible accompaniment; this is a mayonnaise-based sauce containing mixed herbs, finely chopped gherkins, and capers, that is often served as an accompaniment to meat or seafood dishes.

Note: Thinly sliced fillet of beef, rib of beef, and leg of lamb may all be prepared using this method.

SERVES 8
PREPARATION TIME: 40 MINUTES
COOKING TIME:
1 HOUR 30 MINUTES

3 ½ lb. (1.5 kg) center-cut fillet of beef

4 oz. (125 g) fresh lardoons (narrow strips of fat to lard the meat)

4 tablespoons (60 g) butter, divided

9 oz. (250 g) mushrooms

Scant ½ cup (100 ml) Madeira wine

MADEIRA SAUCE

1 small carrot

1 medium onion

7 tablespoons (100 g) butter

7 tablespoons (45 g) flour

¾ cup (200 ml) dry white wine

4 cups (1 liter) stock or very lightly salted veal *jus*, divided

2 tablespoons reduced tomato purée

A few sprigs parsley

A few leaves of thyme and pieces of bay leaf

Beef Fillet with Madeira Sauce and Mushrooms
Filet de bœuf sauce madère et champignons à la ménagère

Prepare the beef for cooking. Remove all visible fat and sinews from the fillet of beef, trim it (keep the trimmings, fat removed, for the sauce), removing the chain, the nerve that runs along the side of the fillet from the head to the tail. Prick the fillet with small 1 ½-in. (4-cm) strips of fresh lardoons. Proceed as follows: Place the beef on an upside-down soup plate on a table. Hold a larding needle in your right hand and thread it through the meat with a strip of fat in it. Work with the grain of the meat, and twist the needle each time so that the lardoons show through at each end of the needle hole.

Prepare the Madeira sauce and mushrooms. Roast or pan-fry the fillet of beef for 20 to 40 minutes.

Present the fillet on a long serving platter, remove the twine, and surround it with the most attractive mushroom caps from the garnish.

Madeira sauce

Cut the carrot and onion into very fine dice. Cook them gently with 2 knobs of butter in a pan big enough to contain the sauce. When they are done, brown them slightly and sprinkle in the flour. Stir well to combine; this will form a roux. Cook the roux gently, stirring constantly, until it turns a dark yellow. Remove from the heat and leave to cool. When the roux is cold, dilute it with the white wine, pouring it in gradually, and then with a generous ⅓ cup (90 ml) stock or veal *jus*. Then add the tomato purée, parsley, thyme, and bits of bay leaf.

Bring to a boil, stirring with a sauce whisk so that no lumps form. Leave to simmer gently for 45 minutes.

Meanwhile clean the mushrooms, reserving 4 to 5 stems, and slice them. Set aside.

Brown the trimmings of the fillet slightly and add them to the sauce, together with the 4 or 5 mushroom stems.

While the Madeira sauce is simmering, skim it from time to time to remove any fat or skin. The end result will be a clarified sauce: the impurities of the flour will be removed. All the sauce retains of the flour is its starchy qualities, and it will be smooth and light. After 45 minutes, strain the sauce through a fine-mesh sieve or chinois and set it aside. Press the aromatic ingredients down hard into another saucepan to extract the maximum amount of cooking juices. Slowly bring to a boil, skimming as for the previous procedure, until clarified. As it cooks, add another spoon or two of the strained sauce that you have set aside. This stage of cooking takes 30 minutes.

Mushrooms

The mushrooms must be firm, white, and unblemished. Cut off the sandy base and wash them quickly in cold water without allowing them to sit in the water. Repeat the procedure once. Drain immediately and pat them dry.

Set aside a few of the more attractive mushroom caps to use as garnish and quarter the remaining mushrooms.

Heat the remaining butter in a sauté pan large enough to contain all the sauce at a later stage. When the butter is nicely browned, throw in the mushrooms and stir them until they are lightly browned. Remove from the heat and pour all the prepared sauce through muslin into the pan. Return to the heat and bring to a boil. Leave to simmer for 5 minutes. Once again, remove from the heat and adjust the seasoning. Keep in warm place, without allowing it to boil, until you are ready to serve.

Then add the Madeira wine and the cooking *jus* used for the fillet of beef. Do not allow the sauce to boil; the flavor of the Madeira wine would vanish as the alcohol evaporates, causing the *jus*, which contains blood, to curdle and form black granules.

When reduced, the final quantity of the Madeira sauce should be about 2 cups (500 ml), half of the initial quantities poured in. This is a result of its being clarified and evaporating.

SERVES 15
PREPARATION TIME: 45 MINUTES
COOKING TIME:
1 HOUR 30 MINUTES TO
2 HOURS 30 MINUTES

1 fillet of beef, weighing 6 ½-7 ½ lb. (3-3.5 kg)

GARNISH

2 ¼ lb. (1 kg) large fresh garden peas

1 handful spinach leaves

1 stick (125 g) butter, and a little extra for the molds

2 tablespoons thick cream

1 pinch caster sugar (if needed)

5 eggs

6 egg yolks

GLAZED CARROTS

1 bunch new baby carrots

1 pinch sugar

2 tablespoons (30 g) butter

Salt

BUTTERED POTATOES

2 ¼ lb. (1 kg) new baby potatoes

2 tablespoons (30 g) butter

Salt

A little chopped parsley for garnish

Special equipment: 15 dariole or small baba molds

Beef Fillet Saint-Germain
Filet de boeuf Saint-Germain

The fillet is roasted and garnished with 15 individual timbales of puréed garden peas, glazed carrots, and potatoes cooked in butter.

While preparing the garnishes, roast the fillet or brown it in a pan. Cook for about 1 ½ to 2 ½ hours; you should count 20 minutes per pound (45 minutes per kg) for a medium roast, a little less if you like it rare.

Garnish

Bring to a boil 12 cups (3 liters) of salted water. Throw in the garden peas and cook them quickly over high heat. Before they are cooked through, add the spinach and leave to boil for 5 minutes. Remove from the heat and drain. Push the peas and spinach through a fine-mesh sieve (the spinach will give a lovely green color to the purée). Allow the purée to drain through into a mixing dish. Work it briskly with a flexible spatula so that it is very smooth and incorporate the butter and the thick cream. If the peas are not sufficiently sweet, add a pinch of caster sugar to finish the seasoning. Mix in 5 eggs beaten with 6 yolks. Be careful not to overmix.

Preheat the oven to 160°F (70°C). Carefully butter 15 dariole or baba molds and fill them to just under ½ in. (1 cm) below the rim with the purée. Transfer them into a large baking dish and pour some boiling water into it so the timbales will cook in a hot water bath. Poach the timbales for 35 minutes in the oven (the water in the dish should on no account boil). They are done when they are firm to the touch. Keep them warm in the water bath until you are ready to turn them out; they will be easier to unmold a few minutes after they are cooked.

Glazed carrots

Peel the carrots, taking off as little peel as possible. If they are small, leave them whole. If you have not been able to find small carrots, cut them into halves or quarters, and trim the angles a little. Wash them and place them snugly in a sauté pan: they should form a thin layer. Just cover them with water. Add a pinch of sugar, a pinch of salt, and two-thirds of the butter (1 tablespoon plus 1 teaspoon, 20 g). Slowly bring to a boil, uncovered, so that almost all the liquid evaporates by the time the carrots are cooked. They should be very tender.

The juices of the vegetables, together with the butter, sugar, and remaining water will form a syrupy liquid. Remove the pan from the heat and add the last knob of butter (2 teaspoons/10 g). Mix through until the carrots are thoroughly coated and are nice and shiny.

Buttered potatoes

Peel the potatoes and cook them in the butter with a pinch of salt in a covered sauté pan. They should be barely browned and very tender.

To serve

Place the fillet of beef on a large, long serving platter. Remove the twine and drizzle it with a little of the cooking juices. At each end of the platter, unmold, in a half-circle, the timbales of puréed peas, and on each side of the beef, alternate small pyramids of glazed carrots and potatoes cooked in butter. Top each pyramid of potatoes with a little chopped parsley.

Serving suggestions: Serve with a sauce dish of Béarnaise Sauce (see p. 530) or Valois sauce. Valois sauce is Béarnaise sauce to which meat glaze is added.

Tournedos Bercy

SERVES 6
PREPARATION TIME: 20 MINUTES
COOKING TIME: 30 MINUTES

6 tournedos

6 round slices of bread, each about 1 in. (2 cm) thick and 3 in. (7–8 cm) in diameter

⅓ cup (75 ml) dry white wine

Veal *jus* as needed

2 teaspoons (10 g) butter, plus a little more to brown the bread

6 teaspoons Bercy butter (see Note)

Brown the slices of bread in butter in a sauté pan, then set aside.

Sauté the tournedos for about 5 minutes on each side, remove from the pan, and keep warm. Place one sautéed tournedos on each round fried piece of bread.

Pour the dry white wine into the sauté pan and reduce it by three-quarters. Add an equal quantity of good veal *jus* and reduce once again by three-quarters. Remove from the heat and incorporate a knob of butter by rotating the sauté pan; this will cause the reduction to swirl.

Pour the reduction over the tournedos and top each one with a teaspoon of softened Bercy butter (see below).

The largest wine market in Europe used to be located in an area of Paris known as Bercy. Many dishes using wine sauces bear its name. Bercy butter contains shallots, white wine, parsley, lemon juice, and an ingredient now almost impossible to obtain: vesiga, the spinal marrow of the sturgeon, or beef marrow.

Tournedos Choron

SERVES 6
PREPARATION TIME: 20 MINUTES
COOKING TIME: 30 MINUTES

6 tournedos, 3 ½ oz. (100 g) apiece

6 artichoke bottoms, pre-cooked in a *blanc* (see Glossary)

2 bunches of very thin green asparagus

1 ⅓ sticks (150 g) butter, divided

2 ¼ lb. (1 kg) large potatoes

6 slices of stale bread

2 tablespoons oil

Scant ½ cup (100 ml) veal *jus*

Salt and pepper

CHORON SAUCE

1 ¼ cups (300 ml) Béarnaise Sauce (see p. 530)

Scant ½ cup (100 ml) reduced tomato purée

Stew the artichoke bottoms in butter for 15 to 20 minutes, ensuring both sides are cooked. Season them with salt and pepper. Cook the asparagus in well-salted boiling water. Drain them and coat them in butter. Check the seasoning.

Peel, wash, and pat dry the potatoes. Using a small scoop, scoop out a ball of potato flesh and drop it into cold water. Repeat as many times as you can with each potato. Cook them in sizzling butter in a sauté pan. These little potatoes are known as *pommes de terre à la parisienne.*

Arrange the potato balls in the center of a round platter.

Prepare the toast: brown the slices of stale bread in butter, arrange them in a circle on the platter, and keep warm.

Combine the béarnaise sauce with the tomato purée.

Cook the tournedos: Sauté them for about 5 minutes on each side.

Place one tournedos on each piece of toast and draw out a circle of tomato-flavored Béarnaise sauce–the Choron sauce–around them.

In between each tournedos, arrange the six seasoned artichoke bottoms and the asparagus.

Deglaze the sauté dish in which you have cooked the tournedos with 6 tablespoons of veal *jus*. Reduce it by half and drizzle a few drops over the tournedos, surrounded by the Choron sauce.

Tournedos Henri IV

SERVES 6
PREPARATION TIME: 20 MINUTES
COOKING TIME: 30 MINUTES

- 6 tournedos, 3 ½ oz. (100 g) apiece
- 2 tablespoons oil
- 6 slices dense stale bread
- 7 tablespoons (100 g) butter, divided
- 1 ½ lb. (700 g) large potatoes
- 6 artichoke bottoms, cooked in a *blanc* (see Glossary)
- ¾ cup (200 ml) Béarnaise Sauce (see p. 530)
- 1 sprig chervil, chopped
- 1 sprig tarragon, chopped

To prepare the toasts, fry them quickly in the oil.

Cook the tournedos on a grill pan.

Scoop out small balls of potato and sauté them in half the butter.

Slice the artichoke bottoms. Melt the remaining butter in a sauté pan and when it is sizzling, brown the artichoke slices slightly.

Place the tournedos on the toasts. Draw out some béarnaise sauce on each one and alternate a pile of potato scoops with a small heap of artichoke bottom slices. Check that the vegetables are well seasoned. Sprinkle the chopped herbs on the potatoes.

Serve the remaining béarnaise sauce on the side.

This classic dish was first prepared in the 1830s in a restaurant named for King Henri IV (1589-1610). He is known to have been a gourmet.

Tournedos Clamart

SERVES 6
PREPARATION TIME: 40 MINUTES
COOKING TIME: 40 MINUTES

6 tournedos, 3 ½ oz. (100 g) apiece

6 individual savory tart shells

3 large oven-baked potatoes

7 tablespoons (100 g) butter, divided

1 lb. (500 g) peas cooked *à la française*, braised in butter with lettuce and baby onions

2 tablespoons oil

Scant ½ cup (100 ml) sherry

¾ cup (200 ml) veal *jus*

Salt and pepper

Prebake the tartlet shells: line them with parchment paper and fill with baking beans so that they retain their shape. Set aside.

Halve the baked potatoes and extract the flesh. In a bowl, season it with salt and pepper. Incorporate 3 tablespoons (50 g) butter using a fork to mash it in. Take the mashed potatoes and fashion six disks the size of the tournedos. Brown them in the oil. Carefully turn them over with a spatula to brown the other side. Arrange them in a circle on a round platter and keep warm.

Cook the tournedos for about 5 minutes on each side. Place one on each potato disk.

Arrange the pre-baked pastry shells around the tournedos. Place a spoonful of buttered peas in each tartlet.

Deglaze the sauté pan in which you have cooked the tournedos with the sherry and veal *jus*. Reduce it by two-thirds. Remove from the heat and add the remaining butter; transfer to a sauce dish. Do not pour this sauce into the serving platter as it would soften the potato disks.

It is the peas that give this dish its name: Clamart, not far from Paris, was famous for its peas and supplied them to the French royal court and to the city.

SERVES 6
PREPARATION TIME: 10 MINUTES
COOKING TIME: 20 MINUTES

6 tournedos, 3 ½ oz. (100 g) apiece

6 thick slices of beef marrow

Scant ½ cup (100 ml) Bordelaise Sauce (see p. 524)

A little butter to cook the tournedos and to add to the sauce

Tournedos with Marrow
Tournedos à la moelle

Grill the tournedos, about 5 minutes on each side.

Poach the marrow slices for 5 minutes in a bowl of salted, almost-boiling water. Reduce the bordelaise sauce a little, remove from the heat, and add a little butter to it.

Arrange the tournedos on a round platter. Place a slice of beef marrow atop each one and drizzle with the reduced bordelaise sauce.

SERVES 2
PREPARATION TIME: 20 MINUTES
COOKING TIME: 20 MINUTES

1 bone-in rib-eye steak weighing 2 ¼ lb. (1 kg)

3 ½ oz. (100 g) beef marrow

1 oz. (30 g) shallot

7 tablespoons (100 g) butter

1 bottle Brouilly wine, or other fruity red wine

1 tablespoon beurre manié (see Glossary)

Salt and freshly ground pepper

Bone-In Rib-Eye Beef with Marrow and Brouilly
Côte de boeuf à la moelle au vin de Brouilly

Ahead of time, soak the beef marrow and then poach it in lightly salted water. Chop the shallots.

Season the rib-eye roast with salt and pepper. In a heavy-bottomed pan, melt half the butter until it is foamy and begins to brown. If you prefer your beef very rare, allow 5 minutes on each side to cook and brown. Then transfer it to a serving platter and keep warm.

Using the cooking butter, sauté the chopped shallots without allowing them to color. Deglaze with the wine, leaving it to simmer until it has reduced by half. To thicken the sauce, incorporate the beurre manié into the wine. Lastly, adjust the seasoning and incorporate the remaining butter until it is creamy.

Top the beef with slices of poached marrow.

Serve the sauce either drizzled over the beef or on the side.

The last-minute addition of a little softened butter to wine-based sauces eliminates their acidity and improves their flavor.

SERVES 80 TO 100
PREPARATION TIME: 40 MINUTES
COOKING TIME: 8 HOURS

Spit-Roasted Haunch of Beef
Cuisse de boeuf rôtie au feu de bois

1 haunch of beef weighing 90–110 lb. (40–50 kg)

1 lb. (500 g) garlic cloves, peeled

Fine sea salt and finely ground pepper

Melted butter if necessary

This is a show-stopping recipe for a grand occasion. It requires the use of a large open fire and spit.

Trim the piece of meat as you would a leg of veal: cut through the knuckle and remove the leg bone.

At 4-in. (10-cm) intervals, prepare small holes using a larding needle. In each hole, place a pinch of salt combined with pepper and a garlic clove.

Season the surface of the meat, rubbing it with your hand to massage the seasoning in.

To cook the haunch, prepare a fire using aromatic wood in a large fireplace with a spit.

When the logs are partially burned and giving off strong heat, place the haunch of beef on the spit about 4 in. (10 cm) away from the flames. Set the spit turning. For a haunch weighing 110 lb. (50 kg), allow 8 hours of cooking over regular heat.

During this period, the fire should be fed regularly and the haunch basted often with the juices and fat that accumulate in the dripping pan.

If necessary, keep the meat from drying out by basting it with melted butter as it cooks.

It is best to allow the haunch to rest for one or two hours before serving. If possible, leave it in an oven at a very low temperature.

Present this magnificent piece to the guests before slicing it. The sliced meat should be pink and slightly rare.

Note: Try to select a haunch of beef that has been hung on the bone to mature.

SERVES 4 TO 6
PREPARATION TIME: 20 MINUTES
COOKING TIME: AT LEAST 3 HOURS

Family-Style Braised Beef
Bœuf mode

- 2 ¼ lb. (1 kg) rump roast
- About 4 oz. (125 g) fatback (for larding)
- ½ calf's foot
- 9 oz. (250 g) salt pork
- 6 carrots
- 6 small onions
- Bouquet garni, made with 3 sprigs parsley, 1 sprig thyme, and ¼ bay leaf
- 4 tablespoons (60 g) butter
- 2 cups (500 ml) dry white wine
- Generous ¾ cup (200 ml) hot water
- Salt and pepper

About 90 minutes ahead of time, take the meat out of the refrigerator. Lard the beef with strips of fatback, using a larding pin (or ask your butcher to do it). Salt and pepper the meat and calf's foot. Remove the rind from the salt pork and cut the salt pork into ½-in. (1-cm) cubes.

Peel the carrots, rinse them quickly and dry them. Cut them into sticks of roughly 2 in. (5 cm). Peel the onions and leave them whole. Carefully wash the parsley, then tie together the thyme, bay leaf, and parsley with twine.

In a large stew pot, preferably enameled cast-iron, melt the butter. When it starts to foam, add the onions and salt pork, and brown over high heat, stirring frequently. Add the beef and calf's foot, brown on all sides, then add the carrots, bouquet garni, and wine. Simmer uncovered for 1 hour, during which time some of the wine should evaporate. Add the water, salt, and pepper. Turn the meat over, bring to a boil, then cover the pot and simmer slowly for 2 hours (this dish must cook very slowly and for a long time).

To serve, discard the bouquet garni, then lift the meat and calf's foot out of the pot. Slice the meat and cut the foot into pieces, then place them on a hot platter, surrounded by the vegetables and salt pork. Use a spoon to skim off the fat on the surface of the cooking liquid, then pour the liquid over the meat and serve.

Serving suggestions: Serve with Mashed Potatoes (see p. 496), Split Pea Purée (see p. 479), or Rice Pilaf (see p. 504).

Variation: Leftovers are delicious eaten cold; in fact, some people always eat this dish cold rather than hot. Place the meat in a deep dish or bowl, arrange the carrots and onions around it and on top of it, then strain the cooking liquid over it. Leave to cool, then refrigerate overnight before serving. Serve with a Green Salad (see p. 68).

SERVES 6
PREPARATION TIME: 30 MINUTES
COOKING TIME:
3 HOURS 30 MINUTES

Beef Stew
Estouffade de boeuf

- 1 ¾ lb. (800 g) upper chuck or shoulder of beef, cut into 3 ½ oz. (100 g) cubes
- 9 oz. (250 g) pork belly or bacon
- 2 tablespoons (30 g) butter or fat, plus 1 tablespoon (15 g) for frying mushrooms
- 3 medium onions
- 2 teaspoons (10 g) salt
- 1 pinch freshly ground pepper
- 2 tablespoons flour
- 2 cloves garlic, crushed
- 2 cups (500 ml) good red wine
- 4 cups (1 liter) veal stock or lightly salted broth
- 1 bouquet garni, comprising 1 sprig parsley, 1 sprig thyme, and a bay leaf
- 9 oz. (250 g) mushrooms

Cut the pork belly or bacon into large dice. Boil and drain. Brown the dice in the butter, using a pan just large enough to contain the beef and the cooking liquid.

When the diced bacon bits are browned, remove them and lightly brown the cubed beef. When it is half done, quarter the onions and add them. Continue cooking until the beef is completely browned, then sprinkle with salt, pepper, and flour. Stir well to combine and allow it to turn a little brown, stirring constantly. Be careful not to allow the onions to become too dark, as this would give a bitter taste to the dish.

Preheat the oven to 300°F (150°C).

Add the crushed garlic and stir for 2 seconds to allow it to develop all of its flavor. Then pour in the 2 cups (500 ml) wine. Reduce it by two-thirds. Pour in the veal stock or broth, ensuring that it wets the top of the pieces of meat. Bring back to a boil, stirring all the time. Add the pork belly pieces and the bouquet garni. Cover with the lid and cook in the oven for 3 hours. It should barely simmer while it cooks.

Wash the mushrooms rapidly and quarter them. Sauté them (use a sauté pan of the same size as the one used previously) for 5 minutes in butter over high heat. Remove from the heat as soon as the mushrooms begin to color.

Remove the stew from the oven and transfer the meat and garnish to the pan containing the mushrooms. The meat and pork belly bits should be placed over the mushrooms. Allow the sauce to rest for 5 minutes. Skim the fat off and adjust the consistency, either diluting it or reducing it. It should be slightly thickened, with enough to half cover the meat and garnish. Check the seasoning and strain it through a chinois over the stew, pushing down hard on the aromatic ingredients with a wooden spoon.

Return the sauté pan to the heat and bring back to a simmer over very low heat. Allow to simmer for 15 to 20 minutes.

Serve in a deep serving dish, accompanied by boiled potatoes.

Variation: You may add 1 lb. (500 g) of peeled, seeded, and chopped tomatoes to the garnish at the same time as the mushrooms.

This fine dish, that has been passed down through the annals of *ancienne cuisine*, can also be made using white wine.

Beef au Gratin
Pot-au-feu au gratin

SERVES 4
PREPARATION TIME: 30 MINUTES
COOKING TIME:
1 HOUR 10 MINUTES

- 2 ¾ lb. (1.2 kg) boiled beef (see Pot-au-Feu p. 264)
- 1 clove garlic
- 2 medium (200 g) onions
- 1 bunch parsley
- 4 ¼ cups (1 liter) broth (see Pot-au-Feu p. 264)
- 2 tablespoons (30 g) butter
- 6 tablespoons (100 ml) red wine vinegar
- 1 tablespoon (6 g) flour
- 4 tablespoons tomato paste
- ½ cup (80 g) bread crumbs

Preheat the oven to 425°F (210°C).

Cut the boiled beef into thin slices (roughly 4 slices per person).

Peel the garlic and onions. Carefully wash and coarsely chop the parsley. Thinly slice the onions. Start reheating the broth.

Melt the butter in a frying pan and cook the onions until soft but not brown. Add the vinegar and boil until it has evaporated completely, then add the flour, stir, add the tomato paste, hot broth, and parsley, and simmer uncovered for 25 minutes. Crush the garlic into a baking dish, preferably earthenware, and rub energetically, spreading it around the dish. Lay the slices of beef in the dish so that they overlap slightly, then add the sauce, spreading it over the meat. Sprinkle with the bread crumbs (they should absorb most of the liquid), then place in the oven and bake for 45 minutes.

Serving suggestions: Serve the beef in the dish it cooked in, with Baked Vermicelli (see p. 517) on the side.

SERVES 6
PREPARATION TIME: 30 MINUTES
COOKING TIME:
3 HOURS 30 MINUTES

1 ¾ lb. (800 g) beef chuck or back ribs

3 tablespoons fat

3 large onions

⅓ cup (30 g) flour

1 ⅔ cups (400 ml) beer

2 cups plus 1 scant cup (600 ml) stock

1 teaspoon sugar

1 tablespoon vinegar

1 bouquet garni comprising parsley, thyme, and a bay leaf

Salt and pepper

Flour and water for the sealing paste

Beef Stewed in Beer
Carbonade à la flamande

Cut the meat into thin pieces of 2 oz. (50 g) each. Season them with salt and pepper.

Heat the fat in a sauté pan. As soon as it begins smoking, brown the beef on each side. Transfer immediately to a dish, retaining the fat.

Finely chop the onions. Sauté them until a light golden color in the fat used to cook the beef. Remove the onions from the pan and stir in the flour. Cook, stirring all the time, over low heat, until the roux begins to darken slightly. Dilute it with the beer and the stock. Add a pinch of salt, a pinch of pepper, the sugar, and the vinegar. Bring to a boil, stirring constantly, and leave to simmer on very low heat for 15 minutes.

Preheat the oven to 300°F (150°C).

Choose an ovenproof cooking pot or casserole dish of the appropriate size to hold the ingredients. Layer the beef alternately with the onions. In the center, place the bouquet garni.

Strain the sauce through a chinois over the dish and bring to a boil. Make a roll of dough using a little flour and water to seal the rim of the lid. Place the lid on the dish or pot and fit the dough around. Place in the oven for 3 hours.

Remove the dish from the oven. Take off the lid and remove the bouquet garni. Leave to rest for 6 minutes and skim the fat off the top of the sauce. Check its seasoning: there should not be too much sauce, and it should be slightly thickened. Serve in the cooking dish.

Alternatively, you can serve your carbonade in a deep serving dish. If you do so, remove the meat and keep warm and covered so that it doesn't dry out. Strain the sauce through a fine-mesh sieve or chinois, pressing down hard on the onions so that they form a purée. Reheat and combine with the meat.

STAUB

SERVES 6
PREPARATION TIME: 20 MINUTES
COOKING TIME: 45 MINUTES

- 1 ½ lb. (700 g) boiled beef
- 2 cups stock or veal *jus*
- 6 large onions
- 4 tablespoons (60 g) butter or grated fatback, plus a little for finishing
- 1 heaped tablespoon flour
- 2 tablespoons vinegar
- 1 tablespoon reduced tomato paste, or 3 tomatoes, peeled, seeded, and chopped
- 2 cloves garlic, crushed
- 1 teaspoon chopped parsley
- 1 tablespoon bread crumbs
- Salt and freshly ground pepper

Beef and Onions au Gratin
Boeuf en miroton

Heat the stock or *jus* and keep it very hot until you need it. Finely slice the onions and drop them in boiling water for 5 minutes to remove their pungency. Drain them and pat them completely dry.

In a pan, earthenware dish, or Dutch oven, heat the butter. Add the onions and color them over low heat, stirring often with a wooden spoon.

Then add the flour and continue to brown gently. When the roux is ready, pour in the vinegar and leave to cool. Then pour in the very hot stock or *jus*, stirring well to dissolve the flour, just as you would for a sauce, so that there are no lumps. Finally, add the tomato paste (or tomatoes) and the crushed garlic cloves. Give a few turns of the pepper mill over all this. Bring to a boil and leave to simmer gently for 20 minutes.

Preheat the oven to 425°F (210°C).

Fifteen minutes before serving, slice the beef very thinly (slices ⅛ in. or 3 mm thick). Spread it out in an oven- and flame-proof dish. Check the seasoning of the sauce and pour it over the beef, which should be well soaked. Place over the heat until it boils. Sprinkle with the chopped parsley and bread crumbs. Drizzle a little melted butter over the top and cook at 425°F (210°C) so that it simmers.

Serve when the top is nicely browned.

SERVES 6 TO 8
PREPARATION TIME: 5 MINUTES
COOKING TIME: ABOUT
15 MINUTES (5 MINUTES PER LB.)

About 3 lb. (1.5 kg) beef fillet
3 ½ tablespoons (50 g) butter
Salt and pepper

Roasted Beef Fillet
Filet de bœuf rôti

Ask your butcher to bard the meat. Its juice will be tastier.

Remember to take the meat out of the refrigerator about 2 hours before cooking.

Preheat the oven to 425°F (210°C).

On a cutting board, season the meat with salt and ground pepper, then place it in an ovenproof dish. Put the dish in the oven.

One minute before the end of the cooking time, take off the bard to allow all the surfaces of the roast to brown, and begin heating the serving platter, the plates, and the sauceboat.

At the end of the cooking time, switch off the oven but leave the roast inside for about another 5 minutes, so that the meat can rest. This will make it more tender and easier to cut.

Take the roast out of the oven, carve on a cutting board, and arrange on the serving platter. Keep the meat warm.

Discard any excess fat in the cooking dish, then heat the dish on a stove. Add juice collected from the carved meat as well as the butter cut into pieces. Also add half a ladleful of hot water, and salt and ground pepper.

When the juice is frothy, pour it into the sauceboat.

Serve hot, accompanied, for example, with a gratin dauphinois and a watercress salad.

If you have any roast fillet left over, you can serve it cold the next day, garnished with pickles, olives, and assorted mustards.

SERVES 4
PREPARATION TIME: 10 MINUTES
COOKING TIME:
ABOUT 25 MINUTES,
ACCORDING TO TASTE

1 boneless rib steak weighing 1 ¾ lb. (800 g)

3 shallots

1 medium onion

1 anchovy fillet in oil

3 ½ tablespoons (50 g) butter

Generous ½ cup (150 ml) red wine

Salt and pepper

Steak with Red Wine Sauce
Entrecôtes vigneronnes

One hour ahead of time, take the meat out of the refrigerator. Cut off any excess fat from around the steak.

Peel the shallots and onion. Finely chop the shallots, onion, and anchovies, either by hand or in a food processor. Place all together in a bowl and reserve for making the sauce. Melt the butter in a large frying pan until very hot, salt and pepper the steak on both sides, then place it in the pan. Cook the steak for 6 minutes on each side over moderately high heat if you like it rare, 8 minutes on each side if you like it medium rare. When done, lift the meat out of the pan and keep warm while making the sauce.

Stir the chopped onion mixture into the pan and cook for about 5 minutes, or until the onions have softened and begun to brown. Stir in the wine, bring to a boil, and boil for 1 to 2 minutes, or until the sauce has thickened slightly; add salt and pepper if needed.

You can either serve the steak as it is on a hot platter and slice it at the table with the sauce in a sauceboat on the side, or slice the meat, strain the sauce, spoon a little onto each dinner plate, place the slices of steak on top, and serve with any extra sauce in a sauceboat.

Bœuf Bourguignon

SERVES 4 TO 6
PREPARATION TIME: 20 MINUTES
COOKING TIME: 3 HOURS

- 2 ¼ lb. (1 kg) blade of beef
- 4 oz. (125 g) salt pork or slab bacon
- 12 baby onions
- About 4 carrots (1 lb./500g)
- Bouquet garni, made with 2 stalks celery, 4 sprigs parsley, 1 sprig thyme, and ¼ bay leaf
- 2 small cloves garlic
- 4 tablespoons (60 g) butter
- 1 tablespoon (6 g) flour
- 1 tablespoon tomato paste
- 1 bottle red wine
- Salt and pepper

At least one hour and a half ahead of time, take the meat out of the refrigerator. Cut the meat into egg-sized pieces and the salt pork into ½ in. (1 cm) cubes.

Peel the onions and leave them whole. Peel the carrots, quickly run them under cold water, and cut them into sticks of roughly 2 in. (5 cm). Carefully wash the celery and parsley. Remove the tough outer fibers of the celery, then tie together the thyme, bay leaf, parsley, and celery. Peel and crush the garlic.

Melt the butter in a large cast-iron pot, add the onions and salt pork, and cook over moderate heat for 3 minutes, or until they begin to brown. Salt and pepper the meat, then add it to the pot and brown over high heat on all sides. Lower the heat, add the carrots and the bouquet garni, cover, and simmer for about 30 minutes; then lift the meat and bacon out of the pot with a slotted spoon and keep them warm. Stir the flour into the pot and heat until it starts to color. Stir in the tomato paste, then add the wine little by little, stirring constantly. Check the seasoning, add the garlic, and bring to a boil, stirring constantly. Return the meat and bacon to the pot, cover, and simmer for 2 ½ hours. Remove the bouquet garni, then serve the stew in its cooking pot.

Serving suggestions: Serve with steamed potatoes or a Potato Crêpe (see p. 499).

Hungarian Goulash
Goulasch hongrois

SERVES 4
PREPARATION TIME: 25 MINUTES
COOKING TIME:
1 HOUR 30 MINUTES

1 ¾ lb. (800g) boneless chuck roast

9 oz. (250 g) slab bacon

2 medium onions

Bouquet garni, made with 1 small bunch parsley, 1 sprig thyme, and ¼ bay leaf

2 medium-sized ripe tomatoes

3 ½ tablespoons (50 g) butter, plus butter to serve

2 tablespoons Hungarian paprika

Generous ½ cup (150 ml) dry white wine

2 ¼ lb. (1 kg) potatoes

6 tablespoons (100 ml) crème fraîche or heavy cream

Salt and pepper

Country-style bread

Ask the butcher to cut the meat into evenly-sized cubes. One hour ahead of time, take the meat out of the refrigerator.

Remove the rinds and cut the bacon into ½ in. (1-cm) cubes.

Peel and slice the onions. Wash the parsley and remove the long stems, and tie together the parsley, thyme and bay leaf with kitchen string. Run the tomatoes under boiling water and peel and chop them. Set aside.

Melt the butter in a large pot or high-sided frying pan, lightly brown the bacon, then add the onions, meat, salt, and pepper. Stir, then sprinkle in the paprika, stir again, and simmer uncovered for 10 to 15 minutes. Add the tomatoes, bouquet garni, and wine. Bring just to a boil, then immediately lower the heat, cover the pot, and cook at a very gentle boil for 1 hour and 15 minutes, stirring occasionally (add a little water if necessary so that the meat is always just barely covered by liquid).

Meanwhile, peel the potatoes, place them in a large pot, cover with cold water, salt lightly, bring to a boil, and boil gently for 30 minutes. Time it so that the meat and potatoes finish cooking at the same time.

Just before serving, remove the meat from the heat and stir in the cream. Return to the heat just long enough to warm the sauce, but don't allow it to boil. Season with salt and pepper.

Serve with the potatoes, slices of country-style bread, and a dish of fresh butter, all on the side.

SERVES 4
PREPARATION TIME: 30 MINUTES
COOKING TIME: 3 HOURS

Saône River Bargemen's Grill
Grillade des Mariniers de la Saône

2 ¾ lb. (1.2 kg) beef eye fillet
5 oz. (150 g) white lard
1 ½ lb. (700 g) onions
4 cloves garlic
1 bouquet garni
2 cups (500 ml) Moulin-à-Vent Beaujolais wine
Generous ½ cup (150 ml) red wine vinegar
Kosher salt and black pepper

Cut the beef into small strips and season with salt and pepper.

Mince the onions and crush the garlic cloves.

At the base of an 8 ½ in (22-cm) cast-iron stew pot, place the slices of white lard, then a layer of meat, followed by a layer of onions and garlic, and so on. Add the bouquet garni and sprinkle with the Moulin-à-Vent and vinegar.

Cover and leave to cook gently in the oven for 3 hours at 230°F (110°C).

Serve with steamed potatoes.

SERVES 4
PREPARATION TIME: 7 MINUTES
COOKING TIME: 15 MINUTES

Pepper Steaks
Steaks au poivre

2 steaks from the tenderloin, weighing 10 oz. (300 g) each
2 tablespoons (15 g) whole peppercorns
2 tablespoons (30 g) butter
1 teaspoon Dijon mustard
6 tablespoons (100 ml) crème fraîche or heavy cream
Salt

One hour ahead of time, take the steaks out of the refrigerator.

Place the peppercorns on a cutting board or table and coarsely crush them with a rolling pin. Lightly salt the steaks, then roll them in the peppercorns, pressing down on them as you do so. Leave for 15 minutes before cooking.

Heat the butter in a large frying pan until very hot, add the steaks, and cook over high heat 5 or 6 minutes on each side, then lift them out of the pan and keep warm on a serving platter while making the sauce.

Remove the pan from the heat, stir in the mustard and the cream, scraping the bottom of the pan to dissolve any meat juices, then place the pan back over the heat just long enough to heat the sauce (don't allow to boil). Add a little salt if needed, then pour over the meat and serve.

Serving suggestions: Serve with Sautéed Potatoes (see p. 492).

Pot-au-Feu

SERVES 12
PREPARATION TIME: 25 MINUTES
COOKING TIME: AT LEAST 3 HOURS

- 7 oz. (200 g) steak bones
- 3 lb. (1.5 kg) beef shanks
- 1 lb. (500 g) beef ribs
- 1 lb. (500 g) flank steak
- 1 lb. (500 g) chuck steak
- 1 lb. (500 g) oxtail
- 1 lb. (500 g) veal shanks
- About 3 lb. (1.5 kg) poultry
- 1 lb. (500 g) sirloin steak
- 10 oz. (300 g) leeks
- 10 oz. (300 g) carrots
- 2 celery heads
- 10 oz. (300 g) round turnips
- 1 bulb fennel
- 1 parsnip
- 3 large tomatoes
- 1 head of garlic
- Bouquet garni, made with bay leaves, parsley, chervil, thyme, and green leek leaves
- 5 marrow bones, about 1-1 ½ in. (3 cm) in length
- 9 oz. (250 g) onions, studded with cloves
- Peppercorns
- Kosher salt
- Pickles, mustard, and toasted bread (for serving)

Take a large stewpot and place in order: the steak bones, beef shanks, ribs, flank steak, chuck steak, oxtail, and veal shanks. Add cold water so that the meat is covered. Do not season. Cook over a high heat without covering.

While the meat is cooking, wash and prepare the vegetables. Prepare the bouquet garni. Wrap the marrow bones in muslin.

After the meat has cooked for 20 minutes, use a ladle to skim off all the foam that has gathered at the surface of the bouillon (broth). Lower the heat and allow to cook for another 20 minutes. Add the peppercorns. Place in the poultry after trussing it. Then add the bouquet garni and the onions studded with cloves. Add the garlic, the leeks tied in a bundle, and all the vegetables except the tomatoes. Skim once again, then allow to simmer for 1 hour. Season with salt.

Take out the vegetables gradually as they cook, checking whether they are ready with the tip of a pointed knife. Keep the vegetables warm in a pot over a low heat, dousing them with two ladlefuls of bouillon or broth. Take out the poultry as soon as it is cooked, keeping it warm with the vegetables. Allow the meat to cook for another 30 minutes, skimming the broth from time to time, then remove the veal shanks, which should be kept warm with the poultry.

Tie a length of string around the sirloin, add the meat to the pot, and attach the loose end of the string to the handle. Allow the remaining meats to cook gently for another hour. Add the marrow bones, as well as the tomatoes. Skim. Cook the sirloin for 15 to 20 minutes, depending on its thickness, and remove.

Remove the remaining meats and arrange them on the serving platter. To warm up the meats taken out first, immerse them in the broth for 5 minutes, then arrange them on the platter along with the vegetables and marrow bones.

Serve at the table with coarse sea salt, black pepper, pickles, and mustard. Serve the broth in bowls accompanied by toasted bread.

COMITÉ
INTERPROFESSIONNEL
DE LA

SERVES 4
PREPARATION TIME: 10 MINUTES
COOKING TIME: 1 HOUR

Tripe Sausage
Andouillettes

- 4 andouillettes (French tripe sausages)
- 2 shallots
- 3 ½ tablespoons (50g) butter
- 2 tablespoons bread crumbs (preferably white–see Note)
- 1 ¼ cups (300 ml) dry white wine
- 1 small bunch parsley
- 6 tablespoons (100 ml) hot water
- Salt and pepper

Preheat the oven to 350°F (180°C).

Peel and roughly chop the shallots. Set aside.

Melt the butter in a small roasting pan, add the sausages, and place in the oven for at least 45 minutes, turning over every 10 to 15 minutes.

Lift the sausages out of the pan and set them aside on a plate. Add the shallots, bread crumbs, salt, and pepper to the pan, stir in the white wine, heat to simmering on top of the stove, then place the sausages back in the pan and cook in the oven 15 minutes more. Turn off the oven but leave the sausages inside for another 10 minutes.

Remove the stems of the parsley, carefully wash the leaves, then coarsely chop.

To serve, remove the sausages from the pan and either slice them on a cutting board or leave them whole. Keep warm on a hot serving platter while making the sauce.

Place the roasting pan on top of the stove over high heat. Add the hot water, and boil, whisking, until the sauce is nice and creamy, then pour over the sausages, sprinkle with the parsley, and serve.

Note: White bread crumbs can be made by pulverizing stale white bread in a mortar or heavy-duty blender, but shop-bought bread crumbs may be used instead. The sauce will simply be brown instead of white.

SERVES 4
PREPARATION TIME:
20 TO 30 MINUTES
COOKING TIME:
1 HOUR 15 MINUTES

1 generous cup (300 g) cooked meat or poultry, or a mixture of both

2 ¼ lb. (1 kg) potatoes

1 ½ cups (350 ml) milk

1 egg

Scant ½ cup (50 g) grated Gruyère cheese

Nutmeg

2 small onions

1 tablespoon tomato paste

3 ½ tablespoons (50 g) softened butter, broken into pieces, plus butter for the dish

Salt and pepper

French Shepherd's Pie
Hachis parmentier

Peel and wash the potatoes. Boil in lightly salted water for 30 minutes, then drain and purée in a food mill or mash until smooth. Add the milk, then beat in the egg, cheese, and a little salt, pepper, and nutmeg. Reserve.

Preheat the oven to 350°F (180°C).

Peel the onions. Place them on a cutting board. Cut the meat into small pieces, then coarsely chop the pieces of meat and the onions, preferably using a food mill.

Place the chopped meat, onions, tomato paste, salt, and pepper in a mixing bowl. Beat together with a wooden spoon and reserve.

Butter a baking dish (preferably porcelain or enameled cast-iron). Spread half of the mashed potatoes evenly over the bottom in a thick layer, then pour in the meat mixture and spread it out evenly over the potatoes. Pour in the remaining potatoes and use a fork to spread them over the meat and to decorate the surface by making lines and patterns over it. Dot the surface with the softened butter (see Variation), then place in the oven and bake for 45 minutes or until brown on top. Serve hot from the oven in the dish.

Serving suggestions: This dish is a meal in itself; serve it with a Green Salad (see p. 68).

Variation: If you like, homemade Tomato Sauce (see p. 544) or grated Gruyère cheese can be spread over the surface of the potatoes instead of butter before baking.

Beef Daube Provençal
Daube de boeuf à la provençale

SERVES 8
PREPARATION TIME: 40 MINUTES
MARINATING TIME: 12 HOURS
COOKING TIME:
5 HOURS 30 MINUTES

1 ¼ lb. (600 g) flank or top leg of beef

1 ¼ lb. (600 g) upper chuck or shoulder of beef

1 ¼ lb. (600 g) beef cheeks

1 piece pork rind

1 calf's foot, soaked and boned

4 carrots

1 celery heart (tender part of innermost ribs)

3 onions

3 cloves garlic

3 tomatoes

10 oz. (300 g) unsmoked slab bacon

5 oz. (150 g) fatback

A few sprigs parsley

1 bouquet garni, made with thyme, bay leaves, and summer savory

Zest of 1 organic orange

1 ¾ tablespoons (15 g) peppercorns

Flour and water sealing paste

2 tablespoons (30 ml) olive oil

Salt and pepper

MARINADE

2 carrots

1 stick celery

1 onion

3 shallots

3 cloves garlic

1 bottle full-bodied red wine

Scant ½ cup (100 ml) cognac

Scant ¼ cup (50 ml) olive oil

A day ahead, cut the three cuts of beef into large cubes. Peel the vegetables for the marinade. Slice the carrots, celery, onion, and shallots. Leave the garlic cloves whole. Place the meat in a large bowl with the wine, cognac, and oil, and then add the other ingredients. Leave to marinate in the refrigerator for 12 hours.

Half a day before serving, blanch the pork rind and calf's foot in salted boiling water for 5 minutes. Refresh under cold water. Cut the foot into small dice.

Prepare the vegetables for the cooking liquid: peel the carrots, celery heart, and onions and cut into very small dice. Peel and crush the garlic cloves. Quarter the tomatoes. Remove the rind from the unsmoked slab bacon and cut it into small cubes. Cut the fatback into sticks. Chop the parsley sprigs and roll the fatback sticks in it. Drain the meat cubes over a bowl and pat them dry using paper towel. Filter the marinade and retain. Drizzle some oil into a pan and brown the meat cubes over high heat. Season with salt and pepper.

Preheat the oven to 250°F (120°C). Line the bottom of a pot with the pork rind. Take one-third of the diced vegetables, the bacon bits, the sticks of fatback, the diced calf's foot, and quartered tomatoes. Make a first layer of these ingredients, and then make a layer of meat cubes. Continue making these layers until you have used up all the ingredients.

Add the aromatics (the bouquet garni, orange zest, and peppercorns in a muslin bag). Pour in the filtered marinade. Prepare a dough with the flour and water. Roll it into a long tube and place it around the rim of the pot. Cover with the lid and press the dough in to seal the pot. Pour a little hot water onto the upper side of the lid.

Place in the oven and leave to simmer gently for 5 hours 30 minutes. After 5 hours, break the dough and lift off the lid. Switch off the oven and return the pot for a further 30 minutes. Serve the daube with fresh pasta.

VEAL

SERVES 4
PREPARATION TIME: 15 MINUTES
COOKING TIME: 15 MINUTES

Veal Chops with Mushrooms
Côtes de veau aux champignons

- 4 veal chops
- 8 oz. (240 g) mushrooms
- 2 tablespoons (30 g) butter, plus an extra knob for the sauce
- 4 tablespoons white wine
- 4 tablespoons veal *jus* or stock
- 1 pinch freshly chopped parsley
- Salt

Quarter the mushrooms.

Sauté the veal chops in the butter and transfer them to a serving platter.

Using the same pan (the butter should still be very hot), lightly brown the mushroom quarters. Season with a pinch of salt and add 1 tablespoon of white wine for every chop you have cooked. Reduce the liquid by half and add the veal *jus* or stock (or water if you have neither). Bring quickly to a brisk boil, remove from the heat, and whisk in the extra butter.

Take the juice that has come from the veal chops while they were resting and spoon it over the mushrooms. Mix well and pour the mushrooms and juices back over the chops.

Sprinkle with a pinch of chopped parsley.

SERVES 6
PREPARATION TIME: 5 MINUTES
COOKING TIME: 8 MINUTES

6 scaloppine (veal escalopes), about 4 oz. (120 g) apiece
1 pinch paprika
1 egg
2 ½ tablespoons oil, divided
4 oz. (125 g) stale white bread, crusts removed and reduced to crumbs
8 tablespoons (120 g) butter, divided
Juice of ½ lemon
2 teaspoons capers
2 teaspoons chopped parsley
2 hard-boiled eggs, still hot
Salt and pepper

Breaded Scaloppine with Browned Butter
Escalopes panées au beurre noisette

Flatten the veal scaloppine. This procedure will break the fibers of the meat and thin the scaloppine. They should be beaten until they are about ¼ in. (7-8 mm) thick. Season them on both sides with salt and paprika (or pepper).

Beat the egg in a soup plate with a pinch of salt and ½ tablespoon oil. Dip the scaloppine first in the egg mixture and then in the bread crumbs, ensuring that both sides are coated. Press down the crumbs with the flat of a knife so that the bread crumbs stick well.

Place 4 tablespoons (60 g) butter and 2 tablespoons oil in a pan large enough to contain the scaloppine so that they do not lie on one another (each one must be fully in contact with the base of the pan). Heat over high heat and then sear the scaloppine well. When the bread crumbs on both sides are a nice golden color, finish cooking over minimal heat.

Transfer them to a well-warmed dish. Discard the fat from the pan and brown the remaining 4 tablespoons (60 g) butter. Pour this, with the juice of ½ lemon, over them. Surround with the capers, chopped parsley, and hard-boiled egg whites and yolks chopped separately. The breaded scaloppine should be served crispy.

SERVES 6
PREPARATION TIME: 30 MINUTES
COOKING TIME:
1 HOUR 15 MINUTES

- 1 ¾ lb. (800 g) fillet of veal, or boned rack of veal
- 3 oz. (100 g) fresh fatback for the lardoons
- 4 pieces of fresh pork rind
- 1 medium carrot
- 1 large onion
- 1 stick (125 g) butter
- 1 bouquet garni, comprising a few sprigs parsley, 1 sprig thyme, and ½ bay leaf
- ⅓ cup (75 ml) dry white wine
- 2 cups (500 ml) veal *jus* or lightly salted stock
- Salt and pepper

Veal Grenadins
Grenadins

Cut the fillets (grenadins, see Note) to a thickness of just over 1 in. (3 cm). Cut the fatback into small pieces, season, and insert them into the slices of veal. Blanch the pieces of rind and drain them. Finely slice the carrots and onions into rounds.

Heat the butter in a sauté pan and allow the fillets to brown gently on both sides. Remove them from the pan and transfer to a dish. Soften the carrot and onion slices over very low heat in the same pan–any higher and the butter would burn and the pan juices caramelize.

Preheat the oven to 325°F-350°F (160°C).

When the vegetables are cooked, add the pieces of rind to the pan. Arrange the fillets side by side over the garnish. Cover with a lid and sweat in the oven for 15 minutes. If you continue cooking over the burner, remove the lid and spoon the pan juices over frequently for 10 minutes. Keep an eye on the pan to check that the juices do not reduce. If they do, add a few spoonfuls of *jus* or stock.

Raise the oven temperature to 375°F (190°C).

To braise the grenadins once they have sweated, pour the white wine into the pan. Reduce the cooking liquid by two-thirds, and then add just enough veal *jus* (or stock) to cover the meat. Add the bouquet garni, and continue cooking in the hotter oven with the lid on to reduce the juices by two-thirds; this should take 40 minutes. Towards the end, remove the lid, place the pan on the burner and allow the fatback to brown. This will glaze the surface of the grenadins, giving them a lovely shiny coating.

Arrange the garnish in an attractive circle around the meat. Strain the juices through a fine-mesh sieve and check the seasoning; drizzle it over the meat and garnish.

Note: A grenadin is a narrow, thick fillet in which small sticks of fresh fatback are inserted. It is then pan-fried or braised like a fricandeau, a classic veal dish; in fact, it is a miniature version of this dish.

SERVES 6
PREPARATION TIME: 30 MINUTES
COOKING TIME: 1 HOUR

Veal Paupiettes
Paupiettes de veau

6 veal scaloppine, each 3 ½ oz. (100 g)

STUFFING

3 ½ oz. (100 g) veal to mince

1 medium potato

A little freshly grated nutmeg

Milk

2 tablespoons (30 g) unsalted butter, plus extra for the mushrooms

1 egg

Crème fraîche or heavy cream

2 shallots

4 oz. (125 g) mushrooms

1 teaspoon chopped parsley

1 small carrot

1 onion

A few strips of fresh pork rind

1 bouquet garni comprising 5 to 6 sprigs parsley, 1 sprig thyme, and ½ bay leaf

⅔ cup (150 ml) dry white wine

⅔ cup (150 ml) veal *jus* or low-salt broth

6 strips of fresh lard, cut thinly, for bard

Butter, for greasing

Salt and freshly ground pepper

Veal stuffing

Cook the potato in boiling water. Remove the sinews from the piece of veal and mince it finely with a pinch of salt, a pinch of freshly ground pepper, and a little freshly grated nutmeg. Place it in a dish.

When the potato is cooked, slice it thinly. Place the slices in a small sauté pan, pour over enough milk to just cover them, and boil for 10 to 15 minutes, just so the milk reduces enough to form a fairly firm paste with the potato slices. Mash the potato and milk mixture while it is still hot. Add the ground veal and the butter. Mix well and incorporate the egg. Adjust the consistency by adding a little cream (or even béchamel sauce if you have some).

Push the stuffing through a sieve and smooth it using a spatula in a mixing dish. Chop 1 shallot. Wash the mushrooms, dry them well, and chop them. Brown a knob of butter in a sauté pan and cook the mushrooms over high heat with the shallot. Incorporate them into the stuffing. Lastly, stir in the chopped parsley. Taste to check the seasoning.

Paupiettes

Flatten the scaloppine until they are very thin, about ¼ in. (7 mm) thick. Sprinkle them with a little fine table salt and then on each one spread out one-sixth of the stuffing. Roll them up and tuck in the ends. Wrap them in bard and tie with twine.

Preheat the oven to 325°F (160°C).

Generously butter an ovenproof pot that is small and has high sides–one in which the paupiettes will fit snugly.

Slice the carrot and onion very thinly and place them in the pot to soften and color just a little. Place the pork rind, and then the paupiettes on top, next to one another. Place the bouquet garni in the center.

(Continued overleaf)

Cover with the lid and cook in the oven for 15 minutes so that the liquid contained in the meat will evaporate and condense. This procedure is known as "sweating the meat."

Pour in the white wine, transfer to the burner, and turn the heat up to high until it is almost completely reduced. Then pour in the *jus* or stock to the top of the paupiettes. Bring to a boil, cover with parchment paper or buttered wax paper and the lid, and leave to simmer in the oven for 1 hour 15 minutes.

You will need to spoon the cooking liquid over the meat frequently, particularly as the cooking progresses and the liquid reduces.

To serve, carefully remove the paupiettes. Cut off the twine and remove the bard. Arrange them in a circle on a warmed round platter with your chosen accompaniment in the center. Strain the juices through a chinois and pour over the paupiettes–make sure the liquid has reduced sufficiently before you strain it.

The accompaniments that are especially recommended for paupiettes are: mushrooms with cream or béchamel; cucumbers sautéed in butter; softened tomatoes; spaghetti (or other pasta) Milanese-style; dauphine potatoes (which should be served separately so that the sauce does not make them soggy); boiled asparagus tips or peas with butter; sliced artichokes sautéed in butter; puréed mushrooms, etc.

MAKES 1 LB. (500 G) STUFFING
PREPARATION TIME: 30 MINUTES
COOKING TIME: 20 MINUTES

9 oz. (250 g) filleted cushion of veal, or bottom silverside of veal (from the leg)

2 eggs, beaten

1 pinch pepper

1 pinch freshly grated nutmeg

PANADA (see Glossary)

¾ cup (200 ml) water

2 teaspoons (10 g) salt

1 stick plus 2 teaspoons (135 g) butter, divided

1 scant cup (100 g) flour, sifted

Veal Quenelles with Butter
Quenelles de veau au beurre

Panada

In a pot, bring the water with the salt and 2 knobs of butter to a boil. Remove from the heat and stir in the flour until the mixture is quite smooth. Return to high heat, stirring constantly until some of the water evaporates. The paste will pull away from the sides of the pot when it has dried out sufficiently. Turn it out onto a plate and leave to cool.

Forcemeat

Cut the veal into small cubes and chop it finely in a blender or food mill. Place the minced meat in a mortar and pound it energetically, or process in a food processor. Incorporate the cooled panada and mix until thoroughly combined. Add the remaining butter and continue to mix until smooth. Then season with salt, pepper, and nutmeg, and gradually stir in the 2 beaten eggs.

Push the mixture through a sieve into a bowl. Work it again with a wooden spoon, cover with plastic wrap, and chill until needed.

Quenelles

Using a pastry scraper or spoon, transfer the forcemeat to a pastry bag fitted with a ¼-in. (5-mm) tip. Fold the top edge of the bag down to close it and pipe out small log shapes into a roasting pan. They should be 3 in. (8 cm) in length with 2 in. (5 cm) spaces between them.

Fifteen minutes before using them, pour over salted boiling water, just covering them, and place the roasting dish on the burner so that the water simmers very gently.

The quenelles are done when they float freely and resist a little pressure from a fingertip.

Use the quenelles to garnish vol-au-vents, bouchées à la reine, and so on, or alone as a starter with sauce, such as a light Mornay sauce.

SERVES 4
PREPARATION TIME: 20 MINUTES
COOKING TIME:
2 HOURS 15 MINUTES

1 piece veal *tendron* (breast [rib cartilages]) about 1 lb. (500 g)
7 tablespoons (100 g) butter
2 carrots
1 onion
⅓ cup (75 ml) dry white wine
⅓ cup (75 ml) low-salt veal stock
Salt and pepper

Braised Veal Tendron
Tendron de veau braisé

Preheat the oven to 300°F (150°C).

Cut the veal into 4 oz. (120 g) pieces; each one should be thicker than its width across.

Heat the butter in a sauté dish large enough to hold all the pieces side by side, and color them lightly on both sides over low heat. While they are cooking, slice the carrots and onion.

Remove the meat from the pan and keep warm. Lightly cook the carrot and onion slices. Season the pieces of veal with salt and pepper and arrange them side by side over the vegetables. Cover with the lid and simmer in the butter in the oven for 1 hour.

Then pour in the white wine, leave the lid off, and reduce it until it is almost dry. Pour in enough veal stock to come halfway up the pieces of veal. Return to the oven without the lid and continue cooking, still at 300°F (150°C), for 1 hour, spooning over the juices frequently.

When the cooking is done, there should be very little sauce. Strain it through a fine-mesh sieve. It should be a lovely light color and as thick as a syrup. The pieces of veal will be meltingly tender.

If you leave them to cool in the sauce, it will form a jelly. Tendrons served in this way make an excellent cold dish when accompanied by a vegetable salad.

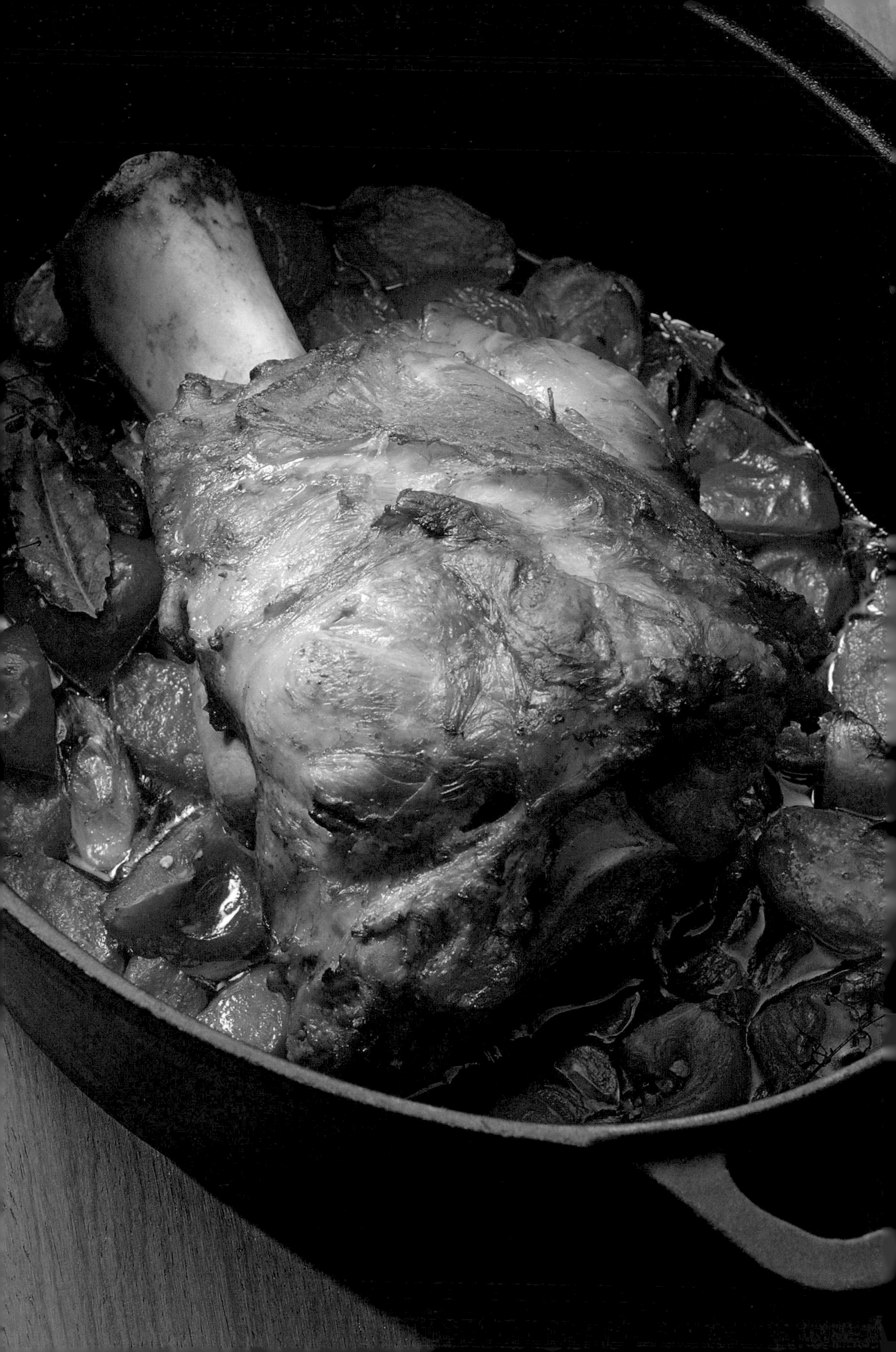

SERVES 4
PREPARATION TIME: 20 MINUTES
COOKING TIME:
1 HOUR 30 MINUTES

1 milk-fed veal shank, about 3 ½ lb. (1.5 kg)
5 ½ tablespoons (80 g) butter
1 large onion
9 oz. (250 g) new carrots
2 ripe tomatoes
Scant ½ cup (100 ml) dry white wine
¾ cup (200 ml) veal stock
1 small bouquet garni
Salt and pepper

Braised Veal Shank
Jarret de veau à la ménagère

Season the veal shank with salt and pepper. Preferably using an oval ovenproof pot, color the veal on all sides in butter. While it is browning, cut the onion into large dice, the carrots into slices, and peel and chop the tomatoes. Add the diced onion and carrot slices and let them sauté a little. Then soften the chopped tomatoes.

Pour in the dry white wine and veal stock. Add the bouquet garni and cover with the lid. Either cook in a 350°F (180°C) oven, or over low heat for about 2 hours. Remove the bouquet garni just before serving.

Serve the veal shank in a deep dish surrounded by the vegetables and drizzled with the pan juices.

This hearty family dish is excellent accompanied by fresh pasta with butter.

SERVES 6
PREPARATION TIME: 1 HOUR
COOKING TIME:
2 HOURS 45 MINUTES

1 ¾ lb. (800 g) good white veal, one-third *tendron* (breast [rib cartilages]); one-third short ribs; one-third shoulder

6 tablespoons (90 g) butter, divided, and a little extra for the sauce

1 medium carrot

1 onion studded with a clove

⅓ cup (30 g) flour

⅔ cup (150 ml) low-salt white stock (or water)

1 bouquet garni comprising 5 sprigs parsley, 1 sprig thyme, and 1 bay leaf

About 12 baby onions

4 ½ oz. (125 g) mushrooms

¼ lemon

2 egg yolks

⅔ cup (150 ml) crème fraîche, whipping cream, or milk

1 pinch freshly grated nutmeg

Salt and pepper

Old-Fashioned Veal Fricassee
Fricassée de veau à l'ancienne

Cut the veal into large cubes. Cut the carrot and onion into quarters. Season the veal cubes with salt and pepper. Heat 4 tablespoons (60 g) butter in a sauté pan and stew the veal, carrot, and onion gently for 15 to 20 minutes, stirring from time to time.

Sprinkle the meat and vegetables in the pan with the flour. Mix it in well and cook gently for 10 minutes as you would for a roux. Do not allow to color. Pour in enough stock (or water) to cover the meat. (If you are using water, add a little salt at this stage.) Bring to a boil, stirring all the time, so that the sauce remains perfectly smooth. Add the bouquet garni. Leave to simmer very gently at the edge of the burner (or over very low heat) for 2 hours.

Blanch the baby onions in boiling water and drain them. Stew them in 1 tablespoon (15 g) butter in a sauté pan until they are cooked. They must remain white, so keep a careful eye on them. Clean the mushrooms: wash them quickly in cold water twice. Drain them and pat them dry. Cut off the stems and place them to simmer with the veal. Quarter the caps and sauté them for 2 minutes over high heat with 1 tablespoon (15 g) butter. Season them with a little salt. When the onions are cooked, squeeze a few drops of lemon juice over the mushrooms and add them to the onions. Cover the pot or sauté pan with a lid and set aside.

Place the 2 egg yolks in a bowl with 3 tablespoons white stock, milk or whipping cream, a few cubes of butter, and a little grated nutmeg. Mix together well.

When the veal is well cooked, remove it from the heat. Using a slotted spoon and a fork, transfer the pieces of meat from the sauté pan to a serving dish and keep warm. Remove the aromatic garnish (carrot, onion, and bouquet garni). Scatter the mushrooms and small onions over the veal, cover with a lid, and keep warm.

Reduce the veal cooking liquid by about half over a high heat. Add the egg-crème-fraîche mixture gradually until you have the desired consistency, then pour the sauce over the veal and vegetables, and serve.

SERVES 6
PREPARATION TIME: 40 MINUTES
COOKING TIME:
2 HOURS 45 MINUTES

1 ¾ lb. (800 g) veal breast (neck end / scrag end)

Herbed salt

1 medium carrot

Rind of fatback

1 bouquet garni comprising parsley, 1 sprig thyme, and 1 sprig bay leaf

⅓ cup (75 ml) dry white wine

2 cups (500 ml) stock, low-salt veal *jus*, or water

STUFFING

4 ½ oz. (125 g) lean pork

5 ¼ oz. (150 g) fresh fatback

1 large onion, cut in half

7 tablespoons (100 g) butter, divided

4 ½ oz. (125 g) mushrooms

Herbed salt

1 egg

1 teaspoon chopped parsley

1 generous pinch chopped tarragon

3 ½ tablespoons (50 ml) cognac

Stuffed Braised Veal Breast
Poitrine de veau farcie et braisée

Stuffing

Finely chop half the onion. Heat a knob of butter in a sauté pan and gently cook half the chopped onion in it.

Quickly wash the mushrooms and drain them immediately. Chop them and add them to the cooked onion. Turn up the heat and cook until dry, about 3 to 4 minutes. Transfer them to a bowl.

Cut the pork and fatback into dice. Chop them and mix together using a mortar and pestle or food processor with a pinch of herbed salt until you have the texture of a smooth stuffing. You can also mix the ingredients together in a dish with a wooden spoon if you do not have a mortar, but the lean meat does not combine so well with the fat. If needs be, you may also buy sausage meat prepared by your butcher.

Combine the stuffing, the chopped, cooked onions and mushrooms, the egg, parsley, tarragon, and cognac. Work together with a wooden spoon until thoroughly mixed. To check the seasoning, take a small quantity (about the size of hazelnut) of stuffing and poach it. Taste and adjust the seasoning if necessary.

Preheat the oven to 350°F (180°C).

Bone the piece of veal, if your butcher has not already done so, slitting it through the thick side without cutting the ends nor the third rib; it should form a pouch. Season the interior with a pinch of herbed salt and fill it with a smooth layer of stuffing. Sew the opening up with trussing twine.

Cut the remaining half-onion into thin rounds and slice the carrot. Lightly cook the vegetables in a little butter in a heavy pot. Cut the rind into small pieces and place them over the vegetables. Add the bouquet garni. Use the remaining butter to brush the veal and add it to the pot. Place in the oven for 15 minutes.

Pour in the white wine and reduce until it is almost dry. Then pour in the *jus* or low-salt stock so that the meat is just covered.

Bring to a boil and cover with a buttered wax paper lid. Cover with the pot lid and leave to simmer gently and regularly for at least 2 hours.

Then remove the lid. The braising liquid should be reduced by two-thirds. If not, leave it to reduce further, spooning the cooking juices over the veal at regular intervals.

Transfer the veal to a rectangular serving platter. Remove the twine. Strain the cooking juices through a fine-mesh sieve and pour it over the veal.

Veal Cutlets with Cream Sauce
Côtes de veau

SERVES 4
PREPARATION TIME: 15 MINUTES
COOKING TIME: 15 TO 20 MINUTES

- 4 veal cutlets weighing about 7-9 oz. (200-250 g) each
- 6 medium (150g) button mushrooms
- Juice of ¼ lemon
- 4 tablespoons (60 g) butter, divided
- Generous ½ cup (150 ml) dry white wine (preferably Pouilly-Fuissé)
- 6 tablespoons (100 ml) crème fraîche or heavy cream
- Salt and pepper

About 90 minutes ahead of time, take the meat out of the refrigerator. Wash the mushrooms in water with a little lemon juice squeezed in.

Melt 1 ⅓ tablespoons (20 g) of butter in a small frying pan, then add the mushrooms and cook slowly until they soften; season with salt and pepper, and reserve.

In a large frying pan, melt the remaining butter. Salt and pepper the cutlets, then place them in the pan when the butter starts to foam. Cook over moderately high heat for 7 to 8 minutes on a side, then remove from the pan and keep warm while making the sauce.

Pour the wine into the pan the veal cooked in, stirring over high heat to detach any meat juices stuck to it, then add the mushrooms, cream, and salt and pepper as needed. Heat the sauce to boiling, pour immediately over the veal, and serve.

Serving suggestions: Serve with Spinach (see p. 474).

SERVES 6
PREPARATION TIME: 40 MINUTES
COOKING TIME: 2 HOURS

Sautéed Veal Marengo
Sauté de veau Marengo

- 1 ¾ lb. (800 g) veal, one-third *tendron* (breast [rib cartilages]); one-third short ribs or neck (UK: scrag end); one-third shoulder
- 1 carrot
- 2 medium onions
- 4 tablespoons (60 g) butter, divided
- 2 tablespoons olive oil
- 3 tablespoons (20 g) flour
- 2 cloves garlic
- ⅓ cup (75 ml) dry white wine
- 1 lb. (500 g) fresh tomatoes, or ⅔ cup (150 ml) tomato purée
- 1 bouquet garni comprising 1 sprig parsley, 1 sprig thyme, and a bay leaf
- 2 cups (500 ml) veal *jus* or low-salt stock, or else water
- 12 small onions
- 4 oz. (125 g) button mushrooms
- ¼ lemon
- 6 slices of sandwich loaf, cut into heart shapes and browned in butter
- 1 tablespoon chopped parsley
- Salt and pepper

Cut the veal into large cubes. Quarter the carrot and onions. Season with salt and pepper. Place 3 ½ tablespoons (50 g) butter and the oil in a sauté pan and when the mixture is smoking, add the veal cubes and vegetables. Stir briskly; it should brown nicely.

Sprinkle the meat with the flour, stirring well as it browns just lightly. Add the crushed garlic, heat for just one second, and then add the white wine. Allow it to reduce by two-thirds. If you are using fresh tomatoes, peel, seed, and chop them. Add the tomatoes or purée and bouquet garni, and pour in the veal *jus* or stock (or water) until it just covers the meat. If you are adding water, add a little salt too. Bring to a boil, stirring all the time. Cover with the lid and simmer over very low heat for 1 hour.

Blanch the small onions, unless they are new, then drain them, and pat them dry. Fry them in a knob of butter until they turn a nice golden color. Clean the mushrooms: wash them carefully but very quickly. Drain them and remove the stems. Add the stems to the veal. Cut the caps into quarters if they are large; if they are small, shape them evenly. If you have any trimmings, add them to the veal.

Prepare a second large sauté pan. Heat a knob of butter well and throw in the mushroom caps. Cook over high heat, stirring until they begin to brown. Remove from the heat.

The veal will now be half done. Remove the meat from its cooking liquid and transfer to the pan containing the mushrooms. Add the onions to the same pan. Leave the cooking liquid to rest for a few minutes then skim off the fat. Strain the liquid, pressing down hard on the vegetables with a spoon, then pour the liquid over the veal, mushrooms, and onions. Check the seasoning and return to the heat to finish cooking, about 20 minutes .

To serve, squeeze a quarter of a lemon over the dish. Place it in timbales or in a large, deep serving platter. Arrange the heart-shaped croutons of bread around the meat and sprinkle with a little parsley.

SERVES 4
PREPARATION TIME: 10 MINUTES
COOKING TIME: ABOUT 1 HOUR

Veal and Olives
Rôti de veau

1 ¾ lb. (800 g) veal rump roast
4 oz. (125 g) veal breast or tail, cut into pieces
1 onion
2 medium-sized ripe tomatoes
4 tablespoons (60 g) butter
1 generous cup (200 g) pitted green olives
Salt

One hour ahead of time, take the meat out of the refrigerator.

Peel and slice the onion. Blanch and peel the tomatoes, then cut them into quarters. Set aside.

Cut off any large pieces of fat from the veal. In a cast-iron pot just large enough for the meat, place the scraps of fat, along with the pieces of veal breast or tail, and brown lightly. Add the butter; when it has melted, add the onions and the veal roast. Cook to brown the meat evenly over moderate heat for 5 to 10 minutes, then add the tomatoes and stir to detach any meat juices stuck to the bottom of the pot. Salt lightly, cover the pot, place over low heat, and simmer for 40 minutes, turning the meat several times as it cooks.

While the meat is cooking, desalt the olives in a bowl of cold water; change the water once or twice.

After 40 minutes, lift the meat out of the pot and place it on a plate. Strain the contents of the pot into a mixing bowl, pressing on the meat and vegetables in the strainer to extract all of their juices. Place the strained liquid back in the pot, add the meat, drain the olives, and add them as well, then cover and simmer 20 minutes longer.

To serve, lift the meat out of the pot and place on a warm platter surrounded by the olives. Serve the sauce in a sauceboat on the side.

Serving suggestions: Serve with Mashed Potatoes (see p. 496).

SERVES 6 TO 8
PREPARATION TIME: 20 MINUTES
COOKING TIME:
1 HOUR 30 MINUTES

Veal Blanquette
Blanquette de veau

- 1 lb. (500 g) neck (UK: scrag end) of veal
- 1 lb. (500 g) breast of veal
- About 3 cups (750 ml) water
- 3 carrots
- 12 baby onions
- Bouquet garni, made with 2 stalks celery, 1 sprig thyme, and ¼ bay leaf tied together
- 3 peppercorns
- 1 tablespoon (15 g) kosher salt
- 4 tablespoons (60 g) butter
- 2 tablespoons (12 g) flour
- 2 egg yolks
- 6 tablespoons (100 ml) whipping cream
- 1 tablespoon lemon juice
- Pepper
- Chopped parsley to garnish

Cut the veal into pieces about the size of an egg. Place in a pot, add the water (the meat should be almost, but not quite, covered by the water), and bring to a boil, skimming off any foam that rises. Peel the carrots, rinse them and cut them into thick sticks. Peel the onions and leave them whole. Remove the tough outer fibers of the celery, then tie together the celery, thyme, and bay leaf. As soon as the water comes to a boil, add the bouquet garni, along with the carrots, onions, peppercorns, and salt. Cover the pot, lower the heat, and simmer slowly for 1 hour.

Lift the meat and vegetables out of the pot with a slotted spoon, place in a serving dish, and keep warm while making the sauce. Discard the bouquet garni.

In a saucepan, melt the butter, then stir in the flour. When the mixture is smooth (do not allow to color), add the cooking liquid from the veal, little by little, whisking constantly. Once all the liquid has been added, bring to a boil and boil rapidly for 2 to 3 minutes to thicken the sauce, then remove the pot from the heat.

In a mixing bowl, whisk together the egg yolks and cream. Ladle in a little of the hot sauce, whisking constantly. Add the lemon juice, then pour back into the pot, stirring constantly. The sauce should be very hot but not boiling. Add a little pepper, pour the sauce over the meat and vegetables, sprinkle with chopped parsley, and serve immediately.

SERVES 4
PREPARATION TIME: 20 MINUTES
COOKING TIME:
1 HOUR 30 MINUTES

1 veal shank, weighing about 1 ¾ lb. (800 g)

6 tablespoons (90 g) butter, divided

2 cloves garlic, whole and unpeeled

3 ripe tomatoes

9 oz. (250 g) new baby carrots

1 lb. (500 g) new baby potatoes

1 tablespoon olive oil

Salt and pepper

Veal Shank with Baby Vegetables
Jarret de veau primeurs

About 90 minutes ahead of time, take the meat out of the refrigerator.

Season the shank with salt and pepper. Blanch the tomatoes, peel them, and cut them into quarters.

Over moderate heat, melt 4 tablespoons (60 g) butter in a pot just large enough to hold the veal. When hot, add the veal and a clove of garlic, and brown for about 15 minutes, turning frequently. Add the tomatoes, cover the pot, lower the heat, and simmer for 1 ½ hours, turning the meat occasionally. If the liquid from the tomatoes evaporates and the meat begins to stick, add a little warm water to the pot.

Peel the carrots and potatoes, preferably by scrubbing them; quickly rinse them, and then wrap them in a clean cloth. Cut the carrots in half lengthwise (larger carrots should be halved lengthwise and quartered). Cut the potatoes in half or leave them whole, depending on their size.

While the meat finishes cooking, heat the remaining butter and the oil in a large frying pan. Add the carrots and potatoes (they should all fit on the bottom of the pan, or almost), the second clove of garlic, salt, and pepper. Cook the vegetables until lightly browned, then lower the heat and cook very slowly for 15 to 20 minutes or until done, shaking the pan frequently.

To serve, lift the veal out of the pot and slice on a cutting board. Season with salt and pepper. Place on a hot platter, surrounded by the vegetables, taste the cooking liquid for salt and pepper, and serve in a sauceboat on the side.

Serving suggestions: Serve with a Green Salad (see p. 68) or whole roasted tomatoes.

SERVES 4
PREPARATION TIME: 30 MINUTES
COOKING TIME: 35 MINUTES

8 thin veal (or turkey) scaloppine (escalopes) weighing about 2 ½-3 oz. (70-80 g) each
8 thin slices ham
9 oz. (250 g) tomatoes
2 onions
1 cup (125 g) pitted green olives
¼ cup (60 ml) olive oil
Bouquet garni, made with 1 sprig thyme, ¼ bay leaf, and parsley
1 clove garlic, whole and unpeeled
Salt and pepper

Veal Birds and Olives
Oiseaux sans tête

Blanch the tomatoes, peel them, and chop them. Peel and chop the onions.

Soak the olives in lukewarm water for 30 minutes.

In the meantime, make the veal birds: place the veal scaloppines on the table, and season with salt and pepper. Place a piece of ham (it should be about the same size as the scaloppine) on top of each one, fold in the ends, then roll each one up like a sausage. Tie with twine, with one piece going around the "bird" lengthwise and the other crosswise, like a little package.

Heat the oil in an enameled cast-iron pot or a high-sided frying pan, add the onions, and cook to color lightly; then add the veal birds and brown on all sides over moderate heat. Add the tomatoes, the bouquet garni, and the garlic. Raise the heat and boil for about 10 minutes, or until the water from the vegetables has all evaporated; then lower the heat, cover the pan, and cook for 8 minutes. Add the olives and cook 7 minutes more, taste for salt and pepper, and serve.

Serving suggestions: These are delicious with Mashed Potatoes (see p. 496) or Potato Soufflé (see p. 500). Veal birds are also very good cold, served with a Green Salad (see p. 68).

SERVES 4 TO 6
PREPARATION TIME: 15 MINUTES
COOKING TIME: 15 MINUTES
RESTING TIME: 15 MINUTES

A piece of calf's liver weighing 1 ¾-2 ¼ lb. (800 g-1 kg)

Bouquet garni, made with 1 sprig thyme, ¼ bay leaf, and 1 stalk celery

4 carrots

4 medium onions

4 tablespoons (60 g) butter

⅓ cup (75 ml) dry white wine (preferably Mâcon)

⅓ cup (75 ml) water

Salt and pepper

Calf's Liver
Rôti de foie de veau

Two hours ahead of time, take the meat out of the refrigerator.

Remove the tough outer fibers of the celery, and wash the celery. Tie together the thyme, bay leaf, and celery with twine. Peel the carrots and cut them into quarters. Peel and slice the onions.

Season the calf's liver on all sides. In a cast-iron pot, melt the butter, then add the liver, carrots, onions, and bouquet garni; brown the liver over moderate heat for about 10 minutes, turning frequently. Add the wine and water, heat almost to boiling, then cover the pot and simmer for 20 minutes. Remove the pot from the heat, season with a little salt and pepper, cover the pot again, and allow to rest for 15 minutes away from the heat before serving.

To serve, lift the liver out of the pot, slice it on a cutting board, then place the slices on a hot serving platter. Pour any juices that come from the liver back into the pot. Bring to a boil (you can add a little hot water if you feel there won't be enough sauce), then strain over the liver and serve immediately, with the carrots and onions in a dish on the side, or arranged around the liver on the platter.

Serving suggestions: Serve with Spinach (see p. 474) or Braised Lettuce (see p. 478).

MUTTON & LAMB

SERVES 6
PREPARATION TIME: 20 MINUTES
COOKING TIME:
1 HOUR 30 MINUTES

Mutton Chops Champvallon
Côtelettes de mouton à la Champvallon

- 6 lamb chops
- 4 tablespoons (60 g) butter
- 2 cloves garlic
- 2 large onions
- 2 cups (500 ml) stock or white veal *jus*
- 1 bouquet garni comprising a few sprigs parsley, 1 sprig thyme, and ½ bay leaf
- 6 medium, yellow-fleshed potatoes
- 1 pinch chopped parsley
- Salt and pepper

Heat the butter in a sauté pan large enough to hold the chops side by side. When it is sizzling, place the chops in it and sprinkle each one with a pinch of salt and a little pepper. Brown them gently so that the butter does not burn. Turn them over, season in the same way, and brown gently. Rub an ovenproof, flameproof dish with a garlic clove.

Preheat the oven to 425°F (210°C).

Remove the chops from the pan and place them in the dish. Cut the onions into thin julienne slices. Sauté them gently until they are pale, stirring often. Pour in half the stock or veal *jus* and leave to boil for 5 minutes. Pour the liquid, with the onions, over the chops, spreading the onions out. If the chops are not completely covered in liquid, add more stock or *jus*. Bring to a boil and place the bouquet garni in the dish. Then put the lid on and transfer it to the oven for 30 minutes.

Peel the potatoes, wash them, and pat them dry. Slice them very finely and, when the chops have cooked for 30 minutes, cover them with a layer of potato slices. Pour in the remaining stock, bring to a boil, and continue cooking with the lid on at the same temperature for 20 minutes.

Chop the remaining garlic cloves. Remove the lid and sprinkle the chopped garlic over the potato slices and pour in some stock or *jus*. Continue cooking for another 30 minutes, spooning over the cooking juices more frequently as they reduce. It should thicken. Most of the juices should be absorbed by the meat and potatoes, which will be very tender. The top of the dish will be covered by a lovely dark golden crust.

Sprinkle with a pinch of chopped parsley and serve in the cooking dish.

This dish of mutton chops dates from the eighteenth century, and is supposed to have been invented by a mistress of Louis XIV.

FOR 1 SHOULDER
PREPARATION TIME: 20 MINUTES
COOKING TIME: 1 HOUR

Lamb Shoulder Boulangère
Epaule de pré-salé boulangère

- 1 shoulder of lamb, boned or not
- 3 medium onions
- 4 large potatoes
- 4 tablespoons (60 g) butter
- Salt and pepper

Preheat the oven to 425°F (220°C).

Prepare the shoulder as you would any roast and place it in an ovenproof dish large enough to hold it comfortably. Brown it quickly in the oven.

Peel the onions and potatoes. Pat them dry. Cut the onions into fine julienne strips and the potatoes into very thin slices. Sprinkle them all with a pinch of salt.

Remove the shoulder of lamb from the dish. Spread out the onions at the bottom of the dish and then make a thin layer of potatoes. Return the shoulder of lamb to the dish and drizzle it with melted butter. Continue cooking in the oven with the temperature lowered slightly until done.

If the roast was trussed, remove the twine before serving. Serve in the cooking dish.

The onions and potatoes brown slightly, absorbing both the butter and the juices from the lamb.

Don't worry if the garnish sticks a little to the dish; just detach with a spoon as you serve your guests.

SERVES 6
PREPARATION TIME: 30 MINUTES
COOKING TIME: 45 MINUTES

Mutton Chops Pompadour
Côtelettes de mouton Pompadour

- 6 lamb chops
- 4 tablespoons (60 g) butter
- Potato Croquettes (see p. 485)
- 6 artichoke bottoms
- Puréed lentils or vegetables
- A few tablespoons veal *jus*, *demi-glace* (see Glossary), or Périgueux Sauce (see p. 96)
- ⅓ cup (75 ml) Madeira wine
- Salt and pepper

Cook the artichoke bottoms and stew them in butter for 15 minutes.

Sauté the chops. When they are cooked, arrange them attractively on a well-warmed round dish. Place a paper frill on the tip of each one.

In the center, arrange a pile of potato croquettes.

Around the chops, arrange one artichoke bottom per guest.

Fill them with well-buttered lentil purée or other pulse or fresh vegetable. Deglaze the sauté pan with a few spoonfuls of veal *jus*, or demi-glace, or Périgueux sauce. Remove from the heat and flavor with the Madeira wine. Serve the sauce in a sauce dish.

The Marquise de Pompadour was Louis XV's mistress. Cookery was among her wide range of interests and this is one of several classic dishes that bear her name.

FOR 1 SHOULDER
PREPARATION TIME: 20 MINUTES
COOKING TIME:
2 HOURS 15 MINUTES

Berry-Style Stuffed Mutton Shoulder
Epaule de mouton farcie à la mode du Berry

1 shoulder of mutton, boned

STUFFING

- 9 oz. (250 g) sausage meat, finely minced
- 1 medium onion
- Butter for frying
- 1 slice bread, crusts removed, soaked in stock
- 1 clove garlic, crushed
- 1 egg
- 1 teaspoon chopped parsley
- Four-spice mixture
- Salt and pepper

GARNISH

- 3 leeks, white part only
- 2 celery sticks
- 1 bouquet garni
- 1 onion
- 1 clove
- 2 medium carrots
- 1 lb. (500 g) celeriac (celery root)
- 3 large potatoes
- 7 tablespoons (100 g) butter
- Peppercorns

To prepare the stuffing, chop the onion and soften it in butter. Squeeze out the excess liquid from the bread. In a mixing bowl, combine the sausage meat, garlic, egg, chopped parsley, bread, spice mixture, and salt and pepper. Mix well and spread it out on the shoulder of mutton where the bone has been removed. Roll the boned shoulder up and truss it with twine so that the stuffing cannot escape.

Place the shoulder in an oval pot. Cover it with water. Season with salt: allow 2 teaspoons (10 g) for every 4 cups (1 liter).

When the cooking liquid is boiling, add the garnish: the leeks, celery sticks, bouquet garni, onion studded with 1 clove, and carrots.

Cook gently for 1 hour 15 minutes. Then quarter the celeriac and place the quarters around the shoulder of mutton. Leave to simmer for a further 25 minutes; lastly add the potatoes.

When the potatoes are cooked (they should remain firm), drain all the vegetables and process them in a food mill. Put the purée in a sauté pan and dry it out over high heat, stirring all the time. When it is fairly thick, remove from the heat and stir in some butter. Season it well with salt and grind 4 or 5 peppercorns over it. Check the consistency, adding a few spoonfuls of cooking juices if necessary.

To serve, place the shoulder on a rectangular dish. Remove the twine and pour over a little of the cooking juices.

Serve the remaining cooking juices in a bowl. Present the puréed vegetables in a vegetable dish.

The Berry is a region in central France where slow-cooked dishes are hearty and rustic.

FOR 1 SHOULDER
PREPARATION TIME: 20 MINUTES
COOKING TIME:
2 HOURS 45 MINUTES

1 shoulder of mutton, boned and trussed
3 tablespoons (50 g) butter
15 small onions
1 lb. (500 g) turnips
1 pinch sugar
⅔ cup (150 ml) dry white wine
2 cups (500 ml) low-salt broth
1 bouquet garni
1 clove garlic

Braised Mutton Shoulder with Turnips
Epaule de mouton braisée aux navets

Heat the butter in an oval Dutch oven. Gently brown the onions. While they are cooking, peel the turnips, quarter them, and trim them so that they are shaped like large walnuts. When the onions are done, remove them from the Dutch oven and replace them with the turnips. Sprinkle with a pinch of sugar and cook until colored. Set them aside with the onions.

Preheat the oven to 425°F (210°C).

Brown the mutton shoulder in the pot and pour in the white wine. When it is almost completely reduced, pour in enough broth to cover three-quarters of the mutton shoulder. Add the bouquet garni and bring to a boil. Cover with the lid and transfer to the oven. Cook for 2 hours.

Spoon the braising liquid over the meat, increasing the frequency as the liquid reduces.

After 2 hours, place the onions and turnips in the dish around the meat. If there is no longer sufficient liquid, add a little broth or water (this prevents the braising liquid becoming too salty).

Leave to simmer for a further 25 to 30 minutes with the lid on, frequently spooning over the braising liquid.

Serve the shoulder of mutton in a deep dish surrounded with the vegetables. Pour over just the quantity of liquid you will need to serve your guests.

SERVES 6
PREPARATION TIME: 30 MINUTES
COOKING TIME:
2 HOURS 40 MINUTES

Classic Mutton Stew
Navarin (recette classique)

- 1 ¾ lb. (800 g) mutton, one-quarter each: breast; neck (UK: scrag); rib (UK: loin); and shoulder
- 1 tablespoon plus 2 teaspoons (25 g) butter
- 1 large onion
- 1 medium carrot
- 1 pinch sugar
- 2 tablespoons flour
- 2 cloves garlic
- 2 tablespoons tomato purée, or 3 fresh tomatoes
- 1 bouquet garni
- 14 oz. (400 g) small potatoes
- 4 ½ oz. (125 g) slab bacon
- 24 small onions
- Salt and pepper

Have the neck (scrag) meat boned and cut into 2 oz. (60 g) chunks and trim them if necessary. Cut the remaining pieces into chunks of the same size, but don't debone them.

Peel and quarter the onion and carrot. Season the meat and vegetables with salt and pepper. Heat the butter until it is sizzling and brown the meat in it. Then discard some of the fat and sprinkle the mutton with sugar. Stir over high heat for 1 minute, just until the sugar caramelizes. This will give an attractive color to the stew. Stir in the flour and mix well. Leave to color very briefly.

Preheat the oven to 350°F (180°C).

Crush the garlic and throw it in. Heat it for a few seconds, stirring all the time, and then pour in just enough water to cover the meat. Add the tomato purée or fresh tomatoes and the bouquet garni.

Bring to a boil and transfer to the oven. Cook with the lid on for 1 hour. During this time, peel the potatoes. If they are large, cut them and trim them to the size of a small egg. Set aside. Cut the slab bacon into dice. Place in a pot of cold water and bring to a boil. Peel the onions. Sauté the bacon bits and then brown the onions in the same pan.

After 1 hour, pour the meat into a colander placed over a large bowl to catch the cooking juices. (Leave the oven switched to 350°F/180°C.) Sort the pieces of meat, picking out any pieces of bone that have become detached and pieces of sinew or skin. Separate the vegetables. Place the meat in a clean sauté pan. Arrange the potatoes and onions over it.

The sauce will have had time to settle; now skim the fat off and adjust the seasoning. If there is not enough of it, add a little water. Pour it over the meat and potatoes. Bring to a boil again and return to the oven. Leave to cook for one more hour before serving.

SERVES 6
PREPARATION TIME: 20 MINUTES
COOKING TIME: 1 HOUR

Lamb Breast
Poitrine ou épigrammes d'agneau

- 1 lb. (500 g) lamb breast
- 6 lamb chops
- ¾ cup (200 ml) dry white wine
- 1 onion
- 1 carrot
- 1 bouquet garni
- 1 egg, beaten
- 1 tablespoon oil
- 4 ½ oz. (125 g) bread crumbs
- 2 tablespoons (30 g) melted butter
- Salt

Special equipment: a clean cloth or tea towel; a weight of approximately 2 lb. (1 kg)

Cut the vegetables into thin slices. In a large sauté pan, place the lamb breast, white wine, sliced vegetables, and bouquet garni.

Pour in just enough water to cover the ingredients. Season with salt, cover with the lid, and simmer gently for 40 minutes.

Before this time is up, check for doneness: the bones should come away easily from the meat.

Drain the meat and place it in a colander over a bowl.

Place the lamb breast flat in a dish and remove the bones. Lay it on one side of a clean cloth and fold the other half of the cloth over it. Transfer this to a baking dish and weigh it down with a 2 lb. (1 kg) weight. Leave it to cool under this weight.

When it has cooled down completely, remove the breast from the cloth and cut it in a zigzag shape to make pieces the size of the mutton chops. There should be one piece per person.

Combine the beaten egg with the oil and a pinch of salt. Dip the pieces of breast meat in this mixture and then in the bread crumbs. Press the bread crumbs down with the back of a knife so that they adhere well to the meat.

Flatten the chops slightly. Dip them in the egg mixture and then in the bread crumbs.

Drizzle the chops and breast pieces with the melted butter. Grill them over very low heat.

Arrange them attractively in a circle, alternating chops and meat triangles, on a round platter.

Serving suggestions: In the center, serve a pyramid of any of the following: garden vegetables, peas, asparagus tips, puréed vegetables, or braised Belgian endives.

SERVES 6
PREPARATION TIME: 30 MINUTES
COOKING TIME:
2 HOURS 30 MINUTES

- 3 ½ lb. (1.5 kg) mutton shoulder, breast, rib (UK: loin), and neck slice (UK: scrag) in equal parts
- 3 large, floury potatoes
- 3 large onions
- 1 bouquet garni, comprising parsley stalks, a sprig thyme, and a piece of bay leaf
- 12 small firm potatoes
- 2 celery stalks, white part only
- 12 small onions
- 1 pinch sage, crushed
- Salt and pepper

Irish Stew
Ragoût de mouton à l'irlandaise

Preheat the oven to 350°F (180°C).

Bone the meat and cut it all into pieces weighing about 2 oz. (60 g) each.

Peel the large potatoes, quarter them, and finely slice the quarters.

Peel the large onions and slice them finely. Set them aside with the bouquet garni.

In an ovenproof sauté pan large enough to contain the stew, place one-third of the finely sliced onions and one-third of the sliced potatoes. Arrange half of the mutton pieces over this layer and season with salt and pepper. Place the bouquet garni in the pan and then cover the meat with the second third of the onion and potato slices. Cover with the remaining meat, season with salt and pepper, and finally make a layer with the last third of onion and potato slices. Generously season with freshly ground pepper–this stew should be well spiced.

Pour in just enough hot water to cover the meat and vegetables. Bring to a boil, cover with the lid, and place in the oven for 1 hour 30 minutes.

Peel the small potatoes (trimming them if they are large) and cut them in half lengthways. Round off the angles to shape them like long olives. Keep them in cold water until you add them to the stew.

Cut the celery into small sticks and set aside. Peel the small onions.

After 1 hour 30 minutes, remove the stew from the oven. Lower the heat to 250°F (120°C). The potatoes and onions should have disintegrated completely. If there are any pieces remaining, press them through a sieve to crush them.

Place the small onions, potatoes, and celery in the stew, pressing them into the thick cooking liquid. Sprinkle with a pinch of sage. If the juices have thickened too much because they have reduced considerably or the potatoes are too floury, add a little boiling water.

Bring the stew to a boil again and check the seasoning. Cut out a piece of parchment paper to the size of the sauté pan, cover, and return to the oven for 45 minutes.

If you wish, you may remove the pieces of mutton and transfer them to a clean sauté pan. Pour the cooking juices through a sieve, pressing down hard. This will give you a smoother sauce, but will not enhance the flavor.

Check the small potatoes for doneness 45 minutes into the second stage of cooking. If they are ready, transfer them to a warmed dish and sprinkle with chopped parsley.

Your guests' plates should also be warmed and the stew must be served boiling hot.

Mutton Curry with Apples
Cary de mouton aux reinettes

SERVES 6
PREPARATION TIME: 35 MINUTES
COOKING TIME: 3 HOURS

- 3 ½ lb. (1.5 kg) mutton shoulder, breast, neck slice (UK: scrag), and rib (UK: loin) in equal parts
- 2 tablespoons lard or butter
- 4 teaspoons (10 g) curry powder
- 2 tablespoons flour
- 1 large onion
- 1 bouquet garni, comprising parsley, a sprig of thyme, and a piece of bay leaf
- 7 oz. (200 g) apples, preferably a small, russet variety
- 1 banana
- A little butter to sauté the fruit
- Scant ½ cup (100 ml) crème fraîche or heavy cream
- 5 oz. (150 g) rice
- Salt and pepper

Preheat the oven to 350°F (180°C).

Bone the meat and cut it all into pieces weighing about 2 oz. (60 g) each. Chop the onion.

Heat the lard or butter in a large sauté pan. Sauté the onions until slightly softened, then remove from the pan. Season the meat with salt, pepper, and curry powder and mix well so that the meat absorbs the spices. Begin searing the meat. When it is half-browned, return the onions to the pan and sprinkle over the flour. Stir well to coat the meat and leave to brown slightly, taking care that the onion does not burn.

Pour in just enough water to cover the meat and add the bouquet garni. Bring to a boil, stirring with a wooden spoon.

Transfer to the oven and cook for 2 hours 30 minutes.

Peel the apples and quarter them. Remove the seeds and core. Peel the banana and cut it into 3 pieces.

Lightly brown the apple quarters and piece of bananas in a little butter in a sauté pan large enough to hold the curry. Remove the curry from the oven and transfer the pieces of meat to the sauté pan with the fruit.

When the sauce has settled, skim the fat off the top, adjust the consistency, and thicken it with the crème fraîche. Check the seasoning and pour the sauce through a fine-mesh sieve over the meat.

Swirl the contents of the pan around so that the meat and garnish are well coated. There should be enough sauce to spoon over the accompanying rice.

Serve the curry in a deep dish with the rice, cooked Indian-style, on the side.

Variation: You may replace the water with coconut milk.

SUN ESTD BRAND
Madras
Curry

SERVES 4 TO 6
PREPARATION TIME: 10 MINUTES
COOKING TIME: 40 TO 45 MINUTES
(15 MINUTES PER LB.)

A 2 ¼ lb. (1 kg) boned shoulder of lamb (weight without bone)

2 cloves garlic

2 tablespoons (30 g) softened butter

Salt and pepper

Roasted Lamb Shoulder
Epaule d'agneau à la broche

Two hours ahead of time, take the meat out of the refrigerator.

Peel the garlic and cut each clove into three wedges. Use a small knife to make six incisions in the meat and slide a wedge of garlic into each one. Salt and pepper the meat generously. Roll and tie into a sausage-like shape if the butcher hasn't already done so.

Roast the lamb on a spit if possible (see Note). Use a stove-top rotisserie or the spit attachment to your oven if it comes with one. Preheat to 425°F (210°C) for about 15 minutes, then spit the lamb, set it into place, pour a generous ½ cup (150 ml) of warm water into the drippings pan under the meat, and roast for 15 minutes per pound. Turn off the heating unit and leave the lamb turning on the spit 5 to 7 minutes more before making the sauce and serving (the meat will be very rare, as it should be).

To serve, remove the meat from the spit, place on a cutting board, and slice, being careful not to lose any of the juices that come out of the meat. Place the meat on a warm platter. Add the meat juices as well as 6 tablespoons (100 ml) of water to the roasting pan and bring to a boil, scraping the bottom of the pan to dissolve anything stuck to it. Break the softened butter into pieces. Stir in the butter, salt and pepper lightly, then pour the sauce into a sauceboat to serve on the side.

Serve immediately.

Serving suggestions: Serve with White Beans Provençale (see p. 461) or Green Beans (see p. 458).

Note: If you don't have a rotisserie, cook the lamb in the oven. Preheat the oven to 425°F (210°C), place the lamb in a roasting pan, and roast for 15 minutes per pound. Turn off the oven but leave the lamb inside for 7 minutes, then carve and make the sauce as described above, but in this case, add ½ cup (120 ml) water to the roasting pan before adding the butter.

Lamb Stew
Sauté d'agneau

SERVES 4
PREPARATION TIME: 20 MINUTES
COOKING TIME: 50 MINUTES

- 14 oz. (400 g) neck of lamb (UK: scrag), cut into 5 or 6 pieces
- 1 ¼ lb. (600 g) shoulder of lamb, cut into 5 or 6 pieces
- 4 carrots
- 10 baby onions
- 3 medium-sized (400 g) ripe tomatoes
- Bouquet garni, made with 2 stalks celery, 1 sprig thyme, and ¼ bay leaf tied together
- 1 lb. (500 g) new baby potatoes
- 5 tablespoons (80 g) butter
- 1 tablespoon (6 g) flour
- Generous ½ cup (150 ml) dry white wine
- Salt and pepper

Two hours ahead of time, take the meat out of the refrigerator.

Peel the carrots and cut them into thick sticks. Peel the onions and leave them whole. Blanch the tomatoes, peel them, chop them, and set them aside. Remove the tough outer fibers of the celery. Make the bouquet garni by tying together the thyme, bay leaf, and celery with twine. Scrub the potatoes, rinse them quickly under running water, and set aside in a clean towel.

Generously season the lamb with salt and pepper.

Melt the butter in a large, high-sided frying pan or stew pot. When it starts to foam, add the meat and brown, turning frequently, over high heat. Add the carrots, onions, and bouquet garni, cook for 5 to 10 minutes to brown the vegetables, then stir in the flour, the wine, and the tomatoes. Bring to a boil, stirring constantly, then immediately lower the heat, cover the pot, and simmer for 10 minutes. Add the potatoes, cover, and cook 30 minutes more, stirring from time to time. Season with salt and pepper when the potatoes are done.

Serve immediately, either in the pot the lamb cooked in or in a serving dish.

Serving suggestions: Serve with a Green Salad (see p. 68) on the side.

SERVES 6 TO 8
PREPARATION TIME: 5 MINUTES
COOKING TIME: 50 TO 55 MINUTES
(15 MINUTES PER LB.)

---

3 ½ lb. (1.6 kg) leg of lamb, excess fat removed

14 cups (3 ½ liters) water

2 ½ tablespoons (40 g) kosher salt

2 carrots

2 onions

1 bouquet garni, made with 2 stalks celery, 1 bunch parsley, 1 sprig thyme and ¼ bay leaf

3 peppercorns

English-Style Leg of Lamb
Gigot à l'anglaise

Two hours ahead of time, take the meat out of the refrigerator.

Bring the water to a boil with the salt in a pot large enough to hold the lamb comfortably. Peel the carrots, then cut them lengthwise into quarters. Peel and quarter the onions. Remove the tough outer fibers of the celery. Wash the parsley, then tie together the thyme, bay leaf, parsley and celery with twine. Add the carrots, onions, parsley, thyme, bay leaf, celery, and peppercorns to the pot. When the liquid is boiling rapidly, add the lamb and cook 15 minutes per pound at a very slow, even boil. Skim off any foam that rises. When the cooking time is up, remove the pot from the heat, but leave the lamb in the liquid an additional 10 minutes, then lift it out and carve into thick slices (they will be nice and rare). Sprinkle with salt and pepper, place on a hot platter, and serve.

Serving suggestions: Serve with Baked Potatoes with Tomatoes (see p. 495) and a Green Salad (see p. 68). Any leftovers are delicious served cold with Vinegar Pickles (see p. 553) and mustard. This dish can be livened up with a Aïoli Sauce (see p. 534) or Gribiche Sauce (see p. 529) served in a sauceboat on the side.

SERVES 4
PREPARATION TIME: 10 MINUTES
COOKING TIME: 15 MINUTES

1 ¾ lb. (800 g) andouille sausage (made of pork intestine filled with chitterlings)
4 medium onions
2 tablespoons (30 g) butter
A little vinegar
1 pinch chopped parsley
Salt and pepper

Chitterling Sausage Sautéed with Onions
Andouilles sautées aux oignons

Cut the onions into julienne strips (allow 1 onion per person) and stew them gently in a little butter.

Cut the sausage into ½-in. (1-cm) slices and brown them in another pan. When they are ready, transfer them to the pan with the onions and turn up the heat to high. Cook for a further 2 minutes. Season with a pinch of freshly ground pepper and drizzle a little vinegar into the very hot pan. Remove from the heat and sprinkle with chopped parsley.

Serve very hot with sautéed potatoes or French fries.

Strasbourg-Style Sauerkraut
Choucroûte à la strasbourgeoise

SERVES 6
SOAKING TIME: 3 HOURS
PREPARATION TIME: 40 MINUTES
COOKING TIME: 2 HOURS

6 Strasbourg sausages (these are smoked; alternatively, use frankfurters)
6 slices poached ham
1 lb. (500 g) smoked bacon
1 ham knuckle taken from an uncooked ham
2 ¼ lb. (1 kg) rack of smoked pork
1 dried sausage, pricked all over so that it does not burst
4 ½ lb. (2 kg) white sauerkraut
1 large carrot
4 wide strips thinly sliced bard
1 bouquet garni
A few juniper berries, tied in a muslin bag
1 clove
8 oz. (200 g) goose fat or lard
1 ¼ cups (300 ml) white wine from Alsace or other dry white wine
4 cups (1 liter) clear stock
Pepper

Three hours ahead, soak the sauerkraut. Wash and drain it and, handful by handful, press out the water. Spread the piles of squeezed sauerkraut out on a clean cloth. Grind the pepper mill over them and mix it in. Blanch the smoked bacon, refresh it under cold water, drain, and trim it a little. Slice the carrot.

Preheat the oven to 425°F (210°C).

Line the bottom and sides of a high-sided pot with the bard. Place one-third of the sauerkraut at the bottom of the pot, and then half of the garnish: the sliced carrot, bouquet garni, juniper berries, and clove, and one-third of the fat or lard.

Then make a layer with the second third of the sauerkraut. Above it, place the remaining garnish and another third of the fat. Then add the bacon, the ham knuckle, the rack of pork, and the dried sausage. Lastly, put in the remaining sauerkraut and spread the fat out over it.

Pour in enough white wine and stock to wet the sauerkraut well; it should cover it. Bring to a boil. Cover with a lid of parchment paper and put the pot lid on. Place in the oven. After 35 minutes, carefully remove the dried sausage. After 1 hour, remove the bacon; after 1 hour 30 minutes, remove the rack of pork. Set these all aside, keeping them warm.

Twenty minutes before serving, put the Strasbourg sausages in boiling water. Remove from the heat and poach them for 10 minutes (they should not boil).

Remove the pot from the oven. Take off the paper lid and return the bacon, dried sausage, and Strasbourg sausages or frankfurters to the pot. Place the lid back on and leave to rest for 10 minutes.

To serve

Remove all the accompaniments from the pot of sauerkraut and keep them warm on a covered serving platter. Add the ham

(*Continued on page 330*)

knuckle. Remove the vegetables and stir the sauerkraut with a fork. Transfer it to a long dish and shape it into a dome. Arrange the slices of poached ham in a row over the sauerkraut, alternating them with slices of bacon, thick slices of dried sausage, and slices of the ham knuckle. Lastly, place the Strasbourg sausages around the edge of the dish. As an accompaniment, serve creamy mashed potatoes or boiled potatoes.

This dish must be served piping hot on well-warmed plates.

Roasted Pork with Mustard
Rôti de porc à la moutarde

SERVES 4
PREPARATION TIME: 20 MINUTES
COOKING TIME:
1 HOUR 30 MINUTES

- 2 ¾ lb. (1.2 kg) boneless blade or pork loin roast
- 8 baby onions
- 1 shallot
- Generous ¾ cup (200 g) Dijon mustard
- About 6 oz. (175 g) pig's caul (lace fat) or thinly sliced fatty bacon
- Generous ½ cup (150 ml) dry white wine
- ⅓ cup (75 ml) hot water
- Salt and pepper

At least one hour ahead of time, take the meat out of the refrigerator.

Preheat the oven to 425°F (210°C).

Peel the onions and shallot, and set aside. Use a small spoon to spread the mustard all over the pork roast, then spread out the lace fat and completely wrap the pork up in it (if using slices of bacon, tie them around the roast from end to end). Tie off both ends of the lace fat, then tie two strings around the roast to hold the fat in place. Place the meat in a roasting pan, surround with the onions and shallot. Season with salt and pepper, add the white wine, and place in the oven. Once the roast begins to brown, baste it every 10 or 15 minutes. Cook for a total of 1 ¼ to 1 ½ hours, then turn off the oven but leave the roast inside for an additional 10 minutes.

Lift the roast out and place on a warm serving platter; place the roasting pan on top of the stove and boil the pan juices over high heat, add the hot water and a little pepper, boil rapidly for about 10 seconds, then pour into a sauceboat and serve with the meat.

Serving suggestions: Serve with Potatoes au Gratin (see p. 503) or Split Pea Purée (see p. 479). Roast pork is also excellent cold with a green salad, so don't be afraid of making too much (if using a larger roast, remember to increase the cooking time proportionally).

Blood Sausage with Onions
Boudin noir

SERVES 4
PREPARATION TIME: 5 MINUTES
COOKING TIME: 30 MINUTES

- 1 lb. (500 g) blood sausage (*boudin*, see Note)
- 2 onions
- 2 tablespoons (30 g) butter
- Salt and pepper

Cut the sausage into pieces about 6 in. (15 cm) long, then prick each one in several places with a pin so they won't burst open while cooking. Peel and slice the onions. Heat the butter in a frying pan until it starts to foam, then add the onions and brown over moderate heat for 10 to 15 minutes. Remove them from the pan with a slotted spoon and keep warm. Place the sausage in the same pan and cook over moderate heat for 15 minutes, turning frequently. Season with a little salt and pepper.

Place the onions on a hot platter with the pieces of *boudin* on top. Serve immediately.

Serving suggestions: Serve with Mashed Potatoes (see p. 496).

Note: Boudin *is a French blood sausage. Although not quite the same,* blutwurst, *when available, could be used instead.*

In a mixing bowl, combine the squares of liver and bacon, the mushroom slices, and the sauce prepared with the chopped mushrooms (*duxelle*). Mix them all together so that the meat and mushrooms slices are well coated.

Take metal skewers and on each one thread a square of liver, a square of bacon, and a mushroom slice. Repeat once more, finishing with a piece of calf's liver. Roll each kebab in the bread crumbs and set aside.

To barbecue the kebabs, fifteen minutes before serving brush them with melted butter and place them on the grill over a low heat. As soon as the bread crumbs are a nice golden color, turn them over to the next side.

Serving suggestions: Serve the kebabs with a bowl of Tomato Sauce (see p. 544) or maître d'hôtel butter (see p. 339).

Lyon-Style Sautéed Calf's Liver
Foie de veau à la lyonnaise

SERVES 5 TO 6
PREPARATION TIME: 40 MINUTES
COOKING TIME: 1 HOUR

- 6 slices calf's liver
- 2 tablespoons (30 g) butter, divided
- 1 tablespoon flour
- 4 large onions
- 1 tablespoon vinegar
- Chopped parsley
- Fine table salt and pepper

Heat half the butter in a sauté pan. While it is heating, season the slices of calf's liver with salt and freshly ground pepper. Dust them with flour and shake off any excess. When the butter is browned, sear the slices of liver in it, cooking over fairly high heat for 2 minutes. Turn the slices over and cook for 2 minutes. Then transfer them to a serving platter. Cover and keep warm.

Slice the onions into thin julienne slices or chop them finely. Place the remaining butter in the same pan. As soon as it is hot, add the onions and cook over medium heat until they are transparent. Stir constantly. When they have softened, add the vinegar, without allowing it to boil, and the juices that drip from the liver in the serving platter. Slide the pan back and forth over the heat until all the bits attached to the bottom dissolve. Spoon the juices and onions over the slices of liver and sprinkle with chopped parsley.

Note: You can cook pork liver in the same way.

SERVES 6
PREPARATION TIME: 15 MINUTES
COOKING TIME: 30 MINUTES

Grilled Calf's Liver Bercy
Foie de veau grillé Bercy

- 6 slices calf's liver, each about 4 oz. (110 g) and about ¾ in. (1.5 cm) thick
- 4 tablespoons (60 g) butter, divided
- 1 level tablespoon flour
- 3 ½ oz. (100 g) beef marrow, well soaked
- 1 shallot
- ⅓ cup (75 ml) dry white wine
- ⅓ cup (75 ml) veal *jus* (see Glossary)
- 4 oz. (120 g) beurre manié (see Glossary)
- 2 teaspoons chopped parsley
- Juice of ¼ lemon
- Salt and pepper

Melt enough butter to brush the slices of calf's liver, then season them with salt and pepper. Dust them with flour, shake off any excess, and then drizzle with a few more drops of melted butter. Place them on a very hot grill or in a very hot griddle pan.

Leave to cook for 2 minutes and then rotate each slice by one-quarter of a circle so that the grill or grill pan leaves a criss-cross pattern on the liver. Cook for a further 2 minutes and turn the slices over. Repeat the procedure to obtain a criss-cross pattern on the other side. Remove the slices from the grill and transfer them to a serving platter. Cover or tent with foil and keep warm while they rest.

Dip a knife into very hot water and cut the marrow into ⅛-in. (3-mm) slices. Place in a pot of well-salted boiling water and poach, away from direct heat, for 5 minutes. After this time, drain the slices well. Meanwhile, finely chop the shallot. Heat a knob of butter in a small pan and gently cook the shallot without browning it. Pour in the white wine and reduce it to 2 to 3 tablespoons. Add the veal *jus* and reduce by half. Dissolve the beurre manié in the reduction, then add the drained marrow slices, a pinch each of salt and pepper, 1 teaspoon of chopped parsley, and the lemon juice.

Heat gently, tilting the pot over the burner so that the ingredients bind well as the butter melts.

Take the juices that have dripped into the platter from the liver and add to the sauce. Spoon the sauce over the slices of liver and sprinkle with more chopped parsley. Serve accompanied by a dish of boiled potatoes.

SERVES 6
PREPARATION TIME: 15 MINUTES
COOKING TIME: 30 MINUTES

Lyon-Style Tripe
Gras-double à la lyonnaise

- 1 ⅓ lb. (700 g) tripe
- 4 large onions
- 4 tablespoons oil
- 2 tablespoons (30 g) butter
- 2 generous pinches chopped parsley
- 1 teaspoon vinegar
- Salt and pepper

Cut the onions finely into julienne strips. Heat the oil in a pan large enough to hold the tripe easily. As soon as the oil begins to smoke, transfer the onions to the pan and turn the heat down. Cook gently, stirring frequently. When they are almost done, raise the heat again to brown them.

Drain the onions on a plate, leaving the oil in the pan and adding the butter to the oil.

Cut the tripe into strips about ¼ in. (5-6 mm) thick. Heat the oil and butter mixture and sear the strips in it. Taste a little to check whether it is properly salted–season if necessary, adding a generous pinch of freshly ground pepper. Sauté the tripe over high heat until lightly browned. Then add the cooked onion and continue to sauté and stir so that the ingredients are well mixed. To finish, sprinkle with chopped parsley.

Transfer the tripe pieces to a timbale and pour the vinegar into the hot pan. Immediately pour it over the tripe. Then add another pinch of fresh parsley and serve on well-heated plates.

SERVES 6
SOAKING TIME: 2 HOURS
PREPARATION TIME: 40 MINUTES
COOKING TIME:
2 HOURS 30 MINUTES

6 mutton tongues
5 oz. (150 g) salt pork
14 oz. (400 g) green or brown lentils
3 oz. (80 g) bacon rind
3-4 tablespoons bacon bits
1 medium carrot
1 medium onion
1 bouquet garni including parsley, 1 sprig thyme, 1 bay leaf
⅔ cup (150 ml) dry white wine
2 cups (500 ml) stock or low-salt veal stock
1 onion studded with 1 clove
1 small carrot
½ head garlic
2 tablespoons (30 g) butter
Salt and pepper

Mutton Tongue with Lentil Purée
Langues de mouton à la purée de lentilles

Soak the tongues in cold water for 2 hours, changing the water several times.

Sort through the lentils, removing any impurities you might find. Wash them thoroughly and soak according to the instructions on the packet.

Place the tongues in a pot and cover with cold water. Bring to a boil and leave to boil for 8 minutes. Remove from the water with a slotted spoon and transfer to a bowl of cold water. When they are quite cool, drain them, and remove the skin. Set them aside on a plate.

Drain the lentils and transfer them to a pot. Cover them well with water, bring to a boil, leave to boil for 5 minutes, and drain again.

Blanch the rind briefly.

Preheat the oven to 300°F (150°C).

Slice the carrot and onion. Using a sauté pan just large enough to hold the tongues side by side, melt a few bacon bits, then brown the sliced carrot and onion. Drain them of their fat and then add the tongues to brown them.

Remove the tongues and arrange the carrot and onion rounds at the bottom of the pan. Add the bouquet garni, the blanched rind, and lastly, the tongues.

Pour in the white wine and gently reduce it by two-thirds. Then pour in the broth until the tongues are just covered.

Top the pot with a buttered piece of parchment paper to fit into the rim. Cover with the lid and transfer to the oven for 2 hours.

Meanwhile cook the lentils. Pour enough water in a pot to just cover the lentils. Add salt, 1 teaspoon (5 g) for every 4 cups (1 liter). Add the clove-studded onion, the carrot cut in two, the bouquet garni, and the fat without the rind (which was used to braise the tongues). Bring to a boil and add the blanched lentils. Skim the surface and place the pot on very low heat (using a heat diffuser if possible) to simmer very gently for 1 hour 45 minutes to 2 hours.

When the lentils are completely cooked and very soft, drain them. Remove the aromatic garnish and push them, still very hot, through a fine-mesh sieve. If you leave them to cool at all, the starch will be hard to purée. Catch the purée in a pot and reduce it over high heat, stirring it with a spatula or wooden spoon. It will thicken, so to bring it to the right consistency, adding some of the cooking liquid from the pot containing the braised tongues. Remove from the heat and grind some fresh pepper over it. Do not allow to boil again.

When the tongues are properly cooked, the cooking liquid will have reduced considerably during the braising process.

At the last moment, remove the lid and baste the tongues thoroughly with the juices. Return them to the oven without the lid. The juices will caramelize a little, coating the tongues in a shiny glaze that is tasty and attractive.

Heap the puréed lentils in the center of a deep round dish. Then arrange the tongues with their tips and glazed sides upwards.

Strain the braising liquid through a chinois and pour a teaspoon of it over each tongue.

Cut the piece of salt pork into six and place the pieces in a circle at the base of the tongues.

Test the remaining strained juice for seasoning and serve it separately in a sauce dish.

You can also serve mutton tongue cold; it is excellent with a Mayonnaise (see p. 552), or a related sauce such as tartare sauce. This is a mayonnaise-based sauce often made with hard-boiled eggs, white wine vinegar, and oil, with finely chopped pickles, capers, onions, and herbs such as chives, tarragon, or parsley.

SERVES 4
SOAKING TIME: OVERNIGHT
PREPARATION TIME: 30 MINUTES
COOKING TIME:
ABOUT 1 HOUR 10 MINUTES

2 ¼ lb. (1 kg) veal sweetbreads (whole)

COURT BOUILLON

3 carrots

3 onions

Bouquet garni made with 2 stalks celery, 1 small bunch parsley, 1 sprig thyme, and ¼ bay leaf tied together

1 tablespoon (25 g) kosher salt

3 peppercorns

2 tablespoons (12 g) flour

4 tablespoons (60 g) butter

⅓ cup (75 ml) white vermouth

Salt and pepper

Sweetbreads with Vermouth *Ris de veau au vermouth*

Place the sweetbreads in a large bowl of cold water and leave in the refrigerator overnight before cooking. Remove from the refrigerator 2 hours before cooking, but leave in the water. Just before cooking, drain the sweetbreads and rinse under cold running water, then leave to drain in a colander.

Meanwhile, prepare the court bouillon. Peel the carrots and cut them into sticks. Peel and halve the onions. Remove the tough outer fibers of the celery and wash the celery. Carefully wash the parsley. Tie together the bay leaf, thyme, celery, and parsley with twine.

Pour 12 cups (3 liters) water into a large pot, add the carrots, onions, and the bouquet garni. Add the salt and peppercorns, then bring to a boil.

Add the sweetbreads, lower the heat, and simmer for 30 minutes. When the time is up, lift the sweetbreads out with a slotted spoon (set aside the cooking liquid), and place them in a sieve over a mixing bowl to catch any juices; allow to cool completely.

When the sweetbreads are cool, roll them in the flour. Heat the butter in a high-sided enameled cast-iron frying pan and brown the sweetbreads for about 10 minutes, turning them over to brown evenly on all sides. Add the vermouth and 1 cup (250 ml) of the cooking liquid set aside earlier, as well as any juices that drained from the sweetbreads as they were cooling. Simmer the sweetbreads for 30 minutes over very low heat, uncovered. Season with salt and pepper just before they are done. Serve them on a hot platter with the sauce they cooked in.

Serving suggestions: Serve with green peas or Braised Lettuce (see p. 478).

SERVES 6
PREPARATION TIME: 20 MINUTES
COOKING TIME: 30 MINUTES

Veal Kidneys with Mustard Sauce
Rognons de veau à la moutarde

- 3 veal kidneys
- 1 shallot
- 7 tablespoons (100 g) butter, divided
- Scant ¼ cup (50 ml) cognac
- 4 tablespoons thick crème fraîche or heavy cream
- 1 teaspoon Dijon mustard
- 1 pinch chopped parsley
- Salt and pepper

Preheat the oven to 450°F-475°F (240°C), or as high as your oven will go.

Remove the membrane and fatty parts from the kidneys and season them with salt and freshly ground pepper.

Chop the shallot finely and cook it, without allowing it to color, in a sauté pan with a knob of butter.

Heat 3 tablespoons (50 g) butter in an ovenproof or cast-iron pot over high heat and brown the kidneys well on all sides.

Place in the oven for 12 minutes and remove when the kidneys are still nice and pink.

Transfer them to a dish and cut them into ¼-in. (5-mm) slices. Return the slices to the pot and pour over two-thirds of the cognac. Flambé it as you stir the kidney slices.

Transfer the kidneys to the sauté pan with the shallot. Cover and keep warm. Pour the cream into the pot, which will still be very hot. Reduce it by half over the burner. Remove from the heat and stir in the mustard and a little freshly ground pepper. Ensure that the mustard does not boil.

Pour the contents of the sauté pan–kidneys, shallot, and juices–into the pot. Dot the remaining butter over this and sprinkle with chopped parsley. Pour in the remaining cognac and stir so that all the kidney pieces are well coated in the thickened sauce.

Check that the dish is sufficiently salted and serve on well-heated plates.

SERVES 6
PREPARATION TIME: 20 MINUTES
COOKING TIME: 30 MINUTES

Veal or Mutton Kidneys with Rice Pilaf
Rognons de veau ou de mouton au riz pilaf

- 6 mutton kidneys or 3 veal kidneys
- 1 lb. (500 g) Carolina rice or other good long-grain rice
- 2 large onions
- 1 ⅓ sticks (150 g) butter, divided
- 4 cups (1 liter) broth or clear stock
- Chopped parsley
- Madeira Sauce (see p. 526)
- Salt and pepper

Preheat the oven to 350°F (180°C).

Rinse the rice thoroughly until the water runs clear. Chop the onions finely. Heat 7 tablespoons (100 g) butter in a sauté pan. When it is sizzling, add the onions and cook gently without allowing them to color. When the onions have softened, add the rice. Stir it over low heat until it has absorbed all the butter. Pour in the broth or clear stock. Bake in the oven, with the lid on and without stirring, for 18 to 20 minutes.

While the rice is cooking, remove the membrane from the kidneys, the fat, and sinews, and slice them. Sauté them in a pan.

Remove the rice from the oven. Cut the remaining butter into cubes and dot over the rice. Work them in carefully with a fork.

Place the rice in a savarin mold (or a bundt pan, i.e. one with a hollow center), press down firmly, and then turn it out on to a round dish. In the center, arrange the sautéed kidney slices and sprinkle them with chopped parsley. Pour the Madeira sauce around the rice.

SERVES 6
SOAKING TIME: 24 HOURS
PREPARATION TIME: 20 MINUTES
COOKING TIME: 30 MINUTES

Veal Sweetbreads with Crayfish and Snow Peas
Ris de veau aux écrevisses et aux pois gourmands

6 veal sweetbreads
2 oz. (50 g) onion
2 oz. (50 g) carrot
7 tablespoons (100 g) butter, divided
Scant ½ cup (100 ml) vermouth
Scant ½ cup (100 ml) dry white wine
2 cups (500 ml) white stock
1 bouquet garni
1 ¼ lb. (600 g) snow peas
2 cups (500 ml) cream
3 ½ oz. (100 g) mushrooms
⅔ oz. (20 g) truffle
14 oz. (400 g) shelled crayfish tails
Salt and pepper

Soak the sweetbreads in cold water for 24 hours. Blanch them very quickly in boiling water, drain, and trim them. Remove the nerves.

Slice the onion and carrot. Sweat them in butter in a pot. Place the sweetbreads over this aromatic garnish and pour in the vermouth, white wine, and white stock. Season with salt and pepper. Add the bouquet garni and cover with the lid. Leave to cook very gently for 20 to 30 minutes.

While they are cooking, boil the snow peas in salted water, sauté them in butter, and season them. Transfer them to a serving dish and keep warm.

Remove the sweetbreads from the pot. Strain the cooking liquid through a chinois and reduce it until it is almost the consistency of a glaze.

Add the cream and mushrooms to the reduced sauce. Reduce again until it thickens and reaches a creamy consistency. In the meanwhile, slice the truffle into julienne sticks.

When the sauce is ready, incorporate the sweetbreads as well as the crayfish tails and julienned truffle.

Arrange the sweetbreads over the snow peas. Coat them generously with the sauce with the crayfish tails, truffle pieces, and mushrooms.

Serve immediately on warmed plates.

Variation: You may replace the snow peas with buttered spinach leaves.

SERVES 12
SOAKING TIME: 24 HOURS
PREPARATION TIME: 15 MINUTES
COOKING TIME: 2 HOURS

1 whole milk-fed calf's head, bones left in
1 lemon
22 ½ pints (10 liters) water
½ cup (50 g) flour
⅔ cup (150 ml) white vinegar
2 carrots
2 medium onions
4 cloves
1 head garlic
1 bouquet garni
Salt and pepper

Milk-Fed Calf's Head
Tête de veau

Trim and clean the calf's head. Leave it to soak for 24 hours in very cold water. Drain it and rub it all over with lemon, including the snout, the cheeks, ears, etc.

Prepare a *blanc*: To do this, pour the water into a large stock pot. Dissolve the flour in a little water and add it to the pot, with all the other ingredients: vinegar, carrots, the onions studded with the cloves, the head of garlic, bouquet garni, salt and pepper.

Dip the calf's head into this flavorful cooking liquid and bring to a boil. The head will take about 2 hours to cook if it simmers gently. Skim the pot regularly as it cooks.

Present the calf's head whole to the guests and cut it at the table.

Serving suggestions: To accompany this dish, serve any of the following sauces: Vinaigrette (see p. 542), Green Sauce (see p. 546), Gribiche Sauce (see p. 529), remoulade sauce (see p. 235), tartare sauce (see page 347), etc.

SERVES 6
PREPARATION TIME: 40 MINUTES
COOKING TIME:
1 HOUR 30 MINUTES

- 1 calf's brain
- ½ calf's head
- 1 calf's tongue
- 1 to 2 tablespoons vinegar
- 1 lemon
- 2 carrots
- Bouquet garni, made with 1 sprig fresh thyme or 2 sprigs of dried thyme, 1 sprig parsley and ¼ bay leaf
- 1 clove garlic, unpeeled
- 1 large onion stuck with 1 clove
- 8 peppercorns
- 1 ½ teaspoons (10 g) kosher salt
- 2 cups (500 ml) dry white wine
- 1 tablespoon (6 g) flour
- Gribiche Sauce (see p. 529)

Calf's Head and Brain
Tête de veau

Half a head is plenty for six people. It should be boned by the butcher, the tongue placed on it, and the head rolled up around the tongue and tied with string so it looks rather like a large, thick sausage.

Place the calf's brain in a bowl of cold water, add the vinegar, and leave to soak while cooking the head.

Rub the head with half a lemon, then wrap it in doubled-over cheesecloth or some other thin white cloth (such as a tea towel) and tie it at both ends and around the middle. Place the head in a large pot (an oval one is preferable). Peel the carrots and slice them lengthwise into quarters, and tie together the parsley, bay leaf, and thyme. Add the carrots, bouquet garni, garlic, onion, peppercorns, salt, and wine to the pot. Mix the flour with enough water to form a thin creamy mixture, then pour into the pot as well. Add enough cold water to completely cover the head, bring to a boil, immediately lower the heat, cover the pot by three-quarters and simmer over moderate heat for 1 hour 15 minutes. Skim off any foam that rises to the surface during this time. Test after about 1 hour by piercing the head with a long trussing needle; it should be tender when done (some people like it more cooked than others, but remember that the ears should be "crunchy" even when completely cooked).

When the head is done, cook the brain. First, hold it under cold running water and use your fingers to remove the membrane that surrounds it. Pat it dry with a clean tea towel. Ladle out about 2 cups (500 ml) of the cooking liquid from the head, place it in a saucepan, and poach the brain for about 8 minutes. Remove the saucepan from the heat and cover to keep the brain warm if you don't serve immediately.

Lift the head out of its cooking liquid, remove the cloth around it, and slice it. Place the slices on a hot platter with the brain, carrots, and a little of the cooking liquid. Serve with a sauceboat of gribiche sauce on the side.

Serving suggestions: Serve with steamed potatoes.

Braised Tongue
Langue de bœuf braisée

SERVES 6 TO 8
SOAKING TIME: 2 HOURS
PREPARATION TIME: 50 MINUTES
COOKING TIME: 2 HOURS 30 MINUTES TO 3 HOURS

- A 3 ¼ lb. (1.6 kg) beef tongue, roots removed
- 3 teaspoons (20 g) salt
- 4 medium (300 g) carrots, peeled
- 10 baby onions
- 5 oz. (150 g) bacon
- 1 ¾ sticks (200 g) butter
- 1 tablespoon (6 g) flour
- 2 cups (500 ml) dry white wine
- ⅓ cups (1.5 liters) bouillon (see Pot-au-Feu, p. 264) or hot water
- 2 veal bones
- Bouquet garni, made with 2 sprigs thyme, 4 sprigs parsley, ¼ bay leaf, and 1 stalk celery tied together
- 1 tablespoon tomato paste
- Salt and pepper

Leave the tongue in a large bowl of cold water for 2 hours; then drain it, place it in a pot, add 12 cups (3 liters) fresh cold water, the salt, and bring to a boil. Skim off any foam that surfaces and boil the tongue for 8 to 10 minutes. Meanwhile, peel the carrots, rinse them, and cut them into thick sticks. Peel the onions and set aside. Remove the rind from the bacon and cut the bacon into cubes of roughly ½ in. (1 cm). Drain the tongue in a colander and cool under cold running water until cool enough to handle. Use a paring knife to scrape off the thick skin that surrounds the tongue (a thin white film will be left in most places), then dry it with a clean towel.

Melt the butter in a pot just large enough to hold the tongue comfortably. Add the carrots, onions, and bacon, and cook for about 3 minutes or until the vegetables begin to soften. Place the tongue in the pot and brown on all sides over moderate heat for about 10 minutes. Sprinkle in the flour, stir to combine, then add the wine, stirring constantly. Add the bouillon or hot water, the veal bones and the bouquet garni; the tongue should be about half-covered by the liquid. Add salt and pepper, bring just to a boil, then immediately lower the heat, cover the pot, and simmer slowly for at least 2 hours. Turn the tongue over five or six times while cooking. To test whether it is cooked, pierce it with a long trussing needle after 2 hours; if the needle goes into the tongue with virtually no resistance, it is done.

To serve, remove the tongue from the sauce, stir in the tomato paste, and simmer the sauce while slicing the tongue. Place the slices on a hot platter. Add any juices to the sauce that came from slicing the tongue. Spoon a little sauce over the tongue and serve with a sauceboat of the sauce on the side.

Serving suggestions: Serve with Rice (see p. 510) or boiled potatoes and butter.

SERVES 6 TO 8
PREPARATION TIME: 15 MINUTES
COOKING TIME: ABOUT 10 MINTUES

- 4 veal kidneys weighing about 12 oz. (350 g) each
- 3 shallots
- 4 tablespoons (60 g) butter
- ⅓ cup (60 ml) cognac
- 6 tablespoons (100 ml) crème fraîche or heavy cream
- 1 tablespoon Dijon mustard
- Salt and pepper

Veal Kidneys *en Cocotte*
Rognons de veau en cocotte

Two hours ahead of time, remove the kidneys from the refrigerator. Remove all the fat and gristle from the kidneys, or ask the butcher to do it for you.

Peel and chop the shallots, and set aside.

Cut the kidneys into thin slices, then sprinkle with salt and pepper.

Melt the butter in a dutch oven or *cocotte* on the stove top; when it starts to foam, add the kidneys and brown over high heat, 3 to 4 minutes on each side.

Lift the slices out of the pan with a slotted spoon. Place on a hot platter and keep warm while making the sauce.

Add the shallots to the pan the kidneys cooked in, stir over high heat until soft, then stir in first the cognac, then the cream, scraping the bottom of the pan to dissolve any meat juices, and finally the mustard. Spoon the sauce over the kidneys and serve immediately.

Serving suggestions: Serve with Rice (see p. 510) or Spinach (see p. 474).

SERVES 4
PREPARATION TIME: 30 MINUTES
COOKING TIME: 45 MINUTES

Chicken Liver Soufflé
Gâteaux aux foies de volaille

At least 3 chicken livers, about 4 ½ oz. (125 g) (see Note)

2 ¼ lb. (1 kg) fresh tomatoes

1 tablespoon olive oil

Bouquet garni, made with 1 sprig fresh and 1 sprig dried thyme, ¼ bay leaf, and 1 stalk celery

1 teaspoon (5 g) granulated sugar

1 small onion (50g)

2 cups (500 ml) milk, plus milk for the onion

1 bunch parsley

1 clove garlic

3 ½ oz. (100 g) stale bread

4 eggs, separated

1 ½ tablespoon (20 g) butter

Salt and pepper

To make the fresh tomato sauce for this recipe, blanch and peel the tomatoes, cut them into wedges, and place in a saucepan with a teaspoon of olive oil and the bouquet garni. Add the sugar, bring to a boil, then lower the heat, and boil gently over moderate heat for about 40 minutes or until thick, stirring frequently. Season with salt and pepper. Just before serving, remove the bouquet garni and stir in the remaining olive oil.

Preheat the oven to 375°F (190°C).

While the sauce is cooking, you can make the soufflé. If possible, buy livers that are light in color–they are the best. Peel and slice the onion. Place the slices in a saucepan, add enough cold milk to cover, bring just to a boil, then drain and set aside.

Carefully wash the parsley and remove its stems. Peel the garlic.

Place the bread in a bowl and add the milk; once the bread has softened, crush it with the prongs of a fork, then pour off any excess milk. Place the bread on a cutting board with the livers, onions, garlic, and parsley, and chop to a paste using a food mill. Place in a mixing bowl, stir in the egg yolks, and season with salt and pepper.

Place the butter in a 7-in. (18-cm) soufflé mold and put it in the oven just long enough for the butter to melt. Remove from the oven and turn the dish to coat the sides with the butter.

Beat the egg whites until stiff and fold them into the liver mixture, then pour the mixture into the soufflé mold. Place in the oven and bake for 45 minutes (check for browning by looking through the window in the oven door, but don't open it until the soufflé is done). Serve the soufflé hot from the oven, with the tomato sauce in a sauceboat on the side.

Note: This recipe, which is made in many homes around Lyon, was devised to use leftover chicken livers, so as not to let them go to waste. It can be made with as few as one liver or as many as six, so if you like chicken livers, don't hesitate to double the amount given in the list of ingredients.

POULTRY

Truffled Roasted Bresse Hen
Poularde de Bresse truffée rôtie

SERVES 6 TO 8
PREPARATION TIME: 45 MINUTES, BUT BEGIN INITIAL PREPARATION THREE TO FOUR DAYS IN ADVANCE
COOKING TIME: 1 HOUR 30 MINUTES

1 hen weighing 4 lb. (1.8 kg), or about 3 lb. (1.4 kg) when gutted through the neck (ask your butcher to do this)

STUFFING

- 1 ¼ lb. (550 g) black truffles
- Scant ¼ cup (50 ml) Madeira wine, divided
- Scant ¼ cup (50 ml) cognac
- 2 tablespoons oil, butter, or other fat
- 1 sprig thyme
- ½ bay leaf
- 1 tablespoon plus 1 teaspoon (20 g) salt
- 3 peppercorns
- A generous pinch (2 g) four-spice mix
- 1 lb. (500 g) very fresh leaf fat (*panne*, the fat lining a hog's abdominal cavity and surrounding the kidneys)
- 4 ½ oz. (125 g) raw foie gras (if you do not have any, add an extra 4 ½ oz. (125 g) leaf fat)
- 2 strips fresh bard
- Salt and pepper

Three or four days ahead, stuff the fattened hen. For the stuffing, carefully brush and wash the truffles. Peel them–cut off as little as possible–and reserve the peel and trimmings. Chop these finely.

Cut about 12 slices from the finest truffles, place them in a bowl, and cover them with at least 1 tablespoon Madeira wine; enough to cover them adequately without completely soaking them. Quarter the remaining truffles and macerate them with the cognac, the remaining Madeira, and oil. Add the thyme, bay leaf, a pinch of salt, pepper, and a pinch of four-spice mix.

Cut the leaf fat into cubes, remove the surrounding membrane, and pound it with a mortar and pestle. When it is ground, add the foie gras and pound until you have a fine paste. Transfer the paste to a mixing bowl and place it in a fairly warm place to soften the fat. This will enable you to push it through a fine-mesh sieve more easily. When it is softened, add the finely chopped truffle trimmings, truffle quarters and the seasonings in which they have macerated. Remove the thyme and bay leaf and mix until thoroughly combined.

For this recipe, the hen must be gutted through the neck. Lift up the skin at the breast and slip the 12 truffle slices between the skin and the meat. Stuff the hen, fold down the skin at the neck over the opening, truss it, and bard it with the strips of fresh bard. Keep it in the refrigerator until you are ready to cook it.

Preheat the oven to 350°F (180°C). Cover the hen in buttered parchment paper. Place it on a rack in a roasting pan. Baste it with butter or poultry fat and place it in the oven for 1 hour 30 minutes. Turn it from time to time. Just 10 minutes before the cooking time is up, remove the paper and bard and allow the hen to brown lightly, spooning over the melted fat from the stuffing. To check for doneness, prick the thickest part of the thigh with a trussing needle. If the juice that comes out is clear, the hen is perfectly cooked. If it is pink, leave the hen to rest for a little while, turning the heat down in the oven and protecting the breasts with the strips of bard again. Remove some of the fat from the cooking juices and serve.

SERVES 6 TO 8
PREPARATION TIME: 40 MINUTES
COOKING TIME: 2 HOURS

Casserole-Roasted Fattened Hen with Chestnuts
Poularde poêlée châtelaine

- 1 fattened hen, weighing 4 lb. (1.8 kg), or about 3 lb. (1.4 kg) when gutted
- A few strips of fresh bard
- 4 tablespoons (60 g) butter, divided
- About 50 chestnuts
- 1 ⅔ cups (400 ml) broth of veal stock
- 1 small stick celery
- Salt and pepper

Season the hen inside and out with salt and pepper, bard it, and truss it. Heat 2 tablespoons (30 g) butter in a large ovenproof pot.

Place the hen in the pot, cover with the lid, and cook either in the oven at 350°F (180°C) or on the stove over very low heat. Keep an eye on how the browning proceeds: brown its thighs and back but make sure the hen stays as little as possible on its breast. Since there is very little evaporation, some juices will form at the bottom of the pot.

Grill the chestnuts lightly, or fry with the remaining butter, and then poach them in a little broth. They should remain fairly firm. Chop the celery and incorporate it into the chestnuts for flavor.

Fifteen minutes before the hen is cooked, remove the bard and twine. Arrange the still-firm chestnuts around the hen and leave to simmer without the lid, basting frequently and carefully. Now the breast of the hen should color slightly.

Transfer it to an oval platter and arrange the chestnuts around it like a necklace of big beads. Spoon the cooking juices over it all.

Joannès Nandron's Truffled Bresse Hen in a Pouch
Poularde de Bresse truffée en vessie Joannès Nandron

SERVES 4
PREPARATION TIME: ABOUT 1 HOUR
SOAKING TIME: 2 HOURS
COOKING TIME: 2 HOURS 15 MINUTES

- 1 pork bladder, plus salt and vinegar for soaking
- 1 Bresse hen, weighing about 4 lb. (1.8 kg)
- 8 large truffle slices
- 4 ¼ oz. (120 g) ground veal
- 5 tablespoons (80 ml) heavy cream
- 2 oz. (50 g) carrots
- 2 oz. (50 g) turnips, turned
- 2 oz. (50 g) celeriac
- 2 oz. (50 g) peas
- 2 oz. (50 g) green beans
- 1 leek, white part only
- 22 ½ pints (10 liters) white chicken stock, preferably prepared with the giblets and bones from the hen
- A little Madeira wine
- Salt and pepper
- Special equipment: a large tureen or stock pot (approximately 12 in. [30 cm] diameter or to hold at least 14 liters)

Ahead of time: Leave the pork bladder to soak in cold water with salt and a little vinegar for 2 hours, then pat dry. Remove the central bone from the hen, but leave the thigh and wing bones. Slip the truffle slices between the skin and the meat, spreading them between the breast and thighs.

Make a veal mousse: place the ground veal in a bowl placed over a larger bowl filled with ice and beat in the cream to make a smooth paste. Season and set aside.

Cook all the vegetables, season them, and combine them, with the exception of the leek, with the veal mousse. Fill the cavity of the hen with the mixture, inserting the leek white in the center.

Bring a pot of 22 ½ pints (10 liters) chicken stock to a boil.

Sew the hen shut and truss it so that it regains its original shape. Turn the pork bladder inside out and place the stuffed hen inside with a pinch of salt, pepper, and a few tablespoons of Madeira wine. Close the bladder tightly with string so that it is perfectly hermetic. Place the enclosed hen in the pot of hot stock and leave it to poach gently, without allowing the liquid to boil, for about 1 hour 30 minutes.

Remove it from the pot and present it to the guests, taking it out of the bladder. To carve, separate the wings and thighs. Serve each guest with a slice of hen accompanied by the vegetable and veal mousse mixture used to stuff the hen.

Note: 2 oz. (50 g) diced truffles and foie gras as well as the liver from the hen may be added to the ingredients listed.

This is one of the signature dishes of Joannès Nandron, a starred Michelin chef in Lyon, and the first chef outside Paris to obtain the prestigious Meilleur Ouvrier de France award in 1949.

SERVES 2
PREPARATION TIME: 10 MINUTES
COOKING TIME: 20 MINUTES

Chicken Breasts Françoise
Suprêmes de volaille Françoise

- 2 chicken breasts
- 4 oz. (110 g) green asparagus
- 3 tablespoons (50 g) butter, divided
- 1 tablespoon flour
- 2 tablespoons crème fraîche or heavy cream
- Salt and pepper

Preheat the oven to 475°F (240°C), or as high as it will go.

Cut the asparagus stems into small ½-in. (1-cm) slices and tie them together. Tie the tips together into several bunches. Throw them into well-salted boiling water and remove as soon as they are cooked–they will be done quickly–and transfer them to a sauté pan to stew with a little butter. Season with a pinch of salt. Just before serving, transfer them to a warmed platter and rub them with a knob of butter.

Ten minutes before serving, season the chicken breasts with table salt and freshly ground pepper. Dust them lightly with flour. Heat two knobs of butter in a suitably sized sauté pan and, when it is sizzling, arrange the chicken breasts flat in the pan. Spoon the melted butter over them, and cover with a tight-fitting lid. Place in the oven for about 5 minutes, depending on the thickness of the breasts.

In the center of a warmed round platter, arrange a heap of asparagus slices and top them with the tips. Place the breasts to either side of the vegetables. Deglaze the pan with crème fraîche and coat the chicken with this sauce.

Hen with Crayfish
Volaille de Bresse aux écrevisses

SERVES 4
PREPARATION TIME: 40 MINUTES
COOKING TIME: 40 MINUTES

1 Bresse or free-range hen, weighing 3 lb. (1.4 kg)

24 crayfish, preferably red-clawed crayfish, in Bordelaise Sauce (see p. 524)

4 tablespoons (60 g) butter, divided

2 oz. (50 g) shallots

2 oz. (50 g) carrots

1 tablespoon plus 1 teaspoon (20 ml) cognac

¾ cup (200 ml) dry white wine

3 ½ oz. (100 g) tomatoes

1 clove garlic

2 tablespoons (30 ml) heavy cream (optional)

1 sprig parsley, finely chopped

1 sprig tarragon, finely chopped

Salt and freshly ground pepper

Cut the hen into eight pieces. Prepare the 24 crayfish in the bordelaise sauce. Shell 20 crayfish and set aside.

Preheat the oven to 350°F (180°C).

Heat 3 tablespoons (50 g) butter in an ovenproof sauté pan. Season the chicken pieces with salt and pepper. As soon as the butter is hot, place them in the pan. Brown them very lightly, turning them over so that they color evenly. While they cook, finely chop the shallots and finely dice the carrots. Add this aromatic base to the pan. Put the lid on and place it in the oven, or else on the stove over low heat, until half cooked, about 15 minutes.

Deglaze the pan with the cognac and white wine. Leave to reduce a little. Roughly chop the tomatoes and crush the garlic. When the cooking liquid has reduced, add the tomatoes and garlic and leave to cook right through with the lid on.

Then transfer the chicken pieces to a serving dish. Again, reduce the cooking liquid a little and add the sauce from the crayfish. Leave to boil for a few minutes. Thicken the sauce with a generous piece of butter or 2 tablespoons (30 ml) heavy cream.

To finish, return the chicken pieces to the sauce with the 20 shelled crayfish tails.

Leave to simmer very briefly so that the flavors meld. If necessary, adjust the seasoning.

To serve, arrange the chicken pieces and the 4 remaining crayfish in a dish, pour the sauce over, and scatter with finely chopped parsley and tarragon.

SERVES 6
PREPARATION TIME: 30 MINUTES
COOKING TIME: 50 MINUTES

Chicken Marengo
Poulet sauté à la Marengo

- 1 chicken weighing about 3 ⅓ lb. (1.5 kg)
- 4 tablespoons (60 g) butter, divided
- 1 clove garlic
- ⅓ cup (75 ml) dry white wine
- ⅔ cup (150 ml) Tomato Sauce (see p. 544)
- ⅓ cup (75 ml) veal *jus*
- 12 mushrooms
- 6 small eggs
- 6 crayfish
- 6 slices bread
- 6 truffle slices
- Juice of ¼ lemon
- 1 sprig parsley, chopped

Preheat the oven to 425°F (210°C).

Roast the chicken in an ovenproof dish with half the butter for 35 minutes. Remove the chicken. Crush the garlic clove and throw it into the hot dish just before deglazing.

Deglaze the dish with the dry white wine and reduce it by two-thirds. Then stir in the tomato sauce and veal *jus*. Carve the chicken roughly into six pieces and keep warm.

Put the carcass and thighs into the dish with the sauce and bring to a boil. Remove from the heat and incorporate some butter.

Sauté the caps of the mushrooms and set aside. Fry the eggs, one per person. Truss the crayfish by pinning the claws to the tail. Cook them in a court bouillon or sauté them in butter. Prepare the toast: cut the bread into heart shapes and brown the slices in butter. Cook the truffle slices in the sauce for 2 minutes at the last minute.

Arrange the chicken pieces on a serving dish and garnish them with the mushroom caps. Pour the sauce over. Then squeeze the lemon juice over the pieces and sprinkle with chopped parsley.

SERVES 4
PREPARATION TIME: 15 MINUTES
COOKING TIME:
1 HOUR 20 MINUTES

1 Bresse or free-range chicken weighing 3 ½ lb. (1.6 kg), ready to cook

9 lb. (4 kg) kosher salt

Pepper

Chicken in a Salt Crust
Poulet de Bresse au sel

Preheat the oven to 475°F-525°F (240°C-270°C), or as high as it will go.

Season the chicken lightly with pepper.

Line the bottom and sides of a large pot, preferably one in cast-iron, with aluminum foil, leaving enough on the sides to fold over the top of the chicken. Pour in a good layer of salt.

Place the chicken in the center, breast downward. Cover it completely with salt and then fold the aluminum foil over to enclose it.

Place the pot in the oven for 1 hour 15 minutes.

To serve, turn the block of salt that forms out of the pot and remove the aluminum foil.

Present the dish to your guests and break the block of salt. The chicken should be perfectly cooked and moist, enhanced by the flavor of the iodine in the salt.

SERVES 4
PREPARATION TIME: 30 MINUTES
COOKING TIME:
1 HOUR 15 MINUTES

Bresse Chicken in a Soup Tureen
Poulet de Bresse en soupière

1 prepared Bresse or free-range chicken weighing 3 ½ lb. (1.6 kg)
2 lettuce hearts
3 ½ oz. (100 g) new carrots
7 oz. (200 g) fresh peas
3 ½ oz. (100 g) extra-fine green beans
2 oz. (60 g) new turnips
4 small white onions
7 tablespoons (3 ½ oz./100 g) butter
1 pinch sugar
7 oz. (200 g) puff pastry
Fine table salt and freshly ground pepper
Special equipment: a large tureen such as one you would use for onion soup, or casserole dish

Preheat the oven to 425°F (210°C).

Place the chicken in a large casserole dish or ovenproof tureen if you have one. Cut the lettuce hearts into quarters and the carrots into sticks. Place all the vegetables (lettuce, peas, beans, turnips, carrots, and onions) in the casserole around the chicken. Add the butter and season with salt, pepper, and a pinch of sugar.

Roll out the puff pastry thinly, until it is large enough to completely seal the casserole. Roll over the top of the casserole.

Place the casserole in the oven. Leave to cook for about 5 to 10 minutes, keeping an eye on the puff pastry. Then cover it with a sheet of aluminum foil so that it does not get too dark. Leave to cook for a further 45 minutes, then switch the oven off and leave the casserole in for another 15 minutes.

To serve, bring the casserole or soup dish to the table. Make an incision in the pastry with the tip of the knife—a wonderful aroma will waft out.

Carve the chicken in the classic way. Serve a portion of chicken to each guest, accompanied by the vegetables and a piece of puff pastry.

SERVES 4
PREPARATION TIME: 35 MINUTES
COOKING TIME: 50 MINUTES

Vallée d'Auge Chicken Fricassee
Fricassée de poulet vallée d'Auge

- 1 chicken weighing about 3 lb. (1.4 kg)
- 4 tablespoons (60 g) butter, divided
- 3 ¼ tablespoons (20 g) flour
- 2 cups (500 ml) clear stock or broth
- 1 small bunch parsley, tied together with ½ bay leaf
- 12 small onions
- 12 medium mushrooms
- Juice of ¼ lemon
- 2 egg yolks
- A little freshly grated nutmeg
- Scant ½ cup (100 ml) crème fraîche
- 4 slices bread
- Salt and pepper

Cut the chicken, separating the upper thighs from the legs, and cutting the breasts into three parts. Cut the carcass into four and add the wings, neck, and giblets.

Season with fine table salt and freshly ground pepper. In a low-sided pot large enough to hold the chicken snugly, heat half the butter and cook the chicken pieces over low heat without browning them. Stir frequently with a wooden spoon.

Sprinkle with flour and mix it through. Cook for a few minutes without allowing the contents of the pan to color. Pour in the stock (or water, if you do not have stock) and stir to dissolve the flour. Add the parsley with the ½ bay leaf. Cover with the lid and leave to simmer gently for 35 minutes.

While the chicken is cooking, barely cover the small onions in a pan with water and add a small knob of butter and a few grains of salt. Cook gently. Wash the mushrooms carefully and quarter them. Pour a tablespoon of boiling water into a pan with a small knob of butter, the juice of ¼ lemon, and a pinch of salt, and throw the quartered mushrooms in. Cook over high heat for 4 minutes. Transfer them to a bowl, reserving some of the liquid.

Prepare the liaison for the sauce: Place the egg yolks in a bowl. Stir in 2 tablespoons of the mushroom cooking liquid, a few knobs of butter, and a little freshly grated nutmeg. Dilute with the cream.

When the chicken is cooked, remove the pieces from the sauce and transfer them to another sauté pan. Top with the onions and drained mushrooms.

Strain the sauce through a muslin cloth over the chicken, rolling the pieces in it to coat them well. Arrange in a warmed serving dish. Cut the bread into heart shapes, brown the slices in butter, and place them around the chicken.

Coq au Vin
Coq au vin à la bourguignonne

SERVES 4 TO 6
PREPARATION TIME: 30 MINUTES
COOKING TIME:
1 HOUR 15 MINUTES

1 rooster or roasting chicken weighing 4 lb. (1.8 kg)

3 ½ oz. (100 g) bacon

4 tablespoons (60 g) butter

12 small onions

4 ½ oz. (125 g) button mushrooms

1 tablespoon flour

2 cloves garlic

8 cups (2 liters) red Burgundy wine, or other full-bodied red wine

1 small bouquet garni comprising parsley, a sprig of thyme, and a small piece of bay leaf

2 cups (500 ml) low-salt broth, or water

3 tablespoons pork blood

3 tablespoons cognac

Fine table salt and freshly ground pepper

Preheat the oven to 425°F (210°C).

Cut the rooster into pieces. Arrange the pieces on a tray with the giblets (but not the liver, which you should set aside for the sauce) and season with salt and freshly ground pepper.

Cut the bacon into small bits. Place them in a pot, cover with cold water, bring to a boil, and allow them to boil for 5 minutes. Drain and pat them dry.

Heat the butter in an ovenproof dish or casserole. Gently sauté the bacon bits and small onions until they are a nice golden color. Remove them, drain, and set aside, keeping the butter used.

Clean the mushrooms well: rinse them quickly in cold water. Cut them into quarters if they are large. Sauté them gently and transfer them to the same dish as the bacon bits and onions.

Turn the heat up to high and, using the same butter, gently brown the rooster pieces. Sprinkle them with flour, mix well, and leave to brown a little, without the lid, in the oven. Crush the garlic and add it to the dish after 5 minutes. Stir for 1 minute and pour in the wine. Reduce the oven temperature to 350°F (180°C).

Return the pot to the stove top and bring to a boil, stirring constantly. Then add the bouquet garni, onions, bacon bits, and mushrooms. Pour in just enough broth or water to cover all the ingredients. Put the lid on and cook for 45 minutes in the oven. When it is cooked, remove the casserole from the oven and transfer the rooster pieces and garnish to a bowl. If necessary, reduce the sauce to the quantity you want, before straining it through a fine chinois.

Clean the casserole dish and return the rooster and garnish to it. Pour the sauce over, bring to a boil again over the heat, and check the seasoning. To thicken the sauce, cut the liver into large cubes and season them with salt and pepper. Sear rapidly in a sauté pan with a small knob of butter. Push it through a sieve using a pestle. The sieve should be placed over the bowl containing the pork blood. Dilute with the cognac.

Remove the casserole with the rooster pieces from the heat to stop it boiling. Pour a little very hot sauce gradually into the bowl of pork blood, whisking as you do so. Then, when it is thoroughly mixed through, return it to the casserole, swirling it around so that it mixes in evenly. Do not allow the sauce to boil as it will curdle the blood: it will thicken anyway as the blood and the liver cook in the heat contained in the casserole dish. The sauce should be very creamy. Once again, check the seasoning.

You can serve the coq au vin in the casserole you have cooked it in, or transfer it to a deep serving dish, but it is better to use the casserole to ensure that this very fine dish remains hot.

Chicken Sautéed in Vinegar
Volaille de Bresse sautée au vinaigre

SERVES 4
PREPARATION TIME: 20 MINUTES
COOKING TIME:
1 HOUR 30 MINUTES

- 1 chicken weighing 3 ¼ lb. (1.5 kg)
- 1 ⅓ sticks (150 g) butter, divided
- 4 shallots
- 1 cup (250 ml) good red wine vinegar
- Salt and pepper

Preheat the oven to 425°F (210°C).

Cut the chicken into eight pieces and season with salt and pepper. Heat 7 tablespoons (100 g) butter in an ovenproof sauté pan large enough to hold all the chicken pieces. Color the chicken pieces just lightly, ensuring that the butter does not darken at all.

Put the lid on, transfer to the oven, and leave for about 20 minutes. While this cooks, chop the shallots.

The chicken pieces will now be just done. Transfer them to a serving platter (you will need the pan for the sauce), cover, and keep in a warm place.

Using the butter that still remains in the sauté dish, fry the chopped shallots until they are translucent. Deglaze with the wine vinegar. Reduce it by half and then whip in the remaining butter. Pour the sauce over the chicken pieces so that they are all coated.

SERVES 3
PREPARATION TIME: 40 MINUTES
COOKING TIME: 50 MINUTES

Squab with Peas
Pigeonneaux aux petits pois

- 3 squabs (young pigeons)
- 4 ½ oz. (125 g) bacon
- 4 ½ tablespoons (70 g) butter, divided
- 12 small white onions
- 1 lb. (500 g) garden peas
- 1 bouquet garni
- 1 pinch sugar

Have your butcher gut the squabs, but leave the liver (it contains no gall).

Truss the squabs, folding the thighs, and slipping the lower joints into an incision made in the fatty skin on either side of the cavity entrance. With a trussing needle, tie twine through the wings and the thighs.

Remove the rind from the bacon and cut it into large dice. Place in a pot of cold water, bring to a boil, and boil for 5 minutes. Drain, pat dry, and fry in a sauté pan with a knob of butter.

Remove the bacon bits with a slotted spoon, allowing the fat to drip off, and reserve on a plate.

Using the same butter, fry the small white onions until they are golden. Drain them and reserve with the bacon bits.

Then place the squabs in the pan, coloring them on all sides. You should put the lid back on every time you turn them. This will take 12 minutes. Remove them from the pan and keep them warm, covered with a dish.

Return the onions and bacon bits to the same pan. Add the peas, bouquet garni, and a pinch of sugar, as well as 2 tablespoons water, and cook over high heat with the lid on until the peas are almost done, about 15 to 20 minutes if they are freshly picked. Return the squabs to the pan and reheat them, ensuring that the liquid does not begin to boil.

Arrange the squabs in a warmed, deep serving dish. Remove the bouquet garni. Remove the pan from the heat, still with the peas in it, and whip in the remaining butter. Adjust the seasoning and spoon the garnish over the squabs. Serve immediately.

SERVES 2
PREPARATION TIME: 40 MINUTES
COOKING TIME:
1 HOUR 30 MINUTES

Duckling with Orange and Bigarade Sauce
Caneton poêlé à l'orange dit "à la bigarade"

1 duckling
5 ½ tablespoons (80 g) unsalted butter, divided
3 oranges
2 large sugar cubes
¼ lemon
2 teaspoons vinegar
2 tablespoons veal stock
1 pinch tapioca
Salt and pepper

Season the cavity of the duckling with salt and pepper, and place a large knob of butter inside. Gently pan-roast the duckling in some butter for 25 minutes, ensuring it remains slightly rare–it should be pink after it has rested for 10 to 15 minutes.

While it is cooking, remove the zest of the first orange. Cut into fine julienne strips and place in boiling water for 5 minutes. Drain the strips and pat them dry; set them aside.

Peel the first and second oranges, removing all the white pith. Cut out the segments between the membranes, remove the pips, and arrange the segments attractively around the dish in which you will be serving the duckling.

Rub the two cubes of sugar over the skin of the third orange and place the cubes directly into a small pan. Then squeeze the juice from the third orange into a bowl with the lemon juice. Strain the juice through a fine-mesh sieve lined with muslin cloth and set aside.

Cook the sugar cubes in the pan until they form a light caramel. Pour in the vinegar and reduce it until it is very thick and syrupy.

When the duckling is cooked, place it in the center of the orange segments. Take the pan juices and add the veal stock. Strain through a muslin cloth into the pan containing the caramelized sugar and bring to a boil briefly with a pinch of tapioca. When this stock is thoroughly cooked, it will be slightly syrupy. Remove from the heat and add the julienned zest and orange and lemon juice. Whip in the remaining butter, check the seasoning, and spoon some of the sauce over the duckling. Serve the remaining sauce in a separate bowl.

SERVES 4
PREPARATION TIME: 40 MINUTES
COOKING TIME: 40 MINUTES

Pigeon with Foie Gras and Truffle Sauce
Pigeon en bécasse à l'assiette

4 squabs (pigeons)
3 ½ oz. (100 g) foie gras
⅔ oz. (20 g) truffle
7 tablespoons (100 g) butter, divided
Scant ¼ cup (50 ml) cognac
1 cup (250 ml) white chicken stock
4 slices sandwich loaf
Salt and pepper

Divide the foie gras into two halves. Purée half and finely dice the other half. Cut the truffle into julienne slices and set aside.

Season the pigeons and roast them in a pot with 5 tablespoons (80 g) butter.

When they are cooked (the flesh should be pink), remove them from the pot and keep warm.

Deglaze the pot with the cognac and pour in the white stock. Leave to boil for a few minutes without allowing the liquid to reduce too much.

To thicken the sauce, whisk in the puréed foie gras. Then stir in the diced foie gras and julienned truffle.

Brown the slices of bread in the remaining butter and place one in each plate. Cut the squabs in half and place a half on each slice of bread. Pour generous servings of sauce over the dishes and serve immediately.

Wood pigeon or rock dove may be prepared using the same method.

SERVES 2
PREPARATION TIME: 20 MINUTES
COOKING TIME: 30 MINUTES

Duck Steaks
Steaks de canard

- 2 duck breasts
- 1 ⅓ sticks (150 g) butter
- 1 tablespoon chopped shallot
- 1 tablespoon aged Armagnac
- 1 cup (250 ml) red Burgundy wine, or other full-bodied wine
- Salt and pepper

Trim the duck breasts. Season them with salt and pepper.

Melt 3 tablespoons (50 g) butter in a sauté pan and color the duck without overcooking it: it should remain pink, almost rare.

When the duck steaks are done, transfer them to a serving dish and slice them.

Sweat the chopped shallot in the same pan and deglaze with the Armagnac and the red wine.

Reduce the sauce by half and then whip in the remaining butter. Adjust the seasoning.

To serve, coat the steaks with this fine sauce.

SERVES 6 TO 8
PREPARATION TIME: 45 MINUTES
COOKING TIME: 3 HOURS

- 1 good-sized goose, less than a year old
- 60 chestnuts
- 2 celery sticks
- Broth to poach the chestnuts
- 3 tablespoons (50 g) butter
- 7 oz. (200 g) fresh leaf fat (*panne*, the fat lining a hog's abdominal cavity and surrounding the kidneys)
- 9 oz. (250 g) fresh pork from a ham
- 12 small chipolata sausages, or other spicy pork sausages flavored with herbs
- 6 small truffled pigs' trotters (ready-made)
- 7 oz. (200 g) small firm white mushrooms
- 2 medium onions
- 2 shallots
- Scant ¼ cup (50 ml) cognac
- 1 egg, beaten
- 1 tablespoon (½ oz./15 g) herbed salt
- ½ teaspoon freshly chopped parsley
- Strips of bard
- Salt and pepper

Festive Stuffed Goose
L'oie du réveillon

Have your butcher gut the goose through the neck and remove the pouch of bile from the liver, which you should reserve. Remove any excess fat, including fat around the intestines, and reserve it.

Roast the chestnuts in the oven or plunge them in a bath of smoking hot oil. Peel them. Divide them into two lots: in one half, set aside the most attractive.

Cook them separately. Begin by cooking the less attractive chestnuts, which you will need for the stuffing. They should be boiled in broth with a stick of celery; keep the lid on as they cook.

Thirty-five minutes before serving, prepare the second batch: Take a sufficiently large sauté pan; the chestnuts should fit in side-by-side without being overcrowded. Finely chop the other celery stalk and sprinkle the pieces over the chestnuts. Dice 3 tablespoons (50 g) butter. Pour in just enough broth to cover the chestnuts and dot the pan with the butter cubes.

When the first lot of chestnuts is cooked but still fairly firm, drain them. Remove the lid from the pan of the second batch and reduce the broth with the butter until it forms a thick syrup (this will be enhanced by the natural sugar of the chestnuts). Then swirl the pan until all the chestnuts are well coated with the syrupy liquid. Do this very carefully so that you do not crush them.

For the stuffing, cut the leaf fat into small pieces and remove the membranes. Pound it with a pestle and mortar and leave in a warm place so that it can soften. When it is soft, push it through a fine-mesh sieve and set it aside.

Finely chop or process the pork and set it aside.

Cut the goose liver into large dice and set them aside.

Take 2 tablespoons of the goose fat that you have set aside and melt it in a sauté pan. When it is smoking, rapidly sear the goose liver pieces and season them with salt and pepper. Cook very briefly so that they remain red, and drain. Return to the plate.

Using the same fat, quickly brown the chipolatas or other sausages and return them to the plate.

Clean the mushrooms well and wash them quickly. Season them with a pinch of fine salt. Chop finely.

Chop the onions and shallots finely and soften them with the mushrooms over low heat. Stir in 3 tablespoons goose fat. As soon as it begins to heat, add the chopped pork and stir briskly for 5 minutes over high heat. Pour in the cognac and flambé. Stop the flames immediately and remove from the heat.

Pound the goose liver using the mortar and pestle or process in a blender. When it forms a paste, add the leaf fat and combine well. Then add the finely chopped pork. Lastly, stir in 2 tablespoons goose fat, the beaten egg, herbed salt, and chopped parsley.

To test the seasoning, poach a very small quantity before tasting.

Transfer the stuffing to a bowl and carefully stir in the mushrooms and the boiled chestnuts. Stuff the goose cavity, inserting the sausages into the stuffing as well as the truffled trotters.

Truss the goose and tie it with strips of bard. To pot-roast the bird, color the goose gently over low heat in melted butter or goose fat in a large cast-iron pot or Dutch oven. Continue cooking it with the lid on for 2-3 hours, spooning the pan juices over regularly. Ten minutes before the end of the cooking, remove the bard and twine. Since the goose will have cooked very slowly, there should be sufficient juices in the pot. However, if it has reduced too much, just add a few tablespoons of water.

Place the goose on an oval dish and surround it with the stewed whole chestnuts. Remove some of the fat from the liquid in the pot. Spoon a little of the sauce over the goose and serve the rest separately in a sauce dish.

SERVES 6 TO 8
PREPARATION TIME: 1 HOUR
MACERATION TIME: 24 HOURS
COOKING TIME:
2 HOURS MINIMUM

1 fat goose

3 ½ oz. (100 g) leaf fat (*panne*, the fat lining a hog's abdominal cavity and surrounding the kidneys), divided

Herbed salt

2 ¼ lb. (1 kg) finely crushed coarse salt

Preserved Goose
Confit d'oie

Have your butcher prepare the goose: it should have no blood remaining. Cut it open at the back from top to bottom. Gut it carefully, ensuring that the liver is not damaged (you can use it for another recipe). Remove the fat from the giblets and intestines and reserve.

Cut the goose into four: two wings with the breasts and two legs.

Rub the pieces both inside and out with the flavored salt. One generous handful is enough for one goose.

Place the quarters in a dish. Cover with the coarse salt and spread a clean dishcloth over the top. Leave to macerate for at least 24 hours in the refrigerator.

The next day, remove the goose pieces and shake off the salt. Carefully pat to remove any remaining salt. Clarify and strain some of the goose fat; do the same with some of the leaf fat. Heat them together until warm and place the pieces of goose in this warmed fat.

Heat slowly until it simmers gently; it should not fry. At first, the fat will be cloudy, but as the goose softens, the fat will gradually clarify. It takes about 2 hours for the goose to reach the right texture, and you will be able to tell that it is done when the fat is clarified, since the cooking is done on low heat. A needle should be able to penetrate the meat without any resistance.

Drain the goose pieces and remove any small bones protruding from the carcass and legs.

Pour a first layer of the fat used for the cooking into a sterilized jar and leave it to harden. Then arrange the pieces over the fat, ensuring they do not touch the sides of the jar. The remaining fat should have begun to harden (if it is completely hard, soften it slightly); spoon it into the dish to completely cover the pieces of

(*Continued overleaf*)

goose. Refrigerate. Two days later, melt some more fat and pour it into the jar so that it will fill any gaps remaining. The next day, cook some of the leaf fat and pour it in. It will harden. Cut out a piece of parchment paper to fit the jar and place on the fat. Seal with the lid and reserve in a cool, dry place.

Every time you take a piece of goose from the dish, first remove the layer of leaf fat and then the cooking fat. As you remove the pieces of goose, replace the initial layers of fat. You will be able to keep the remaining goose from one season to the next.

Chicken Mousseline Quenelles
Quenelles de volailles mousseline

SERVES 6
PREPARATION TIME: 30 MINUTES
RESTING TIME: 2 HOURS
COOKING TIME: 10 TO 15 MINUTES

- 1 lb. (500 g) chicken meat, all skin and sinews removed
- 2 egg whites, or less
- 1 ¾ teaspoons (9 g) salt
- 3 cups (750 ml) thick crème fraîche

Finely mince the chicken meat, gradually working in the egg whites and salt. It is important to remember that the texture of the quenelles is achieved by vigorously processing the meat, and that the only role of the egg whites is to ensure that the creamy mixture coagulates. For the most refined result, it is best to use as little egg white as possible.

The meat, egg whites, and salt will form a paste; push the paste through a sieve into a bowl. Place the bowl over crushed ice and briskly stir the paste until it is smooth. Leave to rest for 2 hours over the ice, changing it regularly so that the mixture remains cold.

Then stir again so that it is completely smooth. Stir in the cream, little by little. When the consistency is creamy, test the seasoning: Poach a little of the mousse in barely simmering water and taste. Adjust if necessary

To shape the quenelles, use 2 teaspoons or tablespoons, depending on the size you require.

Poach the quenelles in barely simmering water for 4-6 minutes depending on their size. Drain and serve.

SERVES 8
PREPARATION TIME: 15 MINUTES
COOKING TIME:
ABOUT 1 HOUR 30 MINUTES

5 ½ lb. (2.5 kg) capon (see Note)

2 cups (250 g) black olives

2 ½ tablespoons (40 g) butter (for the roasting pan)

½ cup (120 ml) warm water

3 ½ tablespoons (50 g) softened butter

Salt and pepper

Roasted Capon with Black Olives
Chapon de Bresse rôti aux olives noires

At least two hours ahead of time, take the capon out of the refrigerator.

Preheat the oven to 450°F-475°F (240°C), or as high as it will go.

Rinse the olives in cold running water and drain. Place them inside the capon, then sew up the bird to keep them inside while roasting. Sprinkle the capon with salt and pepper, place it in a generously buttered roasting pan, and roast for 1 ½ hours (about 17 minutes per pound). Baste after the first 15 minutes and every so often thereafter. Once the cooking time is up, turn off the oven, but leave the bird inside for another 10 minutes before serving.

To serve, lift the capon out of the roasting pan and carve; save any juices that come from it for the sauce. Remove the olives and place in a bowl. Break the softened butter into 10 pieces. Add the warm water and any carving juices to the roasting pan, place over high heat, and add the softened butter. Bring to a boil, whisking constantly; when all the butter has melted, add salt and pepper, and pour into a sauceboat.

Serve with the sauce and the olives on the side.

Serving suggestions: Serve with Sautéed Potatoes (see p. 492) or Green Beans (see p. 458).

Note: If a capon is unavailable, two 3 lb. (1.4 kg) chickens may be used instead. Follow the directions given here, but roast for only 50 minutes.

Languedoc Cassoulet
Cassoulet languedocien

SERVES 8 TO 10
PREPARATION TIME: 1 HOUR
SOAKING TIME: 2 HOURS
COOKING TIME:
3 HOURS 45 MINUTES

- 2 ¼ lb. (1 kg) haricot beans (French white *coco* beans)
- 9 oz. (250 g) bacon
- 9 oz. (250 g) fresh bacon rind
- 1 ¾ lb. (800 g) pork blade shoulder (US) or spare rib (UK)
- 1 dried garlic sausage weighing 7 oz. (200 g), uncooked
- 4 quarters preserved goose
- 2 teaspoons (10 g) salt
- 1 medium carrot
- 1 medium onion studded with 1 clove
- 1 bouquet garni comprising parsley, thyme, and bay leaf
- 3 cloves garlic
- 4 medium onions
- 5 tablespoons tomato purée
- 2 tablespoons light-colored bread crumbs
- Fine table salt and pepper

Wash the haricot beans carefully. Soak them for 2 hours (or according to the instructions on the packet), drain them, and place them in a large pot with 8 ½ pints (16 cups/4 liters) cold water and the bacon. Heat gently until it reaches boiling point. Skim off the scum that rises to the top and leave to boil for 5 minutes, then drain.

Rinse the pot and return the haricot beans to the heat with 8 cups (2 liters) cold water, 2 teaspoons (10 g) salt, the bacon, the bacon rind tied together in a bundle, the carrot, the clove-studded onion, and the bouquet garni.

Simmer over very low heat so that the haricot beans remain whole. This way, they will be properly cooked and not be damaged.

In a sauté or roasting pan, place the blade shoulder (spare rib) and cover it with goose fat from the preserved goose. Season with salt and pepper. Brown it on all sides. When it is nicely colored, transfer to a dish and set aside. Finely chop the four onions. Using the same fat, soften the chopped onions until they are translucent. Then crush the garlic and add it to the pan. Heat for 2 seconds, add the tomato purée, and a scant ½ cup (100 ml) of the haricot cooking liquid. Leave to simmer very gently for 5 minutes over minimum heat, using a heat diffuser if possible.

When the haricot beans are almost done, remove the carrot, onion, and bouquet garni. Leave enough cooking liquid for them to be just covered and add the pork blade shoulder, the dried sausage, the four quarters of preserved goose, and the softened onions.

Simmer over very low heat for 1 hour. The pot should barely bubble. Keep the lid on all the time.

At the end of the cooking time, remove all the pieces of meat from the haricot beans. Cut the pork and bacon into slices, cut the goose quarters into pieces, julienne the pork rind, remove the skin from the sausage and cut it into ⅛-in. (3-mm) slices. Check the seasoning of the haricots.

(*Continued on page 396*)

Fill an ovenproof pot or casserole with a ladleful of haricots and cooking liquid. Over that, spread a few spoonfuls of julienned rind, several slices of pork and bacon, pieces of goose, and sausage slices. Cover them all with haricots and continue creating alternate layers of meat and beans. Over the last layer of haricots, spread out some slices of bacon and dried sausage. Sprinkle with the bread crumbs and pour over some softened fat from the preserved goose. Cover with the lid. Cook in a 350°C (180°F) oven for 2 hours. Remove the lid 15 minutes before serving so a nice crust can form on the top. The cooking liquid should be reduced and thickened with the starch from the haricots.

Boiled Hen
Poule bouillie

SERVES 6
PREPARATION TIME: 15 MINUTES
COOKING TIME:
1 HOUR 30 MINTUES

- 5 ½ lb. (2.5 kg) top-quality stewing hen
- 1 celery heart (tender part of innermost ribs)
- 6 medium carrots
- 3 turnips
- 4 leeks
- Bouquet garni, made with 1 bunch parsley, 1 sprig thyme, and ¼ bay leaf tied together
- 1 tomato
- 2 onions
- 1 clove
- 4 teaspoons (30 g) kosher salt
- 3 peppercorns
- 6 medium potatoes

At least two hours ahead of time, take the hen out of the refrigerator. Cut the wing tips and neck off the hen and chop into small pieces; tie the bird as for roasting, and place with the neck and wings in a large pot. Split the celery lengthwise, remove the tough outer fibers from the larger stalks and wash the celery. Peel the carrots and cut them in half lengthwise. Peel the turnips. Split the leeks in quarters up to the white part, and wash them in hot water. Blanch and peel the tomato. Wash the parsley. Tie the thyme, bay leaf, and parsley together. Tie the leeks and celery together. Peel the onions and stick the clove in one of them. Add all the vegetables to the pot. Pour in enough cold water to cover completely, and add the salt and peppercorns. Bring to a boil, immediately lower the heat, skim off any foam, cover the pot, and simmer for 1 hour. Peel the potatoes, add them to the pot and cook 30 minutes more.

To serve, ladle out and strain enough of the bouillon to serve first as a soup, with slices of toasted country-style bread (save any leftover bouillon for use in other recipes). Remove and discard the bouquet garni, then lift the hen out of the pot and carve. Place on a hot platter, surround with the vegetables, and serve, with various Dijon mustards (flavored and unflavored), a bowl of kosher salt (to sprinkle over the meat), and Vinegar Pickles (see p. 553) on the side.

Boiled Turkey Dinner
Dindonne au pot

SERVES 6 TO 8
PREPARATION TIME: 20 MINUTES
COOKING TIME:
ABOUT 1 HOUR 30 MINUTES

- 4 ½ lb. (2 kg) turkey (see Note)
- 1 veal shank
- 1 oxtail, cut into pieces
- Bouquet garni, made with 1 leek, 2 stalks celery, 1 sprig thyme, and ¼ bay leaf
- 4 carrots
- 2 onions
- 1 clove
- About 16 cups (4 liters) cold water
- 2 tablespoons (30 g) kosher salt
- 5 peppercorns
- ¾ cup (180 ml) walnut oil
- 3 tablespoons red wine vinegar
- Salt and pepper
- 1 small bunch chervil

Two hours ahead of time, take the turkey, veal shank, and oxtail out of the refrigerator. Gut and truss the turkey.

Cut the leek lengthwise into quarters and wash it carefully in lukewarm water. Remove the tough outer fibers of the celery. Tie the leek, celery, thyme and bay leaf together with kitchen string.

Peel and wash the carrots, and cut them lengthwise in half. Peel the onions and stick the clove in one of them.

Fill a very large pot with the cold water, add the bouquet garni, onions, carrots, salt, and peppercorns; then add the turkey, veal, and oxtail and bring to a boil uncovered. Skim off any foam that rises, then immediately lower the heat, cover the pot, and simmer for 1 ½ hours.

Make a sauce by whisking together the oil, vinegar, and a little salt and pepper. Wash and coarsely chop the chervil. Just before serving, sprinkle in the chopped chervil.

First, serve a bowl of the bouillon as a soup, with slices of country-style bread. Then serve the different meats, sliced and arranged on a hot platter, with the sauce in a sauceboat on the side.

Serving suggestions: Thirty minutes before the meat has finished cooking, take some of the cooking liquid out of the pot, and use it to make Rice (see p. 510). Serve at the same time as the meat.

Note: A very small turkey is called for in this recipe; if you can't find one, use turkey legs only, or buy a large turkey and use one breast and one leg, cut apart (the other half of the turkey can be cut into pieces and used to make the Coq au Vin Juliénas, see p. 402).

Save any leftover bouillon and use it in other recipes.

SERVES 4 TO 5
PREPARATION TIME: 30 MINUTES
SOAKING TIME: 1 HOUR
COOKING TIME: 40 MINUTES

Pot-Roasted Chicken
Poulet cocotte

- 2 thin slices salt pork or bacon
- 3 lb. (1.4 kg) broiling or frying chicken (reserve the liver and gizzard)
- 4 tablespoons (60 g) butter, divided
- 6 baby onions, peeled
- 2 ¼ lb. (1 kg) new potatoes
- 1 tablespoon olive oil
- ½ teaspoon thyme leaves
- 4 tablespoons (60 ml) boiling water
- Salt and pepper

Remove the rind from the salt pork or bacon. Soak salt pork for an hour, then drain and pat dry with a clean cloth (bacon doesn't need to be soaked). Cover the thighs of the chicken with the salt pork or bacon (barding), and tie the slices in place with string or attach them with toothpicks.

Melt 2 tablespoons of butter in a pot (preferably cast-iron) slightly larger than the chicken, and add the chicken along with its liver and gizzard. Cook over low heat, turning frequently for even browning, for 20 minutes. Season with salt and pepper.

Peel the baby onions. Scrape the potatoes with a small kitchen knife, wash in cold water, then drain and pat dry with a cloth before cooking.

While the chicken is browning, heat 2 tablespoons of butter and the oil in a frying pan. Add the onions, potatoes, and thyme. Cook for 20 minutes, shaking the pan to brown the vegetables evenly. Season with salt and pepper (the chicken and vegetables should be done at about the same time). When the cooking time is up, lift the vegetables out of the pan with a slotted spoon, add them to the pot with the chicken, and continue cooking for 15 minutes.

To serve, lift the chicken out of the pot, and carve. Place on a hot platter and surround with the vegetables. Pour the boiling water into the pot that the chicken cooked in, bring to a boil, stirring constantly, season with salt and pepper if needed, and serve in a sauceboat on the side.

Serving suggestions: Serve with one of the salads (see pp. 60 or 68-70).

Note: This is ideally a dish for springtime, when new potatoes are in season.

SERVES 3 TO 4
PREPARATION TIME: 1 HOUR
COOKING TIME: 45 MINUTES FOR GUINEA HEN, 1 HOUR FOR PHEASANT

Pheasant or Guinea Fowl with Chestnuts
Poule faisane ou faisan ou pintadeau aux marrons

- 2 ¼ lb. (1 kg) chestnuts
- 3 to 4 thin slices salt pork or bacon
- Guinea hen or pheasant weighing 2–2 ½ lb. (900 g–1.15 kg) prepared for roasting
- 6 ½ tablespoons (100 g) butter, divided
- 4 tablespoons (60 ml) hot water
- Salt and pepper
- 1 truffle, finely chopped (optional)

Begin by preparing the chestnuts: since peeling them takes quite a while, it might be best to do that the day before cooking. Alternatively, use ready-peeled chestnuts. Chestnuts have two skins: a hard outer one and a thin, furry inner one that clings to the nut. To remove the hard outer one, make a slit in it with a sharp knife, then peel it off (be careful not to cut the chestnut in half when making the slit). Place the peeled chestnuts in a large saucepan, add enough water to cover, a little salt, then cover the pot and bring to a boil. Boil for 5 minutes, then remove the pot from the heat, but leave the chestnuts in the hot water. With a slotted spoon, remove the chestnuts from the water three or four at a time, and rub or peel off the inner skin using a clean cloth (this must be done while the nuts are very hot). Leave to cool, then place in a container, close tightly, and put them in the refrigerator overnight, or use them right away if peeling them the same day.

Attach the slices of salt pork or bacon to the guinea hen or pheasant using string or toothpicks to hold them in place.

Melt 2 tablespoons (30 g) of butter in a large pot. Season, and cook over moderate heat for 10 minutes, turning frequently (if the butter blackens, pour it off, wipe the pot clean, and replace with new butter). Butter a piece of parchment paper slightly larger than the pot, place it over the pot buttered side down, then cover the pot and cook about 40 minutes more, turning the bird once or twice.

Just before the bird has finished cooking, melt the remaining butter in a high-sided frying pan and sauté the chestnuts for 10 minutes, gently shaking the pan frequently to roll them in the butter and brown on all sides. Season.

Serve the bird whole or carve it, and place on a hot serving platter surrounded by the chestnuts. Add the hot water to the pot the bird cooked in, bring just to a boil, season and serve on the side.

One truffle, finely chopped, can be added to the sauce just before serving, if you like (but this is strictly optional).

SERVES 4 TO 5
PREPARATION TIME: 30 MINUTES
COOKING TIME: 40 MINUTES

Louhans-Style Chicken in Cream Sauce
Poulet sauté à la crème comme à Louhans

- 3 lb. (1.4 kg) broiling or frying chicken
- 8 white baby onions
- 1 carrot
- 4 tablespoons (60 g) butter
- 3 cloves garlic, whole and unpeeled
- 1 tablespoon (6 g) flour
- 1 ½ cups (½ bottle) dry white wine (preferably a Mâcon)
- 2 cups (500 ml) water
- Bouquet garni, made with thyme, ¼ bay leaf, parsley, leek, and celery
- ¾ cup (200 ml) crème fraîche or heavy cream, or
- 2 egg yolks, 4 tablespoons (60 ml) crème fraîche or heavy cream, and 1 tablespoon lemon juice
- Salt and pepper

Cut the chicken into eight pieces (wings and breasts separated, thighs and drumsticks separated), then chop the back and carcass into several pieces as well. Season well with salt and pepper.

Peel the onions. Peel and slice the carrot.

Melt the butter in a high-sided frying pan just large enough to hold all the pieces of chicken on the bottom. First brown the breast meat and wings. Lift them out and brown the thighs and drumsticks with the onions, garlic, and carrots. Lift these out, leaving the vegetables in the pot, and brown the back and carcass. When the back has browned, place the other pieces of chicken back in the pan, sprinkle in the flour, stirring and turning over the pieces of chicken. Then add the wine, water, and bouquet garni, bring to a boil, stirring, and cook over high heat for 20 minutes, or until two-thirds of the liquid has evaporated. Lift out the onions and the chicken, with the exception of the pieces of back and carcass, and keep warm between two plates while finishing the sauce. Boil the remaining liquid over high heat until half of the liquid has evaporated.

The sauce can be finished in one of two ways. In either case, strain the boiled liquid into a clean saucepan. Then, either simply add ¾ cup (200 ml) of cream and cook for about 4 minutes or until thick and creamy. Or, if thickening the sauce with egg yolks and cream, whisk the egg yolks and 4 tablespoons (60 ml) of cream together in a mixing bowl, add a small ladleful of the strained sauce, whisking rapidly, and pour the mixture into the saucepan, whisking constantly. Heat over low heat until very hot, but do not allow to boil, then add the lemon juice and taste for salt and pepper. The chicken and onions can be reheated in the sauce if need be, but stir the sauce constantly in this case, and do not allow it to boil or it will curdle. When the sauce is ready, spoon it over the chicken and onions on a hot platter and serve.

Serving suggestions: Serve with Spinach (see p. 474).

Coq au Vin Juliénas
Coq au vin de Juliénas

SERVES 6
PREPARATION TIME: 30 MINUTES
COOKING TIME: ABOUT 1 HOUR 10 MINUTES TO 1 HOUR 30 MINUTES

- 4 ¾ lb.-6 ½ lb. (2.2-3 kg) roasting chicken (see Note)
- Blood from the bird (see Note)
- 5 ounces (150 g) salt pork or slab bacon
- 8 medium (200 g) button mushrooms
- 1 medium (40g) carrot
- 8 baby onions
- 2 cloves garlic
- 1 large tomato
- Bouquet garni made with 2 sprigs (dry, or 1 sprig fresh) thyme, ¼ bay leaf, 4 sprigs parsley, 1 stalk celery, and the white of 1 leek
- 2 ½ tablespoons (40 g) butter
- 1 generous tablespoon (10 g) flour
- 3 tablespoons (50 ml) cognac
- 1 ½ bottles red wine (preferably Juliénas)

BEURRE MANIÉ (optional; see Glossary)
- 2 tablespoons (12 g) flour
- 1 ½ tablespoons (20 g) softened butter
- Salt and pepper

A true cock weighs 9-11 lb. (4-5 kg). If you make this recipe with a cock, double all measurements and the cooking time, and brown the bird in batches.

If possible, get a freshly killed bird and ask that its blood be saved for the sauce (see Note). Clean the bird and reserve the liver, heart, and lungs. Cut off the legs and separate the thighs from the drumsticks, cut off the breasts and divide them in half at the wing, then chop the remaining carcass, neck, and back into several large pieces. Sprinkle with salt and set aside.

Remove the rind from the salt pork or slab bacon, and cut into cubes. Cut off any dirt on the stem of each mushroom, and wash the mushrooms in cold water. Cut in half or into quarters. Peel the carrots, onions, and one clove of garlic. Blanch and peel the tomato, and cut into quarters. Cut the carrot into cubes. Tie the bouquet garni.

Chop the liver, heart, lungs, and peeled garlic to a paste and set aside in a bowl, along with the blood.

Melt the butter in a large pot, add the chicken, bacon, and onions, and brown, turning frequently, for about 7 minutes, then add the tomato, carrot, mushrooms, bouquet garni, and whole garlic. Cook slowly uncovered for 7 minutes more, then sprinkle in the flour and stir to combine. Cook 5 minutes, pour in the cognac and boil for a few seconds, stirring to dissolve the juices stuck to the bottom of the pan. Add the wine, bring just to a boil, then immediately lower the heat and cook at a slow boil, uncovered, for about 45 minutes to 1 hour. Test to see if the chicken is done by piercing a drumstick with the tip of a knife–it should go in easily. Remove the chicken from the pan; discard the back and carcass which were just for flavor. Remove the baby onions, bacon, and mushrooms with a slotted spoon and set them aside. Strain the remaining sauce, pour it back into the pot, and boil for 5 to 10 minutes. Then remove from the heat and stir in the

(*Continued on page 404*)

blood-liver mixture. Place over low heat and heat just until the sauce thickens; do not boil. Place the chicken, bacon, onions, and mushrooms back in the pot to warm through, taste for salt and pepper, then serve in the pot it was cooked in.

Note: The blood used does not necessarily need to come from the same bird. Six tablespoons (100 ml) pig's blood may be used instead, but if neither is available, use five chicken livers. Sear them for 1 to 2 minutes, then drain and allow to cool. Blend until smooth with ⅔ cup (150 ml) of the sauce, then whisk this mixture into the sauce. For a thicker sauce, whisk in some beurre manié.

Duck with Turnips
Canard aux navets

SERVES 4
PREPARATION TIME: 35 MINUTES
COOKING TIME: 40 MINUTES

- 3 lb. (1.4 kg) duck with liver, heart, and lungs
- 1 sprig parsley, leaves only
- 4 ½ oz. (125 g) salt pork
- 3 small shallots
- 3 duck or chicken livers
- 1 cup (40 g) coarsely crumbled dry or stale toast (or melba toast)
- 1 sprig thyme, leaves only
- ½ bay leaf, crushed
- Salt and pepper
- 1 egg yolk
- 1 pinch four-spice mixture (see Note) or allspice
- 2 lb. (900 g) turnips
- Nutmeg
- Generous ¾ cup (200 ml) crème fraîche or heavy cream
- 1 tablespoon cognac
- 5 teaspoons (25 g) softened butter, broken into 5 pieces, plus butter for pans

Prepare the duck for roasting and season; save the heart, liver, and lungs for the sauce. Preheat the oven to 425°F (210°C).

Wash the parsley, remove the stems and keep only the leaves.

Remove the rind from the salt pork. Peel the shallots, and roughly chop two shallots and the salt pork on a cutting board, along with the chicken livers. Add the toast, thyme, bay leaf, and parsley to the cutting board, and finely chop using a food mill. Add the egg yolk. Season with the four-spice mixture, then stuff the duck and sew it closed.

When the duck is ready to roast, prepare the turnips. Peel and slice them very thinly, blanch them for 2-3 minutes in lightly salted boiling water, then drain and cool under running water. Pat dry. Lightly butter a baking dish and arrange the turnip slices in an overlapping row. Season the first layer with salt, pepper, and nutmeg, then finish filling the dish. Spoon over the cream, season again, and set aside.

Place the duck in a lightly buttered roasting pan, add 4 tablespoons (60 ml) of water, and roast for a total of 50 minutes. After 30 minutes, place the turnips in the oven as well, and continue cooking for the final 20 minutes.

Chop the duck's liver, heart, and lungs to a paste along with the third shallot. Place in a small saucepan with the cognac, season, and cook over very low heat for 1 minute; remove from the heat. When the duck is done, remove it from the oven and carve it on a cutting board, saving any juices. Remove the legs and thighs, and place them on aluminum foil, skin-side down; place them back in the oven to continue cooking while you finish off.

Place the sliced duck breasts on a hot platter with the stuffing and keep warm. Discard almost all the fat in the roasting pan. Add the carving juices, the cognac-liver mixture, 5 tablespoons (750 ml) warm water, and the softened butter, and heat on top of the stove, stirring constantly. When the butter has melted, pour the sauce into a sauceboat. Remove the legs from the oven, place on the serving platter, and serve, with the turnips and sauce on the side.

Basque Chicken
Poulet basquaise

SERVES 6
PREPARATION TIME: 25 MINUTES
COOKING TIME: 50 MINUTES

- 1 free-range chicken cut into 12 pieces
- Scant ½ cup (100 ml) olive oil, divided
- 2 large onions
- 2 ¼ lb. (1 kg) tomatoes
- 5 cloves garlic
- 4 thick slices (9 oz./250 g) Bayonne ham or other cured ham
- 2 ¼ lb. (1 kg) Espelette peppers, or other small red bell pepper or mild chili pepper
- Salt and freshly ground pepper

Heat half the oil in a pot and brown the chicken pieces. Season them with salt and pepper. Put the lid on and leave to cook over low heat for 15 minutes.

Peel and slice the onions. Peel and seed the tomatoes.

Heat the remaining oil in a sauté pan and gently sauté the onions for 15 minutes. Add the tomatoes, season them with salt and pepper, cook until soft, then set aside and keep warm.

Peel and cut the garlic cloves into pieces. Add them to the chicken. Cut the ham into julienne slices and add them to the pot. Cook for a further 20 minutes.

Pour the softened tomatoes into a warmed serving dish. Arrange the chicken pieces over them, and then scatter with the julienned ham and chili peppers. If you are using Espelette peppers, you may use them either fresh or dried: just remove the seeds.

The chili peppers from Espelette, France's only native chili peppers, rank very low on the Scoville chili heat scale.

SERVES 6 TO 8
PREPARATION TIME: 30 MINUTES
MARINATING TIME: 3 HOURS
COOKING TIME:
1 HOUR 45 MINUTES

1 young hare
A few thyme leaves, crushed
1 bay leaf, crushed
2 large onions
2 tablespoons olive oil
1 tablespoon Armagnac
3 tablespoons (50 g) butter
9 oz. (250 g) bacon
24 small onions
9 oz. (250 g) firm white button mushrooms
2 medium carrots
Scant ½ cup (45 g) flour
2 cloves garlic, crushed
4 cups (1 liter) good red Burgundy wine
1 bouquet garni
12 slices of bread
⅓ cup (75 ml) cognac
4 tablespoons crème fraîche or heavy cream
1 pinch chopped parsley
Salt and pepper

Hare in Red Wine
Civet de lièvre

When you prepare the hare or have it prepared, ensure that the blood accumulated around the lungs and throat is collected. Reserve the liver, making sure that the bile pouch has been removed.

Cut the hare into 10 pieces and season with fine table salt, freshly ground pepper, crushed thyme leaves, and crushed bay leaf. Slice 1 onion into rounds and add them to the meat with the olive oil and Armagnac. Combine all the ingredients well and leave to marinate for 3 hours in the refrigerator, turning the pieces over from time to time.

Cut the bacon into large bits. Place in a pot with 2 cups (500 ml) cold water and bring to a boil. Leave to boil for 5 minutes, drain, and pat dry. Peel the small onions. Wash the mushrooms quickly using cold water, drain, and pat dry. Halve or quarter them if they are large. Heat the butter in a heavy-bottomed ovenproof pan or pot large enough to contain all the pieces of the hare side by side. When the butter is sizzling, add the bacon bits. When they begin browning, add the small onions and leave them to color gently. Then add the mushrooms, season them with a pinch of salt and turn the heat up. Sauté them, then remove with a slotted spoon to a plate or dish.

Chop the other onion and cut the carrots into about 4 large chunks each. Using the same butter and melted fat (adding a little if necessary), sauté the chopped onion and the carrots. Sprinkle with flour and stir constantly with a wooden spoon over low heat until the flour has turned a light golden color.

Preheat the oven to 350°F (180°C).

Drain the pieces of hare and pat them dry. Sear them in the roux (fat and flour mixture), still stirring constantly with a wooden spoon. When this is done, sprinkle the crushed garlic over, mix together, and pour in enough red wine to just cover the hare.

(Continued overleaf)

Bring to a boil, stirring all the time, and continue to stir until the sauce is quite smooth. Check the seasoning, adding salt if necessary, add the bouquet garni, and cover the pot with the lid. Cook in the oven for 45 minutes. Remove the pot from the oven, but leave the oven on at the same temperature.

Transfer the pieces of hare to an ovenproof sauté pan, using a slotted spoon so that the juices drip back into the pot.

Arrange the bacon bits, small onions, and mushrooms over the hare. Strain the sauce through a fine-mesh sieve over the pan, pressing down hard on the garnish (the onion, carrots, and bouquet garni).

Bring to a boil over high heat, check the seasoning, cover with the lid, and then return the sauté pan to the oven for a further 45 minutes.

While it is cooking, cut the slices of bread into heart shapes, brown them in butter, and set them aside in a warm place.

Press the liver over a fine-mesh sieve into a bowl and combine the purée with the blood. Stir in the cognac and crème fraîche and mix thoroughly.

To thicken the sauce: when the stew is cooked, remove it from the oven and place it on the corner of the burner so that it does not boil. Spoon a little of the sauce into the whisked blood, puréed liver, and crème fraîche. The ingredients will combine gradually with the hot sauce and will not curdle if they do not come into sudden contact with heat. Pour all this liquid through a fine-mesh sieve, moving it around above the sauté pan and swirling the pan with the other hand to combine all the ingredients. Press down hard on the contents of the sieve; there should be nothing remaining. Ensure that the stew does not boil at all while you are working.

When the sauce is well blended, increase the heat slightly, still moving the pan back and forth, until the first signs of boiling. Immediately transfer the stew to a serving dish and arrange the browned bread around it. In the center, sprinkle the fresh chopped parsley. The sauce should be thickened, creamy, and a dark ash-gray color.

SERVES 4
PREPARATION TIME: 30 MINUTES
COOKING TIME: 50 MINUTES

Limousine-Style Stuffed Partridges
Perdreaux farcis à la limousine

2 young partridges

STUFFING
1 oz. (30 g) bread
A little milk or broth to soak the bread
1 small onion
2 shallots
2 tablespoons (30 g) butter
3 ½ oz. (100 g) porcini stems taken from the caps for the garnish
2 partridge livers
2 chicken livers
2 oz. (50 g) cooked ham
1 egg, beaten
½ teaspoon chopped parsley
1 small pinch four-spice mix
Salt and pepper

TO ROAST AND GARNISH
2 strips bard
2 vine leaves
4 ½ oz. (125 g) bacon
2 tablespoons (30 g) butter
3 ½ oz. (100 g) fresh porcini caps
2 tablespoons olive oil
2 tablespoons veal *jus*
2 tablespoons chopped parsley
Salt and pepper

For the stuffing, soak the bread in the milk or broth for a few minutes. Squeeze out any excess liquid and set aside. Finely chop the onion and shallots and fry in butter over low heat until transparent. Finely chop the porcini stems and add them to the pan. Season with a pinch of salt. Turn the heat up to maximum and cook, stirring all the time, for 3 minutes. Then leave to cool.

Sear the partridge and chicken livers in butter, but leave them very rare. Dice the ham. Process the onion and mushroom mixture, livers, ham, bread, egg, chopped parsley, salt, pepper, and spice mix together and stuff the cavities of the partridges.

Preheat the oven to 450°F-475°F (240°C), or as high as it will go.

Truss the partridges, season them, and tie them with bard. Under each bard, place a vine leaf. Remove the rind from the bacon and cut it into small bits. Place the bacon pieces in 4 cups (1 liter) cold water, bring to a boil and boil for 5 minutes, drain, and pat dry.

Brown the bacon bits in butter, using an ovenproof pan or casserole large enough to hold the partridges. Drain the bacon bits and replace them with the partridges. Brown them on all sides.

Slice the porcini caps and season them with salt and pepper. Brown them in very hot oil and drain them. Mix them with the bacon bits and surround the partridges with the mixture. Place the lid on the pot and cook in the oven for 25 minutes.

Just a few moments before you remove the casserole from the oven, pour in the veal *jus*. Sprinkle chopped parsley over the top. Replace the lid and transfer to the stove. Boil for 1 minute and serve, over a folded napkin on a dish.

SERVES 2
PREPARATION TIME: 30 MINUTES
MARINATING TIME: 4 HOURS
COOKING TIME: 1 HOUR 30 MINUTES

1 good-sized saddle of hare

3 ½ oz. (100 g) fatback (cut of pork fat from pig's back)

7 tablespoons (100 g) butter

Scant ½ cup (100 ml) cognac

Salt and pepper

MARINADE

1 bottle red Burgundy wine, or other full-bodied red wine

2 carrots

1 medium onion

Thyme

Bay leaf

Crushed pepper

POIVRADE SAUCE

1 lb. (500 g) bones and trimmings from the hare

7 oz. (200 g) diced vegetables for the aromatic garnish (equal parts of finely diced onion, carrot, and celery)

Scant ¼ cup (50 ml) oil

Scant ¼ cup (50 ml) vinegar

1 slightly heaped tablespoon (10 g) black peppercorns, roughly crushed

1 small bouquet garni

2 oz. (50 g) beurre manié (see Glossary)

⅔ cup (150 ml) hare blood

Salt

Hare with Poivrade Sauce
Râble de lièvre, sauce poivrade

Plan the timing of this recipe carefully: the saddle marinates for 4 hours, and you will need the marinade to make the sauce.

Trim the hare and set aside the trimmings for the base of the sauce. Remove all sinews. Cut the fatback into thin lardoons and sew them into the saddle. Prepare the marinade: Cut up the carrots, slice the onion, and combine them with the thyme, bay leaf, and crushed pepper. Pour in the wine. Leave the saddle to marinate for 4 hours in the refrigerator.

When the hare has marinated, drain the saddle, reserving the marinade for the sauce, and season it with salt.

For the poivrade sauce, cut the hare trimmings into small pieces and brown them in the oil with the bones in a pot. Dice the vegetables and add them. Leave to cook for a few moments. Deglaze with the vinegar and leave to reduce until almost dry. Strain the marinade and pour it over. Season with salt and crushed pepper. Add the bouquet garni and cook for 1 hour over low heat. Strain the sauce and thicken it with the beurre manié. Then incorporate the blood (see method on page 415).

Adjust the seasoning and strain again through a fine-mesh sieve. Before using, heat it up over a hot water bath or using a double-boiler (it should not come into contact with direct heat because of the blood). While heating up the sauce, preheat the oven to 375°C (190°F).

Roast the saddle with the butter in a cast-iron dish, for 10 to 15 minutes–the meat must remain pink. Transfer the hare to a serving dish and keep warm, tented with aluminum foil.

Deglaze the roasting pan with cognac. Leave it to reduce by half and add 2 cups (500 ml) of the poivrade sauce.

Cut the saddle into thin slices. To serve, place them over the backbone so that the saddle looks whole. Serve the sauce separately. This dish is excellent when accompanied by puréed chestnuts.

SERVES 4
PREPARATION TIME: 20 MINUTES
COOKING TIME:
1 HOUR 15 MINUTES

1 wild rabbit weighing 3 ½ lb. (1.5 kg)
5 oz. (150 g) bacon
15 small onions
5 oz. (150 g) button mushrooms
2 tablespoons (30 g) butter
1 bay leaf, crushed
1 sprig thyme, leaves crushed
2 scant tablespoons flour
2 cloves garlic, crushed
1 ¼ cups (300 ml) dry white wine
2 cups (500 ml) veal *jus*, broth, or water
1 bouquet garni
Chopped parsley for garnish
Salt and pepper

Wild Rabbit Stewed in White Wine
Lapin de garenne en gibelotte

Cut the bacon into large bits. Place them in a pot with 2 cups (500 ml) water, bring to a boil, and boil for 5 minutes. Drain and pat them dry. Peel the onions and plunge them briefly in boiling water, then drain. Remove the bases from the mushroom stems and wash the mushrooms quickly in cold water.

Heat the butter in a sauté pan large enough to contain the stew. Begin browning the bacon bits and add the onions, stirring frequently. When they are a nice golden brown, add the mushrooms and leave to cook over high heat for 5 minutes. Remove the bacon, onions, and mushrooms with a slotted spoon, allowing the pan juices to drip off, and transfer them to a serving dish.

Preheat the oven to 350°F (180°C).

Cut the rabbit into pieces, setting aside the liver. Remove any green matter from the liver. Brown the rabbit in the same sauté pan as before, adding a little more butter if necessary. Season with salt, pepper, crushed bay leaf, and crushed thyme.

When the pieces are browned, sprinkle them with the flour. Stir well and allow to color a little. Scatter the pan with the crushed garlic, stir through, and pour in the white wine. Add enough veal *jus*, broth, or water to just cover the pieces. Add the bouquet garni and bring to a boil, stirring constantly. Cover with the lid and cook in the oven for 30 minutes.

After 30 minutes, add the bacon bits and cooked onions and mushrooms. Adjust the seasoning and cook for a further 25 minutes. Then add the liver and cook for 5 minutes more.

If there is too much sauce because it has simmered too gently, transfer it to a saucepan and cook over high heat until you have just enough. Arrange the wild rabbit in a serving dish, remove the bouquet garni, and pour the sauce over it.

Sprinkle with the fresh chopped parsley.

SERVES 6
PREPARATION TIME: 20 MINUTES
COOKING TIME: 50 MINUTES

Roasted Pheasant
Faisan rôti

1 young pheasant, with its liver
Strips of bard
3 tablespoons (50 g) butter, melted
1 slice of bread, thick and large enough to hold the pheasant
1 chicken liver
A pinch of four-spice mixture
5 oz. (150 g) bacon
1 tablespoon good cognac
2 tablespoons veal *jus*, broth, or water
Salt and pepper

Set aside the pheasant liver. Preheat the oven to 450°F-475°F (240°C), or as high as it will go. Season the cavity of the pheasant with salt and pepper. Truss it with twine and protect it with strips of bard, as the flesh of the breast meat is very fragile.

Place the bird on its side in a roasting pan on the rack. Moisten it with the melted butter and season it with salt and pepper. Place in the oven and cook for 25 to 30 minutes, depending on the size. Turn it regularly, ensuring that the breast is not exposed to any direct heat. Baste it frequently with the melted butter in the pan. Do not let it overcook; it should be pink.

Five minutes before the cooking is done, remove the pheasant from the oven and take the twines and bard off. Return the pheasant to the oven and allow the breast meat to brown for the last 5 minutes. Keep the bard warm; you can use it later to serve. Leave the pheasant to rest for a few minutes before serving.

Meanwhile prepare the bread: either brown it in butter or cook it in the pheasant cooking juices. The latter gives a better taste, but a less defined color. Next, prepare the mixture to be spread on the bread. Cut the two livers (chicken and pheasant) into two or three pieces. Season them with salt, pepper, and spices. Cut an equal amount of bacon into dice and melt in a small sauté pan. Throw in the pieces of liver. Sear them and cook them over high heat until half cooked through. Remove from the heat and deglaze the pan with the cognac to dissolve the cooking juices. Pour the contents of the pan into a sieve placed over a bowl and push them through. Smooth the purée and spread it over the slice of bread. Place it briefly in the oven so the top forms a light crust. Place the pheasant on the bread.

Deglaze the roasting pan with the veal *jus* or broth. Serve the juices separately in a gravy dish.

Carve the bird at the table. First detach the two thighs, then the two wings, cutting through the breast. Separate the breast from

(*Continued overleaf*)

the carcass and cut in two. Cut the bread with the liver into six pieces and place one piece of the pheasant on each piece to serve. If the pheasant has been correctly cooked, its flesh will be light pink. The drops of juice it will exude when cut will be the same color.

Serving suggestions: To serve, place an attractive bouquet of watercress and 2 lemon halves at each end of the serving dish, and drape the warm bard over the bird. Alternatively, serve with roasted mushrooms, baby onions, and pieces of bacon. This dish is usually accompanied by straw potatoes or homemade potato chips (crisps).

Lyon-Style Rabbit
Lapin sauté à la lyonnaise

SERVES 4
PREPARATION TIME: 30 MINUTES
COOKING TIME: 50 MINUTES

- 3 lb. (1.4 kg) rabbit
- 1 tomato
- 5 oz. (150 g) salt pork or slab bacon
- Bouquet garni, made with 1 sprig fresh or 2 sprigs dried thyme, ¼ bay leaf, and 2 sprigs parsley
- 4 shallots
- 9 oz. (250 g) fresh mushrooms
- 2 cloves garlic, whole and unpeeled
- 7 tablespoons (100 g) butter
- Generous ½ cup (150 ml) dry white wine
- Salt and pepper

Ask your butcher to cut the rabbit into 10 pieces. Season.

Blanch and peel the tomato, and set aside. Remove the rind from the salt pork or slab bacon, and cut into ½-in. (1-cm) cubes. Tie the bouquet garni. Peel the shallots. Cut off the bottom of the mushrooms, wash them and cut them into quarters.

Melt 5 tablespoons (75 g) of butter in a large, high-sided frying pan. When it foams, add the rabbit, shallots, garlic, salt pork, and bouquet garni and cook for 10 minutes, turning frequently, to brown evenly. Cut the tomatoes into quarters, add to the pan and cook very slowly, uncovered, for 25 minutes, turning three to four times. While the rabbit is cooking, melt 2 tablespoons (30 g) of butter in a small frying pan, add the mushrooms, and sauté until all their moisture has evaporated and they begin to brown. Lift them out of the pan and add them to the rabbit.

When the 25 minutes of cooking time is up for the rabbit, add the white wine, stirring to detach any meat juices, cover, and cook for 8 minutes more over very low heat. Taste for salt and pepper, then remove the pan from the heat and leave the rabbit 5 minutes longer in the pan. Place the rabbit in a hot serving dish, pour over the sauce, and serve.

SERVES 6 TO 8
PREPARATION TIME: 20 MINUTES
COOKING TIME: 1 HOUR TO 1 HOUR 30 MINUTES

5 ½ lb.-6 ½ lb. (2.5-3 kg) rabbit or hare
Blood from the animal
5 small onions
3 carrots
2 cloves garlic
Bouquet garni, made with 2 sprigs parsley, 1 sprig thyme, ¼ bay leaf, 1 stalk celery, and the white of 1 leek
7 ounces (200 g) salt pork or slab bacon
2 sprigs parsley, leaves only
3 tablespoons cognac
1 teaspoon vinegar (if using blood)
7 tablespoons (100 g) butter
1 bottle red wine (preferably Burgundy)
2 tablespoons (12 g) flour
4 tablespoons (60 ml) hot water

BEURRE MANIÉ (optional; see Glossary)
2 tablespoons (12 g) flour
1 ½ tablespoons (20 g) softened butter
Salt and pepper

Rabbit Sautéed in Red Wine
Lapin en civet ou civet de lièvre

If possible, use a freshly killed animal and save the blood (mixed with a teaspoon of vinegar) for making the sauce. Save the liver, heart, and lungs for the sauce as well. Cut the rabbit or hare into 8 to 10 pieces. Season with salt and pepper.

Peel the onions, carrots, and one clove of garlic (leave the other clove unpeeled). Prepare and wash the celery and the white of the leek. Tie together the bouquet garni. Remove the rinds from the salt pork or bacon and cut them into ½-in. (1-cm) cubes. Chop the carrots and onion.

Chop the liver, heart, lungs, peeled garlic, and parsley using a food mill. Place this mixture in a bowl, add the cognac, season with salt and pepper, and reserve. In another bowl, place the blood and the vinegar, and reserve.

Melt the butter in a pot large enough to comfortably hold the rabbit. When the butter starts to foam, add the pieces of rabbit and cook for 20 minutes, turning frequently to brown on all sides.

In a saucepan, bring the red wine to a boil. When the pieces if rabbit are well browned, sprinkle the 2 tablespoons of flour over them and stir in the hot water to bind the sauce, then pour in the boiling red wine. Add the onions, carrots, bacon, bouquet garni and the whole garlic, bring to a boil, then immediately lower the heat and boil slowly uncovered for 25 minutes; at the end of this time, place over very low heat (use a heat diffuser if you have one) and simmer very slowly for another 10 minutes.

Lift the pieces of rabbit out of the pot and place in a hot serving dish. Keep warm while making the sauce. Strain the cooking liquid and place back into the pot over moderate heat. Mix the blood with the liver-cognac mixture, stir in a little of the cooking liquid, then pour back into the pot, stirring. Heat until the sauce thickens, but do not allow to boil, stirring constantly. If you feel the sauce should be thicker, whisk in some beurre manié. When smooth, pour the sauce over the rabbit and serve.

SERVES 4
PREPARATION TIME: 30 MINUTES
COOKING TIME:
2 HOURS 30 MINUTES

- 2 partridges
- 1 Savoy cabbage
- 7 oz. (200 g) bacon
- 3 tablespoons chicken fat or lard, divided
- 1 medium carrot
- 1 onion studded with 1 clove
- 1 bouquet garni comprising 1 sprig thyme and 1 piece of bay leaf
- 1 dried garlic sausage weighing approx. 5 oz. (150 g)
- 4 cups (1 liter) broth
- 6 chipolata sausages, or other spicy pork sausages flavored with herbs
- Crushed sea salt and freshly ground pepper

Partridge with Cabbage and Bacon
Perdrix aux choux

Preheat the oven to 450°F-475°F (240°C), or as high as it will go.

Blanch the cabbage leaves with the bacon in a large pot of boiling salted water for 15 minutes. Drain, refresh, and drain again. Spread the leaves on a large tray and season them with crushed sea salt and freshly ground pepper.

Place the partridges in the hot oven to color them, using some of the chicken fat or lard as you would to start off a roast. This should take 8 minutes. Remove from the oven. You will be deglazing the roasting pan, so do not clean it yet. Reduce the heat to 250°F (120°C).

Prepare an ovenproof pot or Dutch oven large enough to hold the cabbage, partridges, and garnish. At the bottom, place the bacon rind, one-third of the cabbage leaves, the partridges, the carrot, the onion, and the bouquet garni. Then set out the second third of the cabbage, the bacon, dried sausage, and top with the last third of the cabbage leaves. Add the remaining fat and pour in enough broth for the ingredients to be just covered. Place over the stove at high heat until boiling.

Take 3 tablespoons of the broth and dissolve the bits at the bottom of the roasting pan with it. Add this to the pot. Cover with a greased piece of parchment paper and put the lid on. Bring to a boil and then transfer to the oven for 1 hour 30 minutes to braise. Remove the dried sausage after 30 minutes and the bacon after 45 minutes, reserving them somewhere warm.

Towards the end of this cooking time, grill the sausages, and cut the bacon into fairly thick rectangles and the dried sausage into thick slices. When the partridges are cooked, transfer them to a tray or plate. Remove the cabbage leaves with a slotted spoon, allowing as much liquid as possible to drip off, and arrange them in a dome shape on a round dish. Remove the carrot and slice into rounds. Arrange the partridges, back to back, over the cabbage leaves, with the legs facing upwards. Place the grilled sausages and bacon between them, and around them arrange a circle of alternating slices of dried sausage and carrot rounds.

SERVES 4
PREPARATION TIME: 20 MINUTES
COOKING TIME: 1 HOUR

Rabbit Sautéed in Dijon Mustard
Lapin à la moutarde

3 lb. (1.4 kg) rabbit
6 medium (150 g) fresh button mushrooms
Bouquet garni, made with 1 sprig thyme, ¼ bay leaf, and 4 sprigs parsley
½ cup (150 g) Dijon mustard
4 ½ oz. (125 g) salt pork or bacon
9 oz. (250 g) baby onions
3 cloves garlic, whole and unpeeled
5 tablespoons (75 g) butter
1 cup (250 ml) dry white wine
6 tablespoons (100 ml) whipping cream
1 tablespoon lemon juice
Salt and pepper

Fresh Dijon mustard is essential for this recipe; buy a new jar the day you are planning to cook the rabbit. It is best to use a cast-iron or enameled cast-iron pan.

Cut off any dirt from the stem of each mushroom, quickly wash the mushrooms, and cut them into four or six pieces, depending on their size. Wash the parsley and tie the bouquet garni.

Use a large knife to cut the rabbit into 10 pieces on a cutting board, or if you prefer ask your supplier to do it for you. Salt and pepper the pieces of rabbit, then use a spoon to coat them on all sides with the mustard. Set aside in a large glass bowl.

Remove the rind from the salt pork and dice the salt pork. Peel the onions. Prepare the garlic, keeping a thin layer of skin on each clove.

Heat the butter in a high-sided frying pan. When it begins to foam, add the rabbit, salt pork, onions, bouquet garni, and garlic. Brown over high heat, turning frequently, for 20 minutes. Add the wine, scraping the bottom of the pan to dissolve any juices stuck to it, and the mushrooms. Cook over moderately low heat for 10 minutes, lower the heat, cover, and simmer very slowly for a further 15 or 20 minutes to finish cooking.

Lift the pieces of rabbit, the onions, the mushrooms, and pork out of the pan with a slotted spoon and place them on a hot platter. Discard the bouquet garni. Whisk the cream into the pan juices (if all the wine has evaporated, add 6 tablespoons (100 ml) of water as well), heat until almost boiling, then stir in the lemon juice, remove from the heat, add salt and pepper if needed, spoon over the rabbit, and serve immediately.

Note: A chicken of the same weight can be cut into pieces and cooked in the same way. For a more pronounced mustard taste, save a generous tablespoon of mustard and, just before serving, stir it into the sauce away from the heat.

VEGETABLES

SERVES 4
PREPARATION TIME: 10 MINUTES
COOKING TIME: 10 MINUTES

Artichokes with Various Sauces
Artichauts avec sauces diverses

4 globe artichokes
1 pinch parsley or chervil
Salt

Cut the artichoke stems at the base of the leaves. Using a pair of scissors, cut off the tips of the outside leaves and trim off the top third. Wash the artichokes and tie them so that the leaves stay in place while they boil. Prepare a pot of boiling water and place the artichokes in it. Leave them to cook for 10 minutes and drain the water off.

Place them in a fresh pot of boiling water, add salt, and cook at a good boil.

To check for doneness, press lightly on the bottom of an artichoke. If it gives way easily, or you can easily detach one of the outside leaves, they are done.

To serve hot:
Drain the artichokes and place them upside down over a dishcloth or towel. Serve them accompanied by a bowl of melted butter, Hollandaise Sauce (see p. 548), mousseline sauce, cream sauce, Béchamel or White Sauce (see p. 536), and so on.

To serve cold:
Allow the artichokes to drain and cool upside down. Remove the central leaves from the artichokes and set them aside. Then scrape out the fuzzy choke. Take the central leaves and put them, tips inside, into the artichoke. Place the chopped parsley or chervil within the little bowl shape formed by the bottom of the leaves. Accompany with a cold sauce, such as a Vinaigrette (see p. 542), light Mayonnaise (see p. 552), with or without mustard, sauce tartare (see Serving suggestions p. 347), and so on.

Note: To eat, pull off each leaf and dip the fleshy end in the dressing before scraping off the flesh between your teeth. Discard the rest of the leaf.

PREPARATION TIME: 5 MINUTES
COOKING TIME: 15 MINUTES

Green asparagus
Salt

Green Asparagus
Pointes d'asperges vertes

Green asparagus are usually used as a garnish in French cuisine.

Cut off the woody part and tie the asparagus into small bundles.

Bring a large pot of well-salted water to a boil and place the asparagus in it. Cook over high heat until the tip of a knife penetrates easily into the thickest part of the spear.

Drain well and then follow your recipe to use them as a garnish.

Note: The tender part, no more than about 3 in. (7-8 cm) long, snaps at its end (just where the woody part begins) between your fingers when you bend it forcefully. About 9 oz. (250 g) of green asparagus will give only about 3 ½ oz. (100 g) of edible tips.

SERVES 1
PREPARATION TIME: 15 MINUTES
COOKING TIME: 40 MINUTES

Provençal Eggplant
Aubergine à la provençale

1 medium eggplant (aubergine)
3 tablespoons olive oil
½ onion
1 tomato
1 level teaspoon flour
½ clove garlic
1 pinch chopped parsley
Salt and pepper

Cut the half onion into julienne slices. Peel the tomato, seed it, and chop it roughly. Set aside. Heat the oil in a pan and sauté the onion in it. Cut the eggplant into 1-in. (2-cm) cubes and season them with a pinch of salt and pepper. Add them to the pan and sprinkle with the flour. Stir and turn constantly so that they color evenly all over.

Crush the garlic clove with the flat side of a knife. Add it to the pan to heat for just 1 second, stirring all the while. Add the chopped tomato. Season with salt and pepper and continue to cook gently, over low heat.

When you add the tomato, its water will change the way the contents of the pan cook: instead of frying, the eggplants and the condiments will stew very gently. Leave them to cook until all the liquid has evaporated. This should take about 30 minutes. The eggplant, tomato, and oil combined will have the consistency of a marmalade. Before serving, adjust the seasoning. Pour the vegetables into a warmed vegetable dish and scatter with a pinch of chopped parsley.

Eggplant au Gratin
Aubergines au gratin

SERVES 6
SALTING TIME: 30 MINUTES
PREPARATION TIME: 10 MINUTES
COOKING TIME: 20 MINUTES

3 large eggplants (aubergines)
Kosher salt for sprinkling
Olive oil for frying
4 ½ oz. (125 g) white button mushrooms
2 shallots
1 medium onion
2 tablespoons (30 g) butter
1 clove garlic
2 tablespoons tomato purée
2 tablespoons veal *jus*, plus a little extra to garnish the dish
2 tablespoons bread crumbs, divided
1 tablespoon chopped parsley
A little butter
Salt and pepper

Cut the eggplant in half lengthways. Using the tip of a knife, lightly score the flesh and make an incision around the edge, about ⅛ in. (3 mm) from the skin. Sprinkle them with salt and leave for 30 minutes.

Drain the eggplants and pat them dry. Heat the olive oil. When it is smoking, place them in the pan and cook until the pulp comes away easily with a spoon. This should take 5 to 8 minutes.

Drain them on a paper towel. Using a spoon, remove the flesh carefully, without damaging the peel. Butter a gratin dish well and spread the peels out side by side on it, skin-side down. Finely chop the flesh and transfer it to a bowl.

Preheat the oven to 400°F- 425°F (210°C).

Clean and quickly wash the mushrooms in cold water. Pat them dry, chop them, and season with salt and pepper. Set aside. Chop the shallots and onion and stew them gently in half the butter and 1 tablespoon of olive oil. When they soften, turn the heat up so that they color just a little. Add the mushrooms, season with salt and pepper, and cook quickly over high heat, stirring constantly with a wooden spoon.

When the mushrooms have lost their water, crush the garlic clove with the back of a knife and add it with the tomato purée, veal *jus*, and eggplant pulp. Simmer for 5 minutes, adding some of the bread crumbs to change the consistency–it should be like puréed potatoes. Remove from the heat and add the chopped parsley and a knob of butter. Check the seasoning and transfer to the gratin dish, arranging in the eggplant peels in a slight dome shape.

Sprinkle with the remaining bread crumbs, drizzle over some olive oil (or melted butter) and cook in the oven until a crust forms. Just before you remove it from the oven, prepare the extra veal *jus*: reduce it and add a little butter. Drizzle this sauce round the eggplants and sprinkle them with a little more chopped parsley.

SERVES 4
PREPARATION TIME: 10 MINUTES
COOKING TIME: 15 MINUTES

Morels in Cream
Morilles à la crème

1 lb. (500 g) morel mushrooms
Juice of 1 lemon
3 tablespoons (50 g) butter
½ cup (100 ml) cream
Salt and pepper

Cut the morels into quarters if they are very large. Clean them and stew them in a pot with salt, pepper, lemon juice, and butter. Cook over fairly high heat with the lid on for about 10 minutes.

Pour almost all the cream into a small pan and reduce it a little. Pour the reduced cream into the morels and leave to simmer for a few minutes.

Just before serving, add the remaining cream to thicken the texture and make it whiter. Adjust the seasoning and serve.

Note: Morels are a popular garnish for fricassees with veal and poultry. They are also excellent in pies and dishes with puff pastry cases.

CRÈME FRAICHE
DU TERROIR

SERVES 8
PREPARATION TIME: 45 MINUTES
COOKING TIME:
6 HOURS 30 MINUTES

1 cabbage, preferably Savoy, weighing about 3 ½ lb. (1.5 kg)

1 lb. (500 g) chestnuts

6 large onions

9 oz. (250 g) butter, divided

1 tablespoon (15 g) salt

About 12 turns of the pepper mill (4 g)

Scant cup (225 ml) milk

Cabbage Stuffed with Chestnuts
Chou farci aux marrons

This dish is both hearty and refined, and requires long, slow cooking.

Peel the chestnuts and place them in a pot of cold water. Place the lid on and bring to a boil. Leave to simmer gently for 12 minutes. Remove from the heat and use a slotted spoon to remove a few chestnuts at a time. As you do so, rub off the white skins using a clean cloth. Set them aside in a dish.

For the stuffing, peel the onions and cut them into thin rings. Place them with 3 tablespoons (50 g) of the butter in a pot large enough to hold the stuffed cabbage when it is prepared. Heat the onion rings gently, then cover with the lid and leave to sweat for 15 minutes, ensuring that they do not color. Add the chestnuts and 1 stick (125 g) butter. Cover with the lid and leave to cook very gently, stirring frequently with a spatula. Stir carefully so as not to break the chestnuts. Continue this gentle cooking for 30 minutes, by which time the chestnuts will look like candied chestnuts. Sprinkle over with half the salt and pepper, and transfer the chestnuts, onions, and butter to the dish used previously.

Cut off the bottom of the core of the cabbage and remove any leaves that are too green or wilted. Prepare a large pot of boiling water and place the cabbage in it to simmer for 30 minutes. Drain it well, pressing on it to extract as much water as possible.

Place the cabbage on a clean cloth and gently open out the leaves, one by one, until you reach the core. At the core, place a generous tablespoon of stuffing. Close the leaves again, placing a spoonful of stuffing each time you come to the end of a layer of leaves. Once you have closed up the cabbage again, tie it with twine as you would a parcel (in a cross-shape). Knot the twine at the top of the cabbage and leave the ends of the twine long enough to be able to lift the cabbage up from the braising pot.

(*Continued overleaf*)

Spread out the remaining butter at the bottom of the pot. Place the cabbage in the pot with the stem side downwards. Sprinkle it with the remaining salt and pepper. Cover with the lid and place over very low heat. The butter will melt and the cabbage will give off some water; this in turn will create steam that condenses at the bottom of the lid and falls back down in a gentle rain of droplets over the cabbage and into the pot. The cabbage will begin to simmer. Continue cooking for 5 hours, preferably at very low heat.

From time to time, spoon the braising liquid over the cabbage, and check that it does not stick to the pot.

After 2 hours 30 minutes, bring the milk to a boil, setting aside 4 tablespoons, and stir it into the pot. Just 15 minutes before you serve the dish, pour the remaining 4 tablespoons of milk into the pot.

To serve, using the ends of the twine and a slotted spoon, remove the cabbage from the pot and place it on a serving platter. Remove the twine. Dilute the brown crust that will have formed around the pot in the braising liquid, check the seasoning, and spoon it over the cabbage.

SERVES 8
PREPARATION TIME: 40 MINUTES
COOKING TIME:
2 HOURS 30 MINUTES

1 medium red cabbage
9 oz. (250 g) smoked bacon
20 chestnuts
1 onion studded with 1 clove
1 bouquet garni, comprising a few parsley stalks, 1 small piece bay leaf, and 1 sprig thyme
Scant ½ cup (100 ml) broth or low-salt white veal *jus*
3 tablespoons wine vinegar
3 heaped tablespoons goose fat or fat from a pork roast
Salt and freshly ground pepper

Paul Haeberlin's Alsatian Red Cabbage
Chou rouge à l'alsacienne Paul Haeberlin

Trim off any wilted cabbage leaves and cut the stem at the base. Cut the cabbage into quarters, wash them, and drain. Core each quarter and cut the leaves into julienne shreds. Bring a large pot of water to a boil and drop the julienned cabbage in. Boil for 6 minutes, then drain.

Remove the rind of the bacon and trim off the outside, which has a more pronounced smoky taste. Cut the remaining part into rectangles measuring 4 x 3 in. (10 x 8 cm), and ½ in. (1 cm) thick.

To prepare the chestnuts, preheat the oven to 425°F (210°C). Make an incision in the shell and place them on a baking dish. Cook for 5 to 6 minutes, until you can lift up the outer shell and the skin. Take 3 or 4 chestnuts at a time from the pan and peel them as you do so. Set aside.

Use a large high-sided pot. Divide the julienned cabbage into three parts and the bacon pieces and chestnuts into two batches. Make a layer of one-third of the cabbage, half of the bacon, and half the chestnuts. Repeat, adding the onion studded with the clove and the bouquet garni. Cover with the last third of the cabbage. Sprinkle with salt and pepper and pour in the broth or *jus* and the vinegar. Add the fat. Cover the pot with the lid and bring to a boil.

Lower the oven temperature to 350°F (180°C). As soon as the pot begins to boil, cover the cabbage with a piece of buttered parchment paper. Seal with the lid, transfer to the oven and cook for 2 hours 30 minutes. This type of cooking should leave very little liquid with the cabbage–about 4 tablespoons.

Remove the onion and bouquet garni and transfer the cabbage to a dish. Arrange the bacon over it. If there is too much juice, reduce it and spoon it over the julienned cabbage.

Paul Haeberlin was the chef of l'Auberge de l'Ill, a three Michelin-starred restaurant in Alsace, eastern France.

Stuffed Onions
Oignons farcis

SERVES 6
PREPARATION TIME: 30 MINUTES
COOKING TIME: 1 HOUR

- 6 large onions, preferably mild, sweet onions
- 3 tablespoons (50 g) butter, melted, plus extra to butter the dish
- 7 oz. (200 g) stuffing, such as minced meat, poultry, or game, or very finely diced fish or crustaceans, flavored with mushrooms, tomatoes, truffles, and so on
- Brown or white stock as needed for the stuffing
- 2 tablespoons bread crumbs
- 3 tablespoons veal *jus*
- Salt and pepper

Carefully peel the onions and make a deep incision all around the stalk.

Prepare a pot of boiling water, adding 2 ½ teaspoons (12 g) salt for every 4 cups (1 liter). Drop the onions in the pot and leave them to boil for 5 minutes, then drain them.

Hollow out each onion, following the incision round the stalk, to make a "container," and reserve the hollowed-out part. Generously butter a sauté pan and arrange the onions in it. Sprinkle them with a pinch of fine table salt.

Preheat the oven to 325°F (160°C).

Chop the part of the onion you have hollowed out and stew it gently in butter for 15 minutes, stirring frequently and carefully ensuring that it does not color, or hardly colors. Add the onion to your chosen stuffing.

Bring the stuffing to the right consistency by adding brown or white stock, or brown or white sauce, depending on what ingredients you are using.

Fill the onions using a spoon or a pastry bag, heaping the stuffing up to form a little dome. Sprinkle with white bread crumbs and pour over the melted butter.

Cook gently, uncovered, in the oven for about 1 hour until the bread crumbs turn a nice golden color. Spoon over frequently with the butter in the dish.

Warm a round serving dish and pour in the veal *jus*. Then arrange the stuffed onions above it and pour in all the juices from the cooking dish.

Add an original touch to these stuffed onions by leaving them unpeeled.

SERVES 4
PREPARATION TIME: 10 MINUTES
COOKING TIME: 40 MINUTES

Snow Peas
Pois gourmands

- 1 ¾ lb. (800 g) snow peas
- 8 baby onions
- 4 ½oz. (125 g) slab bacon
- 4 tablespoons (60 g) butter
- 1 sprig thyme
- Salt and pepper

String the snow peas and rinse quickly in cold water. Peel the onions.

Remove the rind from the bacon and cut it into ½-in. (1-cm) cubes. Fry the bacon in a frying pan (no fat is needed) until it begins to brown.

In a separate frying pan, melt the butter and lightly brown the onions, then add the bacon, thyme, and peas. Cover and cook for 30 minutes over very low heat, stirring occasionally. Taste for salt and pepper, then serve in a warm vegetable dish.

Serving suggestions: Serve with Calf's Liver (see p. 299).

Glazed Carrots and Turnips
Carottes et navets glacés

SERVES 4
PREPARATION TIME: 15 MINUTES
COOKING TIME: 30 MINUTES

- 15 oz. (450 g) baby carrots
- 15 oz. (450 g) baby turnips
- 4 tablespoons (60 g) butter
- 1 tablespoon (15 g) granulated sugar
- Salt and pepper

Bring a large pot of lightly salted water to a boil. It is preferable to use baby carrots and baby turnips that can be left whole or, at most, cut in half. Peel or scrub the vegetables and wash them quickly in cold water. Boil the carrots and turnips in the pot of lightly salted water for 8 to 10 minutes, then drain.

Melt the butter in a high-sided frying pan, add the vegetables, and cook over moderate heat for 10 to 15 minutes, so that they are dried out and coated with butter; shake the pan frequently while the vegetables are cooking.

Lower the heat, sprinkle in the sugar, and cook, shaking the pan, until the sugar coats the vegetables and begins to brown. Season with salt and pepper, and serve.

Serving suggestions: Serve as garnish with meat.

SERVES 4
PREPARATION TIME: 15 MINUTES
COOKING TIME: 10 TO 12 MINUTES

Green Beans
Haricots verts

- 2 lb. (900 g) very thin green beans
- 3 tablespoons (50 g) butter
- Salt and pepper
- Lemon juice (optional)

Bring 12 cups (3 liters) water and 1 tablespoon (25 g) salt to a boil in a large pot.

String the beans and break off the ends of each one. Rinse the beans. Drop them into the boiling water and boil rapidly, uncovered, for 8 to 12 minutes, depending on size and how you like them. Use a slotted spoon to push down any beans that stick out of the water.

Fill a large basin or bowl with cold water and a tray of ice cubes. When the beans are done (taste one–you may want to cook them longer), drain them and drop them immediately into the ice water. Leave for 3 minutes, then lift out and drain completely.

Just before serving, melt the butter in a large frying pan, add the beans, season with salt and pepper, and warm over low heat, shaking the pan frequently. Serve as soon as the beans are nice and hot (if you like, you can sprinkle them with a little lemon juice just before serving).

Cardoons au Gratin
Gratin de cardons

SERVES 4
PREPARATION TIME: 20 MINUTES
COOKING TIME: 45 MINUTES

- 2 small cardoons (see Note)
- 2 cups (500 ml) milk
- 2 marrow bones
- 1 ¼ cups (125 g) grated Gruyère cheese
- 3 tablespoons (50 g) butter, plus a little for buttering the dish
- 1 tablespoon (6 g) flour
- Salt

Peeling the cardoons is a time-consuming process that requires great care. Cut off the hollow ends of the stalks and remove all the strings, as you would with celery. Cut the remaining (solid) part of the stalks into pieces about 1 ¼ in. (3 cm) long; the base, where all the stalks are joined together, can simply be sliced–this is the best part to my mind. Wash under cold running water and drain in a colander.

Heat the milk and 12 cups (3 liters) water in a large pot until boiling, add some salt and the cardoons, partially cover the pot, and cook for 15 to 20 minutes. Lower the heat if it looks as if the milk is rising and will overflow.

Preheat the oven to 350°F (180°C).

Poach the marrow bones. Place them in a small saucepan of lightly salted cold water, and heat almost to boiling. Simmer for 10 minutes. Lift the bones out of the pot with a slotted spoon and take out the marrow; cut it into thick slices and reserve. Reserve 1 cup (250 ml) of the cooking liquid.

Butter a small earthenware baking dish. Drain the cardoons, then put them in the dish and sprinkle them with the grated cheese.

Melt the butter in a saucepan, stir in the flour, and cook until it starts to change color, then, little by little, stir in the reserved marrow-bone water. Boil until the sauce is just thick enough to coat a spoon.

Place the slices of marrow on the cardoons, pour over the sauce, bake for 25 minutes or until beginning to brown, and serve.

Serving suggestions: Cardoons are excellent with any red meat.

Note: The cardoon is a relative of the artichoke that looks rather like a large head of celery. A winter vegetable, it is best from November to February. Choose cardoons that are small and dull white in color–they are generally the most tender.

Provençal White Beans
Haricots blancs à la provençale

SERVES 4
PREPARATION TIME: 15 MINUTES
COOKING TIME:
1 HOUR 10 MINUTES

- 2 ¾ cups (500 g) fresh white beans or 1 ⅓ cups (250 g) dried white beans
- 1 large onion
- 1 clove
- 1 large carrot
- 1 bouquet garni made with 1 sprig thyme, ¼ bay leaf, and 3 sprigs parsley
- 1 tablespoon (25 g) kosher salt
- 4 peppercorns
- 2 ½ tablespoons (40 g) butter

TOMATO SAUCE

- 4 large tomatoes
- 1 bouquet garni made with 2 sprigs thyme and ¼ bay leaf
- Salt and pepper

Peel the onion and stud it with the clove. Peel the carrot and cut it in half lengthwise. Wash the parsley. Tie together the first bouquet garni of thyme, bay leaf, and parsley using twine. Set aside.

If using dried beans, they will have to be soaked overnight in cold water before cooking according to the instructions on the packet. To cook them, place them in fresh cold water, bring to a boil, then add the peppercorns, onion, carrot, and 1 bouquet garni (the cooking time will be longer than for fresh beans).

If using fresh beans, bring the water and salt to a boil, then add the peppercorns and white beans.

Bring back to a boil and add the onion, carrot, and bouquet garni. In either case, simmer for 1 hour, or until the beans are soft. When done, drain, and discard the bouquet garni, onion and carrot.

While the beans are cooking, make a tomato sauce. Blanch, peel, and chop the tomatoes. Place the tomatoes (without any butter or oil) in a saucepan. Add salt, pepper, and the second bouquet garni, and cook until the water from the tomatoes has evaporated and a thick sauce is formed (about 30 minutes). Discard the bouquet garni. When both the beans and the tomato sauce are done, melt the butter in a large frying pan. Add the beans and tomato sauce, shake the pan (or stir gently without crushing the beans) to combine, then serve in a hot dish.

SERVES 4
PREPARATION TIME: 20 MINUTES
COOKING TIME: 55 MINUTES

Baked Pumpkin Flan
Flan au potiron

2 ¼ lb. (1 kg) fresh pumpkin
1 tablespoon (10 g) cornstarch
1 tablespoon water
1 cup (250 ml) milk
6 tablespoons (100 ml) whipping cream
2 eggs
Nutmeg
Salt and pepper

Bring 10 cups (2 ½ liters) salted water to a boil.

Peel the pumpkin and remove the seeds. Cut it into large cubes, then drop them into the pot of boiling salted water and cook at a moderate boil for 20 minutes. Drain in a colander (leave it in the colander for 5 to 10 minutes so that the maximum amount of water will drain off).

Purée the pumpkin in a food mill, blender, or food processor, and reserve.

Preheat the oven to 425°F (210°C).

Mix the cornstarch with the tablespoon of water. Bring the milk to a boil, and add the cornstarch mixture. Remove from the heat and add first the cream, then the eggs, beating constantly. Stir in the pumpkin, then season with salt, pepper, and a little nutmeg.

Lightly butter a small baking dish (enameled cast-iron or porcelain) and pour in the pumpkin mixture, spreading it evenly around the dish. Place in the oven and bake for about 35 minutes or until golden brown on top. Serve hot from the oven in the baking dish.

Variation: You can make a pumpkin dessert by adding ¼ cup (50 g) of granulated sugar and a little vanilla extract to flavor the pumpkin instead of salt, pepper, and nutmeg.

SERVES 4
PREPARATION TIME: 8 MINUTES
COOKING TIME: 25 MINUTES

Provençal Tomatoes
Tomates provençales

- 4 large, ripe tomatoes
- 1 small bunch cilantro
- A few leaves of basil
- 8 teaspoons (10 g) bread crumbs
- 2 cloves garlic
- 5 tablespoons (75 ml) olive oil
- Salt and pepper

Preheat the oven to 450°F-475°F (240°C), or as high as it will go.

Wash the tomatoes, dry with a towel, then cut out the stems. Cut each tomato in half, then place in a baking dish, cut side up. Sprinkle generously with salt. Wash the cilantro, pat it dry, then finely chop it using scissors; prepare the basil in the same way. Sprinkle each tomato half with a teaspoon of cilantro and basil mixed together, and then a teaspoon of bread crumbs. Peel and finely chop the garlic.

Pepper lightly, then place a little freshly chopped garlic on top of each tomato half, pour over the oil, and bake for 25 minutes. Serve hot from the oven in the baking dish.

Serving suggestions: Serve with either meat or fish.

SERVES 4
PREPARATION TIME: 15 MINUTES
COOKING TIME: 35 MINUTES

Cauliflower au Gratin
Gratin de chou-fleur

- 1 cauliflower weighing about 2 lb. (900 g)
- 1 tablespoon olive oil
- A stale breadcrust (optional)
- 2 ½ tablespoons (40 g) butter
- 1 cup (250 ml) milk
- 1 tablespoon (10 g) cornstarch
- 1 tablespoon water
- 6 tablespoons (100 ml) whipping cream
- ⅓ cup (50 g) grated Gruyère cheese
- Nutmeg
- Salt and pepper

Cut the central core from the cauliflower and separate the florets. Wash them carefully in cold water.

Bring lightly salted water to a boil and add the oil; you can also add a stale breadcrust to the water (it will absorb some of the odor of the cauliflower as it cooks). Add the cauliflower, boil for 5 minutes from the time the water comes back to a boil, then drain. Butter a baking dish (enameled cast-iron or porcelain), place the cauliflower in it, and reserve.

Preheat the oven to 350°F (180°C).

Heat the milk in a saucepan; while it's heating, mix the cornstarch and cold water together. Once the milk boils, remove the pot from the heat and stir in the cornstarch mixture. Return to the heat and bring to a boil, stirring constantly. Cook until the sauce is thick enough to coat the spoon. Stir in the cream, salt, pepper, nutmeg, and grated cheese, then pour the sauce over the cauliflower and bake in the oven for 20 minutes, or until golden brown on top.

Serve in the dish it was cooked in.

SERVES 3 TO 4
PREPARATION TIME: 5 MINUTES
COOKING TIME: 10 MINUTES

Broccoli
Brocolis

2 ¼ lb. (1 kg) broccoli
3 tablespoons (50 g) butter
6 tablespoons (100 ml) crème fraîche or heavy cream
Salt and pepper

If necessary, separate the broccoli into florets. Wash and drain the broccoli.

Bring a large pot of lightly salted water to a boil, then drop in the broccoli and boil for 7 to 10 minutes, or until tender but not soft. Lift the broccoli out and leave to drain for a few seconds on a clean cloth (be careful not to damage the florets, which are quite fragile when cooked).

Place the broccoli in a hot serving dish and sprinkle with salt and pepper. Pour a little melted butter over it, and cream that has been boiled until thick, or simply the juices from the meat it's being served with.

Serving suggestions: Broccoli is delicious with the Fricassee of Scallops in Cream Sauce (see p. 227). It is also excellent with meat or poultry.

Variation: The broccoli can be boiled for only 2 or 3 minutes, to finish cooking in either the butter, cream, salt pork, or meat juices. In this case, simmer slowly for 10 to 15 minutes more, gently shaking the pan frequently so as not to damage the broccoli (don't stir with a spoon). Add salt and pepper, and serve.

SERVES 4
PREPARATION TIME: 15 MINUTES
COOKING TIME: 20 MINUTES

Chanterelles
Girolles ou chanterelles

- 1 ¾ lb. (800 g) fresh chanterelles (see Note)
- 3 tablespoons (50 g) butter
- Salt and pepper
- 1 clove garlic, peeled and coarsely crushed (optional)
- 1 shallot, peeled and finely chopped (optional)
- 1 small bunch coarsely chopped parsley (optional)

Cut off the dirt from the base of each mushroom, then wash them quickly under cold running water and drain.

Melt the butter in a frying pan, add the mushrooms, and cook over moderate heat for approximately 20 minutes, or until all the water they give out has evaporated completely. Continue cooking until the mushrooms begin to brown. At this point, they are done (this method of cooking is good for almost all mushrooms).

Salt and pepper the mushrooms, and serve as they are. If you prefer, stir in garlic, peeled and coarsely crushed, shallots, peeled and finely chopped, or both, and sprinkle with chopped parsley just before serving.

Serving suggestions: Chanterelles are marvelous served with Veal and Olives (see p. 294).

Note: Although chanterelles are called for here, many other wild mushrooms could be used instead (e.g., boletus, Japanese shitake mushrooms). About ½ cup (15 g) top-quality dried wild mushrooms may also be used. Soak them for about 20 minutes in warm water (or follow the directions on the package), then add them with 6 tablespoons (100 ml) of their water to the melted butter and cook as described for the fresh mushrooms.

SERVES 4
SOAKING TIME: OVERNIGHT
PREPARATION TIME: 25 MINUTES
COOKING TIME: 45 MINUTES

Stuffed Zucchini
Courgettes farcies

4 large zucchini
9 oz. (250 g) salt pork
2 slices dry toast or melba toast
⅔ cup (150 ml) milk
1 clove garlic
4 small onions
1 small bunch parsley
1 cup (250 g) leftover cooked veal (see Pot-au-Feu p. 264, or Veal and Olives p. 294)
1 egg
Nutmeg
½ cup (120 ml) Tomato Sauce (see p. 544, or canned)
1 sprig thyme, crumbled
¼ bay leaf, crumbled
½ cup (50 g) grated Gruyère cheese
3 tablespoons (50 g) butter
6 tablespoons (100 ml) water
Salt and pepper

Soak the salt pork in a large bowl of cold water overnight before cooking (change the water several times). When the pork has been desalted, take it out of the water, pat it dry with paper towel, and remove the rind. To cook, place the salt pork in a saucepan, add cold water to cover, bring to a boil, then lower the heat and simmer for 1 hour. Drain and cool before using to make the stuffing (the pork may be cooked ahead of time and kept in the refrigerator until ready to use).

The following day, take all the ingredients out of the refrigerator one hour ahead of time.

Remove the stems from the zucchini, wash them and wipe them dry, but do not peel. Cut in half lengthwise, then scoop out all the seeds, being careful not to puncture the skins. Reserve.

Preheat the oven to 350°F (180°C).

Crumble the toast. Place the toast in a mixing bowl, add the milk, and allow to soak for about 10 minutes, then crush it with a fork and pour off any excess milk. Peel the garlic and onions and place them on a cutting board. Wash the parsley and remove the stems, then place the leaves on the cutting board. Chop the salt pork and the leftover cooked veal into thick cubes, then add these to the cutting board and roughly chop along with the garlic, onions, and parsley, using a *mezzaluna* (herb chopper). All the ingredients for the stuffing can be worked through a meat grinder, if preferred. Don't grind too finely. Add this mixture to the bowl with the bread and milk. Stir in the egg, nutmeg, tomato sauce, salt, and pepper, and sprinkle over the crumbled thyme and bay leaf. Mix well, then fill each half zucchini with stuffing.

Place the zucchini in a large roasting pan, sprinkle with the cheese, add the water, dot with the butter, and bake in the oven for 45 minutes. Serve on a hot serving platter.

Serving suggestions: Stuffed zucchini can make a perfect main course especially if you serve them with Rice (see p. 510).

Mixed Vegetables
Jardinière de légumes

SERVES 6 TO 8
PREPARATION TIME: 20 TO 35 MINUTES
COOKING TIME: 35 MINUTES

- 1 ½ lb. (700 g) potatoes
- 6 to 8 baby onions
- 5 medium (400g) carrots
- 2 ⅔ cups (400 g) shelled fresh peas
- 8 lettuce leaves
- Bouquet garni, made with 2 sprigs thyme and ¼ bay leaf
- 4 ½ oz. (125 g) salt pork or bacon
- 3 tablespoons (50 g) butter
- Salt and pepper

If peas are not in season you can use frozen ones; in this case, follow the cooking instructions on the pack.

Bring a large saucepan of salted water to a boil.

Peel the potatoes, wash them quickly and dice them.

Peel the onions. Peel the carrots and cut them into sticks. Shell the peas. Wash the lettuce. Tie together the bouquet garni. Remove the rind from the salt pork or bacon, then dice the meat.

Add the onions, potatoes, carrots, and bouquet garni to the boiling water. Cover and boil gently for about 20 minutes, then add the salt pork, peas, and lettuce, and cook for 15 minutes uncovered.

To serve, drain the vegetables, discard the bouquet garni, and place in a hot serving dish. Season with salt and pepper, stir in the butter, and serve immediately.

SERVES 6
SOAKING TIME: OVERNIGHT
PREPARATION TIME: 40 MINUTES
COOKING TIME:
1 HOUR 30 MINUTES

Stuffed Tomatoes
Tomates farcies

7 oz. (200 g) salt pork
1 generous cup (300 g) leftover boiled beef or veal or pork (see Pot-au-Feu p. 264, or Veal and Olives p. 294)
12 large tomatoes
1 sprig thyme
¼ bay leaf
4 small onions
1 cup (250 ml) milk
3 slices of dry toast or melba toast
1 small bunch parsley
1 clove garlic
1 egg
4 tablespoons (60 g) butter
Salt, pepper, and nutmeg

Soak the salt pork overnight in cold iced water (change the water several times). Once desalted, take the salt pork out and pat it dry. Place the salt pork in a saucepan, cover with cold water, bring to a boil, then lower the heat and simmer for about 1 hour. Drain and leave to cool before using.

One hour ahead of time, take all the ingredients out of the refrigerator. Wash the tomatoes, and cut off the top third of each one. Reserve the tops. Use a spoon to carefully scoop out the seeds and pulp, being careful not to puncture the skins. Reserve the pulp and seeds. Lightly salt the inside of each tomato. Preheat the oven to 350°F (180°C).

Place the seeds and pulp in a small saucepan with a little thyme, bay leaf, salt, and pepper, and simmer for 15 to 20 minutes or until it is the consistency of a thin tomato sauce, stirring frequently. Reserve. While the sauce is cooking, peel and slice the onions. Place the onions in a saucepan with the milk, bring to a boil, then lower the heat and simmer for 7 to 8 minutes. Lift the onions out of the milk with a slotted spoon and chop them coarsely. Save the milk.

Crumble the toast. Place in a mixing bowl and add the onion milk. Soak for 10 minutes, then crush the toast with a fork; pour off any excess milk. Peel the garlic and chop the garlic and parsley leaves. Remove the rind from the salt pork and chop the salt pork and the leftover meat, and add it to the toast along with the onion, garlic, and parsley. All the ingredients for the stuffing can be worked through a meat grinder, if preferred. Don't grind too finely. Mix well, then add the egg, salt, pepper, and nutmeg, and knead with your hands to mix thoroughly.

Butter a baking dish just large enough to hold all the tomatoes. Fill each tomato with stuffing, add a piece of butter to each tomato, then put the top sections back in place and arrange them in the baking dish. Pour the tomato sauce made earlier into the dish around the tomatoes, then place in the oven and bake for 1 hour. Serve hot from the oven in the baking dish.

SERVES 4
PREPARATION TIME: 15 MINUTES
COOKING TIME: 10 MINUTES

Spinach
Épinards

3 ½ lb. (1.5 kg) fresh spinach

1 generous tablespoon (30 g) kosher salt

1 medium onion

3 tablespoons (50 g) butter

6 tablespoons (100 ml) crème fraîche or heavy cream

Salt and pepper

Bring 14 cups (3 ½ liters) water and the salt to a boil in a large pot.

While the water is heating up, carefully clean the spinach: remove the stem and thick rib from each leaf, then wash in several changes of cold water. Carefully drain after washing, then drop the spinach little by little into the boiling water, pushing each addition into the water with a slotted spoon before adding more. Boil for 5 minutes from the time the water comes back to a boil (if you don't have a pot large enough to cook all the spinach at once, cook only as much as you can, remove from the pot with a slotted spoon, drain, cool under running water, and leave in the colander while cooking the rest). When all the spinach is cooked, drain in a colander, cool immediately under cold running water, then squeeze out the water with your hands, and reserve the spinach in a bowl.

Peel and slice the onion. Melt the butter in a high-sided frying pan, brown the onion lightly, then add the spinach, salt, and pepper, and stir over moderate heat with a wooden spoon to heat thoroughly. Add the cream, cook 5 minutes more, and serve immediately on a hot platter.

Serving suggestions: You can serve the spinach garnished with hard-boiled eggs cut in half and squares or triangles of bread fried in butter (croutons), for a nice effect.

Note: Fresh sorrel can be cooked in the same way.

SERVES 4
PREPARATION TIME: 10 MINUTES
COOKING TIME:
ABOUT 15 MINUTES

Glazed Onions
Oignons glacés

- 1 lb. (500 g) new baby onions (weight without greens)
- 3 tablespoons (50 g) butter
- 1 tablespoon (15 g) granulated sugar
- Salt and pepper

Peel the onions, leave them whole, wash in cold water, and dry.

Break the butter into pea-sized pieces. Place the onions in a frying pan large enough to hold them all on the bottom, and add half the butter, the sugar, salt, and pepper. Cook over low heat until the onions start to brown, then pour in just enough water to barely cover them (they should not float). Cover the pan and raise the heat; boil rapidly for about 10 to 15 minutes over moderate heat, or until all the water has evaporated.

When the onions are done, there should be a thick syrup remaining in the pan; shake the pan to glaze the onions by rolling them in the syrup. Add the remaining butter, then season again if necessary and serve.

Serving suggestions: Serve with meat or poultry.

SERVES 5 TO 6
PREPARATION TIME: 15 MINUTES
COOKING TIME: 1 HOUR

Imam Bayildi
Bayaldi

2 small eggplants, weighing about 1 ¼ lb. (600 g) in total

5 medium (600 g) tomatoes

2 medium (250 g) onions

4 medium zucchini, weighing about 1 ½ lb. (700 g) in total

1 clove garlic

¼ bay leaf

1 sprig thyme

5 tablespoons (80 g) butter, plus butter for the dish

1 cup (100 g) grated Gruyère cheese (see Note)

Salt and pepper

Preheat the oven to 350°F (180°C).

Wash the vegetables and wipe them dry. Blanch and peel the tomatoes. Peel the onions. Cut the zucchini, eggplant, tomatoes, and onions into slices about ½ in. (1 cm) thick (if using a large eggplant rather than two smaller ones, cut it in half lengthwise before slicing). Keep all the vegetables separate from each other. Peel the garlic and crush it using the back of a fork. Crush the bay leaf.

Butter a large baking dish (preferably earthenware or enameled cast iron). Cover the bottom of the dish with the onions, then make a layer of zucchini and sprinkle with a little of the garlic, thyme, and bay leaf, salt, and pepper. Next, make a layer of eggplant, and lastly a layer of tomato, seasoning each layer as you did the zucchini. Dot the surface with half of the butter, then place in the oven for 30 minutes. At the end of this time, sprinkle with the cheese, dot with the remaining butter, and bake 20 to 30 minutes more or until golden brown on top. (If the vegetables dry out during the first 30 minutes' baking, cover them with foil; remove the foil for only the last 10 minutes of the baking time).

Serve with roast or boiled meat.

Variation: If preferred, the cheese can be omitted and ⅓ cup (80 ml) of olive oil used instead of butter. In this case, pour all of the oil over the surface of the vegetables before putting them in the oven. Instead of making layers as described here, you can simply make parallel lines of overlapping vegetables as shown in the photo, and bake them in individual baking dishes rather than in one large one.

The name of this Turkish dish means "the imam fainted," although there is disagreement as to whether the cause was its exquisite taste or the extravagant use of expensive olive oil.

SERVES 4
PREPARATION TIME: 10 MINUTES
COOKING TIME: 20 MINUTES

Braised Lettuce
Laitues braisées

5 or 6 small butterhead (Boston) lettuces
12 baby onions
3 tablespoons (50 g) butter
2 egg yolks
6 tablespoons (100 ml) whipping cream
Salt and pepper

Remove any tough outer leaves from the lettuces and cut off the base of the stem. Leave the lettuces whole and gently wash them in cold water. Peel the onions and leave them whole.

Melt the butter in a high-sided frying pan, add the onions, and brown lightly. Add the lettuce, salt, and pepper. Lower the heat, cover, and cook slowly for 15 to 20 minutes, or until tender, turning the lettuces occasionally.

While the lettuce is cooking, beat the egg yolks and cream together in a small mixing bowl. Season with salt and pepper.

When the lettuces are done, lift them out of the pan with a slotted spoon and place them on a hot platter. Keep warm. Remove the pan from the heat and pour the pan juices into the bowl with the egg-cream mixture, stirring constantly. Pour the sauce back into the pan and place over low heat, stirring constantly, just long enough for the sauce to heat and thicken (do not allow to boil), then pour over the lettuces and serve.

Serving suggestions: Serve with any game bird.

Split Pea Purée
Purée de pois cassés

SERVES 4
SOAKING TIME: OVERNIGHT
PREPARATION TIME: 15 MINUTES
COOKING TIME: ABOUT 2 HOURS

---

4 ⅔ cups (700 g) split peas

3 baby onions

Bouquet garni, made with 1 sprig thyme, ¼ bay leaf, and 3 sprigs parsley

2 tablespoons crème fraîche or heavy cream

Salt and pepper

Soak the split peas overnight in a large bowl of cold water before cooking. To cook, drain the peas, place them in a pot, and add enough fresh cold water to barely cover them.

Peel the onions, wash the parsley, and tie together the bouquet garni. Add the bouquet garni, onions, salt, and pepper to the pot. Bring to a boil, then lower the heat and simmer for about 2 hours. Heat extra water and add it to the pot whenever necessary to keep the peas moist. Stir the peas frequently as they cook to make sure they don't stick to the bottom of the pot. By the time they are done, they should have formed a thick, smooth purée, rather like mashed potatoes. Just before serving, stir in the cream and season generously with pepper. Serve in a hot dish.

Serving suggestions: Split peas are the perfect accompaniment to roast pork or sausages; stir the pan juices into the purée before serving.

SERVES 4
PREPARATION TIME: 20 MINUTES
COOKING TIME: 35 MINUTES

Potato Croquettes
Croquettes de pommes de terre

1 lb. (500 g) potatoes
7 tablespoons (100 g) butter
4 egg yolks
1 pinch freshly grated nutmeg
2 tablespoons flour
1 egg
1 tablespoon olive oil
2 tablespoons bread crumbs
Oil for frying
Salt and pepper

Peel the potatoes and cook them in gently simmering salted water until their flesh gives way to pressure. Do not wait until they are so well cooked that they burst or fall apart.

Drain them well and return them to the cooking pot; leave it on the corner of the burner or over minimal heat so that their water evaporates.

Turn them into a sieve and press them through using a potato ricer. Be careful to use pressure on the ricer and not rotate it, as this would cause the mashed potato to become elastic.

Put the hot mashed potato in a pot and, with a spatula or wooden spoon, work in the butter energetically. The potatoes will become white; now incorporate the egg yolks and nutmeg. Check to see if the mixture is sufficiently salted and leave to cool.

Prepare a working surface very lightly dusted with flour. Divide the mashed potato into several parts and roll each one out into a log shape. Cut the logs into shapes the size of a slightly elongated cork.

Beat the whole egg with a small pinch of salt and olive oil. Dip the potato "corks" into this mixture and then into the bread crumbs.

Heat an oil bath until it just begins to smoke. Drop the potato croquettes into the oil and fry until they are golden and crisp. Drain them on paper towel and sprinkle with just a little fine salt.

Fold a napkin on a plate and arrange a mound of croquettes over it.

SERVES 4
PREPARATION TIME: 15 MINUTES
COOKING TIME: 30 MINUTES

Old-Fashioned Gnocchi
Gnocchis à l'ancienne

- 1 cup (250 ml) milk
- 3 tablespoons (50 g) butter
- 1 pinch salt
- 1 pinch freshly grated nutmeg
- 1 ¼ cups (125 g) flour, sifted
- 3 eggs

This recipe uses the method for Choux Pastry (see p. 571).

Dough

In a saucepan, bring to a boil the milk, butter, salt, and nutmeg. As soon as the butter melts, throw in the flour, mixing with a flexible spatula or wooden spoon as you do so. Move the saucepan to the corner of the burner or turn the heat to minimum, continuing to stir for 5 minutes. This will dry out the dough without burning it. Then remove from the heat altogether and stir in the eggs, one by one, until the dough is very smooth and not too thick.

Gnocchi

In a large, deep sauté pan, bring water to a boil, adding 1 ¾ teaspoons salt (8 g) for every 4 cups (1 liter). Leave the water simmering over very low heat.

Spoon the dough into a pastry bag fitted with a plain, medium tip, and with your left hand press it out over the simmering water. With your right hand, cut it into pieces 1 ½ in. (4 cm) long as they are extruded from the tip, using a knife dipped frequently into hot water. Alternatively, you can take a walnut-sized piece of dough with a teaspoon dipped into hot water (you must dip it each time) and slip it into the poaching water.

Return the pan to the heat and leave to boil properly for 1 minute. Then turn down the heat or move the pan to the side of the burner and leave to simmer gently for 15 minutes.

Gradually, the gnocchi will rise to the surface as they finish poaching. Drain one of them and test for doneness by pressing lightly–it should have some elasticity.

Remove the gnocchi with a slotted spoon and drain them on a clean cloth. To serve, follow either the recipe for Parisian-Style Gnocchi (see p. 490) or the recipe for Potato Gnocchi (see p. 489).

SERVES 4
PREPARATION TIME: 20 MINUTES
COOKING TIME:
1 HOUR 15 MINUTES

1 lb. (500 g) yellow, starchy potatoes

5 tablespoons (75 g) butter

Freshly grated nutmeg

1 egg yolk

1 whole egg, beaten

1 ¼ cups (125 g) flour, sifted

1 oz. (25 g) grated Gruyère cheese

Salt and pepper

TO FINISH

3 tablespoons (50 g) butter, plus extra to grease the dish

1 oz. (25 g) grated Gruyère cheese

Potato Gnocchi
Gnocchis Belle-de-Fontenay

Wash the potatoes and bake them in the oven. When they are softened, scrape out the hot flesh and press it through a fine-mesh sieve into a mixing bowl. Stir vigorously with a wooden spoon, and incorporate the butter, a pinch of salt, a pinch of pepper, and a little grated nutmeg.

When the mixture is smooth and white, check the seasoning. Stir in the egg yolk, and then gradually pour in the beaten egg. Lastly, add the flour and the grated cheese. The dough must be perfectly smooth.

Gnocchi

When the dough is mixed and seasoned, leave it to cool. Then divide it into small 1 oz. (30 g) balls. Dust the counter with flour and roll them into balls by rounding your hand and rolling them over the counter. Flatten them with the tines of a knife twice to make a crisscross pattern.

Bring a large pot of salted water (1 ¾ teaspoons salt for every 4 cups; 8 g per liter) to a boil. Drop the gnocchi into boiling water; they should have plenty of room.

When the water begins boiling again, lower the heat to minimum so that the water simmers gently. Cover with the lid and poach for 15 minutes. To test for doneness, take one of the gnocchi and press it with your fingers. If it is elastic, the gnocchi are ready. Remove with a slotted spoon and drain on a clean cloth.

To finish, preheat the oven to 475°F (240°C).

Butter a round ovenproof dish well and sprinkle it generously with grated Gruyère cheese. Arrange a first layer of gnocchi at the bottom of the dish and sprinkle it with a good amount of grated cheese. Repeat the procedure.

In a pan, heat 3 tablespoons (50 g) butter until it begins to turn brown. Pour it over the top layer of cheese and bake for 7 to 8 minutes until a crust forms. Serve immediately.

Paris-Style Gnocchi
Gnocchis à la parisienne

SERVES 4
PREPARATION TIME: 15 MINUTES
COOKING TIME: 30 MINUTES

MORNAY SAUCE

- 2 cups (500 ml) white sauce (see p. 536)
- Scant ½ cup (2 oz./50 g) grated Gruyère cheese
- 2 egg yolks
- 3 tablespoons cream
- 2 tablespoons (30 g) butter, divided

GNOCCHI

- 1 quantity Old-Fashioned Gnocchi (see p. 488)
- 1 scant cup (3 ½ oz./100 g) grated Gruyère cheese
- ⅔ oz. (20 g) pale bread crumbs

For the Mornay sauce, bring the white sauce to a boil. Stir in the grated Gruyere and leave to simmer, stirring constantly, until the cheese has completely melted. Immediately remove from the heat (the sauce should not boil any longer) and whisk in the egg yolks together with 1 tablespoon cream. This will thicken the sauce. If you do not have cream, use milk. Return to the heat and re-heat gently, whisking briskly all the time, until it is about to start boiling.

Remove from the heat and stir in the remaining cream and 1 ½ tablespoons butter.

For the gnocchi, preheat the oven to 350°F (180°C).

Spread out a few spoonfuls of Mornay sauce in an ovenproof dish. Arrange a layer of old-fashioned gnocchi over the sauce and pour over a generous serving of the same sauce.

Combine the bread crumbs with the grated cheese and sprinkle the mixture over the gnocchi.

Melt the remaining butter and drizzle it over the top. Place in the oven and cook until a nice crust forms, about 25 minutes.

The gnocchi will triple in volume as they cook.

Serve very hot.

Sautéed Potatoes
Pommes de terre sautées

SERVES 4 TO 5
PREPARATION TIME: 15 MINUTES
COOKING TIME: 25 MINUTES

- 1 ¾ lb. (800 g) new potatoes, or 2 ¼ lb. (1 kg) large potatoes
- 1 clove garlic
- 1 tablespoon olive oil
- 2 ½ tablespoons (40 g) butter
- 1 sprig thyme (or more, to taste)
- Salt and pepper

It is preferable to use new potatoes for this recipe; their skins can be scraped off with a knife rather than peeled off with a vegetable peeler. If they are very small, they can be left whole or cut in half lengthwise. If you are using large potatoes, peel them, cut them in half, then cut them into slices ½ in. (1 cm) thick. In either case, wash the potatoes in cold water after peeling them and dry in a towel before cooking.

Peel the garlic, leaving the last layer of skin.

Heat the oil and butter in a large frying pan. When it starts to foam, add the potatoes, thyme, and garlic. Cook over moderate heat for about 15 to 20 minutes, or until tender, shaking the pan frequently to brown the potatoes evenly and avoid sticking. When the potatoes are done, season with salt and pepper, and serve immediately.

Baked Potatoes
Pommes de terre en papillotes

SERVES 4
PREPARATION TIME: 10 MINUTES
COOKING TIME: 45 MINUTES

4 large potatoes (preferably bintje)
Butter
Cream
Kosher salt
Pepper
Finely chopped fresh chives (optional)

Preheat the oven to 500°F (260°C), or as high as it will go.

Carefully wash the potatoes and dry them, but don't peel. Use a knife to cut a deep cross into each one, then place it, cross side up, in the center of a piece of aluminum foil. Wrap the potato up, pressing the foil closed above the cross. If using a microwave oven, simply place the potatoes, unwrapped, in a covered, microwave-safe container.

Bake the potatoes for 45 minutes in a traditional oven. Test to see if they are done by sticking them with a needle; if it goes in with no resistance, the potatoes are done.

To serve, open the aluminum foil and spread it out to form a sort of collar around the potato (or simply open microwave-safe container). Press the ends of each potato gently toward each other to open the cross. Serve, with fresh butter, cream, kosher salt, pepper, and fresh chives (if you wish), all on the side.

Serving suggestions: Baked potatoes can be served with any grilled fish or meat.

Baked Potatoes with Tomatoes
Pommes boulangère

SERVES 4
PREPARATION TIME: 10 MINUTES
COOKING TIME: 45 MINUTES

- 4 ½ oz. (125 g) salt pork or bacon
- 2 ¼ lb. (1 kg) potatoes
- 1 lb. (500 g) tomatoes
- 3 tablespoons (50 g) butter, plus butter for the dish
- 1 sprig thyme
- ¼ bay leaf
- About 1 cup (250 ml) water
- Salt and pepper

Preheat the oven to 425°F (210°C).

Remove the rind from the salt pork or bacon, and cut the salt pork or bacon into ½-in. (1-cm) cubes. Brown the salt pork or bacon in an ungreased frying pan, then drain on paper towels and reserve.

Peel the potatoes, wash them, and cut them into thin slices. Blanch the tomatoes, remove the hard part near the stem (peduncle), and slice the tomato. Reserve the juice from the tomato.

Lightly butter an earthenware or enameled cast-iron baking dish just large enough to hold the potatoes, then cover the bottom with a thin layer of potatoes, followed by a layer of tomatoes. Sprinkle over the bacon, thyme, bay leaf, salt, pepper, and a little butter. Cover this with a second layer of potatoes, and season them in the same way as the first. Fill the dish in this manner, layer after layer, then pour in the tomato juice and enough water to come about halfway up the potatoes. Place in the oven and bake 45 minutes to 1 hour, or until the potatoes are tender and the top layer has begun to brown. Serve in the baking dish.

SERVES 4
PREPARATION TIME: 15 MINUTES
COOKING TIME: 15 TO 20 MINUTES

Potato Crêpe
Crique-salade

1 lb. (500 g) potatoes (do not use new potatoes)
1 egg
3 tablespoons olive oil
Salt and pepper

Just before cooking, wash the potatoes, wipe them dry, and peel them (do *not* wash after peeling but wipe them off with a dry cloth if necessary). Grate the potatoes coarsely, place them in a bowl with the egg, salt, and pepper, and mix well.

Heat 2 tablespoons of the oil in a large frying pan (preferably cast-iron). When very hot, add all the grated potatoes and spread them out with the prongs of a fork, pressing down on them lightly to make a large crêpe, or pancake, of even thickness. Cook over moderately high heat for 6 to 8 minutes, or until the underside has browned, then slide the crêpe out into a large plate.

Place 1 more tablespoon of oil in the pan, then place a second plate on top of the crêpe and turn the crêpe upside down. Lift off the first plate and slide the crêpe back into the pan to finish cooking 6 to 8 minutes on the second side. Serve immediately.

Serving suggestions: Serve as a garnish with meat, or as a light lunch, accompanied by a Green Salad (see p. 68) flavored with a little garlic, if you like it, and a Vinaigrette (see p. 542) made with olive oil and seasoned with finely chopped fresh herbs (parsley, chervil, chives, tarragon, etc.), depending on what's in season.

SERVES 4
PREPARATION TIME: 20 TO 30 MINUTES
COOKING TIME FOR THE MASH: 30 MINUTES
COOKING TIME FOR THE SOUFFLÉ: 40 MINUTES

- 1 ¾ lb. (800 g) potatoes
- 1 ⅔ cups (125 g) Gruyère cheese (optional)
- 4 eggs, separated
- ¾ cup (200 ml) cold milk (optional)
- 1 tablespoon crème fraîche or heavy cream (optional)
- 7 tablespoons (105 g) butter
- Salt and pepper

Potato Soufflé
Soufflé de pommes de terre

Preheat the oven to 350°F (180°C).

Take the eggs out of the refrigerator ahead of time in order to use them at room temperature.

Boil the potatoes in a large pot of lightly salted water for 30 minutes, then drain, peel, and purée in a food mill or mash them until smooth. Place them in a large bowl. Grate the cheese (if using). Carefully break the eggs, separating the whites from the yolks. Reserve the egg whites, and add the egg yolks to the bowl with the potatoes. Then stir in 2 tablespoons (30 g) of butter, salt, pepper, and the milk, cream, and cheese (if using).

Put the remaining 5 tablespoons (75 g) butter in a 7-in. (18-cm) soufflé mold or a 6 ¼-in. (16-cm) charlotte mold and place in the oven until the butter has melted. Remove from the oven and turn to coat the sides with butter.

In a large mixing bowl, beat the egg whites until stiff, then fold them into the potatoes. Pour the mixture into the mold and place immediately in the oven to bake for 40 minutes. Do not open the oven door while the soufflé is baking, but check to see if it has browned by looking through the window in the oven door. Serve immediately when done.

SERVES 4
PREPARATION TIME: 20 MINUTES
COOKING TIME: 15 MINUTES

Sarlat-Style Potatoes
Pommes de terre sarladaises

1 ¾ lb. (800 g) firm, yellow potatoes
3 oz. (80 g) goose fat
1 bunch flat-leaf parsley
3 cloves garlic
Salt and pepper

Peel the potatoes and cut them into very thin rounds. Wash them and dry them carefully. Heat a large cast-iron skillet over high heat. When it is hot, add the goose fat and heat it.

Throw in the potato rounds, stirring from time to time. Leave to cook for about 10 minutes. While they cook, chop the parsley leaves and peel and chop the garlic very finely. Combine the parsley and garlic.

When the potatoes are nice and crisp, season them with salt and pepper, and sprinkle them with the parsley and garlic. Serve immediately with Preserved Goose (see p. 391) or other confit.

Instead of serving raw chopped garlic, you can cook the whole cloves, unpeeled, with the potatoes, which will take up their flavor.

SERVES 4
PREPARATION TIME: 10 MINUTES
COOKING TIME: 15 MINUTES PER PANCAKE

1 ⅓ cups (300 g) leftover mashed potatoes
1 tablespoon (10 g) flour
2 tablespoons milk
1 egg
2 tablespoons (30 g) butter
Salt and pepper, or sugar

Mashed Potato Pancakes
Galettes de pommes de terre

It is best to use four little blini pans 5 in. (12 cm) wide for cooking the pancakes (see Note).

About half an hour ahead of time, take the ingredients out of the refrigerator.

Place the mashed potatoes in a mixing bowl, and whisk in the flour, milk, and egg.

Place a quarter of the butter in each blini pan and heat until it starts to foam, then spoon a quarter of the potato mixture into each one, spreading it out evenly. Cook over moderate heat for 7 minutes, then turn over. Use two plates to turn the pancakes over: slide each pancake out into a plate. Place another quarter of the butter in each pan, then place a second plate on top of the pancake and turn it upside down. Lift off the first plate and slide the pancake back into the pan to finish cooking on the second side for another 7 minutes.

Serve the pancakes as soon as they are done. Sprinkle with salt and pepper, or with sugar if you want to use them as a dessert (a favorite with children!).

Note: If you don't have blini pans, form four potato pancakes with your hands and cook them in a large pan. In this case, turn them over with a spatula.

You can make one large potato pancake instead of four small ones, but it will be harder to turn over.

Potatoes au Gratin
Gratin de pommes de terre au lait

SERVES 4
PREPARATION TIME: 20 MINUTES
COOKING TIME: 40 TO 45 MINUTES

- 2 ¼ lb. (1 kg) potatoes
- 3 cups (750 ml) milk
- Nutmeg
- 1 clove garlic
- 1 ¼ cups (125 g) grated Gruyère cheese
- 3 tablespoons (50 ml) crème fraîche or whipping cream
- 2 tablespoons (30 g) butter, broken into small pieces
- Salt and pepper

Preheat the oven to 350°F (180°C).

Peel the potatoes and wash quickly in cold running water, then wipe dry. Cut them into slices about ¼ in. (5 mm) thick and reserve.

Bring the milk to a boil in a large saucepan, add the potatoes, a little nutmeg, and season generously. Shake the pan gently to make the potatoes settle into the milk (they should be just covered by the milk; if not, add a little warm water). Lower the heat and simmer, uncovered, over very low heat for 20 to 25 minutes, or until tender.

Peel the garlic and split it lengthwise.

Rub a baking dish (preferably porcelain or earthenware) with the garlic. When the potatoes are done, lift some out of the milk with a slotted spoon and place them on the bottom of the baking dish. Sprinkle with a little grated cheese, add another layer of potatoes, sprinkle with cheese, and continue filling the dish, layer by layer, ending with cheese.

Measure the milk remaining from cooking the potatoes; there should be about ⅔ cup (150 ml) left. If there is more than that, boil it to reduce to this amount, then pour it over the potatoes. Spoon in the cream, dot the surface with butter, then place the dish in the oven and bake for 20 minutes, or until the surface is golden brown.

Rice Pilaf
Riz pilaf

SERVES 4
PREPARATION TIME: ABOUT 5 MINUTES
COOKING TIME: 20 MINUTES

- 1 ¼ cups (250 g) rice
- 3 ¼ cup (750 ml) bouillon (see Pot-au-Feu p. 264), or water
- 1 onion
- 4 tablespoons (60 g) butter
- 1 ⅓ cups (100 g) grated Gruyère cheese
- Salt and pepper

Heat the bouillon or water in a saucepan.

Peel and slice the onion.

Melt the butter in a second saucepan and brown the onion, then stir in the rice. Use a ladle to add enough of the bouillon or water to barely cover the rice, salt lightly, stir, and boil gently uncovered until the liquid has been absorbed (about 5 minutes). Add half of the remaining liquid; when this has been absorbed, add the rest. Cook the rice for a total of about 20 minutes; when done, all the liquid should have evaporated.

Season to taste, then serve, with a bowl of freshly grated cheese on the side.

Serving suggestions: Rice pilaf can be served with many meat and fish dishes.

SERVES 4
PREPARATION TIME: 20 MINUTES
COOKING TIME: 30 MINUTES

Greek-Style Rice
Riz à la grecque

1 lb. (500 g) rice
7 tablespoons (100 g) butter
3 ½ oz. (100 g) lettuce leaves
1 medium onion
3 ½ oz. (100 g) sweet red bell peppers
3 ½ oz. (100 g) chipolata sausages, or other spicy pork sausages flavored with herbs
¾ cup (200 ml) small fresh garden peas
6 cups (1 ½ liters) broth or stock, boiling hot

Wash the rice carefully and drain it. Cut the lettuce leaves into julienne slices. Chop the onion and dice the peppers. Melt the butter in a heavy-bottomed pot and sweat the onions until a very light golden color. Cut the sausages into small rounds and sear them in the pot. Add the rice and heat, stirring frequently, until it has absorbed the butter. As you stir, be careful not to break up the pieces of sausage. Finally add the julienned lettuce leaves, the diced bell peppers, and the garden peas.

Pour in the stock; the ingredients in the pot should be well covered. Bring to a boil and cover with the lid. Turn the heat down to minimum to simmer.

As the rice swells with the liquid, add small quantities of boiling broth, stirring carefully as you do so. Repeat several times.

The rice will be done when it has absorbed three times its volume in liquid. This should take 20 minutes.

The rice will not stick and will be very creamy. Adjust the seasoning before serving.

SERVES 4
PREPARATION TIME: 15 MINUTES
COOKING TIME: 40 MINUTES

Risotto with Tomatoes
Risotto à la tomate

- 1 ¼ cups (250 g) rice, preferably round-grained
- 1 ½ lb. (700 g) tomatoes
- 4 medium onions
- 5 tablespoons (80 ml) olive oil
- 2 cups (500 ml) bouillon (see Pot-au-Feu p. 264)
- 1 pinch saffron (optional)
- Scant ½ cup (75 g) freshly grated Parmesan
- Salt and pepper

Bring a pot of water to a boil and blanch the tomatoes. Peel and chop them. Peel and chop the onions on a cutting board. Heat 2 tablespoons of oil in a saucepan, add the onion, and cook to brown lightly, then add the tomatoes, stir, and simmer uncovered for 15 to 20 minutes.

When the tomatoes are done, cook the rice. Heat the remaining olive oil in a large saucepan. Heat the bouillon in another saucepan.

When the olive oil is very hot, add the rice. Stir for a few seconds or until translucent, then add the tomato sauce and the hot bouillon. Salt and pepper, add the saffron (if using), stir, and simmer slowly, uncovered, for 25 to 30 minutes. When the rice is done, all the liquid should have been absorbed.

Gently stir in the Parmesan, taste for salt and pepper, and serve immediately.

Serving suggestions: Risotto is an excellent accompaniment to the Pot-au-Feu (see p. 264).

Pasta with Cream and Basil Sauce
Pâtes à la crème et au basilic

SERVES 4 TO 5
PREPARATION TIME: 15 MINUTES
COOKING TIME FOR THE PEAS: 10 MINUTES
COOKING TIME FOR THE PASTA: 7 MINUTES

- About 1 ¼ lb. (600 g) fresh pasta (see Note and Variation)
- ¾ cup (150 g) peas
- 5 oz. (150 g) prosciutto or bacon
- A few leaves of fresh basil
- 2 tablespoons (30 g) butter
- 6 tablespoons (100 ml) crème fraîche or heavy cream
- Salt and pepper

Boil the peas in a pot of lightly salted boiling water for 5 to 10 minutes, drain, and reservc.

Dice the prosciutto or bacon and coarsely chop the basil.

In a pot large enough to comfortably hold the pasta, but not too large, bring lightly salted water to a boil. Add the pasta and cook at a rapid boil for 2 to 7 minutes. Cooking times will vary depending on the pasta used; generally speaking, when all of the pasta floats, it's done. In any case, taste a piece: the pasta should be cooked *al dente*, that is, somewhat firm inside but *never* overcooked and mushy.

When the pasta is cooked, drain in a colander and return to the pot over moderate heat. Add the butter, cooked peas, and prosciutto or bacon, and stir in the cream, salt, pepper, and basil. Heat to warm through, stirring gently, but do not allow the cream to boil. Serve immediately.

Variation: You can use spinach noodles in addition to plain ones. I suggest cooking them separately and mixing the two together once cooked.

Note: If freshly made pasta is unavailable, buy 12-14 oz. (350-400 g) of egg-enriched pasta. Cooking times vary, so follow the instructions given on the package.

PREPARATION TIME: 25 MINUTES
COOKING TIME: 11 TO 12 MINUTES

Gribiche Sauce
Sauce gribiche

5 eggs
2 tablespoons vinegar
1 ⅔ cups (400 ml) oil
1 teaspoon chopped chervil
1 teaspoon chopped tarragon
1 teaspoon capers
1 teaspoon Dijon mustard
3 medium-sized gherkins
Salt and pepper

Place the 5 eggs in a saucepan of gently simmering water. Leave to simmer until hard-boiled, about 11 to 12 minutes, then remove and cool immediately under cold running water.

Cut the eggs open and scoop out the yolks. Reserve the whites. Place the yolks in a bowl with salt and pepper and crush finely. Drizzle in the vinegar and then the oil, very slowly, just as you would to make mayonnaise. To ensure that the texture is creamy, add a little vinegar or warm water if necessary. Finely dice the egg whites. Lastly, add the chopped herbs, capers, mustard, chopped gherkins, and egg whites. Adjust the seasoning.

This sauce is really a mayonnaise in which the egg yolks are cooked instead of raw.

PREPARATION TIME: 10 MINUTES
COOKING TIME: 15 MINUTES

Béarnaise Sauce
Sauce béarnaise

- 3 medium shallots
- 3 tablespoons white wine vinegar
- 2 tablespoons chopped tarragon
- 1 pinch chopped chervil
- 4 egg yolks
- 2 ¼ sticks (250 g) unsalted butter
- Salt and freshly crushed pepper

This sauce must be made over very low heat, just before serving. Making it in a double boiler will ensure good results. Use the top of the double boiler as an ordinary pot for the first stage of making the sauce.

Peel and finely chop the shallots.

Place the vinegar, shallots, chopped tarragon and chervil (setting aside a little of both for the end), a little salt, and a pinch of freshly crushed pepper in the top part of the double boiler. Place over high heat and reduce until you have the equivalent of 2 teaspoons left in the pan.

Remove from the heat and leave to cool completely before finishing the sauce (you can speed cooling by holding the pot in a bowl of ice water).

Whisk the egg yolks, one by one, and 2 tablespoons of cold water into the vinegar mixture. Heat a little water in the bottom of the double boiler and set the top part in place.

Break the butter into small pieces. Whisk in a piece of the butter, then continue adding the rest of the butter little by little, whisking constantly. The sauce should become foamy at first, then thicken as the butter is added.

Keep warm over a warm hot-water bath.

Just before serving, add salt and pepper, if needed, and the remaining tarragon and chervil. Serve in a sauceboat.

This sauce should be much thicker than a Hollandaise sauce; it has more egg yolks. It has the consistency of Dijon mustard.

Serving suggestions: This is the perfect sauce for any grilled meat.

Terre Exotique
Poivre Noir
Tellicherry
Thalassery
Inde
250 ml

PREPARATION TIME: 10 MINUTES

- 1 medium onion
- 1 teaspoon (5 g) fine table salt
- 1 pinch freshly ground pepper
- 2 tablespoons capers, slightly crushed
- 1 teaspoon chopped parsley
- 1 teaspoon chopped chervil
- 1 teaspoon chopped tarragon
- 1 teaspoon Dijon mustard
- 2 tablespoons vinegar
- 5 tablespoons oil

Ravigote Sauce
Sauce ravigote

Finely chop the onion. In a mixing bowl, combine the salt, freshly ground pepper, slightly crushed capers, parsley, chervil, tarragon, mustard, and finely chopped onion. Gradually pour in the vinegar and oil and whisk in briskly to combine all the ingredients.

If you use this sauce to accompany calf's head or knuckles, add 3 tablespoons of the cooking liquid in which they were prepared.

Aïoli Sauce
Sauce aïoli

PREPARATION TIME: 10 MINUTES

8 cloves garlic
2 egg yolks
1 ¼ cups (300 ml) oil
Juice of ½ lemon
Salt

Crush the garlic using a mortar and pestle until they form a paste. Incorporate the egg yolks into the garlic paste and add a pinch of salt. Slowly drizzle the oil in, turning the pestle as you do so. To maintain the creamy consistency, add a few drops of lemon juice (the acidic element) from time to time and a few drops of warm water.

Horseradish Sauce
Sauce raifort

PREPARATION TIME: 10 MINUTES

1 lb. (500 g) white bread, crusts removed
Milk to soak the bread
1 teaspoon Dijon mustard
2 tablespoons vinegar
1 ¾ oz. (50 g) finely grated horseradish
¼ cup (50 g) granulated sugar
2 cups (500 ml) crème fraîche or heavy cream
Fine table salt

Soak the bread in some milk. When it has absorbed as much as possible, squeeze out any excess.

Combine the mustard with the vinegar. Add the horseradish, a pinch of salt, sugar, and bread. Stir the cream into the paste.

PREPARATION TIME: 5 MINUTES
MARINATING TIME: 1 TO 3 DAYS

1 medium carrot
2 onions
4 shallots
1 stick celery
2 cloves garlic
A few sprigs parsley
1 sprig thyme
½ bay leaf
1 pinch peppercorns, crushed
2 cloves
4 cups (1 liter) white wine
1 ¼ cups (300 ml) vinegar
⅔ cup (150 ml) oil

Uncooked Marinade (for meat or game)
Marinade crue

Slice the carrot, onions, and shallots. Arrange half of these vegetables at the bottom of a dish large enough to contain the piece or pieces of meat to marinade, as well as the marinade itself, of course.

Place the piece of meat over the sliced vegetables, and then cover it with the remaining vegetables and aromatic ingredients. Add the white wine, vinegar, and oil. The oil will remain on the surface and protect the marinating food from spoiling; alternatively you can cover with plastic wrap, flush with the surface.

Keep chilled and turn the piece of meat over frequently as it marinates.

PREPARATION TIME: 10 MINUTES
COOKING TIME: 35 MINUTES

Cooked Marinade
Marinade cuite

⅔ cup (150 ml) oil
1 medium carrot
2 onions
4 shallots
1 stick celery
2 cloves garlic
4 cups (1 liter) white wine
1 ¼ cups (300 ml) vinegar
A few sprigs parsley
1 sprig thyme
½ bay leaf
1 pinch peppercorns, crushed
2 cloves

The ingredients for this marinade are the same as those of the raw marinade.

Slice the carrot, onions, and shallots. Heat the oil in a saucepan and brown the vegetables slightly in it. Add the white wine, vinegar, and aromatic ingredients and simmer gently for 30 minutes.

Leave the marinade to cool completely before pouring it over the piece of meat you will be marinating.

PREPARATION TIME: 5 MINUTES

1 teaspoon Dijon mustard
1 tablespoon red wine vinegar
2 tablespoons salad oil
Salt and pepper

Vinaigrette

Place the mustard and vinegar in a mixing bowl and stir to combine, then add the oil in a steady stream, stirring as it is being added. Season with salt and pepper–the sauce is ready to use.

Variations: Vary your vinaigrettes by using different oils and different acids. For instance, use olive oil or walnut oil, sherry vinegar or lemon juice, or a mixture of vinegar and lemon juice.

Serving suggestions: Use with any salad greens, or with cold boiled vegetables, such as asparagus.

Mustard Sauce
Sauce moutarde

PREPARATION TIME: 10 MINUTES
COOKING TIME: 5 MINUTES

- 3 tablespoons (50 g) softened butter
- 2 tablespoons lemon juice
- 2 egg yolks
- 1 tablespoon cold water
- 1 generous tablespoon Dijon mustard
- Salt and pepper
- 1 tablespoon chopped parsley (optional) or 1 tablespoon capers (optional)

It's best to use a double boiler to make this sauce.

Heat a little water in the bottom of the double boiler. Break the butter into ten pieces. Place the butter, lemon juice, egg yolks, and a little salt and pepper in the top; set over the hot water and whisk vigorously until the mixture begins to thicken. Whisk in the cold water, remove the sauce from the heat, pour into a clean bowl, and allow to cool completely.

Once the sauce is cold, stir in the mustard and serve.

Serving suggestions: A tablespoon of chopped parsley may be added to the sauce just before serving with grilled meats, or a tablespoon of capers to go with grilled fish.

PREPARATION TIME: 10 MINUTES
COOKING TIME: 45 MINUTES

1 lb. (500 g) ripe tomatoes

1 small bouquet garni, made with 1 bunch parsley, 1 sprig tarragon, 2 sprigs thyme, and ¼ bay leaf

1 medium onion

1 clove garlic

6 tablespoons (100 ml) olive oil

1 teaspoon (5 g) granulated sugar

Salt and pepper

Tomato Sauce
Sauce tomate

The better the tomatoes, the better the sauce, so use perfectly ripe ones. Wash them, cut each one in half, and squeeze gently to remove the seeds.

Wash the parsley and the tarragon, and tie them together with the bay leaf and thyme to form the bouquet garni. Peel the onion and the garlic, and slice the onion.

Heat the olive oil in a large saucepan; add the garlic, onion, tomatoes, and bouquet garni. Cook uncovered over moderate heat at a rapid boil, crushing the tomatoes at first, then stirring occasionally with a wooden spoon for 35 minutes, or until the water in the tomatoes has evaporated and a thick sauce is formed.

Stir in the sugar, then grind the sauce through a food mill or purée in a blender or food processor. Taste for salt and pepper. If the sauce seems too thin at this point, you can boil it some more to thicken; otherwise it is ready to serve.

This sauce keeps well–up to a week refrigerated in a glass jar or bottle if you add a tablespoon of olive oil on top before closing the container.

Serving suggestions: Serve with pasta, white beans, fish dumplings, or ravioli.

PREPARATION TIME: 15 MINUTES

2 sprigs tarragon
3 sprigs parsley
1 bunch chives
4 sprigs chervil
1 egg yolk
1 cup (250 ml) olive oil
1 tablespoon Dijon mustard
2 tablespoons lemon juice
Salt and pepper

Green Sauce
Sauce verte aux herbes

All the ingredients should be at room temperature for making this sauce.

Carefully wash all the herbs and pat them dry using a clean towel, then use a *mezzaluna* (herb chopper) to finely chop the tarragon, parsley, and chives together on a cutting board. Separately chop the chervil and set aside. Place the egg yolk in a mixing bowl and stir in the olive oil little by little as for a mayonnaise. Once all the oil has been added, stir in the mustard and lemon juice and season with salt and pepper. Just before serving, stir in the tarragon, parsley, and chives, then sprinkle the chervil over the top and serve.

Serving suggestions: This is excellent with any cold meat, hot or cold poached fish, or boiled artichokes, asparagus, or leeks.

Mayonnaise

PREPARATION TIME: 15 MINUTES

- 1 egg yolk
- 2 generous teaspoons Dijon mustard
- 2 tablespoons red wine vinegar or lemon juice
- 1 cup (250 ml) salad oil
- Salt and pepper

All of the ingredients should be left at room temperature for at least an hour before making the sauce.

Place the egg yolk in a bowl with the mustard and half a tablespoon of the vinegar or lemon juice and whisk to combine. Whisking constantly, add the oil little by little (no more than a tablespoon at a time at first, then in a very thin stream once the mayonnaise has begun to thicken). If the mayonnaise becomes too stiff while the oil is being added, add a drizzle of vinegar then continue to add the oil in a thin stream. When all the oil has been added, stir in a little salt and pepper. Another teaspoon (or more) of vinegar or lemon juice may be added to taste if desired. If you like a thinner mayonnaise, a little warm water may be added, a teaspoon at a time, until the sauce is the desired consistency.

Mayonnaise should always be made just before you use it; never refrigerate it.

Serving suggestions: Serve with cold meat or fish, boiled artichokes or asparagus, grilled or poached lobster.

FOR FOUR $^1/_2$-PINT ($^1/_4$-LITER) JARS
PREPARATION TIME: 1 HOUR
SOAKING TIME: 12 HOURS
COOKING TIME: 5 MINUTES
MARINATING TIME: 6 WEEKS

2 ¼ lb. (1 kg) fresh pickling cucumbers, 2 in. (5 cm) long

4 ½ oz. (125 g) kosher salt

4 sprigs fresh tarragon (see Note)

24 baby onions

16-20 peppercorns

4 cups (1 liter) crystal (white) vinegar, 8 percent strength

Vinegar Pickles
Cornichons

Rinse the jars thoroughly and wipe them dry. Fresh little gherkins, also called pickling cucumbers, should be shiny and rigid when purchased. Wash them under cold running water and scrub them if necessary to remove any dirt. Place in a large dish and sprinkle the kosher salt over them, then leave them overnight.

Wipe each cucumber with a clean dry towel, then place them one by one on another towel to dry thoroughly in a cool place for 6 hours before placing them into jars. While drying, the cucumbers should be spread out so that they do not touch each other or pile up.

Place the cucumbers in the jars; do not pack them too tightly, but leave as little space between them as possible. Wash the tarragon and peel the onions. Place a sprig of tarragon, 6 baby onions, and 4 or 5 peppercorns in each jar as well.

Bring the vinegar to a boil, then pour enough into each jar to entirely cover the cucumbers. Leave the jars uncovered until the vinegar has cooled completely, then seal them. Place in a kitchen cabinet (not in the refrigerator); the pickles are ready to serve in 6 weeks.

Note: If fresh tarragon is unavailable, ¼ teaspoon of dried tarragon may be placed in each jar instead. Once opened, store the jars in the refrigerator.

PREPARATION TIME: 20 MINUTES

4 ½ oz. (125 g) anchovy fillets packed in oil
2 cloves garlic
1 tablespoon sherry vinegar
1 cup (250 ml) olive oil
Pepper

Anchovy Paste
Anchoïade

Peel the garlic. Place the anchovies and garlic in a mortar and pound to a paste (or you can purée them in a blender or food processor). Stir in the sherry vinegar, then add the oil little by little, beating in each addition vigorously with the pestle or a wooden spoon until perfectly smooth. The finished mixture should be the consistency of mayonnaise. Add pepper but no salt.

Serving suggestions: Serve in a bowl as an accompaniment to the Mixed Raw Vegetable Platter (see p. 86), or simply with celery sticks and toasted slices of whole-wheat or country-style bread.

Black Olives
Olives noires

FOR A 1-QUART (1-LITER) JAR
PREPARATION TIME: 15 MINUTES
MARINATING TIME: 10 DAYS

- 1 lb. (500 g) black olives
- 1 clove garlic
- 1 small chili pepper
- 1 teaspoon thyme leaves
- Olive oil

To give a nice flavor to ordinary black olives, try this recipe.

Peel and chop the garlic. Wash the chili pepper under running water and wipe it dry using a clean towel. Mix the olives, garlic, and thyme leaves together in a bowl.

Place half of the olives in a stoneware or glass jar, stand the chili pepper up in the middle, and add the rest of the olives. Pour in enough olive oil to cover.

Leave for at least 10 days before using.

Choux Pastry
Pâte à chou

MAKES 1 LB. (500 G)
PREPARATION TIME: 20 MINUTES
COOKING TIME: 20 TO 25 MINUTES

- 2 cups (500 ml) water
- 2 ¼ sticks (9 oz./250 g) butter
- 2 ½ cups (9 oz./250 g) flour, sifted
- 7 to 8 eggs
- 6 tablespoons milk or crème fraîche
- 1 small tablespoon of sugar
- 1 tablespoon orange blossom water
- Salt

Pour the water into a large, heavy-bottomed saucepan. Cut the butter into cubes and throw it into the water with a pinch of salt. Bring to a boil; when it boils, stir with a spatula or wooden spoon and incorporate the flour.

A dough will form; keep it over high heat, continuing to stir. The water will gradually evaporate, drying out the dough. You will be able to tell when it is completely dry when you see the butter dripping. As soon as you see this, remove the saucepan from the heat, continuing to stir as you incorporate the eggs one by one. Lastly, stir in the milk or cream.

The quantity of eggs you will need depends on their weight and on whether or not you add milk. If you add milk, not only do you save an egg, but you also make the dough more tender. Add the orange blossom water for flavor.

Stir the dough vigorously with a spatula or wooden spoon until it is smooth and light. Its consistency should not be too soft. To test whether it is ready for baking, spoon a little of the still-hot dough into a pastry bag and pipe it out. If it collapses just a little, it is ready. Follow your recipe for the shapes to pipe out and baking times.

MAKES 40 GOUGÈRES
PREPARATION TIME: 20 MINUTES
COOKING TIME: 20 TO 25 MINUTES

Gougère Batter
Pâte à gougère

2 cups (500 ml) milk
1 stick (125 g) butter
9 oz. (250 g) flour
7 to 8 eggs
6 tablespoons milk or crème fraîche
3 ½ oz. (100 g) grated Gruyère cheese
Salt

Pour the milk into a fairly large, heavy-bottomed saucepan. Cut the butter into large cubes and add it to the milk with the salt. Bring to a boil, stirring constantly with a wooden spoon. When it is boiling, pour in the flour.

Maintain the saucepan over high heat, continuing to stir vigorously with the wooden spoon while the water evaporates gradually. Continue until it is almost dry.

Then remove from the heat and continue to stir as you add the eggs one by one, and then the milk or the cream.

It is important to stir the batter very briskly to make it smooth and light. The consistency should not be too soft. When it reaches this point, incorporate the grated cheese.

Pipe out and bake for 20 to 25 minutes, or until puffed and golden, at 400°F (200°C).

MAKES 20 SMALL VOL-AU-VENTS
PREPARATION TIME: 30 MINUTES
COOKING TIME: 12 TO 15 MINUTES

Small Vol-au-Vents
Bouchées

1 ½ lb. (750 g) Puff Pastry (see p. 565)

1 egg, beaten

Preheat the oven to 400°F (200°C).

Take 1 lb. (500 g) of the puff pastry and roll it out to a thickness of ⅓ in. (8-9 mm). Using a fluted pastry cutter with a 3-in. (8-cm) diameter, cut out 20 small rounds. Each one should weigh about 1 oz. (25 g).

Lightly wet a baking tray and turn the rounds over onto it.

Brush them with a beaten egg, stopping short of the edge. This would prevent the puff pastry from rising.

Dip a plain 1 ¼-in. (3-cm) diameter pastry cutter into warm water and make a very small incision in the middle of the pastry rounds, no deeper than 1⁄18 in. (1 mm). Dip the cutter into warm water each time you make the incision in the remaining rounds.

Roll out the remaining 9 oz. (250 g) puff pastry and cut out 1 ¼-in. (3-cm) rounds. These will form the lids of the pastry cases. Use the tip of a knife to draw a criss-cross pattern on each small lid.

Bake for 12 to 15 minutes, until golden. When you take them out of the oven, remove the lids and lightly push down the pastry inside to make room for the garnish.

SERVES 6
PREPARATION TIME: 30 MINUTES
COOKING TIME: 25 MINUTES

Kouglopf Batter
Pâte à kouglopf

- 2 ¼ cups (8 oz./225 g) flour
- ⅔ cup (150 ml) milk
- ⅔ oz. (20 g) yeast
- 3 ½ tablespoons (1 ½ oz./40 g) sugar
- 1 egg
- 4 tablespoons plus 1 teaspoon (65 g) butter, softened
- ⅓ cup (1 ¾ oz./50 g) currants
- Salt
- Almonds for lining the mold
- Special equipment: a kouglopf mold

With this Alsatian pastry, dry beer yeast (brewer's yeast)–already long used in Poland and Austria–was introduced into French pastry making. After that, it was used in bread making.

Kouglof batter is similar in composition and consistence to brioche and baba batters.

Sift the flour onto the working surface and shape it into a circle with a well. Dilute the yeast in the milk. Place the sugar, a pinch of salt, egg, milk, and yeast in the center. Mix all the ingredients together until the batter is smooth. Add the butter and currants.

Follow the procedures for fermentation, placing in the mold, and baking, as for the Brioche Dough (see p. 561). Butter the mold and scatter almonds over it. Bake according to instructions for the brioche. Turn out of the kouglopf mold as soon as you remove it from the oven. Serve it as you would a brioche.

The kouglopf requires a special mold. Traditionally earthenware, it is something like a bundt pan: it has high sides with wide, angled fluting, creating a turban effect, and a hollow in the center.

Frying Batter
Pâte à frire

PREPARATION TIME: 10 MINUTES
RESTING TIME: 2 HOURS

- 2 ½ cups (9 oz./250 g) flour, sifted
- 2 eggs, separated
- ⅔ cup (150 ml) beer
- ⅔ cup (150 ml) water or milk
- 2 tablespoons melted butter or olive oil
- Fine salt

In a mixing bowl, combine the flour, a pinch of salt, and egg yolks. Gradually mix in the beer and the water or milk; lastly, stir in the butter or oil.

Leave to rest for 2 hours so that the fermentation can begin. When you are ready to start frying, whip the 2 egg whites to soft peaks and fold them in to the batter.

This frying batter should have the consistency of a light but fairly firm cream.

Pancakes
Pannequets

MAKES 20 PANCAKES
PREPARATION TIME: 15 MINUTES
RESTING TIME: 2 HOURS
COOKING TIME:
1 MINUTE PER PANCAKE

- 9 oz. (250 g) fine wheat flour
- 8 eggs, separated
- 2 cups (500 ml) milk
- Scant ½ cup (100 ml) crème fraîche or heavy cream
- 1 ¾ oz. (50 g) sugar
- 1 stick (4 oz./125 g) butter, softened
- A few drops of bitter almond extract
- 1 teaspoon vanilla-scented sugar (To make your own, leave a vanilla bean in your sugar ahead of time to flavor it.)
- Salt

Sift the flour into a mixing bowl. Mix in the egg yolks, one by one. Then incorporate the milk, cream, sugar, a pinch of salt, and softened butter.

Flavor the mixture with a few drops of bitter almond extract and the vanilla-scented sugar.

Leave to rest for 2 hours.

When you are ready to cook the pancakes, whip the 8 egg whites to firm peaks and fold them into the mixture.

Generously butter a small frying pan, or better, a crêpe pan. When it is hot, pour just enough batter to make a thin layer and spread it out evenly. Cook until it just begins to brown, about 30 seconds, and then flip over.

SERVES 6
PREPARATION TIME: 10 MINUTES
RESTING TIME: 1 HOUR
COOKING TIME:
5 MINUTES PER CRÊPE

3 tablespoons (50 g) butter, plus butter (or oil) for the pan
2 ½ cups (9 oz./250 g) flour
1 tablespoon granulated sugar
3 eggs
2 cups (500 ml) milk
Salt

Crêpes
Pâte à crêpe

At least one hour ahead of time, take the eggs, butter, and milk out of the refrigerator.

Melt the butter in a small saucepan and reserve.

Place the flour, sugar, and salt in a mixing bowl; stir in the eggs, then pour in the milk little by little, stirring at first, then whisking to make a smooth, liquid batter. Finally whisk in the melted butter. Leave the batter at room temperature for about 1 hour before making the crêpes.

Lightly butter or oil a frying pan (preferably cast-iron or nonstick). When very hot, spoon about ¼ cup (60 ml) of the batter into the center of it, and tip and turn the frying pan to cover the bottom with the batter and make a very thin pancake (crêpe). Cook the crêpe for about 2 minutes over moderate heat, turn it over using a flexible-blade spatula, and finish cooking about 3 minutes on the second side. Remove the crêpe and lightly butter the pan before cooking the next one. To keep the crêpes warm after cooking, heat a little water to simmering in a saucepan. Set a large plate on top of the saucepan. As the crêpes finish cooking, put them on the plate and cover with a second plate turned upside down.

Serve the crêpes hot with honey, walnuts, jam, or chestnut cream. They are also delicious simply spread with a little butter and sprinkled with granulated sugar.

COOKIES, CAKES & CONFECTIONS

FOR ABOUT 25 COOKIES
PREPARATION TIME: 10 MINUTES
COOKING TIME: 7 MINUTES PER BATCH

1 egg yolk
⅔ cup (120 g) granulated sugar
½ cup (50 g) flour
1 ½ cup (120 g) slivered almonds
3 egg whites
2 tablespoons (30g) butter (for the baking sheet)
Salt

Almond Cookies
Tuiles

At least one hour ahead of time, take the eggs and butter out of the refrigerator.

Preheat the oven to 350°F (180°C).

In a mixing bowl, beat the egg yolk and sugar until smooth and pale, then stir in the flour, a pinch of salt, and almonds.

In a separate bowl, beat the egg whites until thick and foamy, but not stiff, then pour them into the bowl with the almond mixture. Cut and fold them into the other ingredients.

Generously butter a baking sheet. Place a generous teaspoon of the batter on the sheet and flatten it out completely, spreading out the almonds with the back of the spoon to make a thin disc about 2 in. (5 cm) wide. When the baking sheet is full–leave lots of space between the cookies–place in the oven and bake for 5 to 6 minutes. When done, the edge of each cookie will be golden brown, but the center will remain pale. Remove the cookies three or four at a time and lay them on a lightly floured rolling pin (leave the baking sheet with the remaining cookies in the oven with the door ajar). Drape the cookies over a rolling pin and hold them in place for about 15 seconds so that when they cool they will be arched rather than flat. Alternatively, a tuile mold sheet–an undulating metal sheet made up of several cylinders which allow the cookies to cool in a curved shape–can be used.

Note: You will have to bake the cookies in several batches. Don't make them more than a few hours before you intend to serve them, because they don't keep well. In any case, as soon as they are completely cool, place them in a tightly closed cookie tin.

… Soufflé

PREPA…
C…

…king tray in the

…in-
…the
…the
…gradu-
…chosen
…ites.

…und and at

Fill the mold … rters full, and smooth the surface with … draw a flower shape on the surface.

First place the mold on the baking tray for 1 minute to warm the base. This will help the soufflé rise well. Place in the oven. You will have to keep a careful eye on the soufflé's progress: rotate it a quarter of a turn fairly frequently. Do so as quickly and carefully as possible so you leave the oven door open for the least possible time. The soufflé will be done in 18 to 20 minutes.

Dust lightly with confectioners' sugar and serve immediately.

Almond Cookies
Tuiles

FOR ABOUT 25 COOKIES
PREPARATION TIME: 10 MINUTES
COOKING TIME: 7 MINUTES PER BATCH

---

1 egg yolk
⅔ cup (120 g) granulated sugar
½ cup (50 g) flour
1 ½ cup (120 g) slivered almonds
3 egg whites
2 tablespoons (30g) butter (for the baking sheet)
Salt

At least one hour ahead of time, take the eggs and butter out of the refrigerator.

Preheat the oven to 350°F (180°C).

In a mixing bowl, beat the egg yolk and sugar until smooth and pale, then stir in the flour, a pinch of salt, and almonds.

In a separate bowl, beat the egg whites until thick and foamy, but not stiff, then pour them into the bowl with the almond mixture. Cut and fold them into the other ingredients.

Generously butter a baking sheet. Place a generous teaspoon of the batter on the sheet and flatten it out completely, spreading out the almonds with the back of the spoon to make a thin disc about 2 in. (5 cm) wide. When the baking sheet is full–leave lots of space between the cookies–place in the oven and bake for 5 to 6 minutes. When done, the edge of each cookie will be golden brown, but the center will remain pale. Remove the cookies three or four at a time and lay them on a lightly floured rolling pin (leave the baking sheet with the remaining cookies in the oven with the door ajar). Drape the cookies over a rolling pin and hold them in place for about 15 seconds so that when they cool they will be arched rather than flat. Alternatively, a tuile mold sheet–an undulating metal sheet made up of several cylinders which allow the cookies to cool in a curved shape–can be used.

Note: You will have to bake the cookies in several batches. Don't make them more than a few hours before you intend to serve them, because they don't keep well. In any case, as soon as they are completely cool, place them in a tightly closed cookie tin.

SERVES 6
PREPARATION TIME: 30 MINUTES
COOKING TIME: 30 MINUTES

Chocolate Soufflé
Soufflé au chocolat

- 2 ¾ oz. (80 g) bittersweet chocolate
- 1 tablespoon plus 1 teaspoon (20 g) butter, plus extra for the soufflé dish
- ¾ cup (200 ml) milk
- 4 eggs, separated
- ¼ cup (1 ¾ oz./50 g) sugar, plus 1 tablespoon for the mold
- 1 or 2 tablespoons liqueur of your choice
- 1 egg yolk

Preheat the oven to 350°F (180°C). Place a baking tray in the center to heat–you will need it when you begin baking.

Break up the chocolate and melt it with the butter over a bain-marie, or hot water bath. Cook gently for 10 minutes. Stir in the milk and reduce it until it forms a thick syrup. Remove from the heat and incorporate the egg yolks. Whisk the egg whites, gradually adding the sugar, until they are very firm. Stir your chosen liqueur into the mixture and carefully fold in the egg whites.

Generously butter a soufflé mold and dust it well all round and at the bottom with confectioners' sugar.

Fill the mold with the mixture at least three-quarters full, and smooth the surface with a knife. Use the tip to draw a flower shape on the surface.

First place the mold on the baking tray for 1 minute to warm the base. This will help the soufflé rise well. Place in the oven. You will have to keep a careful eye on the soufflé's progress: rotate it a quarter of a turn fairly frequently. Do so as quickly and carefully as possible so you leave the oven door open for the least possible time. The soufflé will be done in 18 to 20 minutes.

Dust lightly with confectioners' sugar and serve immediately.

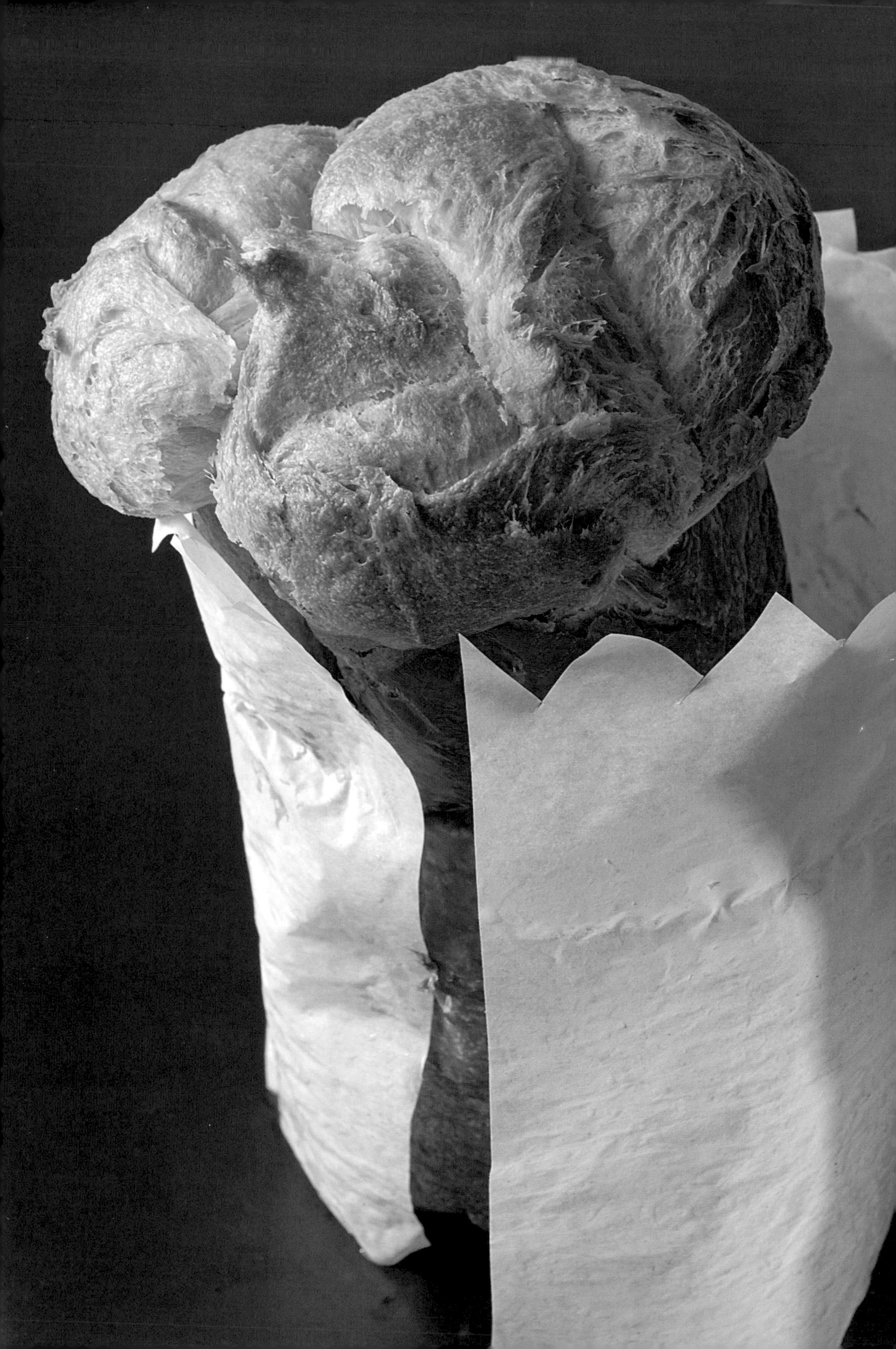

Brioche Mousseline

PREPARATION TIME: 40 MINUTES
COOKING TIME: 25 TO 30 MINUTES

1 lb. (500 g) Brioche Dough (see p. 561)

1 stick plus 2 teaspoons (135 g) butter, softened

Roll out the brioche dough into a thick circle. Spread 1 stick (125 g) softened butter over it and fold it over several times. The butter will eventually be incorporated into the dough. Form the dough into a ball. Butter a plain, round, narrow mold and line it with parchment paper, which should be cut about 1 in. (3 cm) higher than the rim. Cut the edge of the paper into a zigzag.

Leave the dough to rise as you would for the brioche with a head.

Preheat the oven to 350°F (180°C).

Brush it with melted butter and use the scissors to make a cross-shaped incision on the top.

Bake for 25 to 30 minutes, until the top is golden.

Turn the brioche out of the mold, leaving the paper on. It will ensure that this fine pastry remains soft until you serve it.

MAKES ABOUT 20 COOKIES
PREPARATION TIME: 15 MINUTES
COOKING TIME: 8 MINUTES

Classic Cat's Tongue Cookies
Langues de chat (recette commune)

⅔ cup (4 ½ oz./125 g) sugar

1 teaspoon vanilla-scented sugar (To make your own, leave a vanilla bean in your sugar ahead of time to flavor it.)

1 egg

Scant ½ cup (100 ml) whipping cream or milk

1 ¼ cups (4 ½ oz./125 g) flour

Preheat the oven to 350°F (180°C).

In a mixing bowl, dilute the sugar and vanilla-scented sugar in the egg and milk or cream. Sift in the flour and mix until smooth.

Spoon the batter into a pastry bag fitted with a plain ¼-in. (5-mm) tip and pipe it out into lengths of 3-4 in. (8-10 cm), leaving about 2 ¼ in. (6 cm) between each one so that they can spread. Alternatively, an éclair/ladyfinger pan may be used.

Bake for 7 to 8 minutes, until they are a golden color with light brown edges.

Remove the cookies from the baking tray before they cool down completely and, when cool, store in an airtight metal container so that they retain their crumbly texture.

MAKES 30 TO 40 LADYFINGERS
PREPARATION TIME: 40 MINUTES
COOKING TIME: 10 TO 15 MINUTES

2 ⅔ cups (1 lb./500 g) sugar, plus a little extra to sift over the ladyfingers

16 eggs, separated

4 cups (14 oz./400 g) flour

1 teaspoon vanilla-scented sugar (To make your own, leave a vanilla bean in your sugar ahead of time to flavor it.)

Ladyfingers
Biscuits à cuillère

Preheat the oven to 350°F (180°C).

Place the egg yolks in a large mixing bowl and add the sugar.

Mix vigorously until the batter triples in volume and becomes pale in color and creamy. It should reach the ribbon stage, when it slips down from the spoon or spatula to form a thick ribbon.

Then fold in the flour, lifting up the batter as you do so. Whip the egg whites to very firm peaks, add the vanilla-scented sugar, and fold in one-quarter of the whipped egg whites. When they are thoroughly combined, add the remaining whipped egg whites, folding them in delicately so that the batter does not become heavy.

Line a baking tray with parchment paper. Spoon the batter into a pastry bag fitted with a plain 1-in. (2.5-cm) diameter tip. Close the bag and pipe out 5-in. (12-cm) lengths leaving 2 in. (5 cm) between each one. Alternatively, a ladyfinger/éclair pan can be used.

Sift some sugar over the ladyfingers. Leave them for 2 minutes and then tilt the baking tray to remove the excess sugar. Using a brush dipped in cold water (shake off any excess), spray droplets onto the sugar that sticks to the ladyfingers. The drops combined with the sugar will form small beads when baked.

Place the baking trays in the oven and bake. The cookies should barely color. Remove after about 10 to 15 minutes. Leave to cool on the tray. Detach when completely cooked and store in an air-tight container so that they retain their very soft texture.

MAKES 6 PASTRIES
PREPARATION TIME: 40 MINUTES
COOKING TIME: 20 MINUTES

Lattice-Topped Almond Pastries
Jalousies aux amandes

1 lb.(500 g) Puff Pastry (see p. 565)

1 egg, beaten

Confectioners' sugar

ALMOND CREAM

1 cup plus scant ½ cup (4 ½ oz./125 g) ground almonds

⅔ cup (4 ½oz./125 g) sugar

3 eggs

1 stick (125 g) butter

1 teaspoon vanilla-scented sugar (To make your own, leave a vanilla bean in your sugar ahead of time to flavor it.)

1 tablespoon rum

Combine all the ingredients for the almond cream together to make a smooth, creamy paste.

Roll the puff pastry out to form a first rectangle 7 in. (18 cm) wide, 12 to 16 in. (30 to 40 cm) long, and ¼ in. (6 mm) thick.

Gather the trimmings together and roll out a second rectangle of the same dimensions but slightly thinner than the first.

Lightly wet a baking sheet and place the second rectangle on it. Prick it with a fork so that it does not swell when it bakes. Brush the edges with a little water and spread the almond cream over it. It should be just under 1 in. (2 cm) thick and 3 in. (8 cm) wide. Cover this with the first rectangle. Press round the edges with your fingers to seal it, and trim the two sides straight using a knife. Make close, shallow, angled incisions with the tip of a knife along the sides. This helps seal the two layers of pastry together. Brush the top with the beaten egg or sprinkle it with sugar. Using the tip of a knife, draw out divisions 2 ½ to 3 in. (6 to 8 cm) wide. In each section, draw leaf patterns.

Bake at 400°F-425°F (200°C-210°C) until golden, about 20 to 25 minutes.

If you brushed the top with egg, sprinkle with confectioners' sugar as soon as you remove the pastry from the oven.

Leave to cool and cut into the sections to serve.

SERVES 6
PREPARATION TIME: 20 MINUTES
COOKING TIME: 45 MINUTES

Chocolate Marble Cake
Marbré au chocolat

- 1 stick (120 g) softened butter, plus butter for the mold
- 2 large eggs
- ⅔ cup (120 g) granulated sugar
- 1 ¼ cups (125 g) flour
- 1 ¾ oz. (50 g) bittersweet chocolate
- Salt

One hour and a half ahead of time, take the eggs and the butter out of the refrigerator.

Preheat the oven to 350°F (180°C).

Place the butter in a bowl near a source of heat to soften, but don't let it melt.

Break the eggs into a teacup to check they are fresh. Beat the eggs and sugar in a mixing bowl until smooth and a pale yellow color, then sift in the flour, whisking as it is being added. Whisk in the softened butter and a pinch of salt; the finished batter should be smooth.

Melt the chocolate in a double boiler.

Lightly butter a 9 ½-in. (24-cm) pound cake or loaf pan, line it with parchment paper, then lightly butter the paper as well. Pour the melted chocolate over the batter, then barely stir it in, so that there will be light and dark patches. Pour the batter into the mold, smooth the surface, and bake for 45 minutes. Test to see if the cake is done by sticking a needle or knife blade into the center; it should come out clean and dry. If not, bake the cake a little longer.

Turn the mold upside down on a cake rack to cool as soon as you take the cake from the oven, but don't lift it off of the cake until it has cooled completely.

When cool, lift off the mold, peel off the paper, turn right side up and serve on a serving platter.

This cake will stay fresh up to a week wrapped in aluminum foil.

Serving suggestions: Serve with Vanilla Custard Sauce (see p. 699) or Chocolate Mousse (see p. 670) on the side.

SERVES 8
PREPARATION TIME: 30 MINUTES
COOKING TIME: 40 MINUTES

FIRST METHOD

1 ¾ sticks (7 oz./200 g) butter

1 ½ cups (10 oz./300 g) sugar

8 eggs

9 oz. (250 g) blanched ground almonds

A few drops bitter almond extract

2 teaspoons Curaçao

Scant ⅔ cup (2 oz./60 g) flour

SECOND METHOD

9 oz. (250 g) blanched almonds

6 eggs

1 cup plus 1 scant cup (12 oz./350 g) sugar

Scant ⅔ cup (2 oz./60 g) flour

1 stick (125 g) butter, melted

1 teaspoon anise-flavored liqueur

Genovese Loaf
Pain de Gênes

The Genovese loaf is one of the finest sponge desserts. Use either of the two methods given here depending on your kitchen equipment.

First method

Soften the butter in a mixing bowl so that you can work it with a flexible spatula or wooden spoon. Add the sugar and stir energetically with the spatula until the mixture becomes paler in color. Alternatively, a food mixer may be used. Separate 4 eggs and set aside. Then add the ground almonds, and next, 4 whole eggs, one by one, followed by 4 egg yolks. Mix in well.

As the mixture becomes airier it becomes creamy and increases in volume. Carefully add the Curaçao and the flour. Whip the 4 egg whites well and fold them in carefully.

Second method

If the almonds are not already peeled, place them in boiling water for 1 minute and peel them. Then pound or grind them. When they are finely ground, add the eggs, one by one, followed by the sugar. Work energetically with the spoon until the mixture becomes creamy and airy. When it is ready, carefully fold in the flour and the melted butter.

To flavor, add the teaspoon of anise liqueur.

For both methods, butter a cake mold and pour the batter in. Bake at 350°F (180°C) for 40 minutes.

SERVES 6
PREPARATION TIME: 20 MINUTES
COOKING TIME: 45 MINUTES

Chocolate Marble Cake
Marbré au chocolat

- 1 stick (120 g) softened butter, plus butter for the mold
- 2 large eggs
- ⅔ cup (120 g) granulated sugar
- 1 ¼ cups (125 g) flour
- 1 ¾ oz. (50 g) bittersweet chocolate
- Salt

One hour and a half ahead of time, take the eggs and the butter out of the refrigerator.

Preheat the oven to 350°F (180°C).

Place the butter in a bowl near a source of heat to soften, but don't let it melt.

Break the eggs into a teacup to check they are fresh. Beat the eggs and sugar in a mixing bowl until smooth and a pale yellow color, then sift in the flour, whisking as it is being added. Whisk in the softened butter and a pinch of salt; the finished batter should be smooth.

Melt the chocolate in a double boiler.

Lightly butter a 9 ½-in. (24-cm) pound cake or loaf pan, line it with parchment paper, then lightly butter the paper as well. Pour the melted chocolate over the batter, then barely stir it in, so that there will be light and dark patches. Pour the batter into the mold, smooth the surface, and bake for 45 minutes. Test to see if the cake is done by sticking a needle or knife blade into the center; it should come out clean and dry. If not, bake the cake a little longer.

Turn the mold upside down on a cake rack to cool as soon as you take the cake from the oven, but don't lift it off of the cake until it has cooled completely.

When cool, lift off the mold, peel off the paper, turn right side up and serve on a serving platter.

This cake will stay fresh up to a week wrapped in aluminum foil.

Serving suggestions: Serve with Vanilla Custard Sauce (see p. 699) or Chocolate Mousse (see p. 670) on the side.

Rhum
EGRITA
BARDINET
1857

SERVES 6
PREPARATION TIME: 20 MINUTES
COOKING TIME: 45 MINUTES

Chocolate Marble Cake
Marbré au chocolat

- 1 stick (120 g) softened butter, plus butter for the mold
- 2 large eggs
- ⅔ cup (120 g) granulated sugar
- 1 ¼ cups (125 g) flour
- 1 ¾ oz. (50 g) bittersweet chocolate
- Salt

One hour and a half ahead of time, take the eggs and the butter out of the refrigerator.

Preheat the oven to 350°F (180°C).

Place the butter in a bowl near a source of heat to soften, but don't let it melt.

Break the eggs into a teacup to check they are fresh. Beat the eggs and sugar in a mixing bowl until smooth and a pale yellow color, then sift in the flour, whisking as it is being added. Whisk in the softened butter and a pinch of salt; the finished batter should be smooth.

Melt the chocolate in a double boiler.

Lightly butter a 9 ½-in. (24-cm) pound cake or loaf pan, line it with parchment paper, then lightly butter the paper as well. Pour the melted chocolate over the batter, then barely stir it in, so that there will be light and dark patches. Pour the batter into the mold, smooth the surface, and bake for 45 minutes. Test to see if the cake is done by sticking a needle or knife blade into the center; it should come out clean and dry. If not, bake the cake a little longer.

Turn the mold upside down on a cake rack to cool as soon as you take the cake from the oven, but don't lift it off of the cake until it has cooled completely.

When cool, lift off the mold, peel off the paper, turn right side up and serve on a serving platter.

This cake will stay fresh up to a week wrapped in aluminum foil.

Serving suggestions: Serve with Vanilla Custard Sauce (see p. 699) or Chocolate Mousse (see p. 670) on the side.

Rhum
1857

Chocolate Marble Cake
Marbré au chocolat

SERVES 6
PREPARATION TIME: 20 MINUTES
COOKING TIME: 45 MINUTES

1 stick (120 g) softened butter, plus butter for the mold
2 large eggs
⅔ cup (120 g) granulated sugar
1 ¼ cups (125 g) flour
1 ¾ oz. (50 g) bittersweet chocolate
Salt

One hour and a half ahead of time, take the eggs and the butter out of the refrigerator.

Preheat the oven to 350°F (180°C).

Place the butter in a bowl near a source of heat to soften, but don't let it melt.

Break the eggs into a teacup to check they are fresh. Beat the eggs and sugar in a mixing bowl until smooth and a pale yellow color, then sift in the flour, whisking as it is being added. Whisk in the softened butter and a pinch of salt; the finished batter should be smooth.

Melt the chocolate in a double boiler.

Lightly butter a 9 ½-in. (24-cm) pound cake or loaf pan, line it with parchment paper, then lightly butter the paper as well. Pour the melted chocolate over the batter, then barely stir it in, so that there will be light and dark patches. Pour the batter into the mold, smooth the surface, and bake for 45 minutes. Test to see if the cake is done by sticking a needle or knife blade into the center; it should come out clean and dry. If not, bake the cake a little longer.

Turn the mold upside down on a cake rack to cool as soon as you take the cake from the oven, but don't lift it off of the cake until it has cooled completely.

When cool, lift off the mold, peel off the paper, turn right side up and serve on a serving platter.

This cake will stay fresh up to a week wrapped in aluminum foil.

Serving suggestions: Serve with Vanilla Custard Sauce (see p. 699) or Chocolate Mousse (see p. 670) on the side.

Rhum
BARDINET
1857

SERVES 6
PREPARATION TIME: 20 MINUTES
COOKING TIME: 45 MINUTES

Chocolate Marble Cake
Marbré au chocolat

1 stick (120 g) softened butter, plus butter for the mold
2 large eggs
⅔ cup (120 g) granulated sugar
1 ¼ cups (125 g) flour
1 ¾ oz. (50 g) bittersweet chocolate
Salt

One hour and a half ahead of time, take the eggs and the butter out of the refrigerator.

Preheat the oven to 350°F (180°C).

Place the butter in a bowl near a source of heat to soften, but don't let it melt.

Break the eggs into a teacup to check they are fresh. Beat the eggs and sugar in a mixing bowl until smooth and a pale yellow color, then sift in the flour, whisking as it is being added. Whisk in the softened butter and a pinch of salt; the finished batter should be smooth.

Melt the chocolate in a double boiler.

Lightly butter a 9 ½-in. (24-cm) pound cake or loaf pan, line it with parchment paper, then lightly butter the paper as well. Pour the melted chocolate over the batter, then barely stir it in, so that there will be light and dark patches. Pour the batter into the mold, smooth the surface, and bake for 45 minutes. Test to see if the cake is done by sticking a needle or knife blade into the center; it should come out clean and dry. If not, bake the cake a little longer.

Turn the mold upside down on a cake rack to cool as soon as you take the cake from the oven, but don't lift it off of the cake until it has cooled completely.

When cool, lift off the mold, peel off the paper, turn right side up and serve on a serving platter.

This cake will stay fresh up to a week wrapped in aluminum foil.

Serving suggestions: Serve with Vanilla Custard Sauce (see p. 699) or Chocolate Mousse (see p. 670) on the side.

Alsatian Apple Cake
Gâteau alsacien

SERVES 5 TO 6
PREPARATION TIME: 20 MINUTES
COOKING TIME: 45 TO 50 MINUTES

- 9 oz. (250 g) white bread or soft dinner rolls
- 5 large (1 lb./450 g) apples
- 1 vanilla bean
- ¾ cups (200 ml) milk
- 6 tablespoons (75 g) granulated sugar
- 2 eggs, separated
- 1 tablespoon Kirsch (cherry brandy)
- 1 ½ tablespoons (20 g) butter, plus butter for the mold
- 2 tablespoons cinnamon
- 2 tablespoons bread crumbs

Leave the bread out overnight so that it will become stale before using it to make the cake. Cut the bread into ½-in. (1-cm) cubes and place in a mixing bowl.

Peel the apples and thinly slice them. Cut the vanilla bean in half lengthwise.

Place the milk in a saucepan with the vanilla bean and bring to a boil, then pour onto the bread and leave for 30 minutes.

Preheat the oven to 350°F (180°C).

Remove the vanilla bean from the bowl and crush the bread to a paste with a fork. Stir in the sugar, then the egg yolks, and finally the apples and cherry brandy.

Beat the egg whites until stiff and fold them into the other ingredients. Butter an 8-in. (20-cm) square or 9-in. (22-cm) cake pan and pour in the batter. Break the butter into little pieces. Mix the cinnamon and bread crumbs together, then sprinkle over the batter. Dot with the butter, then bake for 40 to 45 minutes, or until a knife stuck into the center comes out clean. Serve cold.

SERVES 4
PREPARATION TIME: 10 MINUTES
COOKING TIME: 40 MINUTES

Sponge Cake
Gâteau manqué

Generous ¾ cup (180 g) granulated sugar, divided
1 cup (100 g) flour
3 eggs
½ cup (120 ml) milk
2 tablespoons (30 g) butter, plus butter for the cake pan

Preheat the oven to 450°F-475°F (240°C), or as high as your oven will go.

Place 150 g of the sugar, the flour, eggs, and milk in a bowl and beat to make a smooth batter. Break the butter into pieces and set aside.

Generously butter an 8-in. (20-cm) cake pan (preferably porcelain), pour in the batter, and place immediately in the hot oven. Bake for 20 minutes, then lower the heat to 350°F (180°C), dot with the butter, sprinkle with the remaining sugar, and bake for 20 minutes more.

Serving suggestions: Serve hot or cold, either plain or with Vanilla Custard Sauce (see p. 699).

Rhum
BARDINET
1857

Maurice Bernachon's Rum Savarins
Savarins au rhum Maurice Bernachon

SERVES 8
PREPARATION TIME: 30 MINUTES
MACERATION TIME: OVERNIGHT
RESTING TIME: 3 HOURS
COOKING TIME: 30 MINUTES

Scant cup (5oz./150 g) currants
Aged rum
9 oz. (250 g) high gluten wheat flour
⅓ oz. (10 g) fresh yeast
4 eggs
1 ⅓ sticks (150 g) butter
¾ teaspoon (7 g) salt
1 ½ tablespoons (20 g) sugar

SAVARIN SYRUP
4 cups (1 liter) water
1 cup (250 ml) aged rum
2 ⅔ cups (1 lb./500 g) sugar

A day ahead, macerate the currants in a little rum.

The next day, sift the flour into a mixing bowl and add the yeast. Dissolve it with just a little water at room temperature and add the eggs. Knead the dough, roll it out, cover it with the butter but do not blend it in. Leave to rise for 2 hours. Then knead in the salt, the sugar, and the drained currants. Shape the dough and place it in a savarin mold. Leave to rise for 1 hour, and then bake for about 30 minutes at 350°F (180°C). Turn out of the mold when baked.

For the Savarin syrup, bring all the ingredients to a boil. Dip the savarins in it and leave them to drip off on a rack. When the excess has dripped off, garnish with fruit and serve with apricot sauce, for example. You may also make the syrup with good maraschino liqueur.

Maurice Bernachon was a renowned chocolatier in Lyon and founder of the Maison Bernachon, which also sells fine pastries.

Madeleines

MAKES 24 LARGE MADELEINES
PREPARATION TIME: 15 MINUTES
COOKING TIME: 20 MINUTES

- 1 ¼ sticks (150 g) butter
- Generous ⅔ cup (150 g) granulated sugar
- 1 tablespoon orange flower water
- 3 eggs
- 1 ½ cups (150 g) flour

At least one hour ahead of time, take the eggs and butter out of the refrigerator.

Preheat the oven to 425°F (210°C).

Melt the butter in a small saucepan. Place the sugar, orange flower water, and eggs in a mixing bowl and beat with a whisk. Whisk in the melted butter, then add the flour little by little, whisking constantly to make a smooth batter.

Lightly butter the madeleine molds, then fill them to about three-quarters with the batter. Bake for 20 minutes, until a rich golden brown, then turn out onto a cake rack and allow to cool before serving.

Variation: Orange flower water can be replaced by a tablespoon of finely grated orange peel or lemon peel if preferred.

Note: Madeleines are usually baked in elongated, shell-shaped molds, but any shallow cupcake or cookie mold could be used for baking them.

MAKES 20 TWISTS
PREPARATION TIME: 20 MINUTES
COOKING TIME: 10 TO 15 MINUTES

Puff Pastry Twists
Sacristains

4 oz. (125 g) Half Puff Pastry (see pp. 565-66)
1 egg, beaten
A handful of chopped almonds
Sugar as needed

Preheat the oven to 400°F-425°F (200°C-210°C).

Preferably use puff pastry trimmings gathered together. Roll out the pastry to form a rectangle ¼ in. (5 mm) thick. Trim with a knife so that it is 6 in. (15 cm) wide.

Brush the pastry with the egg and sprinkle it generously with chopped almonds. Dust generously with sugar. Lightly press the almonds and sugar in with the back of a knife so that they stick.

Lightly sprinkle another working surface with sugar. Turn the piece of dough over onto it and repeat the procedure: brush with egg, sprinkle with chopped almonds, dust with sugar, and press in the almonds and sugar with the back of a knife.

Dampen a baking sheet. Cut out small strips just over 1 in. (3 cm) wide. Take them, one by one, and twist them twice. Place them on the baking sheet and bake for 10-15 minutes until a nice golden color. Keep a careful eye on the sacristains, as the sugar caramelizes very quickly and may burn quickly.

You can also make these puff pastry delicacies in a very small size and serve them as petits fours.

SERVES 8
PREPARATION TIME: 15 MINUTES
COOKING TIME: 35 TO 40 MINUTES

Chocolate Genoese Sponge
Génoise au chocolat

- 8 eggs
- 1 ¼ cups (9 oz./250 g) sugar
- 9 oz. (250 g) fine wheat flour
- 7 tablespoons (1 ¾ oz./50 g) unsweetened cocoa powder
- 1 generous cup (3 ½ oz./100 g) ground almonds
- 1 ⅓ sticks (5 oz./150 g) butter, melted

Preheat the oven to 350°F (180°C).

In a double-boiler, combine the eggs with the sugar. Sift the flour with the cocoa powder and ground almonds and add them to the egg mixture. When this is thoroughly combined, stir in the melted butter.

Bake for 35 to 40 minutes, then turn out onto a wire tray to cool.

SERVES 8
PREPARATION TIME: 30 MINUTES
COOKING TIME: 20 TO 25 MINUTES

Savoy Sponge Cake
Biscuit de Savoie

- 12 eggs, separated
- 2 ⅔ cups (1 lb./500 g) sugar
- 5 cups (1 lb./500 g) flour
- 1 teaspoon vanilla-scented sugar (To make your own, leave a vanilla bean in your sugar ahead of time to flavor it.)
- 1 tablespoon flour or cornstarch
- 1 tablespoon confectioners' or castor sugar
- Butter to grease the mold, clarified

Preheat the oven to 350°F (180°C).

Place the egg yolks in a large mixing bowl and add the sugar.

Mix vigorously until the batter triples in volume and becomes pale in color and creamy. It should reach the ribbon stage, when it slips down from the spoon or spatula to form a thick ribbon.

Then fold in the flour, lifting up the batter as you do so. Whip the egg whites to very firm peaks, add the vanilla-scented sugar, and fold in one-quarter of the whipped egg whites. When they are thoroughly combined, add the remaining whipped egg whites, folding them in delicately so that the batter does not become heavy.

You should use high, round, fluted molds. Traditionally, they are decorated.

Butter the molds carefully with clarified butter and turn them upside down so that the excess can drip off. Make a mixture of half flour or starch, half caster or confectioners' sugar, and dust the inside of the mold.

Bake for 20 to 25 minutes, until a very light yellow. The dusted sugar will form a delicate, crumbly envelope.

Leave to rest for 5 minutes before turning out of the mold.

SERVES 8
PREPARATION TIME: 30 MINUTES
COOKING TIME: 40 MINUTES

FIRST METHOD

- 1 ¾ sticks (7 oz./200 g) butter
- 1 ½ cups (10 oz./300 g) sugar
- 8 eggs
- 9 oz. (250 g) blanched ground almonds
- A few drops bitter almond extract
- 2 teaspoons Curaçao
- Scant ⅔ cup (2 oz./60 g) flour

SECOND METHOD

- 9 oz. (250 g) blanched almonds
- 6 eggs
- 1 cup plus 1 scant cup (12 oz./350 g) sugar
- Scant ⅔ cup (2 oz./60 g) flour
- 1 stick (125 g) butter, melted
- 1 teaspoon anise-flavored liqueur

Genovese Loaf
Pain de Gênes

The Genovese loaf is one of the finest sponge desserts. Use either of the two methods given here depending on your kitchen equipment.

First method

Soften the butter in a mixing bowl so that you can work it with a flexible spatula or wooden spoon. Add the sugar and stir energetically with the spatula until the mixture becomes paler in color. Alternatively, a food mixer may be used. Separate 4 eggs and set aside. Then add the ground almonds, and next, 4 whole eggs, one by one, followed by 4 egg yolks. Mix in well.

As the mixture becomes airier it becomes creamy and increases in volume. Carefully add the Curaçao and the flour. Whip the 4 egg whites well and fold them in carefully.

Second method

If the almonds are not already peeled, place them in boiling water for 1 minute and peel them. Then pound or grind them. When they are finely ground, add the eggs, one by one, followed by the sugar. Work energetically with the spoon until the mixture becomes creamy and airy. When it is ready, carefully fold in the flour and the melted butter.

To flavor, add the teaspoon of anise liqueur.

For both methods, butter a cake mold and pour the batter in. Bake at 350°F (180°C) for 40 minutes.

MAKES 20 COOKIES
PREPARATION TIME: 15 MINUTES
COOKING TIME: 10 TO 15 MINUTES

Sugared Puff Pastry Cookies
Palets au sucre

4 ½ oz. (125 g) Half Puff Pastry (see pp. 565-66)

2 ½ tablespoons (1 oz./30 g) granulated sugar

Preheat the oven to 350°F (180°C).

Roll out the half puff pastry (or trimmings) to a thickness of ¼-⅓ in. (6-7 mm). Cut it out into small disks using a cutter.

Sprinkle the working surface generously with sugar. Drape one pastry disk over the rolling pin and roll it out in the sugar, lengthening it until it becomes oval. Repeat with the remaining disks.

Lightly wet a baking tray and place the cookies on it, sugar side downward. Bake for 10-15 minutes until light golden. Keep a careful eye on them as they bake; the sugar caramelizes quickly and may burn.

MAKES 20 COOKIES
PREPARATION TIME: 15 MINUTES
COOKING TIME: 10 TO 15 MINUTES

4 ½ oz. (125 g) Half Puff Pastry (see pp. 565-66)

2 ½ tablespoons (1 oz./30 g) granulated sugar

Sugared Puff Pastry Cookies
Palets au sucre

Preheat the oven to 350°F (180°C).

Roll out the half puff pastry (or trimmings) to a thickness of ¼-⅓ in. (6-7 mm). Cut it out into small disks using a cutter.

Sprinkle the working surface generously with sugar. Drape one pastry disk over the rolling pin and roll it out in the sugar, lengthening it until it becomes oval. Repeat with the remaining disks.

Lightly wet a baking tray and place the cookies on it, sugar side downward. Bake for 10-15 minutes until light golden. Keep a careful eye on them as they bake; the sugar caramelizes quickly and may burn.

MAKES ABOUT 40 COOKIES
PREPARATION TIME: 20 MINUTES
RESTING TIME: 20 MINUTES
COOKING TIME: 8 TO 10 MINUTES

- 3 ⅓ sticks (13 oz./375 g) butter, room temperature
- 2 eggs
- 5 cups (1 lb./500 g) flour
- 1 ¼ cups (9 oz./250 g) sugar
- 3 cups (9 oz./250 g) ground blanched almonds
- 1 teaspoon vanilla-scented sugar (To make your own, leave a vanilla bean in your sugar ahead of time to flavor it.)
  or
  1 tablespoon rum

Shortbread Cookies
Gâteaux sablés fins

Preheat the oven to 375°F (190°C).

Combine the butter with the eggs. Combine the flour with the sugar and ground almonds.

Working on a counter, rapidly knead the butter-egg mixture into the flour mixture. If the dough is too firm and seems to break easily, add either 1 whole egg or 2 egg yolks.

To flavor, add either the vanilla-scented sugar or the rum.

Wrap the dough up in a clean cloth or plastic wrap and leave to rest for 20 minutes.

Roll it out very thinly, 1/12 to ⅛ in. (3 to 4 mm) thick and use a fluted pastry cutter to cut out small squares. Place them on a baking tray and prick them with a fork so that they do not swell in the oven.

Bake for 8 to 10 minutes, until a lovely golden color. They will be delicate and crumbly. Store in an airtight container.

PREPARATION TIME: 10 MINUTES
COOKING TIME: 25 MINUTES

1 cup (7 oz./200 g) sugar
7 oz. (200 g) blanched, chopped almonds

Almond Nougatine
Nougat aux amandes

Keep the almonds warm as you prepare the syrup. Oil a baking pan lightly.

Place the sugar in a copper or other heavy-bottomed pot. Heat gently, stirring constantly.

Without any liquid added, the sugar will melt at 325°F (160°C), when it changes to a light yellow color. As soon as it turns into a syrup, pour in the chopped almonds and remove immediately from the heat. Stir until thoroughly combined and pour into the oiled pan. Keep the pan in a gently warmed oven while you mold the nougatine pieces in oiled molds.

Leave the nougatine to solidify in the molds and then turn the pieces out.

Plain Meringues
Meringues ordinaires

MAKES 20 MERINGUES
PREPARATION TIME: 15 MINUTES
COOKING TIME: 1 HOUR

- 8 egg whites
- 2 ½ cups (1 lb./500 g) sugar
- A little confectioners' sugar for dusting

Preheat the oven to 250°F (120°C).

Whisk the egg whites. When they begin to firm up, pour in all the sugar and whisk further until glossy.

Line a baking tray with parchment paper. Spoon the preparation into a pastry bag fitted with a ½-in. (12-mm) tip and pipe it out in little heaps onto the baking tray. Sprinkle with just a little confectioners' sugar and spray with a little water before placing in the oven.

Bake for 1 hour, without allowing them to color too much.

When you remove the meringues from the oven, indent the bottom a little by pressing in with your thumb or a teaspoon.

When the meringues have cooled, store them in an airtight metal container, where they will keep for a long time.

MAKES 20 MERINGUES
PREPARATION TIME: 15 MINUTES
COOKING TIME: 1 HOUR

Filled Meringues
Meringues garnies

8 egg whites

2 ½ cups (1 lb./500 g) sugar

A little confectioners' sugar for dusting

Cream or filling of your choice: Chantilly (see p. 710), Saint-Honoré (see p. 709), ice cream, etc.

Preheat the oven to 250°F (120°C).

Whisk the egg whites. When they begin to firm up, pour in all the sugar and whisk further until glossy.

Line a baking tray with parchment paper. Spoon the preparation into a pastry bag fitted with a ½-in. (12-mm) tip and pipe it out in little heaps onto the baking tray. Sprinkle with just a little confectioners' sugar and spray with a little water before placing in the oven.

Bake for 1 hour, without allowing them to color too much.

When you remove the meringues from the oven, indent the bottom a little by pressing in with your thumb or a teaspoon.

Fill pairs of meringues with Chantilly cream, ice cream, or fruit by topping a meringue (on its flat side) with about 1 in. (3 cm) of filling and then sandwiching the other one over it.

This is a delicate dessert that offers endless possibilities for variations. Use your culinary imagination!

DESSERT TARTS

Lemon Tart
Tarte au citron

SERVES 6 TO 8
PREPARATION TIME: 20 MINUTES
RESTING TIME: 1 HOUR
COOKING TIME: 45 MINUTES
CHILLING TIME: 3 HOURS

DOUGH

2 ½ cups (250 g) flour
1 stick (125 g) softened butter
6 tablespoons (75 g) granulated sugar
1 egg

FILLING

Juice of 3 lemons
Zest of 3 lemons
7 tablespoons (100 g) softened butter
⅔ cup (125 g) granulated sugar
3 eggs
2 tablespoons (30 ml) crème fraîche or heavy cream

About one hour and a half ahead of time, take the butter out of the refrigerator. Break the butter into pieces.

First make the dough: place the flour, butter, sugar, and egg in a large mixing bowl. Use your fingers to "pinch" the ingredients together, working quickly, until a ball of dough is formed. Place it on a lightly floured table or plate, cover with a clean towel, and leave for 1 hour before baking.

Preheat the oven to 350°F (180°C).

Lightly butter and flour a 9½-in. (24-cm) pie pan, then roll the dough out into a thin sheet and line the pan. Cut off any excess dough from around the edges (see Note), then prick the bottom in several places with the prongs of a fork. Place a piece of parchment paper on top of the dough; it should be large enough to cover the bottom and sides of the dough and stick up above the edges of the pan. Press the paper well against the dough lining the sides of the pan, then fill the pan with uncooked rice, beans, or lentils. Place in the oven and bake for 15 minutes, then remove from the oven and lower the oven temperature to 250°F (120°C). Carefully lift out the paper containing the rice or beans (save the rice or beans for baking other pie crusts in the same way).

Wash the lemons and carefully dry them. Thinly grate the zest and set aside. Squeeze the juice from the lemons and set aside.

Make the filling by beating together first the butter and sugar, beat in the eggs and cream, then add the lemon juice and zest. Pour the filling into the pie crust, place back in the oven and bake for about 30 minutes or until the filling and crust have begun to brown. Allow to cool completely, then chill in the refrigerator for 3 hours before serving.

Note: Use any leftover pie dough to make cookies: pack it into a ball, roll it out, and cut into any shape you like. Bake about 20 minutes or until golden brown.

SERVES 8
PREPARATION TIME: 20 MINUTES
COOKING TIME: 20 MINUTES

Strawberry Tart
Tarte aux fraises

- 9 oz. (250 g) Sweetened Short Pastry (see p. 568)
- 1 lb. (500 g) strawberries
- 3 oz. (80 g) redcurrant jelly (jam)
- 2 tablespoons kirsch
- A few pistachios, chopped

Roll out the pastry and fit it into an 8-in. (20-cm) tart circle if you have one. Otherwise use a tart pan with a detachable bottom. Make sure it fits the inside of the circle snugly, so push it in gently.

Bake it blind (see Glossary) at 350°F (180°C).

When it is done (it should be nicely browned), leave it to cool. Remove the circle or detach it from the pan when it is almost cool.

Very shortly before serving, brush the pastry crust with half the redcurrant jelly. Arrange the strawberries attractively over it.

Dilute the remaining jelly with the kirsch and glaze the surface with it. Sprinkle with the chopped pistachios.

Lemon Tart
Tarte au citron

SERVES 6 TO 8
PREPARATION TIME: 20 MINUTES
RESTING TIME: 1 HOUR
COOKING TIME: 45 MINUTES
CHILLING TIME: 3 HOURS

DOUGH

2 ½ cups (250 g) flour
1 stick (125 g) softened butter
6 tablespoons (75 g) granulated sugar
1 egg

FILLING

Juice of 3 lemons
Zest of 3 lemons
7 tablespoons (100 g) softened butter
⅔ cup (125 g) granulated sugar
3 eggs
2 tablespoons (30 ml) crème fraîche or heavy cream

About one hour and a half ahead of time, take the butter out of the refrigerator. Break the butter into pieces.

First make the dough: place the flour, butter, sugar, and egg in a large mixing bowl. Use your fingers to "pinch" the ingredients together, working quickly, until a ball of dough is formed. Place it on a lightly floured table or plate, cover with a clean towel, and leave for 1 hour before baking.

Preheat the oven to 350°F (180°C).

Lightly butter and flour a 9½-in. (24-cm) pie pan, then roll the dough out into a thin sheet and line the pan. Cut off any excess dough from around the edges (see Note), then prick the bottom in several places with the prongs of a fork. Place a piece of parchment paper on top of the dough; it should be large enough to cover the bottom and sides of the dough and stick up above the edges of the pan. Press the paper well against the dough lining the sides of the pan, then fill the pan with uncooked rice, beans, or lentils. Place in the oven and bake for 15 minutes, then remove from the oven and lower the oven temperature to 250°F (120°C). Carefully lift out the paper containing the rice or beans (save the rice or beans for baking other pie crusts in the same way).

Wash the lemons and carefully dry them. Thinly grate the zest and set aside. Squeeze the juice from the lemons and set aside.

Make the filling by beating together first the butter and sugar, beat in the eggs and cream, then add the lemon juice and zest. Pour the filling into the pie crust, place back in the oven and bake for about 30 minutes or until the filling and crust have begun to brown. Allow to cool completely, then chill in the refrigerator for 3 hours before serving.

Note: Use any leftover pie dough to make cookies: pack it into a ball, roll it out, and cut into any shape you like. Bake about 20 minutes or until golden brown.

SERVES 8
PREPARATION TIME: 20 MINUTES
COOKING TIME: 20 MINUTES

Strawberry Tart
Tarte aux fraises

- 9 oz. (250 g) Sweetened Short Pastry (see p. 568)
- 1 lb. (500 g) strawberries
- 3 oz. (80 g) redcurrant jelly (jam)
- 2 tablespoons kirsch
- A few pistachios, chopped

Roll out the pastry and fit it into an 8-in. (20-cm) tart circle if you have one. Otherwise use a tart pan with a detachable bottom. Make sure it fits the inside of the circle snugly, so push it in gently.

Bake it blind (see Glossary) at 350°F (180°C).

When it is done (it should be nicely browned), leave it to cool. Remove the circle or detach it from the pan when it is almost cool.

Very shortly before serving, brush the pastry crust with half the redcurrant jelly. Arrange the strawberries attractively over it.

Dilute the remaining jelly with the kirsch and glaze the surface with it. Sprinkle with the chopped pistachios.

Lemon Tart
Tarte au citron

SERVES 6 TO 8
PREPARATION TIME: 20 MINUTES
RESTING TIME: 1 HOUR
COOKING TIME: 45 MINUTES
CHILLING TIME: 3 HOURS

DOUGH

2 ½ cups (250 g) flour
1 stick (125 g) softened butter
6 tablespoons (75 g) granulated sugar
1 egg

FILLING

Juice of 3 lemons
Zest of 3 lemons
7 tablespoons (100 g) softened butter
⅔ cup (125 g) granulated sugar
3 eggs
2 tablespoons (30 ml) crème fraîche or heavy cream

About one hour and a half ahead of time, take the butter out of the refrigerator. Break the butter into pieces.

First make the dough: place the flour, butter, sugar, and egg in a large mixing bowl. Use your fingers to "pinch" the ingredients together, working quickly, until a ball of dough is formed. Place it on a lightly floured table or plate, cover with a clean towel, and leave for 1 hour before baking.

Preheat the oven to 350°F (180°C).

Lightly butter and flour a 9½-in. (24-cm) pie pan, then roll the dough out into a thin sheet and line the pan. Cut off any excess dough from around the edges (see Note), then prick the bottom in several places with the prongs of a fork. Place a piece of parchment paper on top of the dough; it should be large enough to cover the bottom and sides of the dough and stick up above the edges of the pan. Press the paper well against the dough lining the sides of the pan, then fill the pan with uncooked rice, beans, or lentils. Place in the oven and bake for 15 minutes, then remove from the oven and lower the oven temperature to 250°F (120°C). Carefully lift out the paper containing the rice or beans (save the rice or beans for baking other pie crusts in the same way).

Wash the lemons and carefully dry them. Thinly grate the zest and set aside. Squeeze the juice from the lemons and set aside.

Make the filling by beating together first the butter and sugar, beat in the eggs and cream, then add the lemon juice and zest. Pour the filling into the pie crust, place back in the oven and bake for about 30 minutes or until the filling and crust have begun to brown. Allow to cool completely, then chill in the refrigerator for 3 hours before serving.

Note: Use any leftover pie dough to make cookies: pack it into a ball, roll it out, and cut into any shape you like. Bake about 20 minutes or until golden brown.

Rhubarb Tart
Tarte à la rubarbe

SERVES 6
PREPARATION TIME: 25 MINUTES
RESTING TIME: 1 HOUR
COOKING TIME: 50 MINUTES

2 ¼ lb. (1 kg) rhubarb

Generous ⅔ cup (150 g) granulated sugar

Butter (for the pie pan)

1 egg yolk

Generous ½ cup (50 g) slivered almonds

2 tablespoons (20 g) confectioners' sugar

DOUGH

1 ½ cups (150 g) flour

5 tablespoons (75 g) butter

2 tablespoons water

Salt

To prepare the dough, one hour ahead of time, take the butter out of the refrigerator to soften. Break the butter into pieces.

Place the flour, butter, and a pinch of salt in a bowl and "pinch" them together until a crumbly mixture is formed. Add the water and knead lightly to make a smooth dough. Place on a lightly floured plate, cover, and place in the refrigerator for 1 hour before baking.

Discard any rhubarb leaves (they are mildly toxic), peel the rhubarb stalks to remove the fibrous strings, then cut each stalk into pieces about ½ in. (1 cm) long. Place in a saucepan with the sugar and leave for 15 minutes or until the rhubarb has given out water and the sugar has dissolved (stir to help dissolve the sugar). Place the saucepan over moderate heat, bring just to a boil, then lower the heat and simmer for 30 minutes, stirring occasionally (the mixture will thicken and darken in color). Remove from the heat and reserve.

Preheat the oven to 350°F (180°C).

Roll the dough out into a thin sheet on a lightly floured table. Butter an 8-in. (20-cm) pie pan and line with the dough. Place a large sheet of parchment paper on top of the dough–it should be large enough to cover the bottom and sides of the dough and stick up above the edges of the pan. Fill the pan with uncooked rice, beans, or lentils. Brush the edge of the dough with egg yolk (this will make it brown nicely as it bakes), then place it in the oven and bake for 40 to 45 minutes.

Remove the pie pan from the oven; carefully lift out the paper containing the rice or beans (save the rice or beans for baking other pie doughs in the same way). Pour the stewed rhubarb into the pie pan, sprinkle with the slivered almonds, and place back in the oven for 8 to 10 minutes. Remove from the oven and sprinkle with confectioners' sugar. Serve warm.

Note: Alternatively, 7-8 oz. (200-225 g) ready-made puff pastry (chilled or frozen) may be used instead.

Apple Tart
Tarte aux pommes

SERVES 6 TO 8
PREPARATION TIME: 25 MINUTES
RESTING TIME: 1 HOUR
COOKING TIME: 45 MINUTES

1 ¾ lb. (800 g) apples

¼ cup (50 g) granulated sugar

Blackcurrant jelly, or raspberry or apricot jam, melted (optional)

DOUGH

2 ½ cups (250 g) flour, plus flour for the pan

1 stick (125 g) softened butter, plus butter for the pan

3 tablespoons (50 ml) water

Salt

At least one hour ahead of time, take the butter out of the refrigerator. Break the butter into pieces.

Make the dough by placing the flour, butter, and a pinch of salt in a large mixing bowl and "pinching" them together until a crumbly mixture is formed. Add the water and knead lightly to make a smooth dough. Form it into a ball, wrap in a clean, lightly floured towel, and leave for 1 hour before baking.

Preheat the oven to 350°F (180°C).

Peel the apples, halve them, and cut them into slices of 1⁄12 in. (3 mm) thick.

Roll the dough out into a thin sheet on a lightly floured table. Butter and flour a 10-in. (25-cm) pie pan, then line it with the dough. Prick the bottom in several places with a fork. Lay in the slices of apple so that they slightly overlap each other; you can arrange them in concentric circles to make a flower pattern, for example. Sprinkle the apples with the sugar and bake for 35 to 40 minutes.

When the tart comes out of the oven, you can spread a little jelly over the apples if you like, to give them an attractive sheen.

Serve warm or cold.

Note: This tart can also be made without a pie pan. Simply roll out the dough, place it on a buttered and floured baking sheet, and crimp the edges a bit with your fingers to make a slight border before arranging the apples on it.

SERVES 8
PREPARATION TIME: 20 MINUTES
COOKING TIME: 20 MINUTES

Strawberry Tart
Tarte aux fraises

- 9 oz. (250 g) Sweetened Short Pastry (see p. 568)
- 1 lb. (500 g) strawberries
- 3 oz. (80 g) redcurrant jelly (jam)
- 2 tablespoons kirsch
- A few pistachios, chopped

Roll out the pastry and fit it into an 8-in. (20-cm) tart circle if you have one. Otherwise use a tart pan with a detachable bottom. Make sure it fits the inside of the circle snugly, so push it in gently.

Bake it blind (see Glossary) at 350°F (180°C).

When it is done (it should be nicely browned), leave it to cool. Remove the circle or detach it from the pan when it is almost cool.

Very shortly before serving, brush the pastry crust with half the redcurrant jelly. Arrange the strawberries attractively over it.

Dilute the remaining jelly with the kirsch and glaze the surface with it. Sprinkle with the chopped pistachios.

SERVES 8
PREPARATION TIME: 30 MINUTES
MACERATION TIME: 5 MINUTES
COOKING TIME: 25 MINUTES

9 oz. (250 g) Sweetened Short Pastry (see p. 568)

3 ½ oz. (100 g) Pastry Cream (see p. 709)

¾ cup (200 ml) crème fraîche or heavy cream

14 oz. (400 g) cherries

1 tablespoon sugar

1 tablespoon kirsch

Creamy Cherry Tart
Tarte aux cerises à la crème

Preheat the oven to 350°F (180°C).

Roll the pastry out. Line an 8-in. (20-cm) tart circle (or a pan with a detachable bottom) with the dough, pressing it in so that it fits the inside of the circle snugly.

Stir the crème fraîche into the pastry cream and set aside. Pit the cherries and macerate them in a little sugar with the kirsch.

Spoon out half of the pastry cream over the bottom of the pastry. Arrange the cherries over this and cover them with another layer of pastry cream.

Bake for 25 minutes, until golden brown.

SERVES 6 TO 8
PREPARATION TIME: 30 MINUTES
COOKING TIME: 50 MINUTES

Cheese Cake
Tarte au fromage blanc

FILLING

7 oz. (200 g) *fromage blanc* cream cheese (see Note)

6 tablespoons (100 ml) crème fraîche or heavy cream

2 eggs

1 egg yolk

½ cup (100 g) granulated sugar

1 tablespoon (6 g) flour

1 tablespoon vanilla extract

DOUGH

1 ½ cups (150 g) flour

5 tablespoons (75 g) butter

2 tablespoons water

Salt

One hour ahead of time, take the butter out of the refrigerator to soften. Break the butter into pieces.

Make the dough by placing the flour, butter, and a pinch of salt in a bowl and "pinching" them together until a crumbly mixture is formed. Add the water and knead lightly to make a smooth dough. Place on a lightly floured plate, cover, and place in the refrigerator for 1 hour before baking.

Preheat the oven to 350°F (180°C).

Place the *fromage blanc* in a strainer and drain if necessary, then work it through the strainer into a clean bowl to eliminate any lumps. Add the cream and beat until smooth. Beat in the 2 whole eggs, one by one, then the egg yolk. Mix the sugar and flour together, then beat them into the *fromage blanc* little by little; add the vanilla extract.

Roll out the dough on a lightly floured table into a thin sheet. Lightly butter an 8-in. (20-cm) pie pan, line it with the dough, and prick the bottom all over with a fork. Pour in the filling, bake for 20 to 25 minutes; then lower the oven temperature to 300°F (150°C) and bake 25 minutes more. Serve warm.

Note: Fromage blanc *("white cheese") is a light cheese whose consistency is between that of a fairly thick yogurt and cream cheese. The moisture content is anything up to 80 percent. If you cannot find fromage blanc, make your own mix with ricotta, Quark, or farmer's cheese, and sour cream, or blend cottage cheese and yogurt until smooth.*

SERVES 8
PREPARATION TIME: 20 MINUTES
COOKING TIME: 30 MINUTES

Alsatian Fruit Tart
Tarte à l'alsacienne

- 8 apples or pears
- 9 oz. (250 g) Sweetened Short Pastry (see p. 568)
- 3 ½ oz. (100 g) Pastry Cream (see p. 709)
- 2 tablespoons (25 g) granulated sugar
- 1 egg, beaten
- 1 tablespoon apple jelly or apricot preserves, slightly reduced

Preheat the oven to 350°F (180°C).

Roll the pastry out and line an 8-in. (20-cm) pastry circle with it so that it fits snugly in. Shape the edges and prick the base with the tines of a fork. Half fill with the pastry cream.

Cut the apples or pears into quarters, and then into slices lengthways. Arrange the slices so that they overlap closely in successive rings. Sprinkle with the sugar and bake for about 30 minutes.

As soon as the tart is cooked, remove the circle and brush the edges with the beaten egg. Return it to the oven for 2 to 3 minutes to finish the cooking and allow it to brown a little.

To glaze, brush the jelly or preserves over the apples or pears.

Pear Tart
Tarte aux poires

SERVES 8
PREPARATION TIME: 20 MINUTES
COOKING TIME: 30 MINUTES

- 9 oz. (250 g) unsweetened Shortcrust Pastry (see p. 568)
- 6 ripe Williams pears
- 2 cups (500 ml) thick cream
- 4 eggs
- ¾ cup (5 ¼ oz./150 g) sugar
- Salt

Preheat the oven to 350°F (180°C).

Butter an 8-in. (20-cm) tart pan and line it with the pastry. Peel the pears and slice them finely. Arrange them at the base of the pastry.

In a mixing bowl, combine the thick cream with the eggs, sugar, and a pinch of salt. Stir well and pour it over the pears. Bake for 30 minutes.

SERVES 8
PREPARATION TIME: 40 MINUTES
COOKING TIME: 40 MINUTES

Upside-Down Apple Tart
Tarte Tatin

3 ½ lb. (1.5 kg) apples

7 tablespoons (100 g) butter, divided

⅓ cup (2 ½ oz./70 g) sugar, divided

PASTRY

1 ¼ cups (4 ½ oz./125 g) flour

1 egg

5 tablespoons (80 g) butter, softened

Salt

Take a large cake pan or *tarte tatin* pan. Use half the butter (3 tablespoons plus 1 teaspoon/50 g) to butter the bottom of the pan, and sprinkle it with ¼ cup (50 g) sugar.

Peel the apples and cut them into thick slices, or even quarters, and remove the seeds. Arrange them, tightly packed, so that they fill the bottom of the cake pan. Sprinkle the remaining sugar over them. Melt 1 tablespoon and 2 teaspoons (25 g) butter and pour it over. Cook for about 20 minutes, if possible over the burner, otherwise in the oven at 350°F (180°C). The sugar must caramelize, but get no darker than light brown.

While the apples are baking, pour the flour on to a pastry board and make a circle. Make a well in the center and place the egg, butter, and a pich of salt in it. Work the ingredients together, adding a little water if necessary so that the dough is soft. Spread it out as thinly as possible with a rolling pin.

Preheat the oven to 350°F (180°C).

Transfer the dough to the cake pan. Place it over the apples and tuck the edges inside. Bake in the oven for 20 minutes.

When it is done, turn the upside-down cake out onto a cake platter. Allow to cool a little, but serve warm.

Orange Blossom Crêpes
Crêpes à l'eau de fleur d'oranger

MAKES 20 CRÊPES
PREPARATION TIME: 15 MINUTES
RESTING TIME: 2 HOURS
COOKING TIME: 1 MINUTE PER CRÊPE, PLUS 1 MINUTE FOR FINAL FLAVORING

- 2 ½ cups (9 oz./250 g) flour, sifted
- ½ cup (3 ½ oz./100 g) sugar
- 6 eggs
- 2 egg yolks
- 2 tablespoons crème fraîche or heavy cream
- 2 tablespoons cognac
- 1 ¼ cups (300 ml) milk
- 4 tablespoons (60 g) butter, melted
- Light-colored brown sugar
- A few drops of orange blossom water
- Salt

An hour ahead, take the eggs, butter, and milk out of the refrigerator to bring them to room temperature. Melt the butter in a small saucepan and reserve.

Place the flour, sugar, and a pinch of salt in a mixing bowl; stir in the eggs and egg yolks, then pour in the cream, cognac, and milk little by little, stirring at first, then whisking to make a smooth liquid batter. Finally whisk in the melted butter. Leave the batter at room temperature for about 2 hours before making the crêpes.

Before you start cooking, sprinkle a warmed plate with fine light brown sugar. When you cook your crêpes, ensure that they are not too thin. Use two large, well-buttered frying pans so that you can serve them in batches of two, without keeping your guests waiting.

Lightly butter or oil a frying pan (preferably cast-iron or non-stick). When very hot, spoon about ¼ cup (60 ml) of the batter into the center of it, and tip and turn the frying pan to cover the bottom with the batter and make a very thin pancake (crêpe). Before tossing them, prick them with a fork. This will cause any humidity to evaporate immediately. Cook the crêpe for about 2 minutes over moderate heat, turn it over using a flexible-blade spatula, and finish cooking about 3 minutes on the second side. Remove the crêpe and lightly butter the pan before cooking the next one. To keep the crêpes warm after cooking, heat a little water to simmering in a saucepan. Set a large plate on top of the saucepan. As the crêpes finish cooking, put them on the plate and cover with a second plate turned upside down.

Slip the crêpe onto the plate with sugar and sprinkle the top of the crêpe too. Spray it with a few drops of orange blossom water. Then place the next crêpe over it, sprinkle with sugar, and spray with the orange blossom water. Serve immediately. While your guests are enjoying their crêpes, prepare the next batch.

SERVES 8
PREPARATION TIME: 40 MINUTES
COOKING TIME: 40 MINUTES

Upside-Down Apple Tart
Tarte Tatin

3 ½ lb. (1.5 kg) apples
7 tablespoons (100 g) butter, divided
⅓ cup (2 ½ oz./70 g) sugar, divided

PASTRY
1 ¼ cups (4 ½ oz./125 g) flour
1 egg
5 tablespoons (80 g) butter, softened
Salt

Take a large cake pan or *tarte tatin* pan. Use half the butter (3 tablespoons plus 1 teaspoon/50 g) to butter the bottom of the pan, and sprinkle it with ¼ cup (50 g) sugar.

Peel the apples and cut them into thick slices, or even quarters, and remove the seeds. Arrange them, tightly packed, so that they fill the bottom of the cake pan. Sprinkle the remaining sugar over them. Melt 1 tablespoon and 2 teaspoons (25 g) butter and pour it over. Cook for about 20 minutes, if possible over the burner, otherwise in the oven at 350°F (180°C). The sugar must caramelize, but get no darker than light brown.

While the apples are baking, pour the flour on to a pastry board and make a circle. Make a well in the center and place the egg, butter, and a pich of salt in it. Work the ingredients together, adding a little water if necessary so that the dough is soft. Spread it out as thinly as possible with a rolling pin.

Preheat the oven to 350°F (180°C).

Transfer the dough to the cake pan. Place it over the apples and tuck the edges inside. Bake in the oven for 20 minutes.

When it is done, turn the upside-down cake out onto a cake platter. Allow to cool a little, but serve warm.

Apricot Tart with Frangipane Cream
Abricots Bourdaloue

SERVES 6
PREPARATION TIME: 1 HOUR
RESTING TIME: 1 HOUR
COOKING TIME: 50 MINUTES

- 12 large apricots
- Amaretto or other kernel liqueur
- 9 oz. (250 g) Sweetened Short Pastry (see p. 568)
- 2 cups (500 ml) Frangipane Cream (see p. 708)
- 3 almond macaroons
- Confectioners' sugar for dusting
- Apricot Sauce (see p. 716) flavored with kirsch to serve

Poach the 12 apricots in water (see p. 725) and flavor them with the amaretto or other liqueur. While they are poaching, line an 8-in. (20-cm) pan with the short pastry. Bake it blind (see Glossary).

Prepare the frangipane cream. Spoon out a thin layer over the baked pastry.

Preheat the oven to 425°F (210°C).

Cut the apricots in half and drain them well. Arrange them attractively over the frangipane cream. Crush the macaroons and sprinkle the crumbs over the apricots. Dust lightly with confectioners' sugar and bake for a few minutes, until the sugar caramelizes and a fragrant crust forms on top of the tart.

Serve accompanied by apricot sauce flavored with kirsch.

MAKES ABOUT 12 ÉCLAIRS
PREPARATION TIME: 40 MINUTES
COOKING TIME: 20 TO 25 MINUTES

14 oz. (400 g) Choux Pastry (see p. 571)

1 egg, beaten

Coffee- or chocolate-flavored Pastry Cream (see p. 709)

Coffee or chocolate fondant to decorate

Coffee or Chocolate Éclairs
Éclairs au café ou au chocolat

Preheat the oven to 350°F (180°C).

To make one dozen éclairs of the usual size, prepare 14 oz. (400 g) choux pastry. Spoon the pastry into a pastry bag fitted with a ½-in. (1.5-cm) plain tip.

Pipe out lengths of 3 ½ in. (9 cm) on to a baking tray, leaving at least 2 in. (5 cm) between them.

To cut the dough from the tip when you have piped out the required length, all you need to do is stop the pressure on the pastry bag and lift the tip up quickly with the guiding hand.

Each éclair uses up about 1 oz. (30 g) of the dough.

Brush each éclair with the beaten egg. Bake for about 20 minutes. Leave to cool.

Slit them lengthways down the side and fill them with pastry cream flavored with coffee or chocolate extract, or cocoa (see recipe p. 709). Alternatively, you might want to use any of the following: Frangipane Cream (see p. 708), Saint-Honoré Cream (see p. 709), or whipped cream.

When they are filled, replace the top half over the lower half. Warm some coffee or chocolate fondant and dip the top of each éclair in it. Place them on a baking tray while the fondant hardens. Then remove any fondant that might have dripped down the sides and serve the éclairs on cake plates.

SERVES 4
PREPARATION TIME: 20 MINUTES
RESTING TIME: 3 HOURS
COOKING TIME: 30 MINUTES

4 apples (about 12 oz./350 g)
2 cups (200 g) flour
2 eggs
9 tablespoons (120 g) granulated sugar
½ tablespoon cooking oil, plus oil for the pan
½ teaspoon salt
1 cup (250 ml) milk
1 tablespoon cognac, or
1 teaspoon orange flower water or vanilla extract (or more, to taste)

Lyon-Style Apple Pancake
Matefaim lyonnais

The batter must be made 3 hours before cooking. Place the flour and eggs in a mixing bowl, beat with a wooden spoon, and add 6 tablespoons (80 g) of sugar, the oil, and the salt. Continue beating as you pour in the cold milk little by little to make a smooth batter. Add the flavoring of your choice. If there are any lumps in the batter, work it through a fine sieve into another mixing bowl. Leave at room temperature for 3 hours.

Just before cooking, peel the apples and core them. Grate the apples, then stir them into the batter as well as the remaining 3 tablespoons (40 g) of sugar.

Lightly oil a large frying pan (preferably cast iron or nonstick); when very hot, pour in the batter and spread it out to make a thick pancake. Cook over moderate heat for 30 to 45 minutes, turning over every 6 to 8 minutes (to turn over, slide the pancake out onto a plate, then place a second plate on top of the pancake and turn it upside down. Lift off the first plate and slide the pancake back into the pan). When the pancake is done, a knife or needle stuck into it should come out clean and almost dry.

Serve warm with sugar and cream on the side.

Lyon-Style Fritters
Bugnes

SERVES 8
PREPARATION TIME: 15 MINUTES
COOKING TIME: 4 TO 6 MINUTES
RESTING TIME: AT LEAST 2 HOURS

1 ¾ sticks (200 g) butter
Zest of 1 lemon
5 cups (500 g) flour, sifted
1 pinch granulated sugar
1 teaspoon (5 g) baking powder
4 eggs
1 tablespoon (15 ml) rum
8 ½ cups (2 liters) peanut oil
Confectioners' sugar

Leave the butter at room temperature a little in advance, so that it is soft when you begin preparing the dough.

Grate the lemon zest very finely.

In a salad bowl, mix the flour, granulated sugar, and baking powder, then stir in the eggs one by one. Add the softened butter, the grated lemon zest, and the rum.

Work the mixture together with your fingertips until you obtain a malleable dough.

Heat the oil in a deep fryer or a large pan. Make sure that the temperature of the oil never gets too high (it should be simmering and not smoking; no higher than 350°F [180°C]).

On a floured working surface, spread out the dough in a very fine layer. Then, with the help of a scalloped pastry-wheel, cut the dough into more or less evenly shaped rectangles or triangles. Make a slit in the middle of each shape so that the dough swells up readily during cooking.

To check whether the oil has reached the right temperature, drop in a small piece of the dough, which should sizzle in the oil and quickly change color. When the oil is ready, carefully slide in the pieces of dough. As soon as the *bugnes* rise to the surface and turn a beautiful golden color, take them out and place them on paper towels. Dust with confectioners' sugar before serving.

SERVES 10
PREPARATION TIME: 40 MINUTES
COOKING TIME: 30 MINUTES

2 cups (500 ml) milk
2 sticks plus 1 tablespoon (8 ½ oz./240 g) butter
2 teaspoons (10 g) salt
1 ½ tablespoons (⅔ oz./20 g) granulated sugar
4 cups (14 oz./400 g) flour
12 eggs

CREAM
4 cups (1 liter) milk
1 Bourbon vanilla bean
8 egg yolks
1 ½ cups (10 oz./300 g) sugar
¾ cup plus 1 tablespoon (2 ¾ oz./80 g) flour
Salt

DECORATION
1 ½ cups (10 oz./300 g) sugar
A few sugar-coated almonds
1 orange, cut into slices and caramelized

Special equipment:
a croquembouche mold, or other conical or round mold

Croquembouche
Croque en bouche

Pour the milk into a saucepan and add the butter, salt, and sugar. Bring it all to a boil. Pour in the flour, stirring vigorously, and dry out the mixture by stirring for about 4 minutes over the heat. Remove from the heat and incorporate the eggs, one by one, still stirring briskly. Continue to stir until the mixture is perfectly smooth. Butter a baking tray. Spoon the batter into a pastry bag and pipe out 30 small choux pastry shapes on to the tray. Bake at 400°F (200°C) for about 20 minutes.

Cream

Slit the vanilla bean lengthways and infuse it in the 4 cups (1 liter) milk with a pinch of salt. Place the egg yolks into a mixing bowl and stir in the sugar. Then add the flour and whisk it in, followed by the vanilla-infused milk. Transfer the mixture to a saucepan and cook over low heat for 5 minutes at least, stirring all the time until the cream coats the back of a spoon. Leave the cream to cool and then fill the choux pastries with it.

To assemble the croquembouche, you will need a conical or round mold. Melt 1 ½ cups (10 oz./300 g) sugar without adding any water until it turns a caramel color. Grease the mold. Carefully dip a choux pastry puff into the warm caramel and place in the mold. Repeat this process, building up a pyramid around the sides of the mold. When the sides are evenly coated, fill the center with the remaining puffs, dipped in caramel, and let the caramel set before removing the croquembouche from the mold. Special croquembouche molds, around the outside of which the choux pastry puffs are arranged, may also be used. Spin and drizzle some caramel over the choux pastries, and decorate with the sugar-coated almonds and caramelized orange slices.

This elaborate cake is traditionally served at weddings and other festive occasions.

Apple Fritters
Beignets de reinette

SERVES 4
PREPARATION TIME: 20 MINUTES
MACERATION TIME: 20 MINUTES
COOKING TIME: 5 MINUTES

4 large apples, preferably russet apples
Caster sugar as needed
To flavor: cognac, rum, or kirsch
Frying Batter (see p. 578)
Oil for frying
Confectioners' sugar for dusting

Using the tip of a knife or an apple corer, remove the cores of the apples. Peel them and cut them into rounds ¼ in. (8 mm) thick.

Arrange them in a single layer on a large baking dish or tray and sprinkle them on both sides with the sugar. Then sprinkle them generously with the liqueur of your choice. Cover (with another tray or plastic wrap) and leave to macerate for 20 minutes.

Prepare the oil bath. When the oil is smoking, dip the rounds one by one in the frying batter and immerse them in the oil. It is important that they are seared immediately so that they fry rather than boil. Otherwise, the frying batter would absorb too much oil and the fritters would taste unpleasant and be rather hard to digest. When the batter encounters the oil at the right temperature, it is transformed into a crisp, golden crust that protects the fruit inside.

Turn your oven to the "broil" function.

Drain the fritters on sheets of paper towel and dab them gently to absorb any excess oil. Dust them with confectioners' sugar and transfer them to a baking sheet. Broil them for just one minute to lightly caramelize the confectioners' sugar.

Serve the fritters on a warmed platter.

MAKES 20 FRITTERS
PREPARATION TIME: 20 MINUTES
COOKING TIME: 15 MINUTES

Souffléed Fritters
Beignets soufflés

- 2 cups (500 ml) water
- 7 tablespoons (100 g) butter
- 1 teaspoon (5 g) salt
- 2 ½ teaspoons (10 g) sugar
- 3 cups (300 g) flour
- 6 to 7 eggs, depending on their size
- Rum or other liqueur of your choice to flavor
- Oil for frying
- Confectioners' sugar for dusting

The batter used here is the same as the one used to make choux pastry.

Combine the water, butter, salt, and sugar in a saucepan and bring to a boil. Sift the flour to add as soon as the mixture boils. Remove the saucepan from the heat and pour in the flour. Stir well and return to the heat, fairly high, and continue stirring to evaporate the moisture from the batter. Stir until the batter pulls away from the sides of the saucepan.

Remove from the heat and immediately begin stirring in the eggs, one by one. Stir energetically each time.

The batter should be very smooth and of medium consistency. Flavor it with the rum or other liqueur.

Prepare an oil bath, heating the oil to medium heat. Using a tablespoon and a knife, shape small walnut-sized balls of batter to drop into the oil bath. The method is simple: fill the spoon with the batter, dip a knife in hot water, and scrape the batter off with the blade. As you push it, it will form a walnut sized ball and will slip off the damp knife into the hot oil.

As you continue to drop the batter into the pot, increase the temperature of the oil bath. The fritters will, at the very least, double in volume. Fry them until they turn a nice golden color.

Drain them on sheets of paper towel and dust them with confectioners' sugar. Arrange them in a heap on a folded napkin placed on a serving platter.

MAKES 20 WAFFLES
PREPARATION TIME: 20 MINUTES
COOKING TIME: 15 MINUTES

My Grandmother's Waffles
Gaufres de grand-mère Bocuse

5 cups (1 lb./500 g) flour
1 pinch baking powder
1 tablespoon sugar
1 cup (250 ml) milk
3 cup (750 ml) whipping cream (30 percent butterfat)
8 egg yolks
⅓ cup (75 ml) rum
1 ¼ cups (300 g) melted butter
4 egg whites
Salt
Butter to grease the waffle iron

In a mixing bowl, combine the flour, baking powder, sugar, and a pinch of salt.

Pour in first the milk, then the cream, the egg yolks, and the rum, stirring thoroughly each time. Then incorporate the melted butter. Whip the egg whites until they form firm peaks and fold them into the batter.

Heat the waffle iron and butter the plates. Pour some batter onto one of its sides, making sure the dimples are filled. Close the waffle iron and turn it over so that the batter is distributed on both plates.

This will ensure that your waffles are nice and crisp.

Serving suggestions: Serve your waffles simply dusted with confectioners' sugar, topped with Chantilly Cream (see p. 710), or spread with homemade preserves.

MAKES 20 PANCAKES
PREPARATION TIME: 15 MINUTES
RESTING TIME: 2 HOURS
COOKING TIME: 1 MINUTE PER PANCAKE

Pancakes with Preserves
Pannequets aux confitures

- 9 oz. (250 g) fine wheat flour
- 8 eggs, separated
- 2 cups (500 ml) milk
- Scant ½ cup (100 ml) crème fraîche or heavy cream
- ¼ cup (1 ¾ oz./50 g) sugar
- 1 stick (125 g) butter
- A few drops of bitter almond extract
- 1 teaspoon vanilla-scented sugar (To make your own, leave a vanilla bean in your sugar ahead of time to flavor it.)
- Salt

GARNISH

- Preserves of your choice
- Confectioners' sugar
- Fresh fruit of the same sort as your preserves
- Kirsch

To make the pancakes, sift the flour into a mixing bowl. Mix in the egg yolks, one by one. Then incorporate the milk, cream, sugar, softened butter, and a pinch of salt.

Add the bitter almond extract to the mixture with the vanilla-scented sugar.

Leave to rest for 2 hours.

When you are ready to cook the pancakes, whip the 8 egg whites to firm peaks and fold them into the mixture.

Generously butter a small frying pan or crêpe pan. When it is hot, pour just enough batter to make a thin layer and spread it out evenly. Cook until it just begins to brown, about 30 seconds, and then flip over.

Turn the oven to the "broil" function.

You may use any preserves you like. They should be thick enough not to liquefy when they come into contact with heat.

Fold the pancakes in two, spread out a very thin layer of preserves on the upper side, and then fold over again to form triangular shapes.

Arrange them in a circle on a platter and dust with confectioners' sugar. Place the platter in the oven just long enough to allow a glaze to form on the top.

If you like, you may pile some fruit of the same variety as the preserves in the center of the platter. The fruit can be poached whole or in halves, or diced. If you use fruit, drizzle it with a little sauce of the same flavor to which you can add kirsch. Serve more of the same sauce in a jug as an accompaniment.

ARÔME FLEURS D'ORANGER
PRODUCTION 2008
A. MONTEUX
PARFUMEUR DISTILLATEUR
DLUO 12-2009
VALLAURIS (Alpes Mmes)

Chocolate Mousse
Mousse au chocolat

SERVES 4 TO 5
PREPARATION TIME: 15 MINUTES
COOKING TIME: 10 MINUTES
RESTING TIME: AT LEAST 2 HOURS

4 ½ oz. (125 g) bittersweet chocolate

2 tablespoons (30 g) softened butter

4 tablespoons (50 g) granulated sugar

4 eggs, separated

Chocolate mousse should be prepared at least 2 hours before serving; ideally, it should be made 24 hours ahead of time.

At least one hour ahead of time, take the butter and the eggs out of the refrigerator.

Break the chocolate into pieces.

Melt the chocolate and butter in a double boiler over low heat, stirring gently as they begin to melt. Stir in the sugar little by little. When thick and creamy, pour the chocolate mixture into a large mixing bowl and stir until it has cooled to lukewarm, then stir in the egg yolks.

Beat the egg whites until stiff in another mixing bowl, then slide them into the bowl with the chocolate and fold them in, using a wooden spatula or spoon.

When the egg whites have been completely incorporated into the chocolate, place the mousse in the refrigerator for 2 hours or more before serving.

Serving suggestions: Serve with warm Almond Cookies (see p. 585).

DESSERTS

SERVES 4 TO 5
PREPARATION TIME: 15 MINUTES
COOKING TIME: 10 MINUTES
RESTING TIME: AT LEAST 2 HOURS

4 ½ oz. (125 g) bittersweet chocolate

2 tablespoons (30 g) softened butter

4 tablespoons (50 g) granulated sugar

4 eggs, separated

Chocolate Mousse
Mousse au chocolat

Chocolate mousse should be prepared at least 2 hours before serving; ideally, it should be made 24 hours ahead of time.

At least one hour ahead of time, take the butter and the eggs out of the refrigerator.

Break the chocolate into pieces.

Melt the chocolate and butter in a double boiler over low heat, stirring gently as they begin to melt. Stir in the sugar little by little. When thick and creamy, pour the chocolate mixture into a large mixing bowl and stir until it has cooled to lukewarm, then stir in the egg yolks.

Beat the egg whites until stiff in another mixing bowl, then slide them into the bowl with the chocolate and fold them in, using a wooden spatula or spoon.

When the egg whites have been completely incorporated into the chocolate, place the mousse in the refrigerator for 2 hours or more before serving.

Serving suggestions: Serve with warm Almond Cookies (see p. 585).

SERVES 4
PREPARATION TIME: 20 MINUTES
COOKING TIME: 45 MINUTES

My Chestnut Pudding
Pudding de chez nous

- 9 oz. (250 g) candied chestnuts (see Note)
- 3 tablespoons (50 g) softened butter, plus extra for mold
- 1 tablespoon (15 g) granulated sugar
- 3 tablespoons (50 ml) crème fraîche or heavy cream
- 4 egg yolks
- 3 egg whites
- Confectioners' sugar

At least one hour ahead of time, take the butter out of the refrigerator to soften.

Bring a large saucepan of water to a boil. Preheat the oven to 425°F (210°C).

Generously butter a 6 ½-in. (16-cm) charlotte mold or a 7-in. (18 cm) soufflé mold. Sprinkle in the sugar and turn the mold to coat the sides with it. Place the mold in the refrigerator while making the pudding.

Place the chestnuts in a mortar with the butter and pound to a paste, then stir in the cream. Pour the chestnut mixture into a fine sieve and use a wooden spoon or a pestle to work it through and make a fine, smooth paste. Stir in the egg yolks.

Beat the egg whites until stiff, then fold them into the chestnut cream. When all the egg whites have been added and the mixture is smooth, remove the mold from the refrigerator and pour in the chestnut mixture. Place the mold in a roasting pan and pour in enough boiling water to come about one-third of the way up the sides of the mold, then place in the oven and bake for 30 to 45 minutes. Test to see if the pudding is done by sticking the tip of a knife or a trussing needle into it; if it comes out clean and dry, the pudding is done. If not, it needs to cook longer. Either turn out the pudding when it comes from the oven and sprinkle with confectioners' sugar, or serve in the mold (in which case it's preferable to bake it in a porcelain soufflé mold). Serve warm, but not hot.

Serving suggestions: Serve with Apricot Jam (see p. 700) and macaroons.

Note: Candied chestnuts are sold around Christmas in France. In the course of being candied, many of them break, and they are sold at much lower prices than the whole ones. It is these broken ones that are used in this dessert, but whole ones can, of course, be used instead.

Rice Pudding
Riz au lait

SERVES 4
PREPARATION TIME: 10 MINUTES
COOKING TIME: 45 MINUTES

- ½ cup (100 g) round-grained rice
- 1 vanilla bean
- Generous 2 cups (500 ml) milk
- ½ cup (3 ½ oz./100 g) granulated sugar
- ½ teaspoon salt

Split the vanilla bean in half lengthwise. Place the milk, sugar, salt, and vanilla bean in a large saucepan and bring to a boil. Sprinkle in the rice, stirring.

Lower the heat (use a heat diffuser for very low, even heat) and cook the rice 45 minutes to 1 hour or until it is tender and has absorbed practically all of the milk (the milk left over will be absorbed as the rice cools).

Remove the vanilla bean, pour the rice into a bowl, and leave to cool; it can be served either warm or cold.

Serving suggestions: Serve with a homemade jam, poached fruits, or candied fruits.

Almond Blancmange
Blanc-manger amande

SERVES 4
PREPARATION TIME: 30 MINUTES
MACERATION TIME: 1 HOUR
CHILLING TIME: 4 HOURS

- 9 oz. (250 g) sweet almonds, blanched if possible
- A few drops of bitter almond extract
- 1 ¾ cups (400 ml) whipping cream
- 7 ½ sheets (15 g) gelatin
- ½ cup (3 ½ oz./100 g) sugar
- ½ teaspoon vanilla-scented sugar (To make your own, leave a vanilla bean in your sugar ahead of time to flavor it)
- Scant ½ cup (100 ml) thick cream
- 1 teaspoon caster sugar

If the almonds are not blanched, proceed as follows: place them in boiling water then refresh them under cold water. Squeeze them between your thumb and forefinger to remove the skins. Soak them for 1 hour in cold water so that they become very white. Drain them and pat them dry.

Grind the almonds using a mortar and pestle or food processor, gradually drizzling in the almond extract and the 2 tablespoons water. Then dilute the paste by gradually adding the whipping cream.

Set the gelatin sheets to soak in a bowl of very cold water. Transfer the almond paste into a clean cloth and place it over a mixing bowl. Press down hard to extract the almond milk. Dissolve the sugar in the almond milk and add the vanilla-scented sugar. Take just a little of the almond milk and warm it slightly. By now, the gelatin sheets should be soft. Remove them from the water, press the water out, and dissolve them completely in the warmed almond milk.

Together, the almond milk, sugar, and gelatin mixture should make a volume of about 1 ½ cups (350 ml). Chill until the mixture just begins to set. Whip the thick cream and add the caster sugar to it. Carefully fold it in to the almond mixture, pour it all into a mold, and chill until set.

SERVES 6
PREPARATION TIME: 40 MINUTES
CHILLING TIME:
2 HOURS MINIMUM
COOKING TIME: 20 MINUTES

25 Ladyfingers (see p. 595)

3 sheets (6 g) gelatin

1 ¼ cups (300 ml) crème fraîche

2 tablespoons confectioners' sugar

½ teaspoon vanilla sugar

CUSTARD

1 vanilla bean

¾ cup (200 ml) milk

4 egg yolks

½ cup (3 ½ oz./100 g) sugar

Salt

Special equipment: a charlotte mold, diameter 5 in. (12 cm), height 4 ½ in. (11 cm)

Charlotte Russe
Charlotte à la russe

It is best to line the charlotte mold with two pieces of parchment paper: cut out a disk for the bottom and a wide strip for the sides. Arrange the ladyfingers around the edges. You will need about 20, and they should peek out about ½ in. (12 mm) from the rim. If you have made them yourself, trim them so that they are all the same length. Place them in such a way that the charlotte will stand straight when turned out of the mold. Crush the remaining ladyfingers and set aside.

Soak the gelatin sheets in a bowl of very cold water for 5 minutes.

To prepare the custard, split open the vanilla bean lengthwise, place in a medium saucepan (do not use an aluminum pan as this will blacken the sauce) with the milk and bring just to a boil. Remove the pan from the heat and leave to infuse for 7 to 8 minutes, then remove the vanilla bean.

Away from the heat, in the top of a double boiler, whisk together the eggs, sugar, and a pinch of salt, then whisk in the hot milk. Set the top of the double boiler in place and heat, stirring the mixture constantly for about 8 minutes or until it thickens (it should not boil). As soon as the custard coats the back of the spoon, remove the saucepan from the heat. Squeeze the excess water from the gelatin sheets and stir them into the custard until they dissolve. Strain the custard through a fine-mesh sieve into a bowl set over ice.

Sweeten the cream with the confectioners' sugar and vanilla-scented sugar and whip until firm.

Cool the custard by stirring it over ice until it is on the point of setting. Then carefully fold in the whipped cream.

Pour the mixture into the lined charlotte mold. It should be full. Smooth the surface with the back of a knife or an offset spatula. Sprinkle the top with the crushed ladyfingers. Chill for at least 2 hours before serving.

SERVES 6
PREPARATION TIME: 20 MINUTES
COOKING TIME: 30 MINUTES

French Christmas Pudding
Pudding de Noël à la française

- 1 lb. (500 g) candied chestnut pieces (see Note)
- 1 teaspoon vanilla extract
- 7 tablespoons (100 g) butter
- 3 tablespoons crème fraîche or heavy cream
- 8 egg yolks
- 6 egg whites
- Creamy Chocolate Sauce (see p. 715)
- A few soft chocolate-flavored almond macaroons, to garnish

Crush or process the candied chestnuts with the vanilla and butter. Dilute the paste with the crème fraîche; it should now have the consistency of choux pastry batter.

Push the purée through a fine-mesh sieve and mix it through. Incorporate the egg yolks. When they are mixed in, whip the egg whites until very firm and carefully fold them in. To make this easier, first spoon a little of the purée into the egg white and mix through. Then fold in the egg white mixture, one-third at a time, ensuring that you do not deflate it.

Butter a charlotte mold well and prepare a hot water bath large enough to hold the mold. Pour the chestnut mixture in until the mold is two-thirds full. Leave the charlotte mold to simmer gently over medium heat for 30 minutes.

Turn the pudding out of the mold and serve, drizzled with chocolate sauce.

Note: Candied chestnuts are sold around Christmas in France. In the course of being candied, many of them break, and they are sold at much lower prices than the whole ones. It is these broken ones that are used in this dessert, but whole ones can, of course, be used instead.

SERVES 6 TO 8
PREPARATION TIME: 30 MINUTES
COOKING TIME:
1 HOUR 15 MINUTES

⅔ cup (3 ½ oz./100 g) currants
10 oz. (300 g) round-grained rice
4 cups (1 liter) milk
1 vanilla bean
Scant cup (6 oz./170 g) sugar, divided
2 tablespoons (30 g) butter
4 eggs
Salt

Rice Cake
Gâteau de riz

Leave the currants to soak in a little lukewarm water. Rinse the rice under cold water and place it in a saucepan. Cover with water and bring to a boil. Leave to simmer for 5 minutes. Drain, rinse under cold water, and drain again.

Bring the milk to a boil in a large, heavy-bottomed saucepan. Slit the vanilla bean in two lengthways and add it to the milk with a scant ⅔ cup (4 ¼ oz./120 g) sugar. Remove from the heat and leave to infuse for 5 minutes, covered with the lid. Then pour the rice into the milk, adding a pinch of salt and the butter. Return to the burner and gently bring back to a simmer. Leave to simmer, without stirring, for 40 minutes, by which time practically all the milk should be absorbed. Now leave to cool.

Preheat the oven to 350°F (180°C).

Drain the currants and stir them into the rice. Beat the eggs well and gradually stir them into the rice.

With the remaining ⅓ cup (1 ¾ oz./50 g) sugar, make a caramel at the bottom of the cake pan. To do so, put the sugar in the pan, then hold the pan over the burner until it turns a light caramel color, tilting it so that the entire surface is covered. Remove it immediately from the heat and pour the rice over it. Bake for 30 minutes.

Leave to cool a little, but turn it out of the mold while it is still warm. Serve with well-chilled custard.

SERVES 8
PREPARATION TIME: 40 MINUTES
COOKING TIME: 45 MINUTES
CHILLING TIME: 30 MINUTES

- 3 ½ lb. (1.5 kg) chestnuts
- 1 vanilla bean
- 4 cups (1 liter) milk
- 1 cup (7 oz./200 g) sugar
- 7 tablespoons (100 g) butter, cubed
- 1 cup (250 ml) whipping cream, 30-35 percent butterfat
- 1 teaspoon confectioners' sugar
- 1 ¾ teaspoons (7.5 g) vanilla-scented sugar (To make your own, leave a vanilla bean in your sugar ahead of time to flavor it.)

Mont Blanc

Wash the chestnuts and make a cross-shaped incision in the outer skin using a sharp knife. Place them in a pot and cover with cold water.

Bring to a boil and allow to boil for 1 minute. Peel them, removing both the outer and inner skins.

Slit the vanilla bean lengthways, place it in the milk, and bring the milk to a boil. Add the sugar and peeled chestnuts, and turn the heat down to very low. Leave to simmer for 45 minutes.

Drain the chestnuts and process them through a food mill using the coarse blade. As you process, gradually add the cubed butter.

Fill the mold with the chestnut "spaghetti," making sure you don't apply any pressure.

Chill for 30 minutes.

Whip the cream, adding the confectioners' sugar and vanilla-scented sugar, until it reaches a Chantilly texture.

Turn the chilled chestnut preparation on to a serving dish. Spoon the Chantilly cream into a pastry bag and pipe it out into the center of the Mont Blanc.

Cherry Clafoutis
Clafoutis

SERVES 6
PREPARATION TIME: 20 MINUTES
COOKING TIME: ABOUT 1 HOUR

- 1 lb. (500 g) dark, ripe cherries
- 1 ½ teaspoons (5 g) baking powder
- 2 cups (200 g) flour
- 3 eggs
- ¼ cup (50 g) granulated sugar, plus sugar to finish
- 2 cups (500 ml) milk
- Salt
- 2 tablespoons (30 g) butter (for the pan)

Preheat the oven to 350°F (180°C).

Wash the cherries, dry them in a clean cloth and remove the stems, but do not pit them. Reserve.

Mix the baking powder and flour together in a mixing bowl, then push it up against the sides of the bowl to form a well in the center. Break the eggs into the well, add the sugar, milk, and a pinch of salt, and stir, mixing the flour in as it falls from the sides. The finished batter should be smooth; if there are any lumps, work the batter through a sieve to eliminate them.

Butter a 10-in. (25-cm) pie or cake pan (preferably porcelain). Stir the cherries into the batter, then pour it into the pan and bake for 45 minutes to 1 hour. When golden brown, remove the clafoutis from the oven and sprinkle with sugar. Serve either hot or cold in the pan.

Apple Charlotte
Charlotte reine du Canada

SERVES 6
PREPARATION TIME: 30 MINUTES
COOKING TIME: 40 MINUTES

2 ¼ lb. (1 kg) apples, preferably Reinette du Canada, or other russet variety

3 tablespoons (50 g) sugar

3 tablespoons (50 g) butter

1 vanilla bean

Zest of ½ lemon

2 tablespoons dry white wine

1 sandwich loaf

4 tablespoons Apricot Jam (see p. 700)

Melted butter for the slices of bread

Generously butter the charlotte mold.

Peel the apples, quarter them, and remove the seeds and cores. Place the quarters in a saucepan and sprinkle with the sugar. Cut the butter into cubes and dot them among the apple. Slit the vanilla bean lengthways. Add the lemon zest and vanilla bean to the apple mixture and pour in the white wine. Cook gently, stirring from time to time, and then turn up the heat to reduce until very thick. While the apples are cooking, melt the apricot jam and push through a sieve. Mix it into the applesauce and leave to cool.

Preheat the oven to 500°F (260°C), or as high as it will go.

Cut slices of bread ⅛ in. (4 mm) thick–just enough to make 12 right-angled triangles. Dip them in the melted butter. Line the bottom of the charlotte mold with them, butter side down, packing them closely together so that the apple mixture does not seep through.

Then cut ¼-in. (1-cm) thick slices and cut them into rectangles measuring 1 ¼ in. (4 cm) wide and just under 1 in. (2 cm) longer than the side of the mold (unless your mold is very high, in which case they should be the same length). Dip each rectangle in melted butter and place them, butter side towards the side of the mold, overlapping one another until you have lined the sides.

Remove the vanilla bean and lemon zest from the apple mixture and fill the charlotte mold. Cut a piece of bread into a circle ⅛ in. (4 mm) thick (or use enough bread to make a circle), dip it in melted butter, and enclose the apple mixture with it. Immediately place in the very hot oven so that the bread browns instead of going soggy, and cook for about 40 minutes.

Leave to rest for 15 minutes before turning it out of the mold. Unmold it only when you are ready to serve.

SERVES 2
PREPARATION TIME: 15 MINUTES
COOKING TIME: 20 MINUTES

Tahitian Omelet
Omelette tahitienne

3 slices pineapple, fresh or canned
3 tablespoons Apricot Jam (see p. 700)
2 teaspoons Maraschino liqueur

SWEET OMELET
6 eggs
2 egg yolks
½ teaspoon sugar
2 tablespoons crème fraîche or heavy cream
Salt
Butter for cooking
Confectioners' sugar for dusting

Remove the core from the pineapple slices and dice them. Melt the apricot jam in a small pan and add the pineapple cubes. Bring to a boil and then leave to stew very gently for 15 minutes.

Remove from the heat and stir in the liqueur.

Preheat the oven to 475°F (240°C), or as high as it will go.

Prepare a sweetened omelet. Whip the crème fraîche and set aside. Beat the eggs and the egg yolks, but not too much, with a pinch of salt. Add the sugar and fold in the whipped cream.

Cook the omelet in butter, turn it onto a warmed dish, and dust it with confectioners' sugar. Garnish the omelet with the stewed pineapple, setting aside a little apricot syrup. Turn the omelet over it and dust it with confectioners' sugar. Bake at 475°F (240°C) for 2 minutes, just until the sugar melts and begins to turn light brown.

Draw out a line around the omelet using the remaining apricot syrup.

Souffléed Vanilla Omelet
Omelette soufflée à la vanille

SERVES 4
PREPARATION TIME: 25 MINUTES
COOKING TIME: 10 TO 15 MINUTES

- 8 eggs
- 1 vanilla bean
- 4 tablespoons sugar
- 1 dash rum
- Salt
- Butter for the dish
- Confectioners' sugar for dusting

Separate the eggs. Slit a vanilla bean lengthways and scrape out the seeds. In a mixing bowl, whisk together the 8 egg yolks, sugar, and vanilla seeds. Whip the 8 egg whites with a pinch of salt until they are firm.

Heat the oven to 350°F (180°C).

Very carefully fold the egg yolks into the beaten egg whites, taking care not to deflate them. Then stir in the rum.

Butter an ovenproof dish and pour the omelet in. Draw out patterns on the top with a fork.

Cook for 10 to 15 minutes, keeping a careful eye on the omelet to ensure that it does not brown suddenly.

Dust it with confectioners' sugar and return it briefly to the oven so that the surface caramelizes a little.

Serve immediately.

Cherry Omelet
Omelette aux griottes

SERVES 2
PREPARATION TIME: 20 MINUTES
COOKING TIME: 5 MINUTES

7 oz. (200 g) cherries
¾ cup (5 oz./150 g) sugar
1 teaspoon kirsch

SYRUP
Scant ½ cup (100 ml) water
4 tablespoons sugar

SWEET OMELET
6 eggs, or
4 eggs plus 3 yolks
½ teaspoon sugar
2 tablespoons crème fraîche
Salt
Butter for cooking
Confectioners' sugar for dusting
Kirsch to flambé

Remove the stems from the cherries and cut them into two pieces as follows: one-quarter and three-quarters, leaving the pits in the larger part.

Make a syrup using the scant half-cup (100 ml) water and 4 tablespoons sugar. Cook the smaller, quarter-sized pieces in this for 15 minutes.

Crush the three-quarter sized pieces finely, with the pits, and cook the purée with an equal weight of sugar. When this thickens into a coulis, remove it from the heat and strain through a sieve, and then through a very fine-mesh sieve into a bowl. Add the kirsch to flavor it and mix in the stewed quarter-cherries.

Make a sweet omelet. Whip the crème fraîche and set aside. Beat the eggs, but not too much, with a pinch of salt. Add the sugar and fold in the whipped cream.

Cook the omelet in butter and fill it with the cherry purée.

Dust it with confectioners' sugar and flambé it with kirsch.

SERVES 6
PREPARATION TIME: 30 MINUTES
COOKING TIME: 20 MINUTES

Vanilla Custard Sauce
Crème anglaise

1 vanilla bean
2 cups (500 ml) milk
3 eggs
½ cup (3 ½ oz./100 g) granulated sugar
Salt

Split open the vanilla bean lengthwise, place in a medium saucepan (do not use an aluminum pan as this will blacken the sauce) with the milk and bring just to a boil. Remove the pan from the heat and leave to infuse for 7 to 8 minutes, then remove the vanilla bean.

Away from the heat, in the top of a double boiler, whisk together the eggs, sugar, and a pinch of salt, then whisk in the hot milk. Set the top of the double boiler in place and heat, stirring the mixture constantly for about 8 minutes or until it thickens (it should not boil). Immediately pour the sauce into a serving bowl and allow to cool, stirring occasionally before refrigerating.

Serve cold.

Serving suggestions: Serve with Chocolate Marble Cake (see p. 599). Vanilla custard sauce is also excellent with fresh fruit such as strawberries, raspberries, pears, etc.

Variation: Instead of vanilla, various other flavors can be given to the sauce: for example, stir a little chocolate, coffee, caramel, or rum into the sauce after it thickens but before it cools.

Jams and Jellies

Cooking times for jam vary depending on the ripeness of the fruit used. You can use a candy thermometer to test it: generally when it reaches about 220°F (104°C) it is done. When cooked enough, most jams will bead, i.e., dropped onto a clean plate, a drop will hold its shape and not collapse.

FOR FIVE 1-LB. (450-G) JARS
PREPARATION TIME: 20 MINUTES
COOKING TIME: 40 MINUTES

Apricot Jam
Confiture d'abricots

5 lb. (2.25 kg) ripe fresh apricots (see Note)

10 ½ cups (4 ½ lb. / 2 kg) granulated sugar

2 cups (500 ml) water

Wash the fruit in cold water, drain, and pat dry in a towel. Cut open each apricot and remove the pit; you need 4 quarts (2 kg) of apricot halves for making the jam. Place half of the apricots in a preserving pan, add the sugar and water, and bring to a boil, stirring frequently. Once the water boils, add the remaining apricots and boil for 20 minutes or until the jam is bubbling thickly and coats a spoon. The jam has cooked enough when a drop or two allowed to cool on a clean plate will stick to the plate even when turned upside down. When the jam is done, remove it from the heat and ladle into clean jars. Allow to cool completely, then cover the jars with cellophane for storing.

Note: If you like your jam with pieces of fruit in it, use two different varieties of apricot: one very flavorful variety that will soften, and one firmer variety that will not disintegrate. In this case, place the softer variety in the preserving pan first with the sugar and water, and add the firmer apricots once the water boils. Try to find two local varieties of apricot if possible.

FOR ABOUT SEVEN TO EIGHT 1-LB. (450-G) JARS
PREPARATION TIME: 15 MINUTES
COOKING TIME: 50 MINUTES

Raspberry Jam
Confiture de framboises

4 ½ lb. (2 kg) fresh ripe raspberries

10 ½ cups (4 ½ lb. / 2 kg) granulated sugar

2 cups (500 ml) water

Wash and quickly drain the raspberries. Remove any remaining stems. Place the raspberries in a preserving pan with the sugar and water and bring to a boil, stirring gently. Boil for 30 minutes or until the jam coats a spoon and a drop or two allowed to cool on a clean plate will stick to it when turned upside down (see note at top of page). When done, remove the jam from the heat and ladle into clean jars. Allow to cool completely before covering the jars with cellophane for storing.

SERVES 10
PREPARATION TIME: 15 MINUTES
COOKING TIME:
1 HOUR 20 MINUTES

2 ¼ lb. (1 kg) quinces

About 1 ½ lb. (700 g) granulated sugar, plus sugar to sprinkle over and to serve

Quince Jellies
Pâte de coings

Use only perfectly ripe, unbruised quinces. Peel them and cut the pulp off of the hard, central core. Cut the quinces into quarters. Place in a preserving pan with just enough water to barely cover, bring to a boil and boil rapidly for about 20 minutes or until the quinces are very soft and the water has evaporated.

Purée the quinces in a food mill, using a fine grill, or in a blender or food processor. Weigh or measure the purée and place it back in the preserving pan. Add the same weight of sugar to the purée, or for every cup (250 g) of purée, add 1 ¼ cups (250 g) of granulated sugar. Bring to a boil and boil for 40 minutes, or until the jelly is extremely thick, stirring almost constantly; if the jelly splatters while cooking, lower the heat.

Pour the jelly into a shallow porcelain pie dish or earthenware platter–it should be no more than 1 in. (2.5 cm) thick.

Preheat the oven to 250°F (120°C).

Sprinkle the surface of the jelly with a little sugar, then place in the oven for 20 minutes to dry out. Remove from the oven and allow to cool completely, then cut the jelly into long bands. Wrap each band in parchment paper or waxed paper and store in a cool, dry place (do not refrigerate), or serve immediately.

To serve, cut the bands into squares, roll them in granulated sugar, and arrange on a plate or platter.

SERVES 6
PREPARATION TIME: 10 MINUTES

2 cups (500 ml) thick crème fraîche

⅔ cup (4 ½ oz./125 g) sugar

Chantilly Cream
Crème Chantilly

To make Chantilly cream, use fresh, very thick cream.

Pour the cream into a mixing bowl and using a small flexible balloon whisk, begin whisking slowly. The cream will increase in volume. When it has almost doubled, accelerate the whisking, stopping as soon as it becomes firm and stays between the wires of the whisk like stiffly beaten egg whites. Do not beat any longer: with just two or three seconds of extra whisking, you will transform your Chantilly cream into butter.

Carefully stir in the sugar. The amount depends on what you will be using your cream for; generally, you will need about ⅔ cup (125 g) sugar for every 2 cups (500 ml) cream.

PREPARATION TIME: 10 MINUTES
COOKING TIME: 15 MINUTES

Creamy Chocolate Sauce
Sauce crème au chocolat

- 9 oz. (250 g) bittersweet chocolate, or 1 generous cup (4 ½ oz./125 g) unsweetened cocoa powder and ⅓ cup (75 ml) water and ⅔ cup (4 ½ oz./125 g) sugar
- ¾ cup (200 ml) crème fraîche or heavy cream
- 2 tablespoons (30 g) butter

Melt the chocolate in a double-boiler, or heat the cocoa powder with the water and sugar, stirring from time to time.

When the chocolate is melted, or the cocoa comes to a boil, remove from the heat, and add the cream and butter. Whisk briskly for 2 minutes.

PREPARATION TIME: 15 MINUTES
COOKING TIME: 5 MINUTES

Montmorency Sauce
Sauce Montmorency

- 2 oz. (60 g) candied cherries
- 2 tablespoons kirsch
- 9 oz. (250 g) Montmorency or other sour cherries
- 9 oz. (250 g) redcurrant jelly
- 4 ½ oz. (125 g) raspberries
- Juice of 2 oranges
- 1 pinch ground ginger

Macerate the candied cherries in the kirsch with a tablespoon of water. Warm them a little so that they swell.

Pit the cherries and liquidize them. Warm the redcurrant jelly a little and stir in the liquidized cherries.

Purée the raspberries, strain the juice, and add it to the mixture. Pour in the orange juice, a pinch of ground ginger, and stir in the macerated cherries.

PREPARATION TIME: 10 MINUTES
COOKING TIME: 5 MINUTES

2 ¾ cups (700 ml) Apricot Jam (see p. 700)
¾ cup (200 ml) water
¼ cup (1 ¾ oz./50 g) sugar
Liqueur of your choice

Apricot Sauce
Sauce aux abricots

Combine all the ingredients in a saucepan and bring to a boil. Leave to simmer gently for 5 minutes, skim the surface, and strain through a fine-mesh sieve, pressing down hard on the fruit. Keep warm over a hot water bath.

Just before using, flavor the sauce with kirsch or maraschino and vanilla.

For the following fruits, use the same method with the recommended liqueurs:

Strawberry sauce flavored with kirsch.
Raspberry sauce flavored with maraschino.
Redcurrant sauce flavored with kirsch.
Orange sauce flavored with curaçao, to which you should add one-third apricot sauce.

SERVES 4
PREPARATION TIME: 5 MINUTES
COOKING TIME: ABOUT 8 MINUTES

Hot Spiced Wine
Vin chaud

3 ¼ cups (750 ml) good red wine
10 lumps light brown sugar
1 large pinch cinnamon
1 clove
1 lemon

Place the wine, sugar, cinnamon, and clove in a saucepan and bring to a boil.

While the wine is heating up, wash the lemon, dry in a towel, and cut four thin slices from it. Place one slice of lemon in each glass. Squeeze the remaining lemon and add the juice to the pan with the wine.

As soon as the wine boils, remove the clove, then pour the wine into the glasses and serve.

Hot spiced wine is excellent for you when you feel a cold coming on.

Dried Fruit Compote
Compote de fruits secs

SERVES 4
SOAKING TIME: OVERNIGHT
PREPARATION TIME: 10 MINUTES
COOKING TIME: 20 MINUTES

- 7 oz. (200 g) dried apricots
- 5 oz. (150 g) dried figs
- 4 ½ oz. (125 g) prunes
- 4 ½ oz. (125 g) dried bananas
- 3 cups (750 ml) cold water (for cooking)
- 10 hazelnuts
- 10 almonds

The evening before, place the fruit in a bowl, cover with cold water, place in the refrigerator and leave to soak overnight.

The next day, discard the water the fruit soaked in. Place the fruit in a large saucepan and add the 3 cups (750 ml) cold water. Bring just to a boil, then immediately lower the heat, cover, and simmer slowly for 20 to 30 minutes or until very tender. Pour into a salad bowl and leave to cool completely, then chill for at least an hour in the refrigerator.

Just before serving, stir in the nuts.

Serving suggestions: Serve with Madeleines (see p. 604).

SERVES 4
PREPARATION TIME: 10 MINUTES
COOKING TIME: 20 MINUTES

Applesauce
Compote de pommes

- 2 ¼ lb. (1 kg) apples
- 4 tablespoons (60 ml) water
- ¼ cup (50 g) granulated sugar
- Either 1 pinch cinnamon or lemon juice to taste, or
- ½ cup (70 g) light brown sugar and 2 tablespoons water

Peel, quarter, and seed the apples, then cut into thin slices. Place in a saucepan with the water and sugar, and simmer uncovered for 20 minutes, stirring occasionally with a wooden spoon.

You can either flavor the applesauce with cinnamon or lemon juice, or with caramel. In the second case, make a caramel by cooking the brown sugar and water together until the mixture darkens and caramelizes. Stir the hot applesauce into the caramel and serve warm.

SERVES 4
PREPARATION TIME: 10 MINUTES
COOKING TIME: 10 MINUTES

Stewed Apricots
Compote d'abricots

- 12 large fresh apricots, all equally ripe
- ¾ cup (5 oz./150 g) sugar
- 1 cup plus 1 scant cup (350 ml) water
- 1 vanilla bean
- 1 teaspoon kirsch or walnut liqueur

Dip the apricots into boiling water for just 1 second and peel them immediately. Cut them into halves. Prepare a light syrup using the sugar, water, and the vanilla bean, slit in two lengthways. Break 4 pits and split the kernels. Add them to the syrup.

Gently bring to a boil and poach, making sure that the syrup does no more than simmer for about 8 minutes. The apricots should remain firm so that they do not lose their shape or get crushed.

Keep the syrup in a bowl until you are ready to serve the apricots. When it is lukewarm, add the kirsch or walnut liqueur.

SERVES 4
PREPARATION TIME: 10 MINUTES
COOKING TIME: 30 MINUTES

Pears in Red Wine
Poires au vin

- 8 very small or 4 medium pears weighing about 2 lb. (900 g) in total
- Juice of ½ lemon
- ½ cup (100 g) granulated sugar
- 1 ¼ cups (300 ml) red wine
- ½ vanilla bean, split in half lengthwise
- 1 sprig thyme
- 2 peppercorns
- 1 clove
- 4 tablespoons (60 ml) *crème de cassis*

Preferably use a smooth-skinned variety of pear. Small ones need not be peeled (simply rinse them off and dry with a cloth); large ones can be peeled, cored, then halved or quartered (see Note).

Place the pears in a saucepan just large enough to hold them (stand small pears upright). Add the lemon juice, sugar, red wine, vanilla, thyme, peppercorns, clove, and *crème de cassis*. Bring just to a boil, then cover and simmer very slowly for 30 minutes.

Lift the pears out of the pan and stand them upright in a serving bowl. Pour the contents of the saucepan over them and leave to cool before serving (several hours will do, but overnight is best). Baste the pears periodically with the wine as they cool, and before serving.

Serving suggestions: Serve with Lyon-Style Fritters (see p. 651).

Note: Whole pears (even large ones) make for a nicer presentation. Peel them, then place them on their sides in the wine and turn over halfway through the cooking time. When done, stand them upright and baste as described for small pears.

SERVES 4
PREPARATION TIME: 20 MINUTES

Fruit Salad
Salade de fruits

2 apples
2 pears (not too ripe)
1 orange
½ grapefruit
½ pineapple
Juice of 1 lemon
1 cup (100 g) walnut meats
¼ cup (50 g) granulated sugar
2 bananas
6 mint leaves

Peel and core the apples and pears, and cut them into quarters. Place the apples and pears in a large salad bowl.

Use a knife to cut off the peel (including the white inner skin) of the orange and grapefruit, then cut out the wedges and add them to the bowl, along with any juice they gave out.

Cut the skin off of the pineapple, cut out the central core, then cut it into wedges and add to the salad. Add the lemon juice, walnut meats, and sugar. Stir gently, then refrigerate for about 1 hour before serving.

Just before serving, peel and slice the bananas and add them, finely slice the mint and sprinkle over the fruit, and serve.

Serving suggestions: Serve with Almond Cookies (see p. 585).

Variation: All kinds of fruits other than the ones used here can be used in fruit salads; for example tropical fruits such as kiwis or lichees, or fresh grapes are all excellent additions to a fruit salad. If you like, 3 tablespoons (50 ml) of brandy or a fruit brandy can be added to the salad at the same time as the lemon juice.

SERVES 8
PREPARATION TIME: 15 MINUTES
COOKING TIME: 45 MINUTES

Baked Apples
Pommes au four

- 8 large apples
- 2 tablespoons (30 g) butter, plus butter for the dish
- Generous ½ cup (150 ml) water
- ⅓ cup (60 g) granulated sugar
- 4 tablespoons raspberry or redcurrant jelly

Preheat the oven to 350°F (180°C).

Wash the apples and wipe them dry. Cut out the stems, but it is preferable to leave the cores since the seeds give the apples a nice flavor (if you prefer, you can core them, of course).

Place the apples in a lightly buttered earthenware or porcelain baking dish, put a little butter on top of each one, add the water to the dish, and place in the oven. After 15 minutes, sprinkle each apple with sugar, then place back in the oven and bake for 30 minutes more or until tender.

Remove the apples from the oven and allow to cool for 10 to 15 minutes; they should be served warm but not hot. Just before serving, spoon a little jelly into each one, and serve in the baking dish.

SERVES 4
PREPARATION TIME: 20 MINUTES
COOKING TIME: 20 MINUTES

Orange Soufflés
Oranges soufflées

4 large Maltese (blood) oranges
Scant ½ cup (2 ¾ oz./80 g) sugar
4 eggs, separated

Preheat the oven to 350°F (180°C).

Cut off the top third of the oranges. Use a spoon to scrape out the flesh and push it through a sieve. Reduce the strained pulp over low heat. Peel the zest of the cut-off thirds of the oranges, chop it finely, and blanch it in boiling water to remove the bitterness. Drain well and add to the pulp. Then stir in the sugar and leave to cook for a few minutes. Remove from the heat and leave to cool to lukewarm before incorporating the egg yolks, making sure they do not cook.

Whisk the egg whites until firm, and gradually fold them in to the orange preparation, making sure you do not deflate them.

Spoon the orange mixture into the scooped out oranges. Bake for 20 minutes, just as you would cook ordinary soufflés.

Transfer them to a serving dish and serve immediately.

SERVES 6
PREPARATION TIME: 30 MINUTES
COOKING TIME: 15 MINUTES

12 fresh apricots
1 tablespoon sliced almonds
A few teaspoons vanilla-scented sugar (To make your own, leave a vanilla bean in your sugar ahead of time to flavor it.)
1 large pinch cornstarch
6 tablespoons Grand Marnier

APRICOT SAUCE
6 ripe, tasty apricots
¾ cup (200 ml) poaching syrup
Grand Marnier to taste
2 teaspoons (10 g) butter

Flambéed Apricots
Abricots flambés au Grand Marnier

Wash the apricots and poach them whole. When they are done, cut them in half, remove the pits, setting aside two, and transfer them to an ovenproof dish. Keep the apricots warm in a little of the poaching liquid.

Preheat the oven to 400°F (200°C)

Take the kernels of the two apricot pits and combine them with the sliced almonds. Sprinkle them with the vanilla-scented sugar, and grill them lightly in the oven until they are coated.

Scatter the apricots with the sliced sugared almonds. Dilute the cornstarch with a few tablespoons of poaching syrup and pour it into the dish.

Bring the thickened liquid to a boil just before serving and pour it over the apricots. At the table, pour the Grand Marnier over and flambé.

For the apricot sauce, push the apricots through a fine-mesh sieve. Combine the pulp with the poaching syrup and pour it all into a pan. Reduce until thick. When the sauce has cooled down (either lukewarm or cool), flavor with the liqueur you have selected.

If you are serving the sauce lukewarm, add a generous knob of butter once you have removed it from the heat.

Pears in Beaujolais Wine
Poires à la beaujolaise

SERVES 6
PREPARATION TIME: 15 MINUTES
COOKING TIME: 30 MINUTES

6 large pears, Williams if possible

SYRUP

1 bottle full-bodied red wine, Beaujolais Villages if possible

¾ cup (5 oz./150 g) sugar

1 heaped tablespoon (10 g) ground cinnamon

1 clove

2 slices orange

2 slices lemon

1 ½ teaspoons (5 g) black peppercorns

In a saucepan, combine the wine, sugar, cinnamon, clove, orange and lemon slices, and the pepper (which is indispensable).

Bring to a boil and simmer for 5 minutes.

Peel the pears carefully, leaving the stalks, place them in the liquid and poach them for about 20 minutes, turning them over from time to time. Leave them to cool in the wine.

Chill well before serving.

Dried Plums in Red Wine
Pruneaux au vin de Bourgogne

SERVES 6
SOAKING TIME: OVERNIGHT
PREPARATION TIME: 5 MINUTES
COOKING TIME: 7 MINUTES

- 2 ¼ lb. (1 kg) dried plums (prunes)
- 6 cups (1.5 liters) red wine, Burgundy if possible
- ¾ cup (5 oz./150 g) granulated sugar
- ⅔ oz. (20 g) cinnamon stick
- 1 orange, sliced
- 1 lemon, sliced

Soak the dried plums overnight in cold water. The next day, drain them and transfer them to a saucepan. Pour over the red wine and add the sugar, the cinnamon, and the orange and lemon slices.

Bring to a boil. As soon as the liquid boils, remove from the heat and leave to cool.

Serve the dried plums in a serving dish with the syrup they have cooked in, together with the sliced citrus fruits.

SERVES 6
PREPARATION TIME: 15 MINUTES
COOKING TIME: 10 MINUTES

6 small bananas
4 tablespoons (60 g) butter
6 tablespoons sugar
3 tablespoons crushed almond praline or almond macaroons
Confectioners' sugar for dusting

SOUFFLÉ BATTER
Scant ½ cup (100 ml) milk, plus a little extra to dilute the cornstarch
2 tablespoons (25 g) granulated sugar
1 ½ tablespoons (½ oz./15 g) cornstarch
1 egg, separated
2 teaspoons (10 g) butter

Souffléed Bananas with Praline
Bananes soufflées pralinées

Carefully peel the bananas, taking care not to tear the peels too much because you will need them later. Slit the bananas lengthways in two. Melt the butter with the sugar and cook the bananas gently in the pan until they form a purée.

To make the soufflé batter, bring the milk to a boil with the sugar. As soon as it boils, remove from the heat. Dilute the cornstarch with a little milk and stir it into the hot milk. Return the milk to the burner and heat gently until it begins to simmer, whisking all the time. Remove immediately. When the mixture is quite smooth, incorporate the egg yolk (spoon a little of the hot mixture over the egg yolk, stirring as you do so, and then return it to the milk) and butter. Whisk the egg white to very firm peaks and fold it in carefully.

Preheat the oven to 425°F (210°C). Carefully fold this mixture into the puréed bananas and add 2 tablespoons of crushed almond praline or almond macaroons. Spoon the batter into a pastry bag and pipe out the soufflé batter into the banana skins in the shape of a banana. Arrange the filled banana skins in a circle in an ovenproof dish. Dust with the remaining crushed pralines or macaroons and then a little confectioners' sugar.

Bake for about 5 minutes, until the top begins to caramelize.

SERVES 6
PREPARATION TIME: 30 MINUTES
MACERATION TIME: 30 MINUTES

Melon Cups
Melon de la bonne auberge

9 melons (1 ½ per person)
Confectioners' sugar
Port wine
6 glasses fine champagne cognac, or other cognac

Cut off the top of 6 melons so that you have an opening large enough to remove the seeds and stringy parts. Reserve the tops. Then remove the pulp and process it briefly.

Peel the 3 remaining melons and scoop out the flesh using a melon baller.

Place the 6 shells in the refrigerator. Macerate the balls in a mixing bowl with a little confectioners' sugar, a little port wine, and the 6 glasses of fine champagne cognac (1 per person).

Cover the mixing bowl so that it is airtight and chill for 30 minutes.

Fill the melon shells with the macerated melon balls. Share out the port wine equally between the 6 shells.

To serve, arrange the filled melons on a bed of ice. Top with their lids and serve.

Fruit Macédoine
Macédoines de fruits

SERVES 6
PREPARATION TIME: 15 MINUTES
MACERATION TIME: 2 HOURS
CHILLING TIME: 15 MINUTES

2 ¼ lb. (1 kg) assorted ripe fruit of your choice

½ cup (3 ½ oz./100 g) sugar

Liqueur, fruit brandy of your choice, or champagne

Wash, peel, and pit or seed the fruits. Cut them into small dice or slices. If necessary, rinse them in water with a little lemon juice. If you prefer, you may use whole fruit.

Leave the fruit to macerate for at least 2 hours with the sugar and liqueur of your choice in the refrigerator. Stir from time to time so that all the flavors meld.

A quarter of an hour before serving, arrange the fruit salad in a bowl and place it over crushed ice. Serve it over the ice.

Wild Strawberries and Lemon Ice Cream with Curaçao and Champagne
Fraises mignonnes glacées

SERVES 6 TO 8
PREPARATION TIME: 30 MINUTES
MACERATION TIME: 30 MINUTES

- 1 quart (1 liter) Lemon Ice Cream (see p. 755)
- 2 ¼ lb. (1 kg) wild strawberries
- 3 tablespoons sugar
- 1 teaspoon, plus 1 tablespoon vanilla-scented sugar (To make your own, leave a vanilla bean in your sugar ahead of time to flavor it.)
- Scant ½ cup (100 ml) Curaçao
- Scant ½ cup (100 ml) champagne
- 3 ½ oz. (100 g) candied violets
- ½ tablespoon finely diced candied orange peel
- 1 ¼ cups (300 ml) whipping cream, 30-35 percent butterfat
- 20 orange blossoms

Prepare the lemon ice cream. Do not allow it to become too hard; it should be smooth and soft.

Place the wild strawberries in a mixing bowl and sprinkle them with the sugar and 1 teaspoon vanilla-scented sugar. Pour over the curaçao and champagne. Chill for 30 minutes, stirring from time to time so that the strawberries absorb the flavors of the liqueur.

Coarsely crush the candied violets and combine them with the finely diced candied orange peel. Pour the whipping cream into a bowl set over ice and sweeten it with the tablespoon of vanilla-scented sugar. Whip it until it forms soft peaks.

Just before serving, spread the lemon ice cream smoothly into a crystal or silver bowl. Drain the wild strawberries and filter the syrup through cheesecloth. Place the fruit in a layer over the ice cream. Pour the strained liquid over the fruit. Smooth over the whipped cream and scatter the top with the mixed candied orange peel and candied violets. Insert the 20 orange blossoms on the surface, working as quickly as possible. Serve immediately.

ICE CREAM

Coffee Ice Cream
Glace au café

SERVES 8 TO 10
PREPARATION TIME: 10 MINUTES
COOKING TIME: 10 MINUTES
CHILLING TIME:
ABOUT 40 MINUTES

- 3 cups (750 ml) milk
- 2 oz. (50 g) coffee beans
- 1 ½ cups (10 oz./300 g) sugar
- 8 egg yolks

Bring the milk to a boil, remove it from the heat, and drop the coffee beans in to infuse. Make sure they are completely covered.

In the meanwhile, combine the sugar and egg yolks in a mixing bowl and beat energetically until the mixture thickens and becomes pale, forming a ribbon when the beater is lifted up from the bowl.

Gradually pour the milk over the mixture, straining it through a sieve to remove the coffee beans, stirring as you do so. When thoroughly combined, return it to the saucepan and place over moderate heat. Stir constantly, ensuring that it does not boil, and as soon as the mixture begins to thicken and coat the back of the spoon, remove it from the heat. Strain through a fine-mesh sieve into a bowl.

Stir to accelerate the cooling.

When it is completely cooled, pour it into the bowl of your ice-cream maker and proceed according to the manufacturer's instructions.

SERVES 8 TO 10
PREPARATION TIME: 10 MINUTES
COOKING TIME: 10 MINUTES
CHILLING TIME:
ABOUT 40 MINUTES

3 cups (750 ml) milk

9 oz. (250 g) bittersweet chocolate

1 cup (7 oz. / 200 g) sugar

8 egg yolks

Chocolate Ice Cream
Glace au chocolat

Bring the milk to boil and melt the chocolate with it. Beat the sugar with the egg yolks until the mixture is pale and thick. Pour this gradually into the milk and chocolate mixture, stirring as you do so, and gently simmer for 10 minutes, until the mixture coats the back of a spoon. Remove from the heat and stir frequently until the mixture has cooled down.

Pour into the ice-cream maker and proceed according to the manufacturer's instructions.

SERVES 6
PREPARATION TIME: 15 MINUTES
CHILLING TIME: 30 MINUTES

8 egg yolks

⅔ cup (125 g) granulated sugar

2 cups (500 ml) plain yogurt

6 tablespoons (100 ml) crème fraîche or heavy cream

¼ cup (50 g) mixed candied fruit

Yogurt Ice Cream
Glace au yaourt

Place the egg yolks in a bowl with the sugar and whisk until the mixture becomes smooth and pale in color. Stir in the yogurt, then the cream. Chop the candied fruit and add to the mixture. Pour into an ice cream maker and churn for 30 minutes or until stiff. You can serve the ice cream straightaway (it's best this way), or put it in containers and keep in a deep freezer for later use.

Serving suggestions: Serve with cookies, and a sauce made with fresh raspberries and a little sugar blended until smooth in a blender or food processor.

Lemon Ice Cream
Glace aux citrons

SERVES 8 TO 10
PREPARATION TIME: 15 MINUTES
COOKING TIME: 10 MINUTES
CHILLING TIME:
ABOUT 40 MINUTES

3 lemons
4 cups (1 liter) milk
1 vanilla bean
2 cups (14 oz./400 g) sugar
10 egg yolks

Grate the zest of the lemons and squeeze their juice. Slit the vanilla bean lengthways and place it in a saucepan with the milk. When it comes to a boil, leave to infuse for 5 minutes. Add the lemon zest and juice and leave to cool.

Beat the egg yolks and sugar together until the mixture is pale and thick. Pour just a little milk over the mixture, whisk it, and then return it all to the saucepan. Return to the burner, stirring all the time, until the mixture thickens and coats the back of the spoon.

Remove from the heat and stir frequently until cooled. Pour into the bowl of the ice-cream maker and proceed according to the manufacturer's instructions.

SERVES 4
PREPARATION TIME: 40 MINUTES
CHILLING TIME: 3 HOURS

Iced Cherry Soufflé
Soufflé glacé aux cerises

- 2 cups (500 ml) puréed cherries
- Cherries for garnish
- 2 tablespoons maraschino liqueur, plus a little extra to poach the cherries
- 16 egg yolks
- 2 ⅔ cups (1 lb./500 g) sugar
- 2 cups (500 ml) milk
- 2 cups (500 ml) crème fraîche or heavy cream
- ⅔ oz. (20 g) gum tragacanth, finely crushed (available from specialty cake decorating stores or online; see Note)
- Raspberry coulis

Remove the stems and pits from the cherries you will be using for garnish. Poach them in a syrup flavored with maraschino liqueur. Leave them to cool completely.

Beat the egg yolks and sugar together until the mixture is pale and thick. Pour just a little milk over the mixture, whisk it, and then return it all to the saucepan. Return to moderate heat, stirring all the time, until the mixture thickens and coats the back of the spoon. Remove from the heat and stir frequently until cooled.

Then stir in the crème fraîche, finely crushed gum tragacanth, and puréed cherries.

Place the mixing bowl over ice and whisk vigorously until very frothy and slightly thickened.

Line the sides of four soufflé molds with parchment paper; it should be 2 in. (5 cm) higher than the rim.

Fill the soufflé molds to just under ½ in. (1 cm) from the top of the strip of parchment paper. Smooth the surface with an offset spatula. Top with the poached cherries and chill for 3 hours in the refrigerator.

Just before serving, remove the strip of parchment paper and drizzle lightly with very cold raspberry coulis.

Note: Gum tragacanth is the dried sap or gum obtained from a Middle-Eastern plant, often used in gum paste for cake decoration. An alternative that is slightly more widely available (but synthetic) is tylose powder.

Orange Granita
Granité à l'orange

SERVES 8
PREPARATION TIME: 15 MINUTES
FREEZING TIME: 3 HOURS

4 ½ lbs. (2 kg) juice oranges
1 ¼ cups (9 oz./250 g) sugar
1 small glass cognac or splash of grenadine syrup (optional)

Squeeze the oranges.

Measure the volume of orange juice. Measure out half that volume of water. Add the sugar, dissolving it completely, and liqueur or grenadine syrup if using.

Combine the ingredients well and pour into a plastic tray. Freeze for 3 hours, stirring and scraping frequently with a fork so that it retains its icy texture.

Orange-Scented Oranges
L'orange à l'orange

SERVES 6
PREPARATION TIME: 10 MINUTES
COOKING TIME: 5 MINUTES
CHILLING TIME: 1 HOUR

6 large unsprayed or organic oranges
1 ¼ cups (9 oz./250 g) sugar
⅔ cup (150 ml) grenadine syrup
2 lemons
Sliced or chopped pistachios for garnish

Peel the oranges using a vegetable or citrus peeler, making sure you do not include the bitter white pith, and slice the zest into fine julienne slices.

Cook the slices with the sugar, ¾ cup (200 ml) water, and the grenadine syrup.

Remove the white pith of the 6 oranges. Finely slice them and place the slices in a dish. Pour over the syrup with the julienned zest. Chill for at least 1 hour.

To serve, scatter with a few sliced or chopped pistachios.

Spooms

SERVES 4
PREPARATION TIME: 10 MINUTES
CHILLING TIME: 1 HOUR

Scant ¼ cup (50 ml) cold syrup at 20 degrees Baumé, made from 3 cups (700 ml) water and 2 ⅔ cups (500 g) sugar (see Note)

⅔ cup (150 ml) dry champagne, Muscat, or Sauternes

2 cups (500 ml) ice cream of your choice

ITALIAN MERINGUE

½ cup (3 ½ oz./100 g) sugar

2 tablespoons water

4 egg whites

Salt

Special equipment: an instant-read or candy thermometer

Process the syrup, champagne or other wine, with ice cream in an ice-cream maker. While the machine is running, prepare an Italian meringue: heat the sugar and water together. While the syrup is heating, whisk the egg whites with a pinch of salt. When the syrup has reached 230°F (110°C), begin pouring it slowly but steadily into the beaten egg whites, whisking as you do so. Then continue to whisk until the mixture has cooled completely. It will now be dense and shiny with numerous little peaks. Carefully fold the Italian meringue into the ice cream mixture, and serve (preferably) or freeze.

Note: A spoom is a thick, frothy sorbet. The name comes from the Italian spuma, *meaning foam.*

Degrees Baumé are used to measure the density of certain liquids. In dessert-making, they indicate the sugar density in sugar-liquid mixtures or syrups. The density can be measured using a baumé scale, or by calculating the:

- *weight of sugar required: 1 liter of syrup at 1 degree Baumé contains 25 g of sugar. Multiply the desired number of degrees by 25 g to find the weight of sugar needed for 1 liter of syrup. (1 liter of syrup at 20 degrees Baumé contains 25 g x 20 = 500 g of sugar.)*
- *volume of dissolved sugar: The volume of 1 g of dissolved sugar is 0.6 ml. (The volume of 500 g of dissolved sugar will therefore be 300 ml.)*
- *volume of water required: for 1 liter of syrup at 20 degrees Baumé, use 300 ml dissolved sugar (which corresponds to 500 g) and 700 ml of water (1 liter of syrup - 300 ml of dissolved sugar = 700 ml of water).*

The dissolution may be done from cold or by boiling the sugar and water together in a pan, and then removing it from the heat immediately and skimming or filtering. If the latter method is used, note that the solution will have a lower reading on the baumé scale at boiling point than when it has completely cooled down; typically, a syrup measuring 30 degrees Baumé at boiling point will measure 34 degrees when cooled down. Take this second, higher reading into account for preparations using cold syrup.

APPENDIXES

GLOSSARY

ALMOND MEAL *see* Ground Almonds (Almond Meal)

ASPIC
Clarified stock combined with gelatin make a savory jelly used to coat cold meat, fish, or vegetables, as a base for molded dishes, or cubed, as an accompaniment.

BAKE BLIND
To prepare a tart shell for filling, either if the filling is not cooked or if it is very moist and will not allow the dough to bake properly, the raw pastry is pre-baked. To prevent the dough from rising, it may be necessary to line it with parchment or waxed paper and fill it with pie weights or dry beans. The dough is then baked until ready to eat, in the case of an uncooked filling, or until almost done, if it is going to be filled and returned to the oven.

BARD
Bard refers to the thin strips of pork or bacon fat placed round meat, game, and poultry to protect the flesh from drying out when cooked in the oven. The strips of bard are held in place with kitchen twine. To bard is to surround the piece to be cooked with strips of fat. *See also* Lardoons.

BASTE
Food roasting in the oven is basted to moisten it so that it does not dry out. To baste, spoon over the cooking juices from the pan or brush the roast with them, and repeat several times during the cooking process.

BEAT
When the term "beat" is used, either a wire whisk or electric mixer may be used, unless a specific utensil is mentioned. The term is used most often in connection with egg whites, which are usually beaten until firm or stiff (*see* Beating Egg Whites).

BEATING EGG WHITES
Beating or whisking egg whites involves using a whisk or electric mixer until they stiffen and form soft or firm peaks, depending on what the recipe calls for. If firm peaks are required, the whites should be beaten until they peak and do not slide out of the mixing bowl when the bowl is turned upside down. Stiffly beaten egg whites are folded, not stirred, into other ingredients (*see* Fold); they must be used immediately after being beaten or they will separate and become watery.

BEURRES COMPOSÉS *see* Compound Butters (*Beurres Composés*)

BEURRE MANIÉ *see* Thickening, or Enriching

***BLANC* (TO COOK IN)**
Some vegetables that discolor during cooking, such as artichoke hearts, and white offal should be cooked in a *blanc*–water to which a little flour and lemon juice or vinegar are added.

BLANCH
To blanch a food is to cook it very briefly in boiling water, either to soften it before cooking or remove its bitterness. The food is then refreshed, either by being dipped rapidly in cold or ice water, or held under cold running water, and then drained.

BLENDER
Used for making sauces, soups, purées, mousses, etc., a blender can be either handheld, in which case the blade is plunged into the ingredients for mixing, or fixed on a base, with the ingredients placed in a jug for blending.

BOUQUET GARNI
Unless otherwise specified in particular recipes, the usual components of a bouquet garni are some leek greens, a piece of celery stick, preferably with its leaves, a sprig of thyme, and a bay leaf.

BRAISE
Braising is a slow cooking method that uses a little liquid to gently simmer the meat, vegetables, or even fish, either in the oven or on the stovetop. A variant of braising, known as *cuire à l'étouffée*, requires sealing the pot, usually with a flour-and-water paste, so that no steam escapes.

BREAD CRUMBS
To make your own bread crumbs, remove the crusts of bread and dry it out slowly in the oven, or crush Melba toast.

BREADING
To prepare food for frying (or roasting) by dipping it successively in flour, beaten egg yolk, and then bread crumbs.

BROWN, OR COLOR
These two terms are used interchangeably. They generally refer to cooking a food in fat until the surface takes on a golden or brownish color. Instructions can vary, depending on the degree of color to be attained ("until it begins to color," "until lightly browned," or simply "brown").

Food should be browned in a pan large enough for it to all sit on the bottom without piling up; if this is impossible, the food will have to be browned in several batches. Browning is a preliminary operation, so even if the food is divided into batches to brown, it should all be placed in the pot together to finish cooking.

These terms can also be used in connection with roasting and baking; the meaning is the same, referring to the color the surface should attain.

BUTTER
Use only unsalted butter in these recipes. Butter should always be of the highest quality, and no substitutes (such as margarine) should be used if you want an authentic version of these dishes.

Butter is often said to be "softened." This means that it has been left at room temperature for about an hour or until it can easily be broken into soft pieces with your fingers. It is extremely important that butter be sufficiently soft whenever sauces or doughs are being made. *See* Softening or Creaming Butter.

CARAMELIZE (COOKING SUGAR)
Recipes will call for sugar to be caramelized to various stages or colors, depending on the strength of flavor required. The darker the color, the stronger the flavor. There are two methods for caramelizing sugar: the dry method, when the sugar is cooked directly in the pan, and the wet method, using water. To make a dry caramel, pour the sugar out into an even layer in a heavy bottomed pan or skillet over medium heat and cook until it liquefies and reaches the desired color. The second method is easier to control. Dissolve the specified quantity of sugar in water, bring to a boil, and reduce until the sugar is caramelized. With both methods, great caution should be exercised so that you don't burn yourself, and it should be watched carefully so that it does not burn (sugar burns extremely quickly).

To line a baking pan with a caramel, pour it into the pan as soon as it is ready and swirl it around as quickly as possible until the pan is evenly coated. It will set almost as soon as it comes into contact with the cold surface.

CAUL
Caul, or caul fat, is the membrane laced with fat that surrounds the stomach of animals. Pig's caul in particular is often used to hold together ingredients that might come apart during cooking, such as *paupiettes* (thin slices of meat filled with stuffing) and stuffed cabbage leaves.

CHINOIS
A chinois is a conical sieve, usually perforated metal, used to strain and filter thicker sauces.

CLARIFY
To clarify a liquid is to ensure that it is clear by removing any impurities. This is usually done with careful skimming as it simmers. When it cools, strain it through a fine-mesh sieve or cheesecloth.

To clarify butter, melt it slowly until most of its water content evaporates. The milk solids will sink to the bottom and gold-colored liquid will remain at the top. Skim off the foam and use the clear butter for your cooking.

COAT
To cover a dish smoothly with a sauce or a cream preparation. A sauce or cream preparation is ready when it coats the back of a spoon.

COLOR *see* Brown, or Color

COMPOUND BUTTERS (*BEURRES COMPOSÉS*)
Most compound butters accompany grilled meat and fish and are served cold. To prepare a cold compound butter, first cream the butter (*see* Softening or Creaming Butter) and then incorporate the flavorings. A popular compound butter is maître d'hôtel butter, made with parsley, lemon juice, salt, and pepper. There are a few hot compound butters made with crustacean shells or flesh.

COOKING SUGAR *see* Caramelize (Cooking Sugar)

CREAMING BUTTER *see* Softening or Creaming Butter

CRÈME FRAÎCHE
Crème fraîche is a very thick, rich cream. In most cases–and this is indicated in the recipes concerned–heavy cream can be used instead, but try to use crème fraîche if possible. It is now commercialized on a small scale in the US.

DEGLAZE
To deglaze means to pour liquid (usually wine or other alcoholic beverage, or stock) into a pan at high temperature so that the juices and sediments can be absorbed to make a sauce.

DEGREASING *see* Remove the Fat (Degreasing)

DEMI-GLACE (*Demi-Glaze*) see *Glace* and *Demi-Glace* (Glaze and Demi-Glaze)

DÉTREMPE
The French term for pastry dough in its initial stage when it comprises only flour and water, prior to the addition of other ingredients.

DICE
Many recipes call for diced vegetables, aromatics, and other ingredients. The sizes required vary. A **brunoise** is made of extremely fine dice, cubes of approximately 1/12 in. (2-3 mm). A **salpicon** requires slightly larger dice, approximately ¼-in. (5-mm) cubes. For a **mirepoix**, the size ranges from ¼-½ in. (5-10 mm), depending on whether it is prepared for a sauce or a stock. By dicing all the ingredients to the same size, you will ensure that they cook more evenly. If used as a garnish, they will be all the more attractive.

DOUBLE BOILER
A double boiler consists of two parts: a bottom, in which a little water is placed and brought just below the boiling point to simmer, and a top, in which the ingredients to be cooked over the simmering water are placed. It is important that the water should simmer, not boil, and that it should never touch the bottom of the top section. A double boiler can be improvised by heating water in a saucepan and setting a mixing bowl (preferably stainless steel) over it (make sure the bowl does not touch the water).

DRESS
To prepare whole poultry, game birds, and fish for cooking. Dressing fish involves trimming it, removing the scales, gutting it, and cleaning it. Poultry and game birds must be plucked, singed, trussed, and sometimes barded (*see* Singe; Truss; Bard).

DUTCH OVEN
Known as a *cocotte* in French, this is a large pot with a tight-fitting lid, ideal for stews as it can be used both on the stove top and in the oven. It is usually made of cast iron.

EGGS
Unless otherwise specified, always use 1 ¾-oz. (50-g) eggs, or 21 oz. (596 g) per dozen. These are labeled Medium on the package. If using much smaller or much larger eggs, adjust the number used, as appropriate.

In the chapter on eggs in this book, you can use any size of egg you want.

ENRICHING *see* Thickening, or Enriching

FINE-MESH SIEVE *see* Strainer, or Fine-Mesh Sieve

FLAMBÉ
To pour an alcoholic beverage, often cognac or other liqueur, over a dish and then set light to it. This will intensify the flavor, particularly when the pan juices are required in a sauce.

To flambé desserts, warm the liqueur a little in a deep dish, pour it over the hot food, ignite it using a long match set at the edge of the dish, and allow the flames to burn out. Be careful, of course, not to lean over the dish.

FLOUR
All-purpose flour can be used throughout the book. Do not sift the flour when measuring or when using unless expressly advised to do so.

FOLD
Stiffly beaten egg whites (and whipped cream) are folded into other ingredients rather than stirred,

to keep them from collapsing. To do this, spoon about a third of the beaten egg whites on to the ingredients they are to be mixed with. Using a flat, wooden spatula (a wooden spoon may be used, but it's not as efficient), cut down through the egg whites to the bottom of the bowl, then lift or scoop the other ingredients up onto the egg whites, giving the bowl a quarter-turn as you do so. Repeat this motion over and over until the two are mixed together, then add the remaining egg whites and continue in the same manner. The final mixture should be perfectly homogenous, with no unmixed particles in it.

FOOD PROCESSOR

Electric food processors come in a range of sizes and powers and are able to perform a wide variety of basic tasks, including grating and slicing, puréeing, mixing doughs, and whisking.

FOUR-SPICE MIX

Classic French cuisine uses few spices, but makes frequent use of a blend of ground black pepper, nutmeg, ginger, and cloves.

FUMET

A clear stock used to cook fish, made from fish bones, onions, and other aromatic ingredients.

To make 4 cups (1 liter) of fumet, crush 1 ¼ lb. (600 g) fish bones and leave them to soak in cold water to remove any traces of blood. Peel, wash, and finely slice 2 small shallots (50 g), ½ large onion (50 g), ½ leek (50 g, white part only), ½ carrot (50 g), 1 oz. (30 g) button mushrooms, and place in a large pot with a bouquet garni, 4 cups (1 liter) water, ⅔ cup (150 ml) white wine, and ½ teaspoon (2 g) peppercorns. Bring to a boil, skimming when necessary, then simmer for 25 to 30 minutes, taking care not to stir as this will turn the liquid cloudy. Strain through a chinois or sieve and cool down quickly.

GELATIN SHEETS

Gelatin in thin, transparent sheets (or leaves) weighing precisely 2 grams is the form used in France. They are available from specialty stores or online. To use them, soak them in a bowl of very cold water (unless otherwise specified) until they are softened and very pliable, about 10 to 15 minutes. Then remove them from the water and squeeze all the liquid out with your hands. Dissolve them in the quantity of warm liquid specified in your recipe, stirring until there are no visible traces left. Follow the recipe directions for setting or jelling times. Note that gelatin is an animal-derived product; should you prefer a plant-based jelling agent (such as agar-agar), follow the directions for quantities and times.

***GLACE* AND *DEMI-GLACE* (GLAZE AND DEMI-GLAZE)**

A *glace* is a reduction of a tasty, gelatinous meat stock to about one-tenth of its volume. A *demi-glace* is made by thickening a stock with a roux (butter and flour cooked together) and then reducing it, but by less than for a *glace*. Commercial preparations are available as a substitute for these ingredients.

GRATIN

A gratin is a dish with a topping such as bread crumbs or cheese that is placed under the broiler until crisp and browned.

GRILL PAN

Available in square, rectangular, and round forms, this heavy pan is usually used for high-heat cooking of meat, and sometimes vegetables. It allows individual portions of meat, such as steaks, to be grilled and seared in attractive crisscross patterns, and ensures that they do not cook in their own fat.

GROUND ALMONDS (ALMOND MEAL)

Sweet, blanched, ground almonds are a staple of French pastry making. To make your own, place blanched almonds (peel removed) in a food processor and pulse until they are reduced to a fine powder, essential for best baking results.

HERBS

Various fresh herbs, such as tarragon, chervil, and parsley are frequently called for in these recipes. Whenever possible, try to use the herb in question; otherwise, substitute more available fresh herbs rather than using dried ones. For instance, fresh chives or parsley, or a little mint or basil, could be used in many recipes that call for chervil.

HIGH-SIDED SAUTÉ PAN

This pan is useful for sautéing, searing, and frying,

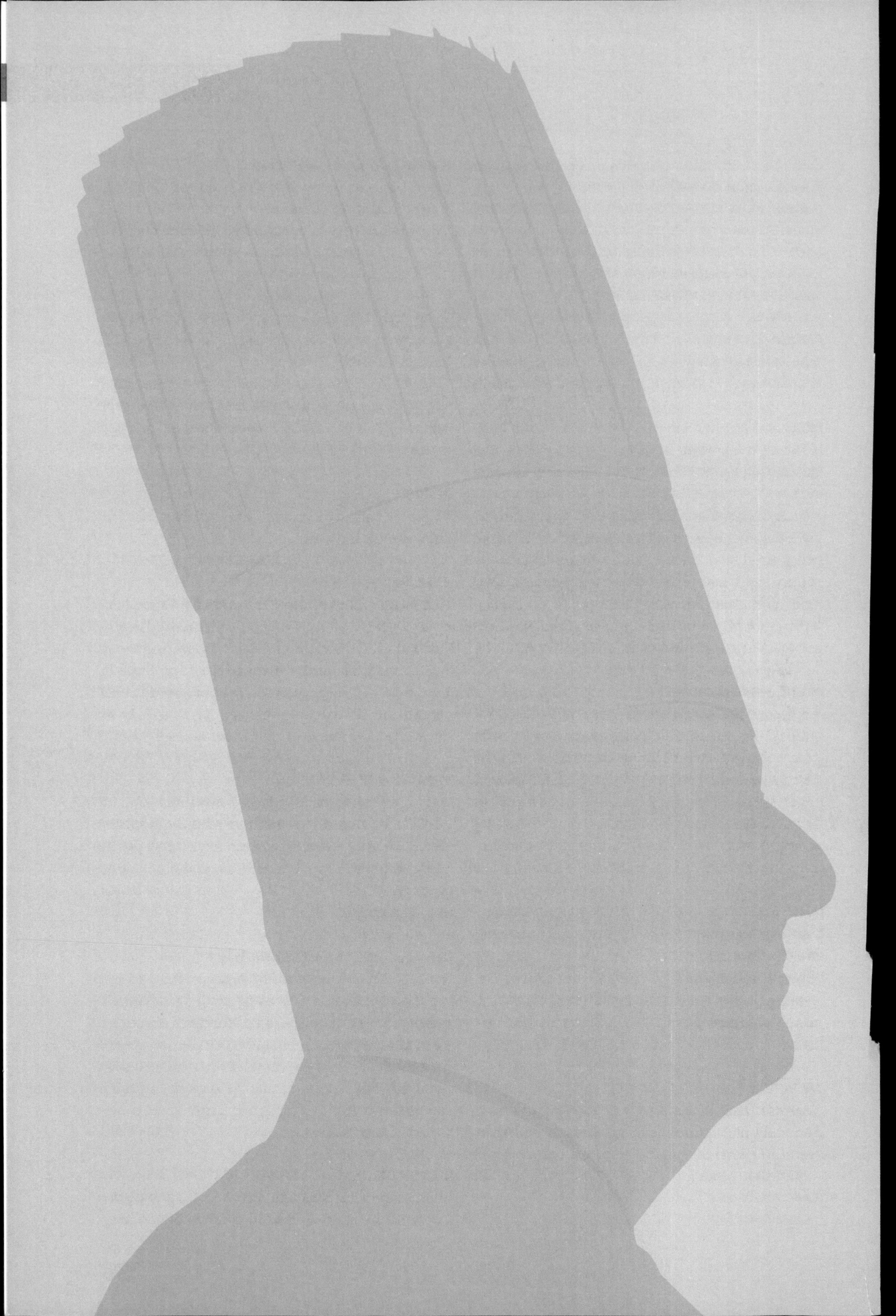